Exploitation and Atrocities on the Dalits in India

EXPLOITATION AND ATROCITIES ON THE DALITS IN INDIA

Prof. Narayan Mishra

KALPAZ PUBLICATIONS
Delhi-110052

ISBN: 978-81-7835-217-6

Price: ₹ 990

Reprinted in 2014 in India by
Kalpaz Publications,
C-30, Satyawati Nagar,
Delhi-110 052
E-mail: kalpaz@hotmail.com
Phone: 9212142040

Printed at: G. Print Process, Delhi

CONTENTS

PREFACE

I consider it to be a privilege to present this volume to every one interested in the welfare of the Harijans (Dalits) of Bihar. I have been associated with the study of Dalits since long. In fact, I was born in a village of North Bihar where the Dusadh, a Scheduled Caste, was the second largest community after the Brahmins. As a child and then as a primary school student. I had some classmates from the Dusadh Caste, though we had to maintain distance outside school as they were untouchables.

Destiny made me an Anthropologist and I took the job of a University teacher in 1963. I took a batch of Honours students for their field work among the Dalits of North Bihar in 1965 after which I developed the desire to specialise in this very area of study and research. My teacher, guide and the then Head of Anthropology Department Late Professor L.P. Vidharthi also wanted me to develop this area of research. Under his leadership I supervised, several batches of P.G. students for their M.A. field work and tried to understand the problems of Dalits of Bihar. After a long brooding, I could make out that there were two basic problems of Dalits, one was the problem of disability, and another was that of inequality, and all other problems had their roots in either of them. To study these two basic problems, I get two very brilliant researchers registered for their Ph.D. level Research. I got several serious research papers published about different aspects of the Dusadh, the Chamars, the Dhobi, the Musahar, the Pasi and the like. Later on about half a dozen Ph.D. research-scholars got themselves registered on different aspects of the Dalits of Bihar under my supervision. I got opportunity to guide several minor and major research projects also. All these gave me inspiration and insight to know them and their problems in better way than before.

In India, socio-economic background of any community has got the maximum value attached to other aspects of life. The Dalits have the lowest socio-economic status in the society. They do not have any right and privilege, but all the duties, to be performed for the benefit of upper caste. Even under earlier Zamindari system, cases of Dalit exploitation and atrocities were not unknown, but their nature and extent were much different from the present day. If an individual Dalit was found guilty of some wrong, he alone was to be punished. But since two decades or more, roughly after 1976, mass atrocities on Dalits on the community basis, often with the help or connivance of the Police, has become a regular feature of Bihar. To the best of my knowledge, organised type of atrocity on Dalits in Bihar started with the Belchi carnage, in which as many as eleven Dalits were massacred and burnt alive by the Kurmis on the 27th May 1977 in the village of Belchi under Barh Block of Patna district. Thereafter in the month of October 1977, four Dalits were murdered in the village of Dharampur in the district of Bhojpur. Then came the Bajidpur incidence in the month of November 1978, in which entire village was razed to the ground. Several Dalit women raped, one person was killed and several injured. In December 1978, in the village of Kaila, three Dalits were killed and property of others looted by the Kurmis of the same village. Mastipur firing in Bodh-Gaya Block of Gaya district took place in 1979, in which two Dalits were killed by the men of the local Mahanta. After this was the shameful carnage of Parasbigha in the district of Jehanabad, in which as many as 12 Dalits were killed by the Bhumihars in the month of January 1980. Soon after this was Pipra massacre in the district of Patna, in which 14 Dalits were killed and many Dalits' houses razed to ground. There has been a chain of Dalit atrocities like those of Gaini, Dherminia, Chhechani, Dalalchak, Baghura, Tartar, Itawa, Arbal, Kansara and the most recent of Lakshmanpur Bathe in Jehanabad, in which 62 Dalit men, women and children were killed by the Ranvir Sena in the 1st week of December 1997.

The mass massacre of poor and innocent Dalits in Bihar compelled me to think seriously about the causes of the carnage. I chose to study the incidences of atrocity and exploitation of the Dalits of two belts, one from Darbhanga which represents the Mithila Culture linguistic zone; and another Gaya, which is core of Maghi culture – linguistic zone. Both of these belts have very good concentration of Dalit population. But the population composition is different. Whereas the Brahmins are the dominant caste of Darbhanga area, in Gaya, it is the Bhumihar and the Rajput somewhere and the Koeri elsewhere. Four blocks, two each from Gaya and Darbhanga, one each a rural and another urban was selected and from each block 20 villages, and from each village 20 households were sampled. Thus the present work is the outcome of an intensive study of 800 households which form the universe of the study.

The present study, based on the facts from the field, reveal that the cases of exploitation of the Dalits in Mithila belt is fearless and atrocity almost nil as compared to the Magahi belt.

In the Magahi belt also, such areas, which have mixed population of the Bhumihar, the Rajputs, the Koeri, the Yadvas and the Dalits, are more prone to atrocities than the one which has only the upper caste and Dalits. Such villages which have the Koeri as the dominant caste and good concentration of Dalit population is equally prone to atrocity. Land dispute, particularly the Gairmajarua and land given in the Bhoodan, demand for the minimum wage as fixed by the government from time to time, election grouping, and protest against outrage the modesty of female folk by the Dalits, plus several other flimsy grounds may be taken as the main causes of atrocity. The Government policy regarding the welfare of the Dalits which is very often to gain cheap popularity than to do real good to them, is also not less responsible for the atrocity and exploitation of Dalits. Government very often launches schemes for the Dalits, which are against the interest of upper caste landholders, but fails to implement them in proper manner.

Now the menace of atrocity has taken a devastative scale. Gang-rape of Dalit women, razing to ground the Dalit settlements, and mass-massacre like Laxmanpur-Bathe in which about 62 Dalits were butchered, speaks of the scale in which the war of Mahabharat is being fought between MCC and Ranvir Sena and several other Senas. This pious land of Janak, Buddha and Gandhi is witnessing the worst ever seen blood bath of own villagers. This has to be stopped by all means with co-operation of every one. These and other issues regarding the problems of atrocities and exploitation of the Dalits have been illustrated in the light of the field data collected and analysed from the two (Magahi and Mithila zones) of the four culture-linguistic zones of Bihar.

In completing this research project, I have received co-operation from different organisations and individuals at different stages of field work, analysis of data and drafting the final report. I am grateful to the University Grants Commission for sanctioning a research grant for this purpose. Dr. P.N. Thakur, the Research Associates, Dr. B.N. Jha and Dr. S.K. Verma the two Junior Research Fellows of the Project did extensive field work. Shri C.S. Prasad and Shri A.K. Thakur helped me in the formulation of the outline of the project and several schedules used for data collection and also in the field work. I am indebted to both of them.

Dr. Gaya Pandey helped me a lot in preparing the preliminary draft. I am thankful to him. I am grateful to Prof. V.S. Upadhyay for his valuable suggestions and academic help.

N. Mishra

INTRODUCTION

The State of Bihar houses about 8 million Dalit population comprising of 23 different scheduled castes, which is 14.11 per cent of the total population of the state. Bihar has greater concentration of the Dalit population than the country as a whole. About the states, Bihar ranks third in India with regard to Dalit population, but economically and educationally, they are most backward. Whereas India in general, 14.67 per cent of scheduled castes are literate. This is only 6.53 per cent in case of Bihar. Similarly, a National survey has revealed that 66 per cent of the bonded labourers in the country belong to the Scheduled Castes.

Bihar is one of the few states where exploitation and atrocities of the Dalits are at apex. Dalits are those people who belong to the last Verna, namely the Sudras and Avarnas include many caste groups which have suffered social and economic disabilities and inequality since ages. The concept of pollution was attached to them and they were treated as untouchable castes. They were called by the names of Patita, Chandala, Achhoota, Antyaja and the like. The term Dalit is an award given to them by late Mahatma Gandhi, the Father of the nation.

Bihar is one of the few states where exploitation and atrocities of the Dalits are very high. The daily newspapers are the recorders of the fact. A look on any newspaper captures one's eyes on the news published about the murder, rape, burning, beating and several other tortures given to the members of the Dalit communities.

The term exploitation may be defined as the utilization of service of any persons for selfish purposes. The exploitation is concerned with at least two persons one is the exploiter and the other is exploitee. The bargaining power of exploitee is completely surrendered. There is no alternative before an exploitee. That is why the exploiter exploits the exploitee for his selfish purpose. The exploiter wants to take more and more work from the exploitee but he likes to make less and less payment. In order to maintain his survival, the exploitee has to accept whatever the exploiter makes payment. Thus, the term exploitation is an economic phenomenon. In this economic relation between exploiter and exploitee, the exploiter behaves like a selfish man. He does not think for the benefit of the exploitee. He always thinks for his own benefit.

There is a close relation between the poverty and exploitation. The poor are dependent upon the rich for their livelihood and survival. That is why the poor are frequently subjected to exploitation in different manner. There may be difference in the degree of exploitation, but the selfish behaviour is prevalent everywhere. It is generally the rich who exploit the poor. But sometimes a reverse situation can be seen in which the poor are able to bargain with the rich. In these situations a rich is also exploited by the poor. During peak agricultural season, there is shortage of labourers. In this situation a labourer becomes able to bargain more wages than the prescribed minimum wages. Here a poor exploits the rich. On the basis of specialisation of work, a poor comes in a position to bargain his wages with the rich. For example, Halwaha (plough-man), kundalwaha (man who handles spade for making boundary of the plot) are able to get more wages than the normal labour.

Nowadays, exploitation of a poor by the poor has also come into existence, Rickshaw-wala, Tangawala, Thelawala etc. not only exploit the rich but they also exploit the poor. They want to bargain more and more fare from the poor as well as the rich.

The nature of the exploitation is economic. There are economic areas like agriculture, construction, brick kiln, tea garden, factory, mines, etc. where the exploiters are landowner, locally called, Malik, moneylender, Mahajan, contractor, brick kiln owners, tea garden owner, industrialists, mine owner middlemen, shopkeeper etc.

It is beyond doubt that the nature of the term exploitation is purely economic, but it has social, psychological, religious and political dimensions. There are certain sections of society like children, women and aged who are easy prey in comparison to young, adults and males. They are exploited not only by outsiders, but even in their own houses. Again, there are certain socially backward and economically deprived sections of society like Dalits, who are subjected to different types of exploitation. Thus, the term exploitation has social dimension also.

From the very beginning the poor are taught that they are meant to serve the rich and bigman. For them the rich and big-man are like God. God gives them birth and the rich give them work and bread. They are taught that the rich do not do injustice, so, they have to receive what they give and to obey what they say. They are taught that taking loan is not a bad thing, but not repaying loan is harmful not only in this world but in the life after death. If a man dies without repaying loan, it is the duty of his son to pay the loan back taken by his father. If his sons do not repay, the departed soul takes birth in oxen and has to work for the man or his family from whom he had taken loan. Thus, the world view of the poor is governed by such psychological factors, that is why they bear their exploitation without any trouble. The poor are not included in many important meetings and decision of the village. But for the building of a temple and celebration of festivals, they are taxed, they have to give subscription and render labour without any payment on those occasions. Thus, exploitation has religious dimension too.

The exploitation has political dimension as well the political authorities who occupy position in traditional and modern political system exploit the poor. Thus, Choukidar, Dafadar, Mukhia, Sarpanch, Karamchari, Gram Sewak, Police, Court, administrative authorities, M.L.A., M.P. etc show their exploitative behavour towards the poor.

The organisation of some activists are also found exploiting the poor. The term atrocity may be defined as wicked, oppressive and cruel behaviour of a person or group against a person or group. The atrocity may be small or big, planned or unplanned, organised or unorganised. Again atrocity may be age based like atrocity on children, atrocity on youth, atrocity on aged. Similarly, atrocity may be sex based like atrocity on women and atrocity on men. According to the Scheduled Castes and Scheduled Tribes (Prevention of the Atrocities) Act 1989, atrocity means an offence punishable under Section 3 which are below :

OFFENCE OF ATROCITIES

3. Punishments for offences of atrocities – (1) Whoever, not being a member of a Scheduled Caste or Scheduled Tribe –

(i) forces a member of Scheduled Caste or a Scheduled Tribe to drink or eat any inedible or obnoxious substance;

(ii) acts with intent to cause injury, insult or annoyance to any member of a Scheduled Caste or a Scheduled Tribe by dumping excreta, waste matter, carcasses or any other obnoxious substance in his premises or neighbourhood;

(iii) forcibly removes clothes from the person of a member of a Scheduled Caste or a Scheduled Tribe or parades him naked or with painted face or body or commits any similar act which is derogatory to human dignity;

(iv) wrongfully occupies or cultivates any land owned by, or allotted to or notified by any competent authority to be allotted to a member of a Scheduled Caste or a Scheduled Tribe or gets the land allotted to him transferred;

(v) wrongfully dispossesses a member of S.C. or S.T. from his land or premises or interferes with the enjoyment of his rights over any land premises or water;

(vi) compels or entices a member of a Scheduled Caste or a Scheduled Tribe to do 'begar' or other similar forms of forced or bonded labour other than any compulsory service for public purposes imposed by Government;

(vii) forces or intimidates a member of a Scheduled Caste or a Scheduled Tribe not to vote or to vote to a particular candidate or to vote in a manner other than that provided by law;

(viii) institutes false, malicious or vexatious suit or criminal or other legal proceedings against a member of a Scheduled Caste or a Scheduled Tribe;

(ix) gives any false or frivolous information to any public servant and thereby cause such public servant to use his lawful power to the injury or annoyance of a member of a Scheduled Caste or a Scheduled Tribe;

(x) intentionally insults or intimidates with intent to humiliate a member of Scheduled Caste or a Scheduled Tribe in any place within public view;

(xi) assaults or uses force to any woman belonging to Scheduled Caste or a Scheduled Tribe with intent to dishonour (outrage) her modesty;

(xii) being in a position to dominate the will of a woman belonging to a Scheduled Caste or a Scheduled Tribe and uses that position to exploit her sexually to which she would not have otherwise agreed;

(xiii) corrupts or fouls the water of any spring, reservoir or any other source ordinarily used by members of the Scheduled Caste or a Scheduled Tribe so as to render it less fit for the purpose for which it is ordinarily used;

(xiv) denies a member of a Scheduled Caste or a Scheduled Tribe any customary right of passage to a place of public resort or having access to a place of public resort to which other members of public or any section thereof have a right to use or access to;

(xv) forces or causes a member of a Scheduled Caste or a Scheduled Tribe to leave his house, village or other place of residence; shall be punishable with imprisonment for a term which shall not be less than six months but which may extend to five years and with fine.

2. Whoever, not being a member of a Scheduled Caste or a Scheduled Tribe :-

(i) gives or fabricates false evidence intending thereby to cause, or knowing it to be likely that he will thereby cause, any member of a Scheduled Caste or a Scheduled Tribe to be convicted of an offence which is capital by the law for the time being in force shall be punished with imprisonment for life and with fine; and if an innocent member of a Scheduled Caste or a Scheduled Tribe be convicted and executed in consequence of such false or fabricated evidence, the person who gives or fabricates such false evidence, shall be punished with death;

(ii) gives or fabricates false evidence intending thereby to cause, or knowing it to be likely that he will thereby cause, any member of a Scheduled Caste or a Scheduled Tribe to be convicted of an offence which is capital but punishable with imprisonment for a term of seven years or upwards, shall be punishable with imprisonment for a term which shall not be less than six months but which may extend to seven years or upwards and with fine;

(iii) commits mischief by fire or any explosive substance intending to cause or knowing it to be likely that he will thereby cause damage to any property belonging to a member of a Scheduled Caste or a Scheduled Tribe, shall be punishable with imprisonment for a term which shall not be less than six months but which may extend to seven years and with fine;

(iv) commits mischief by fire or any explosive substance intending to cause or knowing it to be likely that he will thereby cause destruction of any building which is ordinarily used as place of worship or as a place for human dwelling or as place for custody of the property by a member of a Scheduled Caste or a Scheduled

Tribe shall be punishable with imprisonment for life and with fine;

(v) commits any offence under the Indian Penal Code (45 of 1860) punishable with imprisonment for a term of ten years or more against a person or property on the ground that such person is a member of a Scheduled Caste or a Scheduled Tribe or such member, shall be punishable with imprisonment for life and with fine;

(vi) knowingly or having reason to believe that an offence has been committed under this Chapter, causes any evidence of the commission of that offence to disappear with the intention of screening the offender from legal punishment, or with that intention gives any information respecting the offence which he knows or believes to be false, shall be punishable with the punishment provided for that offence; or

(vii) being a public servant, commits any offence under this section, shall be punishable with imprisonment for a term which shall not be less than one year but which may extend to the punishment provided for that offence.

Thus atrocity is wicked, oppressive and cruel behaviour, but it has social, economic and political dimension. There are certain sections of society who are subject to atrocity frequently. For example, Dalits. Our state of Bihar is in-famous for atrocity on Dalits, from seventies till now, the incidence of atrocity on Dalits is increasing day by day.

The Dalits have been socially backward and economically deprived since centuries. After independence several schemes for the betterment of Dalits have been implemented. Educational facilities have been provided to them. They have been benefited by the policy of job reservation, reservation of seats in MLA and MP elections. Due to these development schemes, the status of Dalits has definitely gone up. This has become a painful development for the rich who thought that the survivals of Dalits was dependent upon them. The poor who did not dare to face the rich, now they have started agitating against them. Those who tolerated their exploitation peacefully now they are trying to get their share violently. those who did not dare to sit on cot even in his own house before a rich, now they sit on the cot on which a rich sits. They take tea and food in the hotel with the rich. They travel with them. They study with them. Not only this, they work with them in the office. Such behaviour of present day Dalits have exaggerated the anger of the people who enjoyed high status in traditional society. In order to break down such spirit of Dalits, the rich and powerful persons have taken the help of atrocities. They are subjected to such type of treatment like beating mercilessly, theft of cattle, theft of grains, dacoity in house, setting thrashing floor on fire, setting the house on fire, brutal murder, group killing, rape and gang rape.

Nowadays organised atrocity on Dalit has also come in to existence. There are many local senas which claim support of castemen and rich and powerful persons. Similarly, there are some senas which claim the support of the poor and the Dalits. Thus, organised atrocity takes place by the different types of senas.

It is beyond doubt that atrocity has economic dimension. The Dalit have been subjected to atrocity due to demand of minimum wages through their organisations.

Dalits have been subject to atrocity in the name of saving sacred plots and sacred ponds. Thus, atrocity has religious dimension.

The Dalits have been subject to atrocity because they wanted to cast their votes. Thus, atrocity has political dimension also.

Exploitation and Atrocity

It is beyond doubt that exploitation and atrocity are closely related. Cases related to atrocity indicate to fight against their exploitations. They had raised their voices against the landowners, Thus, exploitation becomes the root cause for the atrocity, but atrocity may take place without exploitation also.

The Present Study

The present study was designed to explore and examine the phenomenon of exploitation and atrocities on Dalit in Bihar, for this purpose the districts of Gaya from Central South Bihar and Darbhanga from North Bihar were chosen purposively because these two districts of Bihar had very high concentration of Dalits population. Two blocks from each district one as urban and another as rural were selected for the data collection. In the district of Gaya, which was representative of the Magahi Culture, field work was done in 20 villages of Bodh-Gaya as urban Block and Imamganj as on rural Block. These blocks have Dalit population 30% to 40%. In Darbhanga, two blocks – Darbhanga Urban as Urban Block and Dahadurpur as rural block having 25% Dalit population were selected as sample blocks and 20 villages from each Block were selected for the ethnographic material collection. It will not be out of place to mention here that Darbhanga is the core of Mithila and Maithili culture. These two different cultural areas were deliberately chosen for a comparative study of the nature, type, mode and extent of exploitation and atrocities on Dalits.

The term Harijan (Dalit) had been given by Bapu, the Father of our nation for those socially backward and economically deprived Hindu communities who have suffered from various disabilities since centuries. They have been listed by our Honourable President as Scheduled Castes (S.C.) since Dalit have been socially backward and economically deprived, they have been victims of exploitation and atrocities.

In Gaya district, there is high concentration of Dalit population. That is why this M.P. seat has been reserved for S.C. The Chamar, the Bhuiyan, the Pasi and the Dusadh are dominant Dalit communities in the district. The Mushar, The Mehtar, The Dhobi and the Nat are the minor Dalit communities. Majority of them are landless labour. Some are now landowners and engaged in government jobs also. The Dusadh, the Musahar and the Chamars are the major Dalits of Bihar.

Significance of Study

The present study is significant in the sense that it attempts to explore and highlight the pattern of exploitation and atrocity on Dalits in Bihar because our state occupies third position in our country so far as the population of Dalit is concerned. Based on anthropological approaches, the study provides knowledge on the dimensions of exploitation and atrocities on Dalit of Bihar.

Objectives of Study

The study was designed to fulfill the following objectives :

(i) To know the present day status of Dalits in Bihar.

(ii) To explore the social area of Dalit exploitation.

(iii) To describe the economic area of Dalit exploitation.

(iv) To highlight the religious area of Dalit exploitation

(v) To study the political area of Dalit exploitation

(vi) To delineate the atrocity on Dalits

(vii) To explain the exploitation of Dalits by Dalits.

Besides these, this study aimed at testing the following hypotheses :

(i) It appears that the causes of these atrocities and exploitations are not sporadic and superficial, but have their roots in obvious socio-economic disabilities of the Dalits.

(ii) Although, Dalit population in Bihar is universally distributed in various proportion, it appears that there are several major trouble spots which are more trouble prone than other areas.

(iii) If the Dalits are adequately represented in the police force at all levels in the trouble prone areas, there is quick investigation of cases and firm preventive measures are imposed these conjointly may check the incidences of atrocities.

RESEARCH METHODOLOGY

The universe of the present study was Gaya district of Central South Bihar and Dharbhanga district of North Bihar. From these districts two blocks each district were chosen purposively on the basis of concentration of Dalit population. These two blocks were Bodh Gaya and Imamganj, in Gaya. From each block 20 villages were selected randomly. Thus, 40 villages belonging to both blocks were taken up for the present study. Again, from each village 10 households of Dalit were selected purposively on the basis of caste, number of households etc. Attempt was made to cover all Dalit castes present in the village. In this way, altogether 400 households were sampled for the purpose of study. Although all members of households were covered in the study, but information were gathered mostly through the heads of the households. In order to study the exploitation and atrocity of women, women investigators were employed to collect case studies.

The same sample size was chosen from two Blocks – Darbhanga urban and Bahadurpur from Darbhanga district.

In this way four blocks, 80 villages and 800 households were sampled purposively and randomly for the present study.

Data Collection

Data from the field were gathered through following techniques of anthropological research.

1. *Schedules* : In order to collect information on the topic of the proposed research, 3 sets of schedule were prepared. These included village schedule, household schedule and case study schedule which were filled by the investigators in the field. all schedules were checked up by the research associate appointed for this purpose.

2. *Interview* : Some information were gathered through individual

and group interview. For this purpose interview guide was prepared by the investigator.

3. *Case Study* : In order to provide deeper understanding of the exploitation and atrocities, case studies of victims were taken.

4. *Non-participant observation* : While staying in field some information were gathered through non-participant observation.

5. *Field work* : The field work for the study was done in the period between June 1990 to May 1991, i.e. for one year completely. for each block one investigator was employed, who moved from village to village. R.A. used to provide supervision work and to collect some vital information from different key informants.

Scrutiny and Data Processing

Data collected from the field were scrutinized thoroughly and the transferred to the master charts for the purpose of tabulation. Simple monovariate and bivariate tables were prepared manually to illustrate the description. Thus, data were processed manually.

Scheme of Writing Report and Analysis of Data

The report contains a general introduction in the beginning and a brief conclusion at the end. The scrutinized and processed data were analysed under the following chapters excluding introduction and conclusion of Gaya district and Darbhanga district on the same pattern.

Chapter 1	:	Description of Sample Village of Gaya
Chapter 2	:	Present Day Status of Dalit of Gaya
Chapter 3	:	Social Area of Dalit Exploitation of Gaya
Chapter 4	:	Economic Area of Dalit Exploitation of Gaya
Chapter 5	:	Religious Area of Dalit Exploitation of Gaya
Chapter 6	:	Political Area of Dalit Exploitation of Gaya
Chapter 7	:	Exploitation of Dalit by Dalit of Gaya
Chapter 8	:	Atrocity on Dalit of Gaya of Gaya
Chapter 9	:	Description of Sample Villages of Darbhanga
Chapter 10	:	Status of Dalit Today of Darbhanga
Chapter 11	:	Social Area of Dalit Exploitation of Darbhanga
Chapter 12	:	Economic Area of Dalit Exploitation of Darbhanga
Chapter 13	:	Religious Area of Dalit Exploitation of Darbhanga
Chapter 14	:	Political Area of Dalit Exploitation of Darbhanga
Chapter 15	:	Exploitation of Dalit by Dalit of Darbhanga
Chapter 16	:	Atrocity on Dalit of Darbhanga

Besides these chapters, the introduction presents the introductory aspects of the present study and the conclusion highlights the useful remarks related to the findings of the study.

PART I – GAYA

1

THE FIELD : DESCRIPTION OF SAMPLE VILLAGES OF GAYA

As referred to earlier the field of study of the present study was Gaya district of South Bihar, from this district two blocks namely, Bodh Gaya and Imamganj were chosen for the purpose of selecting villages. From each block 20 villages where Dalits were residing separately or with other caste population, were chosen randomly. Hence, it will be the fitness of the thing to present here some basic description of the sample-blocks and villages covered under the study. These basic information will provide the background of the phenomenon of exploitation and atrocities of Dalits.

BODH GAYA BLOCK

The Bodh Gaya Block is situated at a distance of 11 Kms from the district quarters in north direction. It spreads over an area of 60,490 acres. 146 revenue villages come under the administrative boundary of this block. The block has 19 Gram Panchayats and 10 Halakas. As per available 1981 census report, the total population of the block is 106,812 persons in which SC were 390,118 persons. After SC, Backward castes come next followed by the Muslims. The population of upper caste is very low. 60 per cent land of the village is cultivable. There are big, medium and small farmers. SC are landless or near landless. They belong to IPF or Sangram Samiti or MCC like activists organisation. Under the banner of these activists organisation, they are fighting against exploitation and oppression and trying to acquire political power not only in the area but in State Assembly as well.

Description of Sample Villages

As stated earlier, 20 villages from this block were selected randomly to get village level information and to select informants. A brief description about these villages are as follows :

Table 1.1 : Distribution of Sample Villages according to Population

Sl. No.	*Villages*	*No. of Households*	*Total Population*	*Average Size*
1.	Amma	309	1602	5
2.	Bakraur	414	2048	5
3.	Bhagwanpur	503	2378	5
4.	Dahariya Bigha	552	2500	5
5.	Hathiyara	401	1421	4
6.	Janpur	211	941	5
7.	Khagbatti	60	300	5
8.	Kulohara	71	538	7
9.	Koshila	473	2378	6
10.	Maharaur	98	683	7
11.	Mastipur	673	3893	6
12.	Mocharein	710	3893	6
13.	Monia	238	1180	5
14.	Nimabasari	185	564	3
15.	Pakardih	89	547	6
16.	Pararia	315	1215	4
17.	Panchahatti	320	1100	3
18.	Qagichak	105	747	7
19.	Rajapur	1253	6660	5
20.	Shirajpur	125	1240	10
	Total	7105	35828	6

The above table reveals that the total population of the sample villages in Bodh Gaya Block was 35828 persons. They were distributed in 7105 households. The average size of family was found as 6 persons including parents. The number of household is increasing due to disintegration of joint family.

Sex Group and Sex Ratio

Table 1.2 : Distribution of Sample Village Population by Sex Group

Sl. No.	*Villages*	*Sex Group*		*Total*	*Sex Ratio*
		Male	*Female*		
1.	Amma	867 (54.12)	735 (45.88)	1602 (100.00)	847
2.	Bakraur	1049 (51.22)	999 (48.78)	2048 (100.00)	952
3.	Bhagwanpur	1185 (49.88)	1193 (50.12)	2378 (100.00)	1007
4.	Dahariya Bigha	1275 (51.00)	1225 (49.00)	2500 (100.00)	970
5.	Hathiyara	684 (48.13)	737 (00.87)	1421 (100.00)	1077
6.	Janpur	500 (53.13)	451 (46.87)	941 (100.00)	902
7.	Khagbatti	155 (51.66)	145 (48.34)	300 (100.00)	999
8.	Kulohara	265 (49.25)	273 (50.75)	538 (100.00)	1030
9.	Koshila	1234 (51.88)	1144 (48.12)	2378 (100.00)	1170
10.	Maharaur	347 (50.05)	336 (49.95)	683 (100.00)	1054
11.	Mastipur	1963 (51.40)	1930 (49.60)	3893 (100.00)	982
12.	Mocharein	1963 (51.40)	1930 (49.60)	3883 (100.00)	982
13.	Monia	595 (50.42)	585 (48.58)	1180 (100.00)	985
14.	Nimabasari	287 (51.02)	264 (49.98)	564 (100.00)	920
15.	Pakardih	288 (52.65)	259 (47.35)	547 (100.00)	863
16.	Pararia	631 (51.93)	584 (49.07)	1215 (100.00)	925
17.	Panchahatti	585 (53.08)	515 (46.82)	1100 (100.00)	880
18.	Qagichak	388 (51.94)	359 (48.09)	747 (100.00)	925
19.	Rajapur	3508 (53.57)	315 (46.43)	6660 (100.00)	898
20.	Shirajpur	820 (66.12)	420 (33.88)	1240 (100.00)	
	Total	18589 (51.06)	14399 (48.94)	35818 (100.00)	931

The study on sex group and sex ratio in sample village is that in total population the percentage of male is greater than the females. The male occupies 51.06 per cent population whereas female constitutes 48.94 per cent population. In total population, there were 931 females for every

Ethnic – Group

Table 1.3 : Distribution of Sample Village Population by Ethnic Group

Sl. No.	*Name of village*	*Ethnic Group*				
		Forward Caste. No. of household	*Backward Caste. No. of household*	*Schedule No. of H.H.*	*Muslim No. H.H.*	*Total*
1.	Amma	195	34	80	-	309
2.	Bakraur	282	27	105	-	414
3.	Bhagwanpur	321	47	135	100	503
4.	Dahariya Bigha	-	145	375	27	552
5.	Hathiyara	-	276	125	-	401
6.	Janpur	-	7	111	93	211
7.	Khagbatti	-	31	29	-	60
8.	Kulohara	36	-	35	-	71
9.	Koshila	250	15	203	5	473
10.	Maharaur	-	54	40	4	98

Contd.

Contd.

Sl. No.	*Name of village*	*Ethnic Group*				
		Forward Caste. No. of household	*Backward Caste. No. of household*	*Schedule No. of H.H.*	*Muslim No. H.H.*	*Total*
11.	Mastipur	-	100	600	10	710
12.	Mocharein	-	145	545	20	710
13	Monia	75	25	138	-	238
14.	Nimabasari	115	20	125	25	185
15.	Pakardih	30	10	45	4	89
16.	Pararia	200	15	85	15	315
17.	Panchahatti	-	180	105	20	320
18.	Qagichak	-	35	70	-	105
19.	Rajapur	753	200	200	100	1253
20.	Shirajpur	-	70	50	5	125
	Total	2257	1436	3201	428	7142

thousand males. The percentage and ratio of males and female differ in different sample villages which can be observed in the Table 1.2.

The above table reveals the distribution of sample village population by the number of households belonging to ethnic groups. Out of total 6195 households, 2257 households belonged to forward castes, 1436 households belonged to backward castes, 3201 households belonged to scheduled castes or Dalits and 428 households belonged to Muslims. A description of various castes under ethnic group is shown in the table below.

Table 1.4 : Distribution of Caste Group According to Villages

Sl. No.	*Name of village*	*Forward Caste*	*Backward Caste*	*Dalits*	*Muslim*
1.	Amma	Rajput	Koeri, Naua	Bhuiyan	-
2.	Bakraur	Brahmin	Koeri, Gareri	— do —	-
3.	Bhagwanpur	Rajput	Yadav, Koeri Naua	— do —	Muslim
4.	Dahariya Bigha	-	Kahar	— do —	— do —
5.	Hathiyara	-	Koeri	— do —	— do —
6.	Janpur	-	Yadav	— do —	— do —
7.	Khagbatti	-	Koeri	— do —	— do —
8.	Kulohara	Rajput	-	— do —	— do —
9.	Koshila	Rajput	Kahar, Naua	Bhuiyan Chamar	— do —
10.	Maharaur	-	Yadav	— do —	— do —
11.	Mastipur	-	Yadav, Koeri, Naua	— do —	— do —
12.	Mocharein	-	— do —	— do —	
13.	Monia	Rajput	Koeri, Naua	— do —	— do —
14.	Nimabasari	Bhumihar	Koeri	— do —	— do —
15.	Pakardih	Bhumihar	Koeri, Naua	— do —	— do —
16.	Pararia	Rajput	— do —	— do —	— do —
17.	Panchahatti	-	Yadav	— do —	— do —
18.	Qagichak	-	-	— do —	— do —
19.	Rajapur	Bhumihar	Koeri, Kurmi, Naua, Garere, Yadav	— do —	— do —

From the Table 1.4 it appears that three castes come under the ethnic group of forward castes namely – Brahmin, Bhumihar and Rajput. Under the ethnic group backward castes Yadav, Koeri, Kurmi, Naua, Barahi, Lohar and Kahar were found. Under the ethnic group Dalits, Bhuiyan and Charmar castes were recorded. In Muslim Shekh, Paithan, Jolaha, Dhunia and Halalkhore were reported.

Landholding

Each village has a definite boundary. The landholding of each village differ from the other. Three types of land are generally found in each village, homestead land, cultivable and uncultivable land. In village the land is distributed among the individual families. A village-wise distribution of acreage and cultive land is as follows :-

Table 1.5 : Village-wise Distribution of Land

Sl. No.	*Name of Village*	*Land in Hectare*
1.	Amma	1229.78
2.	Bakraur	626.60
3.	Bhagwanpur	512.86
4.	Dahariya Bigha	515.17
5.	Hathiyara	240.78
6.	Janpur	286.78
7.	Khagbatti	68.80
8.	Kulohara	204.95
9.	Koshila	707.38
10.	Maharaur	152.14
11.	Mastipur	2327.00
12.	Mocharein	2327.00
13.	Monia	176.29
14.	Nimabasari	114.12
15.	Pakardih	64.85
16.	Pararia	295.42
17.	Panchahatti	200.00
18.	Qagichak	84.58
19.	Rajapur	1150.00
20.	Shirajpur	91.39

The Table 1.5 reveals clearly that there is unequal distribution of land in the village. Again in each village one finds unequal distribution of land at family and caste level. Forward and Backward castes own resources particularly land. Some Muslim families also own good acreage of land but some Muslims are landless also. Members of scheduled castes or Dalits are mostly landless. A caste-wise distribution of landholding is presented in the table below :-

Table 1.6 : Caste wise Distribution of Land

Landholding size in acre	*Forward Caste*	*Backward Caste*	*Scheduled Caste*	*Muslims*	*Total*
Landless	0	9 (0.07)	2400 (84.11)	300 (70.09)	2709
Upto 1 Acre	115 (5.09)	30 (2.42)	300 (10.52)	75 (17.75)	520
1 – 2.5 Acre	575 (25.48)	503 (2.42)	100 (10.52)	20 (17.75)	1198
2.5 – 5 Acre	825 (36.99)	405 (32.77)	51 (1.92)	22 (5.14)	1303
5 – 7.5 Acre	485 (21.48)	152 (12.26)		6 (1.48)	643
7.5 – 10 Acre	157 (6.92)	120 (9.68)		3 (0.70)	280
Above 10 Acre	100 (4.43)	20 (1.62)		2 (0.46)	
	2257 (100.30)	1239 (99.41)	2851 (100.12)	428 (100.10)	6775

The above table reveals that among forward castes no household was landless. In backward castes 0.07 per cent were landless. Among S.C. and Muslims the percentage of landless was 84.11 and 70.09 respectively among F.C. 5.09 per cent household possessed land up to one acre only. Among B.C., S.C. and Muslims percentages of households possessing land up to one acre were 2.42, 10.52 and 17.75 respectively. Among F.C. 25.48 per cent possessed land up to 2.5 acre, 36.99 per cent possessed land up to 5 acres, 21.48 per cent up to 7.5 acre, 6.2 owned land up to 10 acres and only 4.43 per cent had land above 10 acres.

Among B.C. 40.59 per cent households belonged to the category of 1 to 2.5 acre of land, 32.77 percent owned land up to 5 acre 12.26 per cent had land up to 7.5 acres, 9.69 per cent possed land 10 acres and only 1.62 per cent household had land above 10 acres.

The distribution of land among S.C. reveals that majority of households were landless or near landless. 3.57 per cent possessed land up to 2.5 acres and only 1.92 per cent up to 5 acres of land.

Among Muslims the distribution of land indicates some similar pattern with those of S.C. Because majority of Muslims were also landless or near landless. Some of them were ex-zamindars and now big farmers also. 2.64 per cent household possessed land up to 2.5 acres, 5.41 per cent households had land up to 5 acres, 1.48 per cent up to 7.5 acres 0.70 percent up to 10 acres and 0.46 per cent and land above 10 acres.

Means of Irrigation

The villages of Bodh Gaya block has tube wells boring, Rehat, Lathakuri, Pond, Nala, Pokhara, etc. for the purpose of irrigation. For Bhadai and Agahani crop they are dependent upon rain water. But for sugarcane maize and rabi crops, they depend upon diesel pump, boring, pokhara, etc.

Table 1.7 : Distributions of Villages According to Means of Irrigations

Sl. No.	*Name of Village*	*Means of irrigation*		*Diesel Machine*	*Rahat*	*Pokhara*	*Canal*
		No. of Wells	*No. of Pumps*				
1.	Amma	30	42	34	-	5	-
2.	Bakraur	41	52	44	-	2	-
3.	Bhagwanpur	50	62	67	4	7	-
4.	Dahariya Bigha	37	61	55	2	5	-
5.	Hathiyara	25	19	27	2	2	-
6.	Janpur	18	15	21	2	2	-
7.	Khagbatti	16	9	18	2	2	-
8.	Kulohara	25	15	16	1	1	-

Contd.

Contd.

Sl. No.	*Name of Village*	*Means of irrigation*		*Diesel Machine*	*Rahat*	*Pokhara*	*Canal*
		No. of Wells	*No. of Pumps*				
9.	Koshila	29	31	28	2	4	-
10.	Maharaur	25	21	19	-	3	-
11.	Mastipur	42	38	47	2	2	-
12.	Mocharein	39	33	42	4	5	-
13.	Monia	21	21	23	2	3	-
14.	Nimabasari	18	19	21	1	2	-
15.	Pakardih	20	17	19	-	1	-
16.	Pararia	28	26	29	-	2	-
17.	Panchahatti	37	35	39	-	2	1
18.	Qagichak	26	18	17	2	3	-
19.	Rajapur	203	118	300	15	11	-
20.	Shirajpur	21	14	18	-	2	-

The above table shows that farmers of the villages are not totally dependent upon rain. They have pumps, boring wells and diesel pump for the purpose of irrigation. Dalits also have diesel pumps, well for irrigation. They have obtained those means with the help of block authorities.

Crops Sown

Farmers of the villages under study grow three types of crops namely, Bhadai, Aghani and Rabbi. The Bhadai crops include Marua, Maize, Kurathi, Kods. They are variety of grains. Such crops become ready for harvesting in Bhado is called Bhadai crops. These crops are cultivated in those lands which are upland different varieties of paddy come under Agahani crops. The harvesting period of such crops is Agahan. That is why they are called Agahani crops in local parlance. Wheat, gram, pea and other pulses are called Rabi crops. Their harvesting time is Chait Baishakh month. Besides these crops these villages are well attracted towards the vegetables. Vegetables of different seasons are grown round the year to get cash. Middlemen from the block headquarters and district headquarters pay a visit to the field of farmers to purchase vegetables. They also sell vegetables in different local markets.

Occupation

From the survey of villages it appears that the people of villages are engaged in farming, share cropping, service and business. A description of the occupational status of the households is being given in the table below.

Table 1.8 : Occupational Status of the Heads of the Households (Primary Occupation)

Primary Occupation	*No. of Households*	*Percentage*
Labour	3200	47.37
Share-cropping + own cultivation	1000	14.36
Agriculture	2265	33.43
Artisan	50	00.73
Service	200	2.95
Business	60	00.88
Total	6755	99.72

The above table reveals that 47.37 per cent household's primary occupation was labour, 14.76 per cent households were small farmer and share croppers, 33.43 per cent households were agriculturists, 0.73 per cent households were artisans, 2.9 per cent households were engaged in service and only 0.88 per cent households were engaged in business.

Education

Education is an important means of development. It provides varieties of knowledge which are essential for the development of individual and society. It provides different types of modern occupations and ways to fight against exploitation and atrocities. 50 years of our independence have passed but the picture of literacy is not very encouraging. Till now we have not been able to make 50 per cent population of our country literate. Women in general and children of poor families are worst sufferer in this regard. Various programmes for educating children and adults are going on, but reports available suggest that the result is not satisfactory due to lack of proper implementation and follow of programme.

Table 1.9 : Distribution of Village Population According to Educational Status

Educational Status N.A.	*Number*	*Percentage*
Illiterate	20000	56.3
To write signature	1500	4.2
Upto Primary School	2800	7.85
Upto Middle School	3000	8.42
Upto High School	1400	3.93
Upto Intermediate	1500	4.2
Upto Graduation	1225	3.43
Upto Post Graduation	75	0.2
Technical	125	0.35
Total	35625	99.9

The above table reveals that 56.3 per cent population of sample villages is illiterate the percentage of those persons who knew to put signature was 4.2. The educational qualification of 7.8 per cent population was upto primary school. 8.4 per cent population possessed education upto middle school 3.9 per cent population had education upto high school 4.2 per cent possessed education upto intermediate 3.4 per cent population possessed education upto Graduation 0.2 per cent population possessed education upto post graduation and only 0.35 per cent population possessed technical degree.

The distribution of villages according to vehicle type indicates that all villages had cycles for going, coming and carrying small load. Out of 20 villages, 14 villages possessed rickshaws. Rickshaw pullers belonged to Dalit families. They had received rickshaw on loan from institutional credit facility of the government. The traits of bullockart is gradually vanishing. Previously nearly all villages possessed rickshaws but not only in 4 villages there were bullock carts in few numbers. Tanga was found only in three villages. Tanga was found in the house of some Muslims and Kahar. The trait of tractors can be seen in almost all villages. Tractors are used for carrying goods as well as passengers. Tractors have replaced the function of bullock carts. In scooter two wheelers were found in

Different Types of Vehicles

Table 1.10 : Distribution of Villages According to the Number of Vehicle Types Village

Sl. No.	*Name*	*Cycle No.*	*Rickshaw No.*	*Bullock Cart No.*	*Tanga No.*	*Tractor No.*	*Scooter No.*	*Truck No.*	*Bus No.*
1.	Amma	275	4	2	-	2	7	1	-
2.	Bakraur	305	8	1	-	1	2	-	-
3.	Bhagwanpur	375	2	3	-	3	6	-	-
4.	Dahariya Bigha	211	10	-	-	-	1	-	-
5.	Hathiyara	165	-	-	-	-	1	-	-
6.	Janpur	105	-	-	-	2	-	-	-
7.	Khagbatti	30	-	1	-	1	1	-	-
8.	Kulohara	205	-	-	-	1	1	1	-
9.	Koshila	45	5	1	-	1	-	-	-
10.	Maharaur	175	5	2	2	2	-	-	-
11.	Mastipur	103	14	5	3	3	2	-	-

Contd

Contd

Sl. No.	*Name*	*Cycle No.*	*Rickshaw No.*	*Bullock Cart No.*	*Tanga No.*	*Tractor No.*	*Scooter No.*	*Truck No.*	*Bus No.*
12.	Mocharein	70	19	5	5	3	3	-	-
13.	Monia	139	2	-	-	1	1	-	-
14.	Nimabasari	42	-	-	-	3	-	1	-
15.	Pakardih	145	-	1	-	1	3	-	-
16.	Pararia	155	3	2	-	3	1	-	-
17.	Panchahatti	38	1	-	-	1	1	-	-
18.	Qagichak	75	2	-	-	2	1	-	-
19.	Rajapur	385	9	7	-	10	15	3	2
20.	Shirajpur	36	3	-	-	1	1	-	-

16 villages. In some villages auto rickshaws were also seen. auto rickshaws were used for carrying passengers. In four villages truck owners were also found. In only one village two bus owners lived.

Religion and Religious Centres

From the observation of ethnic composition of the villages, it appears that Hindus and Muslims two religious groups resided in the village. Some villages belonged to only Hindu communities while some villages possessed mixed population of Hindu and Muslim households.

Religious Centres

At village level almost all villages possessed a sacred place in the name of Gram devata (Village God). He is popularly known as *Dihawarhaba*. There is also a sacred place in the name of mother Bhagwati and Lord Bhola Baba. In poor villages there was symbolic representation of their Hindu Gods and Goddesses.

At the level of family, there was a sacred spot either in a house or in the courtyard in the name of *Kuldevata* lineage deity. He is also known as *Sokhababa.* Sokhababa is accompanied by Jauharia Dai. In the house of High caste Hindu one finds the existence of Mahabiri Jhanda (a flag in the name of Lord Hanumana) Muslims had Majar and Madarsha as sacred spots. Each Hindu village had a *Samshanghat* (place of cremation) and Muslims possessed *Kabragah* (place of burial).

Festivals

All Hindus celebrate festivals like Holi, Ramnavami, Janamasthami, Durgapuja, Deepawali, Basant Panchami, etc. At family level the festivals are celebrated by cooking varieties of food items, Prasad and putting on new dresses. At village level, the festival is celebrated by singing Bhajan and Kirtan (Prayer songs) at sacred places, worshipping the image of Goddess Durga, Kali, Lakshmi, and Saraswati. At village level drama and Nautanki are also staged. Hindus and Muslims both participate in the festival of each other.

There are some caste based festival also. For example, Yadvas worship Gobardhan Pahar (mountain Gobardhan) on the day of Gaydarh. Each Yadvas village has a symbolic representation of Gobardhan Mountain.

Political Organisation

The political organisations prevalent in sample villages may be broadly divided into three categories; traditional political organisations, modern political organisations and activists political organisation. Under traditional political system comes caste panchayat and traditional village panchayat. Each caste tries to solve its various problems through its caste panchayat in which senior members of castes residing in neighbouring areas participate. Some village level problems are solved by the senior members of different castes residing in the same village. Some inter village level problems are solved by the senior members of the involved villages.

Under modern political system comes modern Gram Panchayat in which Mukhia, Sarpanch and their executives are elected through election. In village one also finds the supporters of various political parties like B.J.P., Congress, J.D., C.P.I. (M.L.), I.P.F., etc. They take active part in the election of MLA and M.P. under activist political organisations come Indian peoples front (IPF) Sangram Samiti (CPIML) Marxists Coordination Centre (MCC), Bhumi Sena (Land Army) Laurik Sena (An army of Yadavas) Naxalite Sena, Savarna Sena, etc. These local armies are trying to grab power in the central Bihar. Some of them have entered the political field too while others enjoy the support of some reputed political parties. The local armies are involved in committing organised crime in which entire village is set on fire, entire family members are killed, etc. They have established a parallel government in entire central Bihar. They claim to fight against exploitations and oppression but are involved in exploiting oppressing and killing the innocent persons. They have become a threat not only for general people but also for the administrators. Generally a clash between the supporters of two armies takes place which ultimately results in bloodshed and blood bath.

Means of Entertainment

Entertainment is essential for all society, whether urban or rural. Previously villagers entertained themselves by singing songs and playing musical instruments. The hearers and the singers used to enjoy themselves. They enjoyed with story telling and story hearing on festival and ceremonial occasion, drama, dance, Ramlila, Krishnaleela were staged. But now the villages have adopted modern means of entertainment, which include hearing radios, seeing T.V. reading newspaper, etc. Among them radio is very common and can be seen in the house of rich as well as poor T.V. is available only in the houses of rich persons. Reading newspapers can be seen in the well-to-do families. In indoor games, they play card, ludo, chess, etc. The children play cricket, badminton, volley ball and football.

Table 1.11 : Village wise Distribution of Modern Means of Entertainment

Sl. No.	*Name of Village*	*Radio No.*	*TV No.*	*News Papers*	*Football Team No.*	*Volleyball Team No.*	*Cricket Team No.*	*Chess team Team*	*Carram Board*
1.	Amma	50	3	3	2	2	1	1	1
2.	Bakraur	39	6	2	2	1	1	1	1
3.	Bhagwanpur	15	1	-	1	1	1	1	1
4.	Dahariya Bigha	19	1	1	1	1	1	-	-
5.	Hathiyara	35	-	-	1	1	-	-	-
6.	Janpur	16	-	-	1	1	-	-	-
7.	Khagbatti	17	-	-	1	1	-	-	-
8.	Kulohara	20	2	-	1	1	-	-	-
9.	Koshila	25	1	-	1	1	-	-	-
10.	Maharaur	29	-	-	-	-	-	1	-
11.	Mastipur	300	2	-	1	1	-	-	1
12..	Mocharein	325	-	-	1	-	-	-	-

Contd.

Contd.

Sl. No.	*Name of Village*	*Radio No.*	*TV No.*	*News Papers*	*Football Team No.*	*Volleyball Team No.*	*Cricket Team No.*	*Chess team Team*	*Carram Board*
13.	Monia	325	-	-	1	-	-	-	-
14.	Nimabasari	45	2	1	1	-	-	-	-
15.	Pakardih	34	-	-	1	1	-	1	1
16.	Pararia	12	-	-	1	1	1	1	-
17.	Panchahatti	18	1	-	1	1	-	-	-
18.	Qagichak	25	-	-	1	1	-	-	-
19.	Rajapur	525	15	11	4	6	4	4	2
20.	Shirajpur	105	12	1	1	-	1	1	1

Location of the Village

Table 1.12 : Distribution of Villages According to Location

Sl. No.	*Name of Village*	*Distance from block headquarters (Km)*	*Direction*
1.	Amma	3	North
2.	Bakraur	2	East
3.	Bhagwanpur	2	West
4.	Dahariya Bigha	2	North
5.	Hathiyara	5	East
6.	Janpur	3	West
7.	Khagbatti	7	North
8.	Kulohara	11	South
9.	Koshila	13	North
10.	Maharaur	8	West
11.	Mastipur	2	North
12.	Mocharein	2	South
13.	Monia	4	North
14.	Nimabasari	9	East
15.	Pakardih	4	South
16.	Pararia	8	North
17.	Panchahatti	3	East
18.	Qagichak	7	South
19.	Rajapur	11	West
20.	Shirajpur	4	North

Imamgunj Block

Imamganj block is situated at a distance of 60 km from district headquarters Gaya in south-west direction. The block spreads over an area of 31070 hectares. There are 210 villages in the block as per 1981 census report, the total population of the block is 1,04,130 among which there were 52,527 males and 510603 females. The total population of scheduled castes in the block was 38,195 persons. The literacy rate in the block was 30.18 per cent. For female it was 11.1 per cent. 17,704 hectares of land is cultivable whereas 13,743 hectare was uncultivable.

The block has 4 high schools, 11 middle schools, 74 primary schools and one affiliated college. Besides, 100 adult centres were also running in the block at the time of field work.

Development programmes like Indira Awas Yojna, IRDP and Jawahar Rojgar Yojna are going on in the block for the development of rural areas.

Description of Sample Village

Table 1.13 : Location of the Sample Villages from the Block Headquarters

Sl. No.	*Name of Village*	*Distance from Block (Km)*	*Direction*
1.	Bara	14	South
2.	Bavandih	1	East
3.	Beduli Dumari	4	East
4.	Bishrampur	3	North
5.	Dargee bigha	5	East
6.	Imamgunj Pathra	2	North
7.	Imamgunj gharha	3	West
8.	Karchoe	2	East
9.	Kochia	5	North-East
10.	Kosamh	6	East
11.	Lavabar	6	Sough
12.	Lunachak	2	West
13.	Nagwan	6	East
14.	Nagmabara	9	East
15.	Pakardih	1	North
16.	Panijan	2	South
17.	Partha	11	East
18.	Purshotampur	8	East
19.	Ranijanj	2	East
20.	Rohwe	7	East

Size of Family

Table 1.14 : Distribution of Sample Villages According to Family Size

Sl. No.	*Name of village*	*No. of households*	*Total population*	*Family size*
1.	Bara	182	909	6
2.	Bavandih	463	2775	6
3.	Beduli Dumari	86	512	6
4.	Bishrampur	604	2427	4
5.	Dargee bigha	105	515	5
6.	Imamgunj Pathra	201	1124	5
7.	Imamgunj gharha	303	1697	7
8.	Karchoe	128	797	6
9.	Kochia	200	1176	4
10.	Kosamh	122	488	6
11.	Lavabar	296	1720	6
12.	Lunachak	86	494	5
13.	Nagwan	205	1166	7
14.	Nagmabara	111	717	5
15.	Pakardih	305	1551	6
16.	Panijan	500	3001	5
17.	Partha	103	535	6
18.	Purshotampur	86	499	5
19.	Ranigunj	501	2580	6
20.	Rohwe	125	744	
	Total	4712	25417	51

The average size of family including parents was found as 5 the average size of family was different for different villages. In Bishrampur village it was found as 4 while in Karchoe village it was found as seven. In eight villages the family size was discovered as 6.

Sex Ratio

Table 1.15 : Distribution of Village Population by Sex Group and Sex Ratio

Sl. No.	*Name of Villages*	*Sex Group*		*Total*	*Sex Ratio*
		Male	*Female*		
1.	Bara	462 (50.82)	447 (49.18)	2795	970
2.	Bavandih	1396 (49.99)	1369 (50.11)	-	908
3.	Beduli Dumari	268 (52.34)	244 (47.66)	512	903
4.	Bishrampur	1207 (49.32)	1220 (50.68)	2427	1010
5.	Dargee bigha	245 (47.63)	270 (52.37)	515	1102
6.	Imamgunj Pathra	560 (49.63)	270 (52.37)	515	1102
7.	Imamgunj gharha	876 (52.21)	821 (47.79)	1697	036
8.	Karchoe	394 (50.06)	393 (49.94)	787	998
9.	Kochia	571 (48.55)	595 (51.45)	1176	1024
10.	Kosamh	242 (49.57)	246 (50.43)	488	1012
11.	Lavabar	879 (51.10)	841 (48.90)	1720	956
12.	Lunachak	253 (51.21)	241 (48.79)	494	951
13.	Nagwan	582 (50.17)	582 (49.83)	1160	1003
14.	Nagmabara	364 (50.76)	353 (49.24)	717	970
15.	Pakardih	767 (49.48)	787 (50.55)	1551	1022
16.	Panijan	1985 (49.48)	1516 (50.52)	3001	1022
17.	Partha	288 (53.83)	247 (46.17)	535	856
18.	Purshotampur	258 (51.70)	241 (48.30)	499	972
19.	Ranigunj	1385 (55.81)	1195 (44.19)	2580	806
20.	Rohwe	369 (48.25)	375 (51.75)	744	1017
	Total	12551 (49.77)	12866 (50.23)	25417	1025

Table 1.16 : Village-Wise Distribution of Land

Sl. No.	*Name of Village*	*Land in Hectare*
1.	Bara	119.38
2.	Bavandih	388.49
3.	Beduli Dumari	29.14
4.	Bishrampur	325.36
5.	Dargee bigha	33.59
6.	Imamgunj Pathra	106.43
7.	Imamgunj gharha	135.97
8.	Karchoe	112.50
9.	Kochia	414.80
10.	Kosamh	58.68
11.	Lavabar	291.37
12.	Lunachak	32.37
13.	Nagwan	123.02
14.	Nagmabara	62.32
15.	Pakardih	284.49
16.	Panijan	588.00
17.	Partha	46.13
18.	Purshotampur	65.16
19.	Ranijunj	97.12
20.	Rohwe	108.45

The above table reveals that acreage is not same for all villages under study. The acreage differs from village to village which shows that there is no equal distribution of land in the villages. Again at the level of the family, there is unequal distribution of the land.

Table 1.17 : Land Holding Caste Wise

Land holding size	*Forward Caste*	*Backward Caste*	*Schedule Caste*	*Muslim*
Landless (only home stead)		25 (1.69)	1000 (43.54)	150 (47.02)
Upto 1 Acre				
1 – 2.5 Acre	19 (3.06)	275 (18.64)	800 (34.44)	50 (15.67)
2.5 – 5.00 Acre	175 (28.27)	475 (32.20)	300 (13.05)	35 (10.97)
5 – 7.5 Acre	225 (36.34)	500 (33.90)	100 (4.35)	25 (7.83)
7.5 – 10 Acre	60 (9.69)	65 (4.40)	—	19 (5.95)
Above 10 Acre	40 (6.46)	25 (1.69)	—	20 (6.26)
	619 (100.97)	1475 (99.97)	2299 (99.57)	319 (99.96)

The above table reveals that in total population under sample village male constituted 49.87 per cent and female represented 50.23 per cent. Thus, percentage of female was greater than the male. There were 1025 females for every thousand males. The percentage and male female ratio was different for different villages which can be observed in the table presented above.

The above table reveals that in total 4712 households in sample villages, 619 households belonged to forward caste, i.e. Brahmin, Bhumihar and Rajput, 1475 households belonged to Backward castes, i.e. Yadav, Koeri, Naua, Barahi, Lohar, Malah, Kandu, Kahar, etc. and 2299 households belonged to scheduled castes, i.e. Dusadh, Chamar, Bhuiyan and Pasi. Only 319 among forward castes 3.06 per cent households possessed land up to 1 acre, 28.27 per cent between 1 acre to 2.5 acre, 36.34 per cent between 2.5 to 5 acre, 16.15 per cent between 5 acre to 7.5 acre, 9.69 per cent between 7.5 acre and 10 acre and 6.46 per cent had land above 10 acre.

Among backward castes, 1.69 per cent households were landless, 18.64 per cent had land up to 1 acre, 32.20 per cent possessed land between 1 acre to 2.5 acre, 33.90 per cent possessed land between 2.5 to 5 acre, 7.45

Ethnic Group

Table 1.18 : Distribution of Sample Village Population by Ethnic Group

Sl. No.	Name of Villages	Ethnic Group		S.C.	Muslims	Total
		Forward Caste	Backward Caste			
1.	Bara	12	70	100	—	082
2.	Bavandih	63	175	200	25	463
3.	Beduli Dumari	—	36	40	10	086
4.	Bishrampur	105	95	400	04	604
5.	Dargee bigha	15	05	35	50	105
6.	Imamgunj Pathra	15	15	101	10	201
7.	Imamgunj gharha	111	39	100	03	303
8.	Karchoe	28	22	78	—	128
9.	Kochia	85	15	95	05	200
10.	Kosamh	02	52	68	—	122
11.	Lavabar	06	20	130	96	296
12.	Lunachak	06	30	50	—	186
13.	Nagwan	—	104	101	—	205
14.	Nagmabara	30	20	50	11	111
15.	Pakardih	-	145	130	—	305
16.	Panijan	45	255	150	50	500
17.	Partha	40	27	36	—	103
18.	Purshotampur	26	20	40	—	086
19.	Ranigunj	15	185	250	05	501
20.	Rohwe	15	35	75	—	125
	Total	619	1475	2299	319	4712

per cent had land between 5 to 7.5 acre, 4.40 per cent had land between 7.5 to 10 acre and 1.69 per cent above 10 acres.

Among Scheduled Castes, 43.54 per cent households were landless. They had only house-stead land 34.44 per cent households had land up to 1 acre, 32.20 per cent possessed land between 5 to 7.5 acre, 4.40 per cent had land between 7.5 to 10 acre and 1.69 per cent above 10 acres.

Among Muslims, 47.02 per cent households were landless, 15.67 per cent possessed land up to 1 acre 10.97 per cent households had land between 2.5 to 5 acre, 6.26 per cent possessed land between 5 to 7.5 acre, 5.95 per cent between 7.5 to 10 acre and 6.26 per cent households had land above 10 acres.

Observation on distribution of land among households reveal that among forward caste, there was no case of landlessness among backward castes, 1.69 per cent households was landless, along scheduled castes 43.54 per cent households were landless and among Muslims 47.02 per cent households were landless.

Among forward castes 3.06 per cent households possessed land up to 1 acre, among backward castes 18.64 per cent possessed land up to 1 acre, among Dalits to scheduled castes 34.44 per cent households had land up to 1 acre. Thus, among scheduled castes and Muslims and cases of near landlessness were more in comparison to Backward and forward castes. Among backward and forward castes, there were good numbers of small and big farmers. Among scheduled castes and Muslims, there were less number of small farmers. Among Dalits, there was no case of big farmer, but among Muslims, there were some big farmers too.

Means of Irrigation

The people residing in villages are completely dependent upon agriculture for their livelihood and survival. But agriculture in their villages is solely dependent upon rainfall. They lack assured means of irrigation like canal. However, some well to do farmers have their own electric pump and diesel machine for the purpose of irrigation. Some farmers have own wells and fetch water for irrigation with the help of Rehat. Traditional source of irrigation are ponds and tanks. A list of means of irrigation for each villages has been furnished in the table below :

Table 1.19 : Distribution of Villages According to Means of Irrigation

Sl. No.	*Name of village*	*No. of wells*	*Means of no. of electric pumps*	*Irrigation diesel Machine*	*Rehat*	*Pokhra*	*Nala*
1.	Bara	16	—	18	1	3	1
2.	Bavandih	52	18	29	12	2	—
3.	Beduli Dumari	14	12	17	6	4	2
4.	Bishrampur	117	40	60	15	7	—
5.	Dargee bigha	19	21	21	5	6	—
6.	Imamgunj Pathra	30	26	19	4	8	—
7.	Imamgunj gharha	33	27	29	3	5	—
8.	Karchoe	21	18	21	2	9	1
9.	Kochia	17	16	16	1	3	1
10.	Kosamh	23	14	17	4	2	—
11.	Lavabar	27	11	15	6	1	2
12.	Lunachak	25	23	21	8	5	—
13.	Nagwan	45	27	29	10	7	3
14.	Nagmabara	48	25	27	3	3	—
15.	Pakardih	52	37	23	4	8	4
16.	Panijan	43	32	19	7	10	—
17.	Partha	31	17	14	2	3	6
18.	Purshotampur	28	21	15	6	4	8
19.	Ranigunj	19	16	21	3	2	9
20.	Rohwe	31	28	21	3	2	9

Crops Sown

Three types of crops are generally sown in the villages. These are Bhadai crops, Agahani crops and Rabi crops. In Bhadai crops, Marua,

Makeya, Kodo Kurthi, Seraho, Salhi, etc. are sown. In Agahani crops, paddy are generally sown. Different varieties of paddy become ready for harvesting in the month of Agahan, that is why they are known as Agahani crops. In rabi crops come wheat pulses and oil. They become ready for harvesting in the month of Chait.

Besides these crops, villagers have been attracted towards the cultivation of vegetable round the year. Vegetables are sown not only for household consumption but for gaining cash by selling in local market. In some villages sugar canes are also grown. But the crop is gradually vanishing because this takes one complete year for the crop only.

Occupation

Agriculture is the main occupation of the villagers. Those who have very small acreage of land do sharecropping. Those who neither have own land nor do share cropping they earn wages as different types of labour. There are some artisan castes who supply different types of commodities to villagers either on payment of cash and kind. They are tied with the other castes through Jajmani relationship. Nowaday some are engaged in service and business. The occupational status of the heads of the households under study is as follows.

Table 1.20 : Occupational Status of the Head of the Households

Name Occupational Status Labour	*No.*	*Percentage*
Labour	2400	50.90
Share cropper	312	06.62
Farmer	1800	38.22
Artisan	25	50.00
Service	140	02.92
Business	35	00.74
Total	4712	99.98

The above table reveals that the occupation of 50.90 per cent heads of the households was labour. They earned livelihood by means of their labour. They were mostly Dalits and backward castes having only homestead land and 6.6 per cent heads of the households were engaged in share cropping. They were marginal farmer or near landless. They took land from bit land owners on lease or on share cropping. They were some Dalits, some backward castes and few forward castes also. 38.8 per cent heads of the households were farmer. They hired labour to do agriculture along with their own labour. 2.92 per cent heads of the households earned livelihood by service in private and government job. 0.50 per cent heads of the households were artisans and 0.74 per cent heads of the households subsisted on business.

Education

Since the independence our democratic government is making its all efforts to eradicate illiteracy from our country. For this purpose, education upto 14 years of age has been made free for all castes/communities. But due to difference in social and economic structure prevalent in our country, illiteracy is still prevailing in our country. The table presented below furnishes the educational status of the population under study villages.

Table 1.21 : Educational Status of the Population

Educational Status	*Number*	*Percentage*
No Applicable	1417	5.57
Illiterate	1,0080	39.65
Just to put signature	3021	12.26
Upto Primary School	4075	16.03
Upto Middle School	3025	11.58
Upto High School	1500	5.81
Upto Intermediate	1300	5.11
Upto Graduation	500	1.96
Upto Post Graduation	300	1.18
Upto Technical	200	0.78
Total	25417	99.94

The table reveals that 39.65 per cent population of the villages understudy is illiterate. They do not known to read and write anything. Whenever a letter comes in their name, they have to seek a literate person. 5.57 per cent population belonged to the children below the age of 4 years. That is why educational status was not applicable for them, 12.26 per cent population know just to put their signature, 16.03 per cent population possessed education up primary school. They know to read and write letters and to count the bundless of paddy and wheat, 11.58 per cent population had education up to middle school, 5.81 percent had education up to high school. The persons having education up to intermediate constituted 5.11 per cent, 1.96 percent persons possessed education up to graduation and 1.18 per cent had education up to post graduation level only 0.18 per cent persons had technical education.

Vehicle Types in the Village

With the advent of modern technology, modern vehicles have also reached in the villages. Previously head load, shoulder load, oxen, horses, asses, donkey, etc. were used for carrying goods and persons. Grooms and brides were carried in Palake (palangum queen) bullock carts, horses, camels, tanga asses, donkeys were used for carrying goods and passengers. Gradually bicycles reached in the village which was useful for carry person as well as small loads. Rickshaw also came in the village. Rickshaws are owned by Dalits of backward castes. They carry goods as well as passengers. Tempo can also be seen in some villages situated near by the road, station and bus stand. Tempo is owned even by persons belonging to forward castes. Some well to do persons also have scooters. Some well to do businessmen have trucks and buses too.

The Table 1.21 reveals the distribution of modern which types in the village the type any other reveals the traditional types like Palaki, Bullock cart, Tanga, etc.

Sacred Centres and Festivals

Each village has a common village deity called Dihawarbaba represented by a mud hill or stone piece. He is accompanied by his wife. Entire members of the village are regarded as their offsprings. His worship is done at the village level in which all members beyond caste participate. There are also symbolic representation of Shivalingam or temples dedicated in the name of Lord Shiva. Each village has a place or a temple in the name of Goddess Bhagwati. Each Hindu family has a *Mahabiri* flag in the house. In each house, there is a sacred place in the name of lineage deity called Sokhababa or Kuldevata.

Generally festivals are celebrated at village level in which all heads of the families contribute in the expenditure on celebration of festivals. But in villages, where intra caste or intercaste conflict are evident there the celebration is done at group level. In the festivals of Hindus, Muslim also cooperate and participate similarly, in the festivals of Muslims, Hindu also

Table 1.21 : Distribution of Villages According Vehicle Types

Sl. No.	Name of Village	Bicycle	Rickshaw	Tempo	Scooter	Tractor	Bus/Truck	Any other
1.	Bara	52	-	2	1	1	-	2
2.	Bavandih	207	-	1	1	2	-	3
3.	Beduli Dumari	51	3	1	2	-	-	-
4.	Bishrampur	309	2	3	3	4	1	1
5.	Dargee bigha	64	1	-	1	-	-	3
6.	Imamgunj Pathra	129	16	-	-	2	-	4
7.	Imamgunj gharha	132	14	4	3	1	-	6
8.	Karchoe	157	15	-	4	1	-	5
9.	Kochia	100	5	-	-	1	-	3
10.	Kosamh	41	6	2	-	2	-	2
11.	Lavabar	39	-	-	1	1	-	1
12.	Lunachak	107	3	-	-	3	-	4
13.	Nagwan	49	1	-	-	1	-	3
14.	Nagmabara	61	7	3	1	-	-	2
15.	Pakardih	33	-	1	-	-	-	1
16.	Panijan	225	11	2	2	2	-	3
17.	Partha	29	13	1	1	3	-	1
18.	Purshotampur	38	7	-	-	-	-	4
19.	Ranigunj	321	16	4	5	3	-	5
20.	Rohwe	55	5	-	1	1	-	1

participate in procession and other activities. But nowaday, due to various activities of organisation, religious unity of the village is being threatened.

Political Organisations

Each village is politically organised on the basis of traditional Gram Panchayat and caste panchayat. Through these traditional political institutions conflict between two families, two castes, two tolas or two villages are settled even to day. Besides, there is modern political institutions like Gram Panchayat in which, Mukhia, Sarpanch and their executive are elected. Various developmental programmes are being implemented in the village through modern Gram Panchayat. Modern Gram Panchayat has opened the scope for Dalits and women to become Mukhia and sarpanch on the basis of election. In traditional power structure, Dalits and women did not enjoy high status, though they had numerical strength. But now numerical strength is playing significant role in winning election.

In recent decades, the political unity of the village is being threatened due to the development of Naxalism in the area. It is an ideology to gain power on the basis of violent means. Various political organisations such as IPF, CPI (ML), MCC have emerged which claim support of Dalits and other weaker sections. Their main target of attack is high caste Hindus who own resources particularly land. To counter the attack of Naxalities, some local armies of landowners have also come into existence. Due to clashes between two armies, the incidence of blood bath, murder, rape, arson, etc. is increasing day by day. The development of such violent local armies is not good for the societies. These armies run parallel government and take law and order in their hands. They kill innocent persons like women, children and aged. Thus, they become a threat for social harmony in the area under study.

Means of Entertainment

Entertainment is essential for every society. Children, young, aged, men and women all need entertainment. In traditional society there were traditional means of entertainment. Children and aged enjoy by folktales, riddles, idioms, etc. Young men and women sing song and play musical instrument to enjoy the occasion. They see Ramleela, Krishnaleela, etc. played by folk artists. But nowadays modern means of entertainment has reached the village. The Table 1.22 indicates the village wise distribution of means of entertainment.

Table 1.22 : Distribution of Means of Entertainment According to Villages

Sl. No.	*Name of Village*	*Means of Entertainment*							
		Radio	*Tape*	*T.V.*	*Football*	*Volleyball*	*Cricket*	*Kabaddi*	*Newspaper*
1.	Bara	41	2	1	2	1	-	-	1
2.	Bavandih	111	5	5	1	1	1	1	-
3.	Beduli Dumari	31	1	5	3	1	1	1	1
4.	Bishrampur	54	3	-	1	2	-	1	-
5.	Dargee bigha	131	7	1	1	1	1	1	1
6.	Imamgunj Pathra	137	9	-	1	1	-	-	-
7.	Imamgunj gharha	40	1	2	1	1	1	1	-
8.	Karchoe	28	5	-	1	-	-	-	2
9	Kochia	35	4	1	1	1	1	-	1
10.	Kosamh	125	1	-	1	1	1	-	-
11.	Lavabar	37	-	-	1	1	-	-	-

Contd.

Contd.

Sl. No.	*Name of Village*	*Means of Entertainment*							
		Radio	*Tape*	*T.V.*	*Football*	*Volleyball*	*Cricket*	*Kabaddi*	*Newspaper*
12.	Lunachak	17	-	-	2	1	-	1	-
13.	Nagwan	27	5	1	2	2	1	1	1
14.	Nagmabara	29	3	3	1	1	1	1	1
15.	Pakardih	36	2	-	2	1	-	1	-
16.	Panijan	32	1	1	2	1	-	1	-
17.	Partha	28	-	-	1	1	1	1	-
18.	Purshotampur	21	-	-	1	1	1	-	1
19.	Ranigunj	141	5	11	3	1	2	-	1
20.	Rohwe	45	3	2	1	1	1	1	1

2

PRESENT DAY STATUS OF DALITS TODAY OF GAYA

Status is position occupied by a person in society. In traditional Hindu society, males and females have enjoyed status differently. Again in traditional Hindu society, the status of a person was deeply related to his birth in a particular caste. Different Hindu castes were placed in hierarchical order. The status was related to the position of caste in social structure.

Literature available reveals that Dalit, a name given to untouchable castes by our father of Nation, Bapu and who have been listed as scheduled castes by our honourable President of India, have suffered from social religious, political, educational and economic disabilities since centuries, virtually, they have enjoyed no status. They were treated like commodities and accordingly, they were mortgaged, sold and purchased. But if one pays his attention towards Varnavyavastha, he does not find such type of discrimination. Varnavyavastha was based on division of labour and the concept of Karma (work). In order to provide dynamism in Hindu society the system of varna was introduced. Birth was not criteria for ones belonging to a particular varna. If a son of Brahman was not Brahman by Karma, he was excluded from the Brahman varna. Similarly a son of Kshtriya was not included in Kshtriya varna, if his Karma was not like a Kshtriya. Similar was the case with Vaishya and Shudra varna. There was no taboo on intervarna marriages. There was also no prohibition on food and water relation among different varnas. Thus, each varna enjoyed status in the society. There was no feeling of high and low. They were interrelated and interdependent. Survivals of such traits as worship of Doma at the time of Agnishanskar of a person, the worship of Dobi on 10th day of death of a person, worship of Chamar and his Mandar on the occasion of marriage even by high caste Hindus bear testimony in this regard. Again several folk stories prevalent in oral traditions of the area under study relating to the inter varna marriage like marriage of a Brahman girl with a

Kshatriya boy, a Kshatriya girl with Brahman boy, a girl of Setha with a Brahman boy, a girl of king with a boy of a Setha, a girl of Raja with a Shundra boy, a girl of Shundra with a boy of Raja etc., bear witness regarding the equal status of all in course of time. Varna Vyavastha was transformed in Jati Vyavastha (caste system). In caste system, the status of a person was determined by his birth in a particular caste. Now the son of a Brahman was Brahman, the son a Kshatriya was a Kshatriya, the son of a Vaishya was Vaishya and the son of a Shudra was a Shudra. In each Varna several caste groups emerged. Thus, Brahman, Kshatriya, Vaishya and Shudra caste came into existence. They began to maintain their ethnic identity by practicing caste and sub-caste endogamy. Now there was taboo on the exchange of Betic (daughter) and acceptance of Rotic (food). Daughters were exchanged with the same castes but in different clans. Thus, caste endogamy and clan exogamy two important characteristics of caste system came into existence. Each caste eccepted Kachcha food (Bhat, Rice, Dal, Pulse, etc.) from the member of own castes. With other castes, food relation was maintained by Pucca foods, puri vegetable, etc. Shudras, now Dalits or scheduled castes accepted Kachcha and Pucca food from other castes. But other castes did not accept food and even water from shudras because they were deprived of any kind of status in the then society.

Although all Hindu castes maintained their own ethnic identity by endogamy and food relation but they were tied together by another system called *jujmani* system. This system governed social and economic relations among different castes. Depressed castes, now Dalits, were associated with unclean occupation like throwing night soil, throwing dead body of animals, etc. Through this system, social and economic relation in the society was maintained which continued for centuries.

During Mughal period, the system of feudalism was introduced. This system proved to be exploitative and oppressive for the depressed castes. The survival of these castes was dependent upon the landlord. During this period the system of Begar and forced labour also came into existence. These castes were not allowed to have any movable and immovable property. They were also subjected to forceful conversion.

During British period, the system of Zamindari was introduced. It was a slightly changed system of feudalism. This system was exploitative and oppressive for the depressed castes in the same manner. These low status castes did not possess any property. They were given a piece of land by the then Zamindars to erect houses. They were known as the men of the Zamindars. They worked day and night for the benefit of Zamindars only on food or on nominal wages. They were treated like slaves and were mortgaged or sold. British Government banned slavery and Begar labour, but due to the existence of Zamindari system, slavery and Begar system continued.

After independence, our democratic Government is making its efforts to better the conditions of those depressed castes. Several programmes of their social religious, educational, political and economic upliftment have been launched. They are dignified citizen of our country like other citizens. They have been provided with fundamental rights. They have been given voting rights. Slavery, begar and bonded labour have been abolished. The practice of untouchability has been banned. They have been given homestead land, and land for cultivation. Education facilities have been given to them. Seats in Government's jobs have been reserved for them. In the election of MLA and MP, they have obtained reservation. Such activities have certainly brought changes in the status of Dalits. Now it will be in the fitness of the thing to present day status of Dalits on the basis of field data gathered from the villages and informants understudy.

Present Day Social Status of Dalits

In order to know the present day status of Dalits, the heads of the Dalit families chosen for the studies were asked to reply on a series of questions dealing with their status in the society. Their reply has been helpful in assessing their present day status.

Although all Hindu castes maintained their own ethnic identity by endogamy and food relation but they were tied together by another system called jujmani system. This system governed social and economic relations among different castes. Depressed castes, now Dalits, were associated with unclean occupation like throwing night soil, throwing dead body of animals, etc. Through this system, social and economic relation in the society was maintained which continued for centuries.

During Mughal period, the system of feudalism was introduced. This system proved to be exploitative and oppressive for the depressed castes. The survival of these castes was dependent upon the landlord. During this period the system of Begar and forced labour also came into existence. These castes were not allowed to have any movable and immovable property. They were also subjected to forceful conversion.

During British period, the system of Zamindari was introduced. It was a slightly changed system of feudalism. This system was exploitative and oppressive for the depressed castes in the same manner. These low status castes did not possess any property. They were given a piece of land by the then Zamindars to erect houses. They were known as the men of the Zamindars. They worked day and night for the benefit of Zamindars only on food or on nominal wages. They were treated like slaves and were mortgaged or sold. British Government banned slavery and Begar labour, but due to the existence of Zamindari system, slavery and Begar system continued.

After independence, our democratic government is making its efforts to better the conditions of those depressed castes. Several programmes of their social religious, educational, political and economic upliftment have been launched. They are dignified citizen of our country like other citizens. They have been provided with fundamental rights. They have been given voting rights. Slavery, begar and bonded labour have been abolished. The practice of untouchability has been banned. They have been given homestead land, and land for cultivation. Education facilities have been given to them. Seats in Government's jobs have obtained reservation. Such activities have certainly brought changes in the status of Dalits. Now it will be in the fitness of the thing to present day status of Dalits on the basis of field data gathered from the villages and informants understudy.

Present Day Social Status of Dalits

In order to know the present day status of Dalits, the heads of the Dalit families chosen for the studies were asked to reply on a series of questions dealing with their status in the society. Their reply has been helpful in assessing their present day status.

Food and water relation determines status of a caste in the society. Previously Dalits had food and water relationship with other Hindu castes occupying upper and middle strata of the society. At top stratum were high caste Hindus like Brahmin, Rajput, Bhumihar, Kayastha. Kayasthas have left the village and almost settled in urban areas. The urban mobility in Brahmin, Bhumihar and Rajput can also be seen, but they still own resources particularly Kurmi, Lohar, Barahi, Dalit, etc. occupied middle stratum in Hindu caste hierarchy. Dusadh, Chamar, Bhuiyan, Pasi, etc. occupied lower stratum of the society because they were untouchables. Being untouchables, the castes occupying middle and upper stratum did not have food and water relations with them but they had food and water relations with other Hindu castes. Another reason was that they were very

Table 2.1 : Opinion of Heads of Dalit Family on Food and Water Relationship

	Opinion	Yes	Opinion		Total
			No.	N.R.	
1.	Do you have food and water relation with forward Hindu castes ?	300 (75.00)	100 (25.00)	—	400 (100.00)
2.	Do you have food and water relation with backward Hindu castes ?	300 (75.00)	100 75.00)	—	400 (100.00)
3.	Do you have food and water relation with other scheduled castes ?	200 (50.00)	200 (50.00)	—	400 (100.00)

poor and had no property. They subsisted on the mercy of other castes. That is why they gladly accepted food and water of other Hindu castes. Nowadays, they have also become status conscious. Since High and middle stratum Hindu caste do not have food relations with Dalits, many Dalits have also broken food and water relationship with other Hindu castes. This view clearly appear from the observation of Table 1.1 in which 250 per cent heads of the Dalits families did not opine that no family member visit in the house of any caste on the occasion of marriage feast and death feast.

Table 2.2 : Opinion of Heads of Dalit Family on Invitation of Feast

Invitation	Number	Percentage
Oral Invitation	325	81.25
Written Invitation	35	8.75
Visit without Invitation	400	(100.00)

Invitation and manner in which invitation is served determined the status of the caste in the society. In villages understudy the lineage members called Gotia Bhai are invited orally to participate in any kind of feast. But oral invitation is served by the head of the family or in his absence any male member of the family. Relatives residing in other villages are served written invitation in which date and time of the feast is written clearly. The invitation is served by Nai (barbers). The Nai gets money grains, clothes etc. for this purpose. Members of other castes residing in villages get oral invitation by Nai on behalf of the head of the family concerned. Friends residing in other villages and belonging to other castes receive written invitation. In some villages Dalits receive oral invitation while in some places they are expected to visit without any invitation. Modern education and political system have changed the status of Dalits, though very few in number. Dalits occupying posts like Mukhia, Sarpanch, Choukidar, Dafadar, Zamadar, Teacher, Karmachari, VLW, etc. get written invitation even by high caste Hindus to participate in the function.

81.25 per cent heads of the Dalit families informed that they get oral invitation to participate in the function by the other Hindu castes, only then they participate. 8.75 heads of the households informed that they received written invitation or *Nimantran Patra* only then they participated. They were such Dalits who held responsible posts in local Government bodies. Only 10 per cent heads of the family informed that they did not receive any kind of invitation but even then they visited there to get food along with their children. They belonged to Nat and Mushar castes. They move village to village for eating death feast. They seek such information from any person of the village or neighbouring villages.

Tables 2.3 : Opinion of Heads on the Invitation served to High Castes

Question	*Yes*	*No*	*Total*
Do you serve invitation to high caste Hindus	35 (10.00)	365 (90.00)	400
Do you serve invitation to Backward Hindu castes	35 (10.00)	365 (90.00)	400 (100.00)
Do you serve invitation to other scheduled caste	200 (50.00)	200 (50.00)	400 (100.00)

Previously a head of the Dalits family was not expected to serve even written invitation in the name of high castes or backward Hindu castes. It was not taken good by the castes occupying upper and middle position in caste hierarchy. But the participation of Dalits in local Government bodies have raised their status. They invite other Hindu caste to participate in their functions. 10 per cent heads of Dalit family informed that they maintain reciprocal relationship of invitation.

When asked whether other Hindu castes eat food items in their house, they said that on invitation the members of High Hindu castes paid a visit to their houses. They gave some cash as Nevata. They also send rice, wheat flour, vegetable, etc. as Nevata. But, we do not compel them to eat in the courtyard of our house. We serve some items of breakfast which is prepared by the Haluai (sweet makers).

Majority of Dalit families do not invite High caste Hindus and backward Hindu castes though they gladly accept the invitation of other Hindu castes.

Among Dalits, the food water relationship of Dalit caste to other Dalit caste is not acceptable. Chamars do not accept food and water of Dusadh and vice versa. The Dom whose status is lowermost among Dalit do not accept food and water of Dhobi (washer man). This untouchability in terms of food and water exist within the untouchable. Nowadays, some change in this direction has taken place. All Dalits living in a village are trying to unite themselves through food and water relationship. But this is taking place among Chamar, Dusadh, Bhuiyan and Pasi. Dhobi and Dom have been excluded. This also appears true from the information given by heads in which 50 per cent have accepted that they maintain food water relation with other scheduled castes.

Table 2.4 : Opinion of Heads on Sitting Arrangement at the Time of Feast

Sitting Arrangement	*Yes*	*No*	*Total*
Do you sit in the line of other Hindu castes at the time of feast ?	35 (10.00)	365 (90.00)	400 (100.00)
Do you sit in the courtyard of house at the time of feast ?	275 (68.75)	125 (31.35)	400 (100.00)
Do you leave the plate after eating like other High caste Hindus ?	100 (25.00)	300 (75.00)	400 (100.00)
Do you throw the plate after eating yourself ?	300 (75.00)	100 (25.00)	400 (100.00)

At the time of feast special attention is given at sitting arrangement High caste Hindus, Gotiabhai are brought in the courtyard of house. They are asked to sit in a separate line. The members of other backward castes take seat in another line and the members of scheduled castes occupy seat in a separate line. Each line maintains some distance from the other.

Previously only Gotiabhai and other High caste members were brought in the courtyard for serving food items. Other Backward Hindu caste and scheduled castes were served food items in space available in front of the door of the house. But nowadays, this arrangement is not followed strictly. The members of all castes are brought in the courtyard to serve food. 10 per cent heads of Dalit family reported that they set in the same line at the time of feast. 90 per cent heads reported that for them there was separate line arrangement. They did not sit with other Hindus in the same line.

68.75 per cent heads of the households informed that they sit in the courtyard at the time of feat. Only 31.25 per cent heads reported that they had to sit at door at the time of feast. They were not allowed to visit in the courtyard.

25.00 per cent heads of the household reported that they left the patal (plate left after eating) like other Hindus and 75.00 per cent heads reported that they had to throw Patal themselves.

The reply of heads of the Dalit families differed for different items. 90.00 per cent heads informed that they did not sit on cot whenever they visit to the house of a high caste Hindus. But they sit on Chouki and bench without any hesitation, only 10 per cent heads informed that they sit on cot with High Castes.

75.00 per cent heads of the households informed that they sit easily at the cot whenever a high caste Hindu paid visit to his house. 10.00 per cent informed that they did not sit on cots in front of a high caste either at his house or at their own house.

75.00 per cent heads of the Dalit family informed that they sit with high caste Hindus without any hesitation while traveling in bus or train. Only 25.0 per cent heads reported that they fell hesitation in sitting with high castes while travelling in train/bus.

93.75 per cent heads informed that they sit freely with high caste at public place. Only 6.25 per cent heads reported that they did not sit with high castes on public place.

66.25 per cent heads reported that they fetched water freely from the same well or hand pumps from where other Hindu castes also fetched. They were not prohibited in fetching water from any well or hand pump.

Table 2.5 : Opinion of Heads of Social Distance

Question of Social Distance	*Opinion of Head*		
	Yes	*No*	*Total*
Do you sit on cot in front of a high caste Hindu at his house	35 (10.00)	365 (90.00)	400 (100.00)
Do you sit on cot in front of a high caste Hindu at your own house	275 (65.00)	125 (35.00)	400 (100.00)
Do you sit with high caste Hindus on seat in train/bus	300 (75.00)	100 (25.00)	400 (100.00)
Do you sit with high castes in public place ?	375 (93.75)	25 (6.25)	400 (100.00)
Do you fetch water from the same well or hand pump	265 (66.25)	135 (33.75)	400 (100.00)
Do you eat with high castes in a hotel ?	390 (97.50)	10 (2.50)	400 (100.00)
Do you have talk freely with high castes	380 (95.00)	20 (5.00)	400 (100.00)
Do your children play with children of high caste Hindus	350 (87.50)	50 (12.50)	400 (100.00)

33.75 per cent heads of households reported that they had separate wells and hand pumps for drinking water.

95.00 per cent heads of the household opined that they had free talks with the members of High castes residing in the village. Only 5.00 per cent heads reported that they did not have free talks with high caste Hindus.

87.50 per cent heads reported that their children played freely with the children of high castes or other backward castes, residing in the village. But this happens when they start going to school 12.50 per cent heads informed that their children did not like in play with the children of High castes.

Table 2.6 : Opinion of Heads on the Acceptance of Raw Food Items by High Castes and Backward Castes

Raw / Cooked Food Items	*Acceptance by high castes*		
	Yes	*No*	*Total*
Paddy	400 (100.00)	—	400 (100.00)
Wheat	400	—	400 (100.00)
Pulses	400	—	400 (100.00)
Sunfried Rice	400	—	400 (100.00)
Sattu	275 (65.50)	125 (34.50)	400 (100.00)
Chura	250 (60.25)	150 (39.75)	400 (100.00)
Boiled rice	100 (25.00)	300 (75.00)	400 (100.00)
Milk	380 (90.50)	20 (9.50)	400 (100.00)
Curd	160 (40.00)	240 (60.00)	400 (100.00)
Matha (churned curd)	115 (27.25)	285 (72.75)	400 (100.00)
Ghee385	(96.25)	15 (3.75)	400 (100.00)
Butter	205 (51.25)	195 (48.75)	400 (100.00)
Loaf Sugar	300 (75.00)	100 (25.00)	400 (100.00)
Vegetables	400	—	400 (100.00)
Tobacoo	365 (91.25)	35 (8.75)	400 (100.00)
Cocks hens + eggs	400	—	400 (100.00)
Goat	400	—	400 (100.00)

High Hindu castes observe taboo on food items cooked by Dalits in their houses. But this taboo does not exist in case of raw food items in majority of cases. All heads of Dalit households informed that till upper and backward castes accepted paddy, wheat, pulses and sunfried rice from their house. They took these commodities from upper castes or back ward as loan and repaid them.

65.50 per cent heads of the households informed that upper castes and backward castes accepted sattu (fried flour of gram or pulses) but 34-50 per cent reported about non acceptance of sattu from their houses.

25.00 per cent heads of the households informed that high castes and backward castes accepted Usina Chawal (boiled rice) from their houses but 75.00 per cent heads reported about non-acceptance of boiled rice. When asked whether the high caste Hindus and either backward castes accept meals from your house, 90.50 per cent heads reported about the acceptance of meals. Only 9.50 per cent heads reported about the non-acceptance.

About curd, 40.00 per cent heads reported in favour of acceptance and 60.00 per cent heads reported against the acceptance. For Matha (churned curd), 27.25 per cent heads reported in favour of acceptance and 72.75% heads reported against the acceptance. For Ghee, 96.25 per cent heads reported infavour of acceptance and only 3.95 per cent heads reported against the accceptance. For butter, 51.24 per cent heads opined in favour of acceptance and 48.75 per cent heads against the acceptance. For Gur (loaf sugar), 75.00 per cent informed about the acceptance and 25.00 per cent about the non-acceptance. All heads reported about the acceptance of green vegetables by the High Castes and Backward castes. For chicken hens, eggs and goats, all heads reported in favour of acceptance.

For taboo, 91.25 per cent heads reported in favour of acceptance. Previously neither raw food items nor cooked items of Dalits were accepted, but now this taboo is not existing. Non-acceptance of cooked food items like rice, pulse, vegetable can be seen. But raw food items are being accepted.

Over all picture of social status of Dalits reveal that due to break in taboo on untouchability, the social status of Dalits is being enhanced. This is more true for the new generations. The young generations of high castes and backward castes are not so rigid towards the practice of untouchability. Many of them have friendly relationship with Dalits family. They participate in each other's joys and sorrows. Thus, the social distance between them is gradually coming closer. However such instances are not in majority but break in taboos on untouchability is certainly a praiseworthy step.

Present Day Educational Status of Dalits

Literature available on educational status of Dalits reveal a gloomy picture. Various reports highlight that they were not allowed to educate themselves. In ancient Brahmacharya Ashram Vyavastha there was no Gurukul when the children of then depressed castes were allowed to read and educate for them. The education of vedas and archery was completely banned. During Mughal period, there was no arrangement for the education of depressed castes. The British Government started schools, but during British period very few Dalits could be able to attain education. Because educational centres were located largely in urban centres and it was beyond the capacity of poor communities like Dalits to go there for education.

After independence several steps have been taken by the central as well as state governments to educate the children in general and children of scheduled castes and scheduled tribes in particular. Child labour has been prohibited. Education upto 14 years of age has been made free. S.T. and S.C. Children are getting food, clothes, books, copies, etc. free of cost. Lower Primary schools have been started nearly in all villages. Some residential schools have been started specially for the children of S.C. and S.T. These efforts have brought positive results, though not up to mark modern education has opened modern means of occupation for the Dalits. Some are employed in Government job as teacher, Gram Sevak, Karmachari, Police, B.D.O., Engineer, Doctor, etc. New let us see the educational status of Dalits under study.

Table 2.7 : Educational Status of Dalits Under Study

Educational Status	*Number*	*Percentage*
Illiterate	115	28.75
Just to put signature	100	25.00
Upto primary school	45	11.00
Upto middle school	40	10.00
Upto high school	30	7.50
Upto Intermediate	25	6.25
Upto Graduation	15	3.75
Upto Post Graduation	11	2.75
Technical	19	4.75
Total	400	99.90

The above table reveals that 28.75 per cent heads of the Dalit family were illiterate. 25.00 per cent heads knew just to put their signature. 11.00 per cent heads possessed education up to primary school and 10.00 per cent had education up to middle school, 7.50 per cent heads had education up to high school, 3.25 per cent possessed education upto intermediate only 6.25 per cent heads were graduate. 2.75 per cent heads were post graduate and 4.75 per cent heads possessed technical degree.

Table 2.8 : Education Status of Parents of Heads of Households

Educational Status	*Parents*	
	Father	*Mother*
Illiterate	315 (78.75)	390 (97.50)
Just to write signature	30 (7.50)	10 (2.50)
Upto primary school	15 (3.75)	—
Upto middle school	15 (3.75)	—
Upto high school	15 (3.75)	—
Above high school	10 (2.50)	—
Total	400 (100.00)	400

The above table reveals that the father of 78.75 per cent heads were illiterate, father of 7.50 percent heads knew to put signature, father of 3.75 per cent heads possessed education up to primary school, middle school and high school each. The father of 2.50 per cent heads had education above high school. About the education of mother of heads, the table reveals that mothers of 97.50 per cent heads were illiterate and only 2.50 know to put their signature.

Table 2.9 : Education Status of Wives of the Heads of the Households

Education status	Number	Percentage
Illiterate	275	68.75
Just to write name	45	11.25
Upto primary school	30	7.50
Upto middle school	25	6.25
Upto high school	20	5.00
Upto Intermediate	5	1.25
Upto Graduation		
	400	100.00

The Table 2.9 reveals that the wives of 68.75 per cent heads were illiterate. The wives of 11.25 percent heads knew to write their names. The wives of 7.50 per cent heads possessed education up to primary school, while wives of 6.25 per cent heads had education upto middle school. Wives of 5.00 per cent heads possessed education upto high school, while the wives of 1.25 per cent heads had education upto intermediate.

Table 2.10 Opinion of Heads on the Education of Children

Opinion	*Education of Children*					
	Boy			*Girl*		
	Yes	*No*	*Total*	*Yes*	*No*	*Total*
Do you want to educate your children	385 96.23	15 3.75	100 3.75	270 67.50	130 32.5	400 100.00
Do you sent your children to school	300 75.00	25 25.00	400 100.00	200 50.00	200 50.00	400 100.00

The above table reveals that 96.25 percent heads of the households were in favour of providing education in their male child and 67.50% heads were in favour of providing education to their female child. 15% heads were not infavour of providing education due to utter poverty, while 32.50 percent heads were infavour of not giving education to female child due to the same reason.

Table 2.11 : Opinion of Head on the Level of Education of Children

Education Level	*Male Child*		*Female Child*	
	Number	*Percentage*	*Number*	*Percentage*
Upto Middle School	100	26.15	50	18.51
Upto High School	185	48.58	130	48.14
Upto Intermediate	50	13.08	50	18.51
Upto Graduation	30	7.88	20	7.40
Technical	20	5.23	20	7.40
	385	100.90	270	99.96

Among those heads who wanted to educate their male children, 26.15 per cent wanted to provide education to male child up to middle class only. 48.58 per cent heads wanted to educate their male child up to high school, 13.08 per cent head wanted to educate their male child up to intermediate and 7.88 per cent heads wanted to make their male child graduates, 5.23 per cent heads wanted to provide technical education to their male children.

About female children, 18.51 per cent heads wanted to educate their girls upto middle school. Half of heads (48.14 per cent) wanted to educate their girls upto high school, 18.51 per cent heads wanted to educate their girls upto intermediate. 7.40 per cent heads wanted to make their girls graduate and 7.40 per cent heads wanted to make their girls graduate and 7.40 per cent heads wanted to provide technical education to their girls.

Table 2.12 : Opinion of Heads on Occupation of Children

Occupation of Male Child	*Number*	*Occupation of Female Child*	*Number*	
Household work	100 (26.15)	Housewife	50	19.51
Chaprasi (4th Gr.)	85 (22.25)	Chaprasi Nurse	45 39	16.66 11.11
Clerk (3rd Gr.)	100 (26.15)	Clerk	55	20.34
Lower School Teacher	50 (13.08)	Lower School Teacher	50	18.51
High School Teacher	30 (7.88)	High School Teacher	25	9.30
B.D.O.	10 (2.61)	B.D.O.	5	1.50
Engineer	5 (1.31)	Engineer	5	1.50
Doctor	5 (1.31)	Doctor	5	1.50
Total	385 (100.74)		270	(98.93)

When heads of the households were asked as to what kind of job they expected from their sons, 26.15 per cent opined in favour of household work, 22.25 per cent heads wanted to make their sons chaprasi (4th grade staff) in government office. 26.15 per cent heads wanted to see their sons as clerk, 13.08 per cent wanted to see their sons as lower school teachers and 7.88 per cent as high school teacher, 2.61 per cent heads wanted to see their sons as B.D.O. The percentage of heads who wanted to see their sons are engineer and doctor was 1.31 each.

In case of girls, 18.51 per cent heads wanted to see their girls as housewife, 11.11 per cent heads wanted to see their girls as nurses. 16.66 per cent heads wanted to see their girls as chaprasi, 20.34 per cent heads wanted to see their daughters as clerks, 18.51 per cent heads wanted to make their girls as lower school teachers and 9.30 per cent heads wanted to see their girls as high school teachers. The percentage of heads who wanted to see their girls as B.D.O., engineer and doctor was 1.50 for each category.

Present Day Economic Status of Dalits

Literature dealing with the economic status of Dalits per cent very poor economic condition. Literature highlights that they were not allowed to possess any property. They were rather treated as commodity. Like commodity, they were sold, mortgaged and purchased. Their economic conditions resembled to that of a slave. But after independence, several steps have been taken by our Central as well as State Governments to up-lift the socio-economic condition of the Dalits or scheduled castes. Slavery, bonded labour, Begar and similar types of forced labour has been banned completely. House-stead lands have been recorded in their names. Garrmauzarua lands have been distributed among them. Oxen, agricultural implements, seeds and fertilizer are being given to them under land based scheme. Buffaloes, cows, chicks, goats and pigs are being distributed under various schemes. Institutional credit facilities are being made available to them. They are being educated free of cost. Seats in Government jobs have been reserved for them. A change in economic status of Dalits has taken place.

Now, let us see the economic status of Dalits in present context on the basis of study.

The Table 2.13 reveals that all head possessed own homestead land, 67.00 per cent heads possessed Bari land in front of the house but 33.00 per cent heads did not possess Bari land. Not only this, 93.75 per cent heads possessed own cultivable land.

Table 2.13 : Opinion of Heads on Ownership of Land

Ownership of land	*Yes*	*No*	*Total*
Homestead land	400 (100.00)	—	400 (100.00)
Bari land	268 (67.00)	132 (33.00)	400 (100.00)
Cultivable land	375 (93.75)	25 (6.25)	400 (100.00)

Table 2.14 : Opinion of Heads on Possession of Land by their Father

Opinion on did your father possess	*Yes*	*No*	*Total*
Homestead land	125 (31.25)	275 (68.75)	400 (100.00)
Bari land	100 (25.00)	300 (75.00)	400 (100.00)
Cultivatable land	168 (42.09)	232 (58.00)	400 (100.00)

The above table reveals that 400 the primary occupation of 5.00 per cent heads was traditionally caste based. The primary occupation of majority of heads was agriculture labour. 4.50 per cent heads were engaged in share cropping and 3.00 per cent heads engaged in contract cropping 7.05 per cent heads were engaged in own agriculture. The percentage of heads subsisting on the basis of small shops, and pangumati was 5.00 per cent each, 3.0 per cent heads subsisted on the basis of loud speaker and band party. 6.25 per cent heads were engaged in vegetable selling and as feriwala. 1.25 per cent heads were earning by working as driver of tractors of land owners. The primary occupation of 6.25 per cent heads was service 3.75 heads were subsisting on rickshaw and thela pulling. 3.75 per cent heads were also engaged as coolie.

Secondary Occupation

Besides primary occupation each heads were carrying on secondary occupation as well. The most popular secondary occupation was wage earning, harvesting crops, casual labour in construction work and seasonal labour.

Table 2.17 : Distribution of Secondary Occupation by Primary Occupation

Primary Occupation	*— Secondary Occupation*				
	Wage earning	*Harves-ting*	*Brickkiln labour*	*Casual labour in construc-tion work*	*Total*
Caste based occupation	10 (50.00)	10 (50.00	—	—	20 (100.00)
Agriculture labour	—	120	30	30	180
Share cropper	—	10 (55.55)	—	8 (44.45)	18 (100.00)
Contract cropper	—	12	—	—	12
Own Agriculture	—	15	—	15	30
Small shop + Mill	—	10	—	10	20
Pangumati	—	10	—	10	20
Loud Speaker + Band Party	5	5	—	5	15
Vegetable selling + Feriwala	5	10	—	10	25
Driver	—	5	—	—	5
Service	—	—	—	—	5
Rickshaw + Thela	—	15	—	—	15
Coolie	—	15	—	—	15
Total		237	30	88	400

The above reveals that the heads whose primary occupation was traditionally caste based were engaged in secondary occupation like wage earning, harvesting and brick kiln labour. The heads, whose primary occupation was agriculture labour, were engaged secondary occupation of brick kiln labour and as casual labour in construction work. Share croppers were carrying on wage earning, harvesting and casual labour.

Similarly contract croppers were engaged in wage earning harvesting, brick kiln and construction work. Heads whose primary occupation was small crops, Gumati, loudspeaker, vegetables selling, etc., harvesting there whose primary occupation was service, were carrying on share cropping or contract cropping. Similarly rickshaw wala, Thelawala, Coolie etc. were carrying on harvesting and wage earning.

Table 2.18 : Distribution of Cultivable Land

Cultivable land in Acre	*Number*	*Percentage*
Upto one Acre	200	53.33
1 to 2.5	150	40.00
2.5 Acre to 5 Acre	25	6.64
Total	375	99.97

This table reveals that 53.33 per cent heads possessed cultivable land up to one acre only. 40.00 per cent heads possessed land between one acre to 2.5 to 5 acre. Thus, majority of heads were near landless. 40.00 per cent heads were small farmers and 6.64 per cent heads were middle farmers.

Table II.19 : Distribution of Heads According to Domestic Animals

Animals	*Yes*	*No*	*Total*
Single	125 (91.25)	275 (68.75)	400 (100.00)
Pair of oxen	111 (27.75)	289 (72.25)	400 (100.00)
Cows	175 (41.25)	225 (58.75)	400 (100.00)
Buffaloes	115 (28.75)	285 (71.25)	400 (100.00)
Goats	365 (91.25)	35 (8.75)	400 (100.00)
Cock + Hen	334 (83.50)	66 (16.50)	400 (100.00)
Pigs	112 (28.00)	288 (82.00)	400 (100.00)

House

House is essential for each individual and family. It protects individuals from cold, rain and heat. That is why it comes under basic needs. Each Dalit family owns homestead land and a house. The type of house differs from family to family.

Table 2.20 : Distribution of Heads According to Types of House

	Types of House	*Number*	*Percentage*
1.	Made up of mud and thatched with phoos (straw)	142	35.50
2.	Made up of mud and thatched with tiles	158	39.50
3.	Made up of brick and mud and thatched with phoos	20	5.00
4.	Made up of bricks + mud and thatched with tiles	54	13.50
5.	Made up of brick + mud and thatched with lintel	15	3.75
6.	Cemented and lintel	11	2.75

Observation on types of house reveals that 35.50 per cent heads possessed house made up of mud and thatched with phoos. 39.50 per cent heads possessed house made up of mud and thatched with tiles. 5.00 per cent heads had house made up of brick + mud and thatched with phoos. 13.50 per cent heads possessed house made up of brick and thatched with tiles. 3.75 per cent heads were residing in brick made lintel house, 2.75 per cent heads were residing in cemented and lintel house.

For house construction, they prepare bricks and tiles themselves. They prepare house on the basis of exchange of labour. Those who are in jobs have constructed brick cemented lintel house some have been given cemented lintel house under Awas Yojna.

Income

Attempts were made to assess the annual income of the Dalit families under study on the basis of their primary, secondary and tertiary occupation. The pattern of income was not similar for all families. It was found ranging between five thousand to fifty thousand and even above.

Table 2.21 : Distribution of Heads According to Annual Income

Annual Household Income in Rs.	*Number*	*Percentage*
Upto 5000	54	13.50
5001 – 7500	100	25.00
7501 – 10000	156	39.00
10001 – 15000	24	6.00
15001 – 20000	17	4.25
20001 – 25000	15	3.75
25001 – 30000	12	3.00
30001 – 40000	10	2.50
40001 – 50000	7	1.75
Above 50000	5	1.25
Total	400	100.00

Observation on annual income of heads reveals that greater number of heads possessed annual income between Rs. 7500 to Rs. 10000. The percentage of heads coming in this category of annual income was 39.00. The annual income of 13-50 per cent head was up to Rs. 5000. The annual income of 25.00 per cent heads was between Rs. 5001 to 7500. The annual income of 6 per cent heads was between Rs. 10001 to 15000, while the annual income of 4.25 per cent was observed between Rs. 15001 to 20,000. The annual income of 3.75 per cent heads was between Rs. 20001 to 25000, while the annual income of 3.00 per cent heads was between 25001 to 30,000. The annual income or 2.50 per cent heads was between Rs. 30001 to 40000, 1.75 and 1.25 per cent heads annual income was between Rs. 40001 to 50000 and above 50,000 respectively.

Annual Expenditure

An attempt was made to come near the annual expenditure pattern of the Dalits families. The pattern of expenditure was different for different families. Items of expenditure were generally related to household consumption, marriage, treatment, education, etc. The distribution of annual income pattern is shown in the table below.

Table 2.22 : Distribution of Heads According to Annual Household Expenditure

Annual Household Income in Rs.	*Number*	*Percentage*
Upto 5000	45	11.25
5001 – 7500	95	23.75
7501 – 10000	100	25.00
10001 – 15000	61	15.25
15001 – 20000	30	7.50
20001 – 25000	25	6.25
25001 – 30000	22	5.50
30001 – 40000	10	2.50
40001 – 50000	7	1.75
Above 50000	5	1.25
	400	100.00

Observation on annual expenditure pattern of heads of households reveals that the annual expenditure of 11.25 per cent heads was up to Rs. 5000. 23.75 per cent heads reported their annual expenditure between Rs. 5000 to 7501. 25.00 per cent heads reported their expenditure in between Rs. 75001 to 10000. 15.00 per cent heads reported their annual expenditure in between Rs. 10001 to 15000. The annual expenditure of 7.50 per cent head was observed in between Rs. 15000 to 20000. 6.25 per cent heads reported their expenditure in between Rs. 20001 to 25000. The annual expenditure of 5.50 per cent head was Rs. 25001 to 30000. 2.50 per cent heads reported their annual expenditure between 30001 to 40000. 1.75 per cent heads reported their annual expenditure between 40001 to 50000 and 1.25 per cent heads reported their annual expenditure above Rs. 50000.

Loan

Loan is an important source of income. No heads of Dalit family reported about their saving. But they all reported about the loan. The amount of loan was found different for different family.

Table 2.23 : Distribution of Heads According to Amount of Loan

Amount of loan in Rs.	*Number*	*Percentage*
500 – 1000	35	8.75
1001 – 1500	46	11.50
1501 – 2000	59	14.75
2001 – 2500	60	15.00
2501 – 3000	51	12.75
3001 – 3500	49	12.25
3501 – 4000	35	8.75
4001 – 4500	24	6.00
4501 – 5000	26	6.50
5000+	25	6.25
	400	100.00

Observation on amount of loan reveals that 8.75 per cent heads had taken a loan in between Rs. 500 to 1000. 11.50 per cent heads reported about loan in between Rs. 1001 to 1500, while 14.75 per cent head reported the amount of loan inbetween Rs. 2001 to 2500. 12.75 per heads reported their amount of loan in between Rs. 2501 to 3000, while 12.25 per cent reported in between Rs. 3001 to 3500. The annual income of 8.75 per cent heads was seen as between Rs. 3501 to 4000. 6.00 per cent heads reported their loan in between Rs. 4001 to 4500, while 6.50 and 6.25 per cent heads reported their loan in between 4501 to 5000 above Rs. 5000 respectively.

Source of Loan

The source of loan is also important. When loan is taken from traditional sources, more interest is to be paid. When loan is taken from institutional sources, less interest is to be paid. They had taken loan from traditional as well as institutional sources.

Source of loan	*Number*	*Percentage*
Malik or Mahajan	178	44.50
Dukandar (shop keeper)	122	30.50
Friend	15	3.75
Relative	10	2.50
Bank	50	12.50
Cooperative	25	6.25
	400	100.00

Rate of Interest

The rate of interest on loan varies according to sources. Some get loan from Malik, dukandar, Friends or relative without any interest. But such loans are to be paid back within short period, for the loan of long period interest is charged on the loan.

Table 2.24 : Distribution of Heads According to Rate of Interest on Loan

Annual Interest on Loan	*Number*	*Percentage*
10%	15	3.75
12%	20	5.00
13%	25	6.25
15%	35	8.75
25%	80	20.00
36%	125	41.25
48%	40	10.00
60%	25	8.75
No Interest	25	6.25
	400	100.00

Observation on Table 2.24 reveals that the heads of the households had taken loan annual rate of interest from 10 per cent to 60 per cent, 3.75 percent heads had taken loan at 10 per cent per annum rate of interest 5.0 percent heads had taken loan at 12 per cent per annum rate. 6.25 percent heads were able to get interest at 13 per cent per annum rate, 8.75 percent heads were able to obtain loan at 15 per cent per annum rate, 20.0 per cent heads were able to get loan at 36 per cent per year. 41.25 per cent heads were able to get loan at 48 per cent per annum rate of interest, 8.75 per cent heads had taken loan at 60 per cent per annum rate of interest, 6.25 per cent heads were able to obtain loan without any interest.

Purpose of Loan

Different heads had taken loan for different purposes. The purpose of loan has been shown in the table below :

Table 2.25 : Distribution of Heads According to Purpose of Loan

Purpose of loan	*Number*	*Percentage*
Household expenditure	175	43.75
House construction	21	5.25
Marriage ritual	125	91.25
Death ritual	40	10.00
To purchase animal	20	5.00
Education of children	19	4.75
	400	100.00

The table reveals that 43.75 per cent heads had taken loan for household expenditure and 5.25 per cent heads had taken loan for the construction of house, 31.25 per cent heads had taken loan for meeting expenses on marriage rituals and 10.00 per cent heads had taken loans for meeting expenses on death rituals. 5.0 per cent heads had taken loan for purchasing animals and 4.75 per cent heads had taken loan for meeting expenses on education of children.

Religious Status of Dalit Today

Literature dealing with the status of Dalits yesterday reveals that Dalits have virtually enjoyed no religious status. They were not allowed to visit temples and pilgrimage centres. They did not celebrate festival together with other castes. They were not allowed to hear Satyanarayan Swami Katha. No Brahman visited their houses to conduct worship. The milk and ghee of their houses were not accepted for worship. Although some of them were ritual specialists, like doma, the ritual specialist of cremation, Dhobi, the ritual specialist of 10th day of death and *chathi* of birth, Chamar, the ritual specialist of marriage, but they were not enjoying high religious status in the society.

After independence, the practice of untouchability was banned. Discrimination on the basis of caste creed, religion, etc. has been prohibited. Such prohibitive measure have played significant role in enhancing the religious status of the Dalits. Now let us see the present religious status of the Dalits in our sample villages.

Table 2.26 : Opinion of Heads on Religious Status

Question on religious status Does anybody prohibit you	*Opinion*		
	Yes	*No*	*Total*
(a) In visit to temples in the village ?	400 (100.00)	00	400 (100.00)
(b) In visit to sacred pond of the village ?	400 (100.00)	00	400 (100.00)
(c) In visit to sacred well of the village ?	400 (100.00)	00	400 (100.00)
(d) In visit to the sacred Ghat of the river ?	400 (100.00)	00	400 (100.00)
(e) In visit to a sacred place for pilgrimage ?	400 (100.00)	00	400 (100.00)

Each Hindu village has places dedicated in the name of Gods and Goddesses. Some are represented by mud heap, stone pieces, wooden poles, etc. Besides there are some temples dedicated to Lord Shiva, Mother Goddess Bhagwati, Satimai, Lord Hanumana, Lord Ramlakshmana, Lord Radha Krishna, etc. These temples are erected by the villagers on the basis of raising fund by contributing themselves. Over such temples, the village has common ownership. In the erection of such temples, each households contribute on their basis of its economic status. By the side of such temples, there are sacred ponds and wells whose water is used for the bathing purposes and worship purposes. Resides common temples there are some temple over which particulars family of the village have ownership. They treat temples as their property. In such temples the common villagers do not visit to offer worship.

All heads of Dalit families reported that they were not prohibited to visits to general temples, ponds, wells, Ghat, pilgrimage centres for offering worship. But in private temples, like other villagers they do not visit to offer worship.

When asked whether Dalits of neighbouring villages or your own any relatives are prohibited in visiting the general temples or other religious centres of the village, they replied that such type of discrimination was not in practice nowadays.

Table 2.27 : Opinion of Heads on Religious Participation

Religious participation	*Yes*	*No*	*Total*
Worship of Gram Devata	400	—	400 (100.00)
Worship of Bhagwati Mai	400 (100.00)	—	400 (100.00)
Worship of Durga Mai	400 (100.00)	—	400 (100.00)
Worship of Lord Shiva	400 (100.00)	—	400 (100.00)
Worship of Ramnavami	400 (100.00)	—	400 (100.00)
Worship of Janamasthami	400 (100.00)	—	400 (100.00)
Worship of Lakshmi Mai	400 (100.00)	—	400 (100.00)
Worship of Saraswati Mai	400 (100.00)	—	400 (100.00)
Akhanda Harikirtan	400 (100.00)	—	400 (100.00)
Nawaratri Yagya	400 (100.00)	—	400 (100.00)

In villages, some worships are made at the level of villages. Such worship includes the worship of Gramdevata, Bhagwati mai, Durga mai, Siva baba, Ramnawami, Janmasthami, Lakshmi puja, Saraswati puja, Akhanda Harikirtan, Yagya, etc. to celebrate such festivals, a village level committee is constituted in which members of each caste get representation. The fund is raised from each household. The rate of Chanda subscription is decided on the basis of economic condition of the family. If a family is not able to contribute, his case is considered sympathetically and its members are also included in the celebration of worship. The heads of the households reported that they participated whole heartedly in the religious function of the village.

Table 2.28 : Opinion of Heads on Participation in Religious Performances

Participation in religious performances	*Yes*	*No*	*Total*
1. Does Dalit of your village take parts as			
(a) *Shrota* (heārer) of Gram Devata worship ?	380 (95.00)	20 (5.00)	400 (100.00)
(b) *Shrota* of Bhagwati Mai worship ?	380 (95.00)	20 (5.00)	400 (100.00)
(c) *Shrota* of Durga mai worship ?	380 (95.00)	20 (5.00)	400 (100.00)
(d) *Shrota* of Ramnawami worship ?	380 (95.00)	20 (5.00)	400 (100.00)
(e) *Shrota* of Janamasthami worship ?	380 (95.00)	20 (5.00)	400 (100.00)
(f) *Shrota* of Akhanda Dalits ?	380 (95.00)	20 (5.00)	400 (100.00)
(g) Participant of Hawana ritual worship ?	380 (95.00)	20 (5.00)	400 (100.00)
(h) *Shrota* of a Yagna ?	380 (95.00)	20 (5.00)	400 (100.00)
(i) Participant of carrying Images at the time of procession ?	380 (95.00)	20 (5.00)	400 (100.00)
(j) Participant of carrying *prasad* ?	380 (95.00)	20 (5.00)	400 (100.00)
(k) Participant of singing Bhajan and Kirtan ?	380 (95.00)	20 (5.00)	400 (100.00)

The above table reveals that the Dalits of the village get proper representation in village level religious performance. They participate as *shrota* (hearer) of the worship. The village level worship includes many *shrota* (one who hears) in which Dalits are also included. They participate in the ritual of Hawana carrying images, *prasad* and in singing Bhajan and Kirtan. 95.00 per cent heads reported about the participation of Dalit in different rituals related to village level worship.

Table 2.29 : Opinion of Heads on Acceptance of Prasad Items of Worship

Acceptance of prasad	*Yes*	*No*	*Total*
The following items of *prasad* of your house accepted at the time of worship ?			
Milk	400 (100.00)		400 (100.00)
Curd	400 (100.00)		400 (100.00)
Sun-fried rice	400 (100.00)		400 (100.00)
Oat 400 (100.00)	400 (100.00)		
Dhup	400 (100.00)		400 (100.00)
Agarbatti	400 (100.00)		400 (100.00)
Mitha (loaf sugar)	400 (100.00)		400 (100.00)
Fruits	400 (100.00)		400 (100.00)
Thenkua (cooked items Prasad)	400 (100.00)		400 (100.00)
Sweets	400 (100.00)		400 (100.00)

The heads of the Dalit households reported that *prasad* and items of worship like milk, ghee, curd, sun-fried rice, oat, dhup, agarbatti, mitha, fruits, thenkua, sweets, etc. of their houses are accepted at the time of great worship in the village.

The *prasad* of *chhatha* and Satyanarayan Swami Katha is accepted by high caste Hindus too. There is no taboo on the acceptance of *prasad*.

Table 2.30 : Opinion of Heads on the Acceptance of Prasad of Family Level Worship

Acceptance of prasad of household level worship

Do the High Castes of the village accept the prasad of worship made in your house ?	*Yes*	*No*	*Total*
Prasad of Chhatha worship	400 (100.00)		400 (100.00)
Prasad of Satyanarayan Katha	400 (100.00)		400 (100.00)

Table 2.31 : Opinion of Heads on Specialists of Worship

Worship	*Specialists*		
	Brahman	*Nauna (Barber)*	*Total*
Village level	400 (100.00)	00	400 (100.00)
Household level	100 (25.00)	300 (75.00)	400 (100.00)

Village level worship is done in front of a sacred centre, therefore such worships are performed with the help of Brahman priest. For household level worship in Dalits, Barbers used to act as sacred specialist. They act as specialist of different rituals in the Dalit families nowaday, some Brahmin priests have also started visiting in the house of Dalits for conducting rituals. Now, this taboo on Brahman priest is also breaking.

Political Status of Dalits Today

Various reports and literatures highlight that Dalits have been deprived of political status since centuries. As they were untouchables and were known as a men a particular feudal lord or Zamindar, they did not enjoy majority, but they were not ruler, rather, they were meant to be ruled. After independence, our country adopted secular constitution. Now discrimination on the basis of caste creed, sex, religion, etc. has been prohibited. Not only this, our central and state governments have launched several democratic programmes to incorporate the participation of Dalits in political system. The seats for Dalits have been reserved in the election of M.P. and M.L.A. They have been given voting rights. They also participate in the election of Mukhia, Sarpanch and their executives. In the election they not only fight election but also play significant role in making alliance with other castes at the time of election. They enjoy representation in village thana, block and district level administration. Now let us see the political status of Dalit in the villages, under study.

Table 2.32 : Opinion of Heads on Participation of Dalits in Village Level Decision Making

Decision making	*Participation*		
	Yes	*No*	*Total*
Have you participated in decision making as.			
1. Pancha in caste conflict ?	269 (67.75)	131 (32.25)	400 (100.00)
2. Pancha in inter caste conflict ?	195 (48.75)	205 (51.25)	400 (100.00)
3. Pancha in inter caste conflict ?	164 (41.00)	236 (59.00)	400 (100.00)
4. Pancha in inter village conflict ?	125 (31.25)	275 (68.75)	400 (100.00)

Table reveals that the Dalits of today are requested to act as Panch whenever a conflict arises in the village or in neighbouring villages. 67.25 per cent heads reported that they had acted as Pancha in inter-caste conflict, 48.75 per cent heads had acted as Pancha in caste conflict 41.00 per cent heads reported about their participation as Pancha in inter-tola conflict and 31.25 per cent heads had participated as Pancha in inter-village conflict.

There was time when Dalits did not dare to face with even Choukidar and Police. But now the situation has changed. At present they do not hesitate in meeting with different political and administrative authorities. All heads informed about their meeting with Choukidar and Dafadar. 36.25 per cent head reported about their meeting with Daroga or Jamadar of the thana on different occasions. About Mukhia and Sarpanch, all head informed about their meeting, 16.25 per cent heads had met with B.D.O. 12.50 per cent heads had met with S.P. and 13.5 per cent heads had met with D.M. on different occasions, 44.75 per cent heads had met with MLA and 18.75 heads had met with M.P.

Table 2.33 : Opinion of Heads on Meeting with Authorities have You Met these Authorities

	Yes	*No*	*Total*
Chowkidar	400 (100.00)	—	400 (100.00)
Dafadar	400 (100.00)	—	400 (100.00)
Daroga Jamadar of Thana	225 (65.25)	175 (43.75)	400 (100.00)
Mukhia	400 (100.00)	—	400 (100.00)
Sarpancha	400 (100.00)	—	400 (100.00)
Labour Inspector	100 (25.00)	300 (75.00)	400 (100.00)
B.D.O.	65 (16.25)	385 (83.75)	400 (100.00)
S.P.	50 (12.50)	350 (87.50)	400 (100.00)
D.M.	54 (12.50)	346 (76.50)	400 (100.00)
MLA	135 (44.75)	265 (55.25)	400 (100.00)
MP	75 (18.75)	325 (81.25)	400 (100.00)

Table 2.34 : Statement of Heads on the Castes of the Local Political Authority

Local Political Authority	*Forward Caste*	*Backward Caste*	*Schedule Caste*	*Muslim Caste*
Choukidar	—	110(27.50)	170(72.50)	—
Dafadar	260(65.00)	140(35.00)	—	—
Mukhia	185(46.25)	115(28.75)	60(15.00)	40(10.00)
Sarpanch	167(41.75)	133(33.25)	65(16.25)	35(8.75)
Upmukhia	125(31.25)	170(42.50)	75(18.75)	30(7.50)
Up Sarpanch	169(42.25)	200(50.00)	25(6.25)	6(1.50)
Gram Sewak	183(45.75)	200(50.00)	12(3.00)	5(1.55)
Panchayat Sewak	175(43.75)	155(38.75)	45(11.25)	25(6.25)

The above table reveals the distribution of local authorities according to caste group. The table shows clearly that Dalits are getting representation in local political and administrative authorities like Choukidar, Dafadar, Mukhia, Upmukhia, Sarpanch, Upsarpanch, Gramsewak, Panchayat Sewak, etc.

Table 2.35 : Opinion of Heads on Membership of Political Parties

Political Parties	*Number*	*Percentage*
BJP	125	31.25
JD	60	15.00
Cong. I	40	10.00
CPI	20	2.50
CPI ML	70	17.50
MCC	65	46.25
BSP	11	4.75
SP	11	2.75
	400	100.00

The distribution of heads according to the membership political parties reveal that a present Dalits are members of all political parties. 31.25 per cent heads were members of BJP, 15.00 per cent heads were member of JD 10.00 per cent heads belonged to the member of Congress I, 2.50 per cent were members of CPI, 17.50 per cent heads possessed membership of CPI (ML) and 16.25 per cent heads belonged to the member of MCC 4.75 percent belonged to BSP and only 2.75 per cent heads belonged to SP.

Table 2.36 : Knowledge of Heads about Symbols of Political Parties

Symbol of Parties	*Yes*	*No*	*Total*
BJP	300 (75.00)	—	400 (100.00)
JD	400 (100.00)	—	400 (100.00)
Cong. I	400 (100.00)	—	400 (100.00)
CPI	400 (100.00)	—	400 (100.00)
CPI ML	170 (42.50)	230	400 (100.00)
MCC	300 (75.00)	100	400 (100.00)
BSP	175 (43.75)	225 (56.25)	400 (100.00)
SP	60 (15.00)	340 (85.00)	400 (100.00)

All heads of the households know about the symbols of political parties like BJP, JD Cong I and CPI 42.50 per cent heads know about CPI (ML) 75.00 per cent heads know about MCC, 43.75 per cent know the symbol of MCC, 43.75 per cent know about BSP and only 15 per cent heads know about SP.

Table 2.37 : Opinion of Heads on Voting

Do you cast your vote	*Number*	*Percentage*
Yes	260	65.00
No	140	35.00
Total	400	100.00

65.00 per cent heads reported that they cast their votes in the election of MLA, MP and panchayat, while 35.00 per cent reported that they never caste their votes at the time of election. They reported that some other persons looted their booths and voted in their names. Thus, they were prohibited from voting. Due to the fear of Poll violence, they did not want to visit the polling centre. According to them, the incidence of both looting is not a new phenomenon. They are hearing such news ever since they became also to understand the thing. Previously forward caste criminals used to loot our booth. Local armies also make looting of our votes. Thus, booth looting of Dalit voters is still going on.

Table 2.38. Opinion of Heads about the Political Status of Dalit Women

Do women of your community hold any post in the following category ?	*Yes*	*No*	*Total*
Mukhia	—	400 (100.00)	400 (100.00)
Sarpancha	—	400 (100.00)	400 (100.00)
Upmukhia	—	400 (100.00)	400 (100.00)
Upsarpancha	—	400 (100.00)	400 (100.00)
Gramsewak	—	400 (100.00)	400 (100.00)
Gram Panchayat Sewak	—	400 (100.00)	400 (100.00)
Chowkidar	—	400 (100.00)	400 (100.00)
Dafadar	—	400 (100.00)	400 (100.00)
Police	—	400 (100.00)	400 (100.00)

The Table 2.38 reveals clearly that Dalit Women do not enjoy political status like other women of the village. They do not fight election of local political institution. They do not hold any post in caste panchayat. They are not allowed to mediate in any type of conflict.

Table 2.39 : Opinion of Heads on the Membership of Dalit Women of Political Parties

Whether any women of your family is a member of	*No*	*Yes*	*Total*
Political parties	309 (77.50)	91 (22.50)	400 (100.00)
Activities organisation	130 (42.50)	370 (47.50)	400 (100.00)
Mahila Mandal	400 (100.00)	—	400 (100.00)
Anganbari	325 (81.25)	75 (19.25)	400 (100.00)

The above table reveals clearly that very few Dalit women are members of political parties, activists political organisation Mahila Mandal and Anganbari.

Table 2.40 : Opinion of Heads on the Voting of Women

Do women of your family caste vote in following election	*Yes*	*No*	*Total*
Election of Mukhia	318 (79.50)	82 (20.50)	400 (100.00)
Election of MLA	265 (66.75)	135 (93.25)	400 (100.00)
Election of Bazar Samiti	205 (51.25)	195 (48.75)	400 (100.00)
Election of MP	200 (50.00)	200 (50.00)	400 (100.00)

The above table reveals clearly that more number of Dalit women takes part in the election of Mukhia 79.50 per cent, 66.75 per cent heads reported about the participation of women in the election of MLA, 51.25 per cent heads reported their participation in election of Bazar Samiti, 50.00 per cent heads reported about the participation of women in MP election.

3

THE SOCIAL AREA OF DALIT EXPLOITATION OF GAYA

In social areas three sections of Dalit community are worst sufferer of exploitation. These are children, women and aged. They are exploited not only by the member of other castes but by their own castes and in their own houses. It will be proper here to discuss the exploitation of each group one by one.

EXPLOITATION OF CHILDREN.

The children are the backbone of a nation. The children of today are the youth of tomorrow. They are the future of a nation. The prosperity and development of a nation depend upon the development of the children. But unequal distribution of resources compel parents to exploit their children for own household works to send their children to be exploited in the house of others. Although 50 years of our independence has brought some Dalits families in the life of developed families, but still majority of them are yet to be developed. It is true the children of developed Dalit families are enjoying status equal to the children of other developed castes, but the children of poor and underdeveloped Dalit families are worst victim of exploitation and suppression. Since their parents are poor and don't own any resources, they are used as a source of family-income from very beginning when they are expected to attend school. For them bread is more important than education. The exploitation of children takes place in the following ways.

Charwaha (Herd Boy)

The boy who is engaged as cattleherder is known as Charwaha. In order to graze them, they employ a child. As a charwaha he receives breakfast and food of both ends. He also gets clothes on festive and ceremonial occasions. Besides, food and clothes, his parents receive nominal wages. The payment of wages is made at annual basis. The parents bring their boy before a landowner. He takes some loan advance from the Malik, a general term for the landowner. The Malik and the parents or only father of the boy make a verbal agreement. The Malik agrees to pay a fixed annual payment in cash or kind.

The parents agree on behalf of the child to graze the cattle round the year. At the end of the agricultural year, i.e., on the full moon day of Jayestha month a charwaha is free to select another Malik. But he has to clear the dues of the previous Malik. Some times, being unable to repay previous loans, he prefers to work in the house of the same Malik. In some cases, he takes loan from another Malik to pay the loan of previous Malik back.

During the period of contract, a charwaha is not expected to be absent. On illness or absence, his parents have to do the work of a charwaha. The expenditure of treatment is not made by the Malik but by the parents. It is true that the Malik gains sympathy by providing loan for treatment.

If a charwaha leaves work before the period of contract, no payment is made. Rather his parents have to pay some penalty fixed by the Malik. The day a boy accepts the job of a charwaha, he looses freedom to lead life according to his own will. He has to lead life at the mercy of the Malik. The parents of charwaha don't take it ill. They become glad because the problem of food, clothes and shelter of the boy is solved by the Malik. Sometimes female child is also kept as charwahin.

Gharelu Naukar (Domestic Servant)

The Malik or the land owners require a helping child to assist in the feeding of cattle, cleaning shed, taking oxen to field and bringing them back. They require a helping-hand to perform various types of domestic hands. It is not that they do not have children as working hand. But their children attend school. That is why they require a working hand. These helping hands are known as Gharelu naukar (domestic servant). The male children of poor Dalit family serves this purpose of the Malik like Charwaha, they are also employed on the basis of one year contract. The Malik and the guardian of the child agrees upon a verbal contract. The father of the child takes some advance either interest free or on interest to accept the terms and conditions of working in the house of the Malik. Besides loan, Malik agrees to pay some annual payment as wages. He also agrees to pay breakfast, food and cloths.

The day a boy becomes Naukar of a Malik he looses freedom to play with the children of his own age group. He has to stay in the house of Malik 24 hours. He has to get up early in the morning to feed the cattle and to clean the cattle shed. Then he has to take oxen at the field for ploughing. He takes breakfast and carries breakfast of other labourers at the field. In the mid-day he has to carry meals of the labourers at the working place. He has also to feed the labourers. In the evening he has to bring cattle in the shed and feed them. After supper he sleeps with cattle in the shed. Besides, he has to bring grasses for the cattle, fuels for the household consumption. He has to throw ashes and dung in the field. He has also to look after the small kids. Crops and harvesting field of the Malik.

As Naukar a child forgets his parents and community members, though they live in the same village or in a neighbouring village. A Naukar is not expected to Jeave the house of the Malik without prior permission of the Malik. The parents of Naukar become glad to see that their child is learning work. They also become pleased because now they do not worry about the food, clothes and shelter of the child.

Generally a Naukar is employed on a yearly basis, but inability to repay previous loan and incurring more loan before the expiry period compels a Naukar to continue for years to come. Female children are also employed for cleaning shed.

Hotel Naukar

The development of road communication and mobility towards urban areas, has provided an occasion for opening of Bhojnalaya, Jalpangriha and Chaya dukan nearby the urban centres. In order to run such type of hotels, the services of children is required. The children of rich family attend school. They never bother for food, cloth and shelter. But the children of poor Dalit have to think about food and cloth. Being unable to meet both ends meal and clothes once in a year, the father or guardian of such children approach the hotel owners, who generally belong to the same or neighbouring villages. They request the Malik to employ their children as a servant. The Malik agrees to employ the child because he also needs such a boy to clean the utensils and to serve food and water. The water of Dalit boy is not accepted for cooking and drinking purposes in the house of some Hindu castes. But in hotels, their water is accepted because hotel visitors do not care for the caste of the servant.

The hotel owners and the father of the child inter into oral agreement for the payment and the rendering of services. The child receives breakfast and food. The payment is given to the father of the child.

As Khatal Servant

In neighbouring urban centre, *Khatals* are being established not only by the Yadvas, who are famous for opening *Khatal,* but other castes have also taken up this means of earning. In khatal cows and buffaloes are kept for Malik. Malik is supplied in the households residing nearby the Khatal. In order to feed the cattle and to clean the shed and also to send milk in different houses, the Khatal owner requires a servant. Generally, the children of the poor Dalit family accept the job of Khatal servant. The khatal owners, who are generally residents of the same village or neighbouring villages, approaches to the father of such a child. They give some money as advance. This advance amount is treated as loan. The loan may be on interest or interest free or partly interest free and partly on interest. They also agree to pay to some monthly wages besides both ends breakfast and meals. The wages is adjusted against the loan already taken. The child is brought to the Khatal. He is asked to render services in the Khatal. He gets up early in the morning takes the cows and the buffaloes out of the Khatal, cleans the Khatal, helps the Malik in milking the cattle. Thereafter, he has to serve fodder to the cattle and carry milk to the houses of purchasers. In the mid-day, he has to bring cattle to the grazing ground. In the evening he has to assist the Malik in milking them and he has again to carry milk to the houses of purchasers. Then, he has to provide fodder to the cattle. At night, he has to sleep in the shed along with cattle and has to bear the attach of mosquitoes and flies. Besides providing services to the cattle in Khatal he has to render domestic work as well in the house of the Khatal Malik. He assists in bringing ratio, fuel, vegetables, etc.

From dawn to dusk, he remains busy in the work of the Khatal Malik. He remains quite away from his parents, friends and relatives. He forgets his childhood. He gets up with the work of the Malik and sleeps with his work. Even on festive and ceremonial occasions, he is not allowed to pay a visit in his house. Sometimes, his father comes to see him and goes back taking some money in the name of the wages earned by the child.

As Khalasi in Bus/Truck

The bus/truck owner requires a servant to clean and wash the truck/ bus at the time of rest. This is such a work where children are preferred because they do such work more actively. Another reason is that owner has to pay less wages to the children. Still another reason is that children are eager to make journey by bus and truck, so they are available without wages, too. The owner has to pay only food, breakfast and clothes. They have to remain day and night in the bus or truck to render service, but they neither get proper wages, nor food and respect. Not only this, they are abused by the driver and the Malik of the truck too. Being poor, they have to forget their childhood, parents, friends and community members. They have to work in humiliating condition and lead a sub-human life.

As Garage Servant

The children are also exploited as servant in the garage. The garage owner requires the services of children not only for cleaning and brooming the garage, but for different types of work related to the garage. The garage servants can be seen wearing dirty clothes wet in mobile and diesel. They have to perform work in the garage day and night on many occasions. They have to work for the whole night. They work so efficiently, but they do not get proper clothes and payment. They do not get respect and sympathy. The garage owner exploit them for selfish purposes. He is abused frequently. He has to request again and again to get payment. He is not allowed to visit home. Thus, he forgets his childhood for work. If he runs away, the is blamed as a thief. The garage owner approaches is parents and abuse them for the so called theft committed by the child. This is done so that the parents of the child may not demand the payment.

As Servants in the House of Officials

Nowaday many Dalits are service holders. They are earning good fortune by other profession also. They keep servant in their houses for performing household works. They promise the parents to school them during the school hours. But their such promises prove false because they keep the boy engaged in the household work and send their own children to school and colleges. Not only this, they do not behave well with the boy. When the boy requests them to send house, they do not allow them to go. If he runs away, a charge of theft is hooked in their names. Not only Dalit officials, but officials belonging to other castes are also exploiting the children of Dalit in their houses for households works. Previously a servant belonging to low caste was not preferred due to the practice of untouchability. But now, a child servant of any caste is accepted.

As Contract Labour

Dalit children are also exploited by the contractors as contract labour in loading and unloading truck/tractor, carrying bricks, sands, chips, manures etc. They also work in road construction and dam construction. The children work more, but they are paid less.

As Seasonal Labour

During the transplantation of paddy seedlings, the services of children is required to carry bundles of seedlings to the field. The children do this work very efficiently. They are available at low wages.

AGENCIES OF CHILD EXPLOITATION

The Family

It is the first agency responsible for the exploitation of children. It is true that majority of Dalit families are poor. They subsist on the basis of their labour. They want to earn more to maintain the family. In maintaining the family, they utilize the services of children also for selfish purpose children are not sent to school. Rather they are kept engaged in household work and work as labour in the house of other. They have to look after the house and small kids. When the parents are any for some job.

They have to carry the food of parents at the place of work. Their parent want to earn more and more wages during peak agricultural season. They bring with them their children to work and to earn wages. During harvesting crops, they utilize the services of children. At the time of thrashing and winnowing, they use the services of children. Their parents, too, have some cattle like cow, calves, goat, etc. They utilize the services of children in grazing the cattle. They are kept engaged in fishing as well in Nala, Pokhra, canal, river, etc. Not only this, they send their children to work in the house of landowner, khatalowner, garage owner, officials, contractors etc. to work as servant. There is no harm in performing work for the benefit and betterment of the family. And for this, there is division of labour according to age and sex in every family, where family works as unit of production and consumption. But the bad aspect is that they are prohibited to attend the school. They remain uneducated for nominal wages on account of apathy shown by the parents.

The Malik

Landowner, khatal owner, garage owner, lethe machine owner, truck owner, bus owner, mill owner, official are termed locally as Malik by the Dalits. The Malik are resourceful persons and the Dalits are resource-less. The sons of Malik are called as Babu. The Malik and Babu exploit the Dalit children for their selfish purposes. They employ the children of Dalits in their houses to perform different kinds of work. They send their won children in different kinds of school for education. They want to make their own children doctor, engineer, professor, teacher, clerk, B.D.O., etc. But they make the future of Dalit children dark by engaging them to work at a time when they are expected to attend the school. The Government has banned the child labour and has made the education free upto the age of 14 years. Even then, neither the parents of the children nor he Malik are paying any attention towards the future of the poor Dalit children. Their parents say openly that for their children bread is more important than education. Their Malik say that who will perform their work, if they attend the school. Thus, the parents and the Malik snatch the childhood of the children by employing them in various work. Not only this, they are engaged in such types of work which are expected to be performed by young and adult persons.

In spite of performing hard labour, the children as servants do not enjoy any status. They are kept semi-fed, semi-clothed and tortured physically. They are oppressed and abused. They are always on duty. They do not enjoy any rest and holidays. Illness provide them chance to meet their parents and community members. They work hard but receive very nominal wages or in some cases no wages, but only breakfast and both ends meal are given to them.

Contractor

Contractors also engage the children of Dalits for their selfish purposes. These contractors are not only private contractors but Governments contractors also do not lag behind in exploiting and oppressing the children of Dalits. The private contractors associated with brick kiln, stone chips, sand, road construction, dam building, building construction, bridge construction etc. utilize the services of children for their selfish purposes. They do not prohibit the children in performing work. They rather encourage, the child labourers to perform more and more. They also praise the children verbally. Hearing praise the children work more and more. But they do not receive proper payments. They work more than a young and adult, but receive half the wages received by a young labourer. This is true not only for the private contractors, but it stands true also for the Government contractors. Many works like digging wells, embankment of river, dam building, road construction, bridge construction, etc. performed by the Government contractor. They utilize the services of the children but pay them very little in return.

Nowadays the work of street construction, drainage construction, Nali repair etc. are being done by the panchayat. In those works also the services of children are being utilized.

Officials

Many Government officials reside in the village or in neighbouring urban areas, they utilize the services of the children for their selfish purposes. They employ the poor children as servants for performing their household work like cleaning utensils, cooking food, washing clothes, rooms, floor, etc. They keep them engaged for whole day and night. They take hard work but pay very little.

Table 3.1 : The Mode of Payment of Different Type of Children

Types of child labour	*Mode of Payment*
1. Charwaha	10 kg paddy per cattle in a year plus break fast, food and clothes on festive occasion.
2. Domestic servant	10 to 15 Mounds of paddy in a year plus breakfast food and clothes.
3. Casual labour	1.5 kg rice per day plus breakfast and midday meal or Rs. 8 to 10 per day plus breakfast and midday meals.
4. Hotel servant	Rs. 50 to Rs. 100 per month plus food and clothes.
5. Khatal servant	Rs. 30 to 50 per month plus food and clothes.
6. Garage servant	Rs. 50 to 70 per month plus food and clothes.
7. Khalasi	Rs. 30 to 70 per months plus food and clothes.
8. In construction work	Rs. 8 to 12 per day.

EXPLOITATION OF WOMEN

Women are custodian of family. They not only bear the children but nourish the children and other family members. They not only perform the domestic works but do not lag behind in performing work outside the house. In case of Dalit family, both male and female have to work hard to maintain the family. Besides cooking and rearing children, they help husband in agriculture and earn wages to raises the family income. But they do not enjoy prestige and respect in the family. Their exploitation starts from the family. Wherever they pay visit to work, they have to face exploitation and oppression. The exploitation of women takes place in the following ways.

Charwahin

It is a local name given to a woman engaged in the work of grazing cattle. Two or more women together take the responsibility to herd the cattle of the entire village. All agricultural families have cattle to till the land and to get milk. For herding buffalo a separate herd boy is kept at the family level. But for cows, calf, goats, oxen a charwahin is kept commonly. The charwahin takes the cattle of the village to grazing ground in the morning and brings them back in the evening. In course of grazing, she gathers dung for fuel, which she use in her house for cooking. She gets a fixed quantity of paddy for each cattle head from each household. She does not get food and clothes. She gets generally 5 to 10 kg per cattle head annually but for such a nominal payment she has to remain engaged round the year from morning to evening. She does not get even food and clothes. But on festive occasion she gets cooked food and some used old clothes from her Malik and Malkin.

Dai

It is a local name given to a woman who cleans the cattle shed of a Malik. Each Malik has his own cattle. The Dai is kept to clean the dung from the cattle shed in the morning. It is her duty to make Goitha (a kind of fuel coke prepared from the dung). For this work a Dai gets annual payment in kind which depends upon the age and type of cattle. She gets food at the end of each week. On festive and ceremonial occasion she gets food for the entire family members. She also gets Sari once in a year.

A Dai can take an advance from the Malik. The advance is treated as loan may be without interest or with interest. On the basis of loan, she enters into an oral agreement with the Malik to work as Dai round the year. Generally the terms and conditions to work as Dai continues for a period of one complete years. It begins in the month of Asharh (the first month of our national calendar) and ends in the month of Jyestha (the last month of our national calendar) on the fullmoon day. If a Dai pays back all the previous loan of a Malik, she becomes free to work as Dai in the house of the Malik or not. She is also free to change her Malik. But if she is unable to pay the loan or if she takes more loan before the expiry period, she has to continue to work as Dai for the next year. If a Dai repays all previous loan and refuses to continue to work as Dai for the next year, the Malik employs another Dai. It can be seen that a Dai can take loan from a new Malik to repay the loan of previous Malik but before the last day of the Jyestha month.

If a Dai becomes ill for long time, her husband or children has to complete the work in the house of the Malik. If there is nobody to do work in place of her, she is treated as absent. No payment is made for the period of her absence. Rather she has to pay some penalty in the form of more interest on the loan. If due to any reason, she becomes unable to work and repay loan, her property is confiscated. Her goats, chicks, cows, etc. are brought and sold to recover the loan back.

Lauri

It is a local name given to a woman who performs household work in the house of a Malik. She is associated with such work as cleaning courtyard, gate, floor, utensils, etc. She is also expected to bring water for cleaning purposes. Generally Lauri for cooking purposes belong to clean caste like Kahar, Dhanu, Mahto, etc. But Lauri for cleaning houses, walls, floor, clothes, and to look after the small kids may belong to Dalits. Lauri assists the Malkin in various kind of domestic work. She works as a helping hand for the Malkin. She remains with the Malkin from dawn to dusk and assist in cleaning houses, clothes, grains, etc. She takes every care of a newly born child and her mother. For her work, she gets payment in kind on annual basis. She also gets breakfast and both ends meal. On festive occasion, she gets food for her entire family members. She receives new clothes on festive occasion. She enjoys a status like a family members. She is called by the kinship term like Dadi, Chachi, Bhabhi, etc. She can take loan any time from the Malkin.

The exploitative aspect of a Lauri is that she is exploited for selfish purposes and nominal wages. She works from the dawn to dusk for the benefit and the battlement of the family of the Malik, but she receives very nominal wages. Virtually, she has to work on food and clothes only.

Reja

Reja is a local name given to women who perform work on truck for loading and unloading brick, cement, chips, sand, etc. and in construction work done by the contractors such as building construction, road construction, bridge construction, etc. They work as Reja along with male members or alone. But they are exploited in many ways by the contractor. They work not less than men in any respect, but receive payment always less than men. Generally they receive payment at week end, but all wages is not cleared some is always kept so that they may always remain in clutch of the contractor. Sometimes, they have to approach many times, to contractor for the payment of wages. The contractor tells lie that they have not received any payment from the party. He can make payment only on receiving payment from the party. In absence of timely payment, they have to take loan from other agencies on exorbitant rate of interest. In construction work, they have to remain many days at the site of work away from family members. There they work even during night. But they neither get good food nor good payment. Not only this, for petty amount they are exploited sexually as well.

Brick Kiln Labour

The brick kiln owner prefers the services of women who work efficiently and dedicatedly. Nearby the brick kiln, they erect a hut. This hut becomes house for them. In this hut, they live with their husbands and children. Some women of neighbouring houses also join the group of brick kiln labour. They stay in the group, while their husbands stay in villages.

The brick kiln labour do the work like preparing mud paste for brick, preparing kiln for baked bricks, arranging the baked brick at other places loading and unloading the trucks carrying bricks, for such work they get payment on contract basis for each thousand of bricks.

They remain day and night at the brick kiln and perform services whenever required. There is not fixed time of work and fixed date of payment. They have to request many times to get payment from the owner. They are given loan which is adjusted against their payment of wages. They are generally illiterate, the owner of the brick kiln manipulates the register containing loan taken and payment made against the name of each labour. Being illiterate the labours have to accept what the owner says and gives.

Sometimes a woman wants to go back home, but she is usually prevented due to the non-payment of wages. The payment against wages is never cleared off. Some amount is always kept as arrears, the owner knows it well that on receiving total payment they may leave the place for visiting home and may not come back again. If the arrear of payment is with the owner, the labourers are bound to visit again at kiln to work. Thus, once in contact with the brick kiln, becomes labourer for ever or a labourer can break the contact by forgetting the arrear.

On festive and ceremonial occasions, the behaviour of owner is definitely changed. He distributes sweets and local made liquor free of cost. This is done to gain the sympathy of the labourers. They perform work equal to men, but receive less payment. In contract work, they extend cooperation to their husband, but they do not get recognition.

Agriculture Labour

Dalit women form potential agriculture labour force. Only ploughing is tabooed for them, but in other kinds of agricultural work, they do not lag behind in comparison to male. They do the work of uprooting seedlings, trans-planting seedlings, weeding, harvesting, thrashing, winnowing and carrying the grains to houses. Thus, in family, the role of women in Dalit family is no less than those of males. But the most sorrowful aspect is that they are paid less for the same kind of work and for the same hours of work in comparison to men.

Table 3.2 : Mode of Payment to Women Labour

	Women Labour	*Mode of Payment*
1.	Charawahin	5 to 10 kg paddy per year per cattle head.
2.	Dai	5 to 10 kg paddy per year per cattle + week end food + sari.
3.	Lauri	3 to 5 Maunds paddy + breakfast and food + clothes.
4.	Reja	Rs. 20 without breakfast and food per day or as per contract.
5.	Brick kiln labour	Rs. 30 to 40 per thousand brick.
6.	Agriculture labour	3 kg paddy or 2 kg rice + food and breakfast per day or Rs. 15 without food and breakfast.

AGENCIES OF WOMEN EXPLOITATION

The agencies involved in the exploitation of women are as follows :

The Family

Family is the first agency involved in the exploitation the women for selfish purposes. Being poor and resourceless, Dalit women have to struggle hard in running the family and rearing the children. From dawn to late night they have to work hard. They get-up early in the morning, clean stores, courtyards and houses, clean cattle shed, provide foder to cattle. Then they prepare food and serve the children and other members. Then they share food themselves. They have to fetch water for cooking and washing utensils and clothes. They have to bring water for drinking purposes from 8 a.m. They have to visit at the place of work along with food and water. They come back in the evening and have to fetch water for cooking and drinking. They cook food and serve food among family members. Then they do some work like boiling paddy for rice, cleaning wheat and pulse etc. only then they go to bed. It is also true that children and other members sometimes cooperate them, but many time, they have to do those works alone. They have to go to perform hard work, when they are expectant and nursing mothers. They neglect their heath to run the family. They feel lucky when their husbands and children are active, cooperative and without drinking habit. Because in majority of cases, their husbands are in idle, inactive, indulged in drinking and non-cooperative. On these issues, husbands and wives can be seen quarreling. Thus, they have to fed not only their children but also husbands who do not share the responsibility of running the household. They have to incur loan at exorbitant rate of interest and have to perform work on less wages.

The Malik

The land owner are termed as Malik in local term. They exploit the Dalit women for their selfish purposes. They want to exploit the services of women for their own benefit. They provide them loan at high rate of interest and brought them under contract to perform work round the year at nominal wages. As daily labour, women receive less wages than men. Their ruthless behaviour can be seen with the expectant and nourishing mothers who on account of poverty join work to earn wages. Some of them are found indulged in immoral behaviour with the women. For petty amount Dalit women have to become victims of sexual exploitation.

The Contractors

The contractors, private or public are involved in the exploitation of Dalit women. They employ Dalit women in construction work. Women labour working in construction work are termed as Reja. As Reja, they have to visit far off places for rendering work. The contractors have Metha to look after the work of Reja and building materials. Not only contractors, but his men as Metha do not lag behind in exploiting the Reja. They are illiterate and do not know any calculation. At the time of payment, they were paid less and have to put thumb impression on more payment. The Reja have to accept whatever is paid by the contractor. Contractors and his men are also involved in the sexual exploitation of the Reja.

Bricks Kiln Owner

The brick kiln owners exploit women in the same manner as contractors. They also do not make proper payment to women labourers working in brick kiln. They also pay less and have thumb impression at high rate of payment. Being illiterate, labourers do not go verify the mode of payment. They accept without any grievances whatever is paid by the owner.

EXPLOITATION OF THE DALIT AGED

In our culture aged occupies significant place. They are not treated as liability but are recognised as asset because it is believed that their blessings bring peace, harmony and wealth in the family. Dalits, too, have every regard and respect for their aged. But being poor and resourceless, they have to exploit aged for family work or for the work of the other. It can be seen that aged are more active that other members of the family. So long as they are capable of walking and working they do not want to place their liabilities at the shoulder of their sons. Rather they work more and more to supplement the family income. The services of male and female aged are utilized for selfish purpose. The male and female aged are exploited in the following ways.

Barahil

It is local term given to male aged labour who are engaged by a Malik to look after the agricultural works. He provides supervision work to other labourers in place of Malik. An old and experienced labourer is treated suitable for this post. This a status oriented post given to a labourer by the Malik. A labourer as a Barahil becomes the family members of the Malik. He remains twentyfour hours in the house of Malik and provide supervision works to charwaha, Banihara, lauri and other labourers performing works in the field or in the house of the Malik. Expenditure on his illness is also met by the Malik. He also gets new clothes twice a year. He gets payment on annual basis. The payment may be 10 to 15 Maunds of paddy per year. But he enjoys this status till he is able to walk and perform some minor work. As soon as he becomes disable, he does not get work as Barahil. He does not receive any support from the Malik. In this state, he has to depend upon his family members.

Khalihan Agora (Watchman of Thrashing Field)

When bundles of crops are brought in the Khalihan, a watchman is required to look after the thrashing field in the day as well as in the night. Those owners who are able to do this job themselves, do not employ any watchman. But those who are unable to look after the Khalihan themselves have to employ a watchman. For this kind of job an aged male labour is preferred. He gets food, clothes, some payment in kind for the period concerned. His payment varies one maund to maunds of paddy per month. Not all aged get this kind of job. Only faithful aged can get this kind of job.

Metha

This is a local term given to a loyal labourer of a contractors or a brick kiln owner. He remains in charge of labourers working in construction work or in brick kiln. For this kind of work, an aged and experienced labourer is required. He own the respect of the labourers as well the contractors or the brick kiln owners. He gets food, clothes and some nominal wages fixed by the Malik.

Agriculture Labour

Agriculture requires more and more number of labourers at the time of uprooting the paddy seedlings, transplanting the paddy seedlings, weeding, harvesting, carrying bundles of harvested crops at thrashing field, thrashing and winnowing etc. In such kind of work, the services of children, women and aged are utilized.

Table 3.3 : Mode of Payment to Aged Labour.

	Aged labour	*Mode of Payment*
1.	Barahil	10 to 15 Maunds of paddy + food and clothes.
2.	Agora (watchman)	One to 2 Maunds of paddy per month + food.
3.	Metha	Rs. 10 to Rs. 15 per day + food.
4.	Agriculture labour	3 kg. paddy or 2 kg. rice + mid day food and breakfast.
5.	Dai	3 Maunds to 4 Maunds of paddy per year.
6.	Lauri	5 to 10 Maunds of paddy per year.

In agriculture, the services of aged are taken in uprooting seedlings, weeding, harvesting and thrashing, winnowing, etc. They generally work like a young person but as they become aged, their payment of wages becomes less. They are employed on works when young and adults are not available. Some owners prefer aged labour because they know the quality of the aged. They have to pay less wages to aged but receive the work not less than the adults.

The aged females get work as Dai and Lauri. About Dai and Lauri and detail description has been given earlier in exploitation of women.

4

ECONOMIC AREA OF DALIT EXPLOITATION OF GAYA

In the area under study, the Dalit constitute the major labour force in agriculture sector as well in non-agricultural sector like brick kiln, construction work, etc. Thus, agriculture, construction work and brick kiln are the main economic areas where exploitation of Dalit takes place. About exploitation of Dalit women, aged and children in brick kiln, construction work and agriculture, a description has been furnished in the previous chapter. Here, we are going to discuss the exploitation of Dalit labour who are young and adult. A discussion on exploitation of Dalits as share-croppers and contract croppers will also be presented here.

EXPLOITATION OF DALITS AS AGRICULTURAL LABOUR

Our country is agricultùral rcountry. Here more than 80 per cent population resides in villages and are engaged in agriculture. From the study of occupation of Dalit households, it appears that majority of them are agricultural labour because majority of them are landless or near landless. The exploitation of agriculture labour takes place in the following ways.

Bonded Labour

The bonded labour in the area under study is locally known by the term Kamia. The Kamia takes loan from the landowner, who belong to high castes, Backward castes or even Muslims. The landowners are known by the term Malik. The Kamia borrow loan from the Malik on oral agreement to render labour in the house of the Malik so long as the loan is not paid back. He gets breakfast, food, clothes and some nominal wages which is much less than the other kinds of labourers.

The loan is the root cause behind the persistence of bonded labour. A landless labourer has nothing to mortgage except his labour to obtain loan from the Malik. If he refuses to mortgage his labour, he will not be able to obtain loan. It is not that the Mahajan does not charge any interest on loan for mortgaging the labour. The Malik provides loan at a very high rate of interest at one hand and utilizes the services of the Kamia at normal wages, on the other hand. Thus, this system is in both ways beneficial to the Malik and exploitative for the Kamia.

The Kamia knows it well that as bonded labour he will be exploited and oppressed, but inability to obtain loan from other sources compels him to visit the house of the Malik to get loan and to accept the terms and conditions of a bonded labour. In this system, he gets security to obtain food, clothes and loan any time he needs. His wife also gets work as Dai, Laure and agriculture labour in the house of the Malik. His children may also get job as charwaha or domestic servant in the house of the Malik. Thus, a Kamia has not to visit door to door in search of work. He and his family members visit the house of own Malik to perform works. He can take loan any time from the Malik in cash and kind. He is also recognised as the men of the Malik. He and his family members never face the situation of unemployment because it becomes the duty of the Malik to provide them work, breakfast and food daily.

As bonded labour, a Kamia looses freedom of various kind. He can work freely in the field of his Malik, but he cannot work in the house and field of another Malik. He can not sell labour in open market at market-value. He cannot work for his own house. He is not expected to be absent in peak agricultural season. He cannot visit his friends and relative without the permission of the Malik. Even on festive occasion he is not given leave. On such occasions he has to work more. He has to clean house gadgets and to wash animal. Only then he can visit his house to celebrate festival for some time. He has to work from dawn to dusk. He has to perform agricultural as well as domestic work. There is no rest and holidays in the conditions associated with the bonded labour.

The Government has taken prohibitive, protective and rehabilitative measures to uproot the system of bonded labour, but improper implementation of rehabilitation scheme has frustrated the labourers.

In absence of institutional facilities for the advance of loan a labourer accepts the terms and conditions of bonded labour. The prohibitive measures have created difficulty for labourers to get loan on bonded labour. According to this, the Malik cannot enforce the labourer to take the loan back. Rather it has made the labourers free even without payment of loan back. Now the Malik does not want to provide loan on boded labour. They provide loan by taking land or ornaments in mortgage. Thus, the system of bonded labour is gradually on the way to vanish. But there are same labourers who are fully dependent upon the Malik in absence of other means of livelihood. They accept to work on terms and conditions of bonded labour.

According to the terms and conditions of bonded labour, a labourer can become free by paying the loan back. But inability to pay previous loan back or to incur more loan time to time increases the duration of bondedness. Thus, once in bondage becomes bondage for many years.

Table 4.1 : Mode of Payment of Bonded Labour

Work	*Mode of Payment*
Ploughing	1.5 kg. paddy + breakfast + both ends meal.
Spading	1.5 kg. paddy + breakfast + both ends meal.
Uprooting seedling	1.5 kg. paddy + breakfast + both ends meal.
Weeding	1.5 kg. paddy + breakfast + both ends meal.
Harvesting	One bundle in 16 bundles of crops harvested.
Thrashing	1.5 kg. paddy + breakfast + both ends meal.
Other works	Only breakfast and meals.

Banihar (Attached Labour)

Banihar is a local term given to an attached labour who enters into agreement with the Malik to render labour for round the year. Banihar is employed on the basis of one year contract. He is employed in the month of Asarh and continues till the month of Jyestha. After completion of one year, an attached labour becomes free. He may continue as attached labour or he may not continue. He may continue in the house of same Malik or in the house of another Malik. The only condition is that all loans and interest of Malik should be cleared in the month of Jyestha and the Malik should also clear all the wages of the labourer in the month of Jyestha.

An attached labour is given a piece of land to cultivate on this plot the labourer has right to cultivate the crops he like for one complete year. Besides, he gets 1.5 kg. paddy per day for daily work. He also gets breakfast and midday meal, for daily work. The meal of night is given on festive and ceremonial occasion, they receive food for entire family members.

An attached labour can take the loan from the Malik any time. But he has to pay the interest on the loan. The interest is much more than the rate of bank. For few days, he can take interest free loan. The attached labour has not to search for work daily by visiting door to door. He visits in the house of the Malik and the Malik provides him work daily. He performs agriculture and domestic works for the Malik. In transplantation, weeding, harvesting, thrashing and winnowing, the services of other family members of the attached labour is also utilized. The Malik keeps attached labour because he does not want to visit daily to search for a labourer. It is the duty of the attached labour to pay a visit at the door of the Malik and to ask about the work of the day.

The attached labour enjoys no treedom. During peak season, they are not expected to be absent. But in off season, they can remain absent. During this period, he can work for his own house. He can also visit to relatives. In absence no penalty is charged.

Table 4.2 : Work and Mode of Payment of Attached Labour

Work	*Mode of Payment of Attached Labour*
Ploughing	1.5 kg. Paddy + breakfast + midday meal.
Spading	1.5 kg. Paddy + breakfast + midday meal.
Transplanting	1.5 kg. Paddy + breakfast + midday meal.
Weeding	1.5 kg. Paddy + breakfast + midday meal.
Harvesting	One bundles in every 12 bundles of harvested crops.
Thrashing	1.5 kg. Paddy + breakfast + midday meal.
Winnowing	1.5 kg. Paddy + breakfast + midday meal.
Carrying grain	1.5 kg. Paddy + breakfast + midday meal to house.

Besides the above wages, attached labour gets 10 to 15 katha of land to cultivate. They get food for entire family members on festive and ceremonial occasion.

Majdoora (Daily Wage Earning Labour)

The labourers who earn daily wages, are known by the local term Majdoora. They are hired on daily wage. At the time of transplantation more and more labourers are required. Only bonded and attached labour cannot complete the work of transplantation. For this purpose labourers are hired on daily wages. Similarly for ploughing and spading, Majdooras are hired. For thrashing also Majdooras are required. They are free to work or not to work. They can work daily for whole period in one house or daily in the house of a new Malik. They do not work under any type of bondage. They are completely free. They definitely get more wages in comparison to other labourers but they cannot enjoy lone facilities in the house of the Malik. In peak season, they get work, but in off season they have to face unemployment problem. Their wages was 2 kg rice per day breakfast and midday meal.

Contract Labour

In agricultural works Dalits are exploited as contract labour. For throwing particular manure heap, they take contract at a fixed amount. They receive payment after the completion of work. Similarly they do work like ploughing, spading, uprooting, transplanting and weeding, etc. on contract basis. The Malik keeps watch on the performance of work of the labourers. The table below will present the nature of work of the labourers, and payment of contract labour.

Table 4.3 : Mode of Payment of Contract Labour

Work	*Mode of Payment*
For manuring 1 bigha land	Rs. 50
For ploughing 1 bigha with OX	Rs. 50
For spading 1 bigha	Rs. 20
For uprooting 1 katha seedling	Rs. 30
For transplanting 1 bigha	Rs. 50
For weeding 1 bigha	Rs. 30
For harvesting	1 bundle out of 12 bundle
For thrashing	1 Maund out of every 10 Maund
For loading and unloading tractor	Rs. 20 per trip
For cutting soil	Rs. 20 per cubic ft.
For making kuchha brick	Rs. 30 per thousand
For making kiln of bricks	Rs. 30 per thousand

EXPLOITATION IN BATAIDARI SYSTEM (SHARE CROPPING)

Those Dalit families which do not won land sufficiently for cultivation are engaged as share croppers. They have own plough and oxen. They approach to the Malik for land to do share cropping. The Malik gives them land and the share cropper invests seed, fertilizer and labour when the crops are ready, the Malik takes the half share and the half share remains with the share croppers. Nowadays, Dalits employed in Government's job do also share cropping to add the family income. They do job but their family members remain in village. They can earn wages as casual labour. But they want to remain engaged in share cropping. They have oxen, cows and buffalo. They also have cash with them. So they do share cropping.

In order to do share cropping a share cropper has to approach the Malik. He has to convince the Malik that he has plough, oxen and other capital required for share cropping. Only then he can get land for share cropping. In order to get the required acreage for share cropping, he has to visit many Mahajans. When the Malik agrees to give the land, and oral agreement prevails between the Malik and the share cropper.

There are two types of share cropping : 1. Adha Batai (half share) and 2. Tisari (one third share).

Adha Batai

In this system, after thrashing and winnowing the total produce is divided into two equal parts. The Malik gets one part and the share cropper gets the another half part. Here the share cropper has to meet expenses on seed, fertilizer, watering, ploughing, spading, uprooting seedlings, transplanting, harvesting, carrying the bundles in thrashing field, thrashing, winnowing. The share cropper has to inform the Malik time to time about the cultivation of crops. For harvesting, he has to seek the permission of the Malik. The Malik visits himself or sends any family members to see the harvesting. He counts the bundle in the field. He again counts bundles in the thrashing ground. When the grains are ready, the Hatawe (the man who does the work of measuring or weighing) or Bania to divide the produce. The Hatawe makes two equal parts. The share cropper has to carry the grains in the house of Malik. Only then he carries his own part in his own house.

If the Malik gives half share in seed and fertilizer, he takes half share in straw and if not, he leaves the entire heap of straw for the share cropper. In the same way, share cropper divides the produce of Rabi crops. The share cropper cannot keep the bundles of crops according to his own wishes. He has to keep the bundles at a place where the Malik desires to keep. After completion of one year, the Malik may allot the land to the same share cropper or he may change the share cropper or he may cultivate the land himself. If a share cropper gives good share by produce of the crops, the Malik considers sympathetically for his next year share cropping. But if the produce is not satisfactory, the Malik refuses to pay the land to share cropper. In this situation, the share cropper has to approach other Malik to get land for share cropping.

Tisari Batai (One Third Share)

In this type of share cropping, the Malik invests two parts and the co-sharer invests the one part in every expenses. In seed, fertilizer, ploughing, transplanting weeding, harvesting, thrashing two parts of expenditure are met by the land owner and one part is met by the sharer. In produce also two parts go in the hand of landowner and one part goes in the hand of sharer.

Table 4.4 : Table Showing Expenditure Met by Owner and Sharer in Half Share Cropping

Item of expenditure	*Expenditure met by the owner of land*	*Expenditure met by the sharer*
Seed	No share	Total expenditure
Fertilizer	No share	Total expenditure
Rent of Watering	Half share	Half Share
Labour cost	No share	Total expenditure

Table 4.5 : Table Showing Share in Agricultural Produce of Malik and Sharer

Agricultural Produce	*Share of Malik*	*Sharer*
Paddy	Half of the yield	Half of the yield
Wheat	Half of the yield	Half of the yield
Pulses	Half of the yield	Half of the yield
Oil Seeds	Half of the yield	Half of the yield
Straw	No share	Total share

In case of sugarcane and potato, there is also a system of Tisari Batai. In case of these two crops, the owner of the land provides only land to the sharer. The sharer has to meet the entire expenses. In produce, two share goes in hand of the sharer and one share goes in the hand of land owner.

Table 4.6 : Table Showing System of Expenditure in Tisari Batai

Item of Expenditure	*Expenses Share by Malik*	*Expense Shared by Bataidar*
Seed	Two part	One part
Fertilizer	Two part	One part
Rent of watering	Two part	One part
Labour cost	Two part	One part

Table 4.7 : Table Showing Share in Agriculture in Tisari Batai System

Agriculture	*Share of Malik*	*Share of Bataidar*
Paddy	Two part of yield	One part of the yield
Wheat	Two part of yield	One part of the yield
Pulses	Two part of yield	One part of the yield
Oil seeds	Two part of yield	One part of the yield
Straw	Two part of yield	One part of the yield

Table 4.8 : Table Showing the System of Tisari Batai in Sugarcane and Potato

Expenditure	*Met by Malik*	*Met by Bataidar*
Seed	No Share	Total Expenditure
Fertilizer	No Share	Total Expenditure
Rent of Water	No Share	Total Expenditure
Labour Cost	No Share	Total Expenditure

Table 4.9 : Table Showing Share of Malik and Bataidar in Sugarcane and Potato

Produce	*Share of Malik*	*Share of Bataidar*
Sugarcane	3rd part of the yield	Two parts of the yield
Potato	3rd part of the yield	Two parts of the yield

Exploitation in Contract Cropping

Besides share cropping, there is system of contract cropping. In this system a person who wants to do cropping on the land of other, gets land on contract for one year. The contract is verbal. The contractor agrees to pay a fixed amount for a particular plot. He pays the amount in advance. Thereafter, he becomes free to do cropping like his own land. Like share cropper, he does not have to take permission from the Malik to harvest. He is free to cultivate any crop he likes. But in share cropping the Bataidar has to ask about the types and varieties of crops to be cultivated.

Nowadays Dalits are also leasing in land for the purpose of cultivation. The persons leasing in land are known as Manidar in local term and the person leasing out land are known as Malik. The system begins in the month of Asharh. The Manidar approaches to the Malik and requests him to provide a particular plot of land on the basis of land. The Malik puts the rate of Mani of that plot before the Manidar. If the Manidar becomes ready to pay the Mani demanded by the Malik, he becomes the owner of the land for cultivation for one complete year. The Mani is taken in cash or in kind. Previously Mani was taken in kind. In this case the Manidar agrees to pay to particular maunds of rice or paddy or wheat for a particular plot. Here the Mani is paid by the Manidar after harvesting and thrashing the crop. Many Manidars did not move as per agreement. So to avoid this, nowadays, the Malik leases out land on cash basis. The cash is taken in advance. So the question of non-payment of Mani does not arise here. Those who have cash can easily get land for cultivation.

The rate of Mani depends upon the type of land and facility of irrigation. A land which is nearby the village with good irrigation facility gives more Mani. A land situated away from the village without irrigation facility gives less Mani. Again a plot which attract more Manidar gives more Mani because there is competition among the Manidar for that plot of land.

Table 4.10 : Showing Pattern of Expenditure in Manidari System

Expenditure	*Malik*	*Manidar*
Seed	No	Total Expenditure
Fertilizer	No	Total Expenditure
Water rent	No	Total Expenditure
Labour cost	No	Total Expenditure

Table 4.11 : Table Showing the Rate of Mani in Cash or Kind

Rate of Mani	*Mani in Kind*	*Mani in cash*
Paddy	10-20 Maunds per Bigha	Rs. 1000 – 2000
Wheat	05-10 Maunds per Bigha	Rs. 500 – 1000
Pulses	02-05 Maunds per Bigha	Rs. 300 – 1000
Potato	10-30 Maunds	Rs. 1500 – 2500

EXPLOITATION AS MIGRANT LABOUR

Dalits of the village understudy have to move place to place in search of work. During peak agricultural reason, they visit other neighbouring districts where assured means of irrigation is available. They go there to work as agricultural labour. As they are migrant, they have to live at the mercy of the Malik. They have to stay in shade or in old houses which is not suitable for health. Not only this, they have to work more but have to receive less wages than other labourers. It is true that they get breakfast and both ends meal and 1.5 kg. rice per day. But they have to work from dawn to dusk according to the mercy of the Malik, in whose house they get shelter.

They visit other places within or outside the district to work in brick kiln. At the place of brick kiln, they visit along with family members. They erect temporary huts and stay at the site of kiln. They prepare mud brick, prepare kiln for making the mud brick pucca. Then they arrange the pucca brick in rows for sale. In performing such works the labour of entire family members is involved because they get payment on contract basis for preparing one thousand bricks, they receive Rs. 35 to Rs. 45. If bricks become dried and they are arranged in Khewals of 1000 piece, only then they are entitled to get payment. But if bricks are damaged before preparing Khewals of kuchcha bricks, the damage goes with the labour. They work even at night to earn more and more but sometimes heavy rain causes great damage to their labour. Not only this, in receiving payment they are cheated due to illiteracy. They do not know to calculate and count in proper way. They have to believe upon the statement of the Malik.

They visit other places in search of work in construction of road and building. They erect temporary settlement at nearby the place of work. They live there day and night to work. But they are exploited by the contractors. They do not receive proper wages. They have to request many time to receive payment. They never get full payment. They cannot leave the site without the order of the contractor.

5

RELIGIOUS AREA OF DALIT EXPLOITATION OF GAYA

Dalit have to suffer from religious disabilities since centuries though they have been an integral part of Hindu society and religion, on account of practice of untouchability, they have been deprived from many religious rights which other Hindu castes are enjoying. They cannot be a priest of temple or Matha, though now they are enjoying this status at several places in Ayodhya, Prayagraj, Vrindaban and Mathura. They do not wear sacred thread, they cannot be involved in *karmakanda*, they cannot be principal *shrota* of Durga Puja, Ramayan Path, Akhanda Harikirtan, etc. Brahman priests do not visit their houses to conduct worship, *katha*, ritual, etc. But services of Dalits have been utilize and are being utilized at the time of religious activities. They are religiously tabooed in performance of many worships, but their manual labour is not tabooed on the occasion of worship. They contributed in the erection and maintenance of temple or matha, but they cannot work as priest. Because priesthood is based on specialised division of labour based on the concept of purity and pollution.

The villages under study Dalits are exploited in the following manner in the performance of religious activities.

Exploitation in Erection of Temple

Temples are places where Gods and Goddesses of Hindus take their abode. They are regarded as Deolok on the part of the earth. Hindus attach so much value to the temples that they want to project them at any cost. Dalits are poor but in the erection of temple and in its maintenance, they do not lag behind the other Hindu castes.

When a temple is to be repaired or erected, a general meeting is held in the village in which heads of all Hindu household take part. Mutually they decide the amount expected to be spent on erection. Then they elect a treasurer on consensus basis. The treasurer keeps the account of the temple construction. All heads of the households express their desire to contribute in the name of erection of the temple either in cash or in kind. They are not compelled to pay a particular amount in cash or in kind. Every body tells the amount. The amount in cash or kind. Everybody tells the amount according to his socio-economic status. As Dalits they do not possess money, they generally contributed their labour in the name of erection of the temple. The become ready to offer five days labour without any wages.

With their labour they erect the temple. Dalit labour are also hired to erect the temple but they are paid less than the existing wages in the name of Gods and Goddesses.

In the ritual o Pranpratistha, they bring materials of worship on their head, Play Dhol, Singha and musical instruments. They sing variety of prayer, songs. They make the ritual of Pranprathistha (ritual of giving life in the images) enjoyable for other as well.

In the maintenance of the temple, the priest collects sun-fried rice, ghee, dhup, Agarbatti and cash or kind to purchase prasad for daily offering in the temple. He also visits at the door of the Dalits. They also contributed sun-fried rice, dhup, ghee, Agarbati, etc. for the maintenance of worship. Thus, their religious sentiment is exploited in the name of religion. They become ready to offer labour on religious occasion without any wages or nominal wages, but they are not allowed entry in it.

Exploitation in Digging Sacred Well

Every temple is accompanied by a sacred well whose water is used for the purpose of worship in the temple. It is believed that wells are abode of Ganga Maiya who appears in the water of well to serve the Gods and Goddesses on the earth. With this religious sentiment a well is dug nearby the temple.

In digging the well services of Dalits are utilized. In the name of religion they are asked to do this job without any wages or on nominal wages. They are taught that for this kind of job, they will be paid by the Gods and Goddesses not only in this life but also in life after death. Dalits are poor but sentimental religiously. They become ready to this job free of cost or on much reduced wages.

Exploitation in Digging Sacred Pond

Sometimes nearby the temple a small pond is also dug. The pond is regarded very pious. Because its water is used not only for the purpose of worship but it quenches the thrust of other animals and birds as well. It is treated pious for offering worship to sun God. For digging a sacred ponds funds are raised by visiting door to door in many villages. Unable to pay cash, Dalits become ready to offer labour. They offer labour either free of cost or on nominal wages. They believe that for such kind of work, they have to be rewarded by the Gods and Goddesses.

Exploitation in Celebration of Durga Puja

Durga puja is very famous festival of Hindus. In villages under study, this festival is celebrated. On this occasion, the images of Goddess Durga are established to worship. The festivals begins on 1st bright day of Ashwin month. On this occasion drama and Nautanki are staged. For this great worship funds are raised. Each household of the village contributes subscription in the name of Durga Puja. Dalits of the village also contribute in subscription for Durga puja. Besides, they are requested to clean, the site where images are established. They are told to sing prayer song in day and night turn-wise. They are told to bring images from the town. They are engaged in carrying the images, flags, etc. at the time of procession of puja on the day of Vijayadasmi. For this kind of work, they are paid nothing, but they are kept engaged on all 10 days of worship. In the name of Goddess, they do not deny to do those works.

Exploitation in Celebration of Lakshmipuja or Dipawali

Dipawali is one of the greatest festivals of our country. This festival is also celebrated at village level. On this occasion, the worship of Goddess Lakshmi is held with great pump and show. Drama and Nautanki, dance etc. are staged on this occasion. In celebration of these festival Dalits have to pay cash as subscription in the name of Lakshmi puja. They not only pay subscription, but their service is utilized for carrying images from market upto village and at different places at the time of procession. They are told to clean the place where image of Lakshmi Mata is to be established and the place where drama is to be staged. They are engaged in carrying chauki, bamboos and wood pillars for erecting a stage for the image and also for the drama. For these works, they do not receive any payment. They are expected to perform such works in the name of the great puja.

Exploitation in Celebration of Chhath Puja

Chhath puja is also a great puja in villages under study. It takes place twice in a year. For Chhath worship the villagers clean the street of the village and the Ghats of ponds and rivers. They also make arrangement of light. For this purpose, they hire a diesel machine and coloured bulbs. In this ways they decorate the street and the Ghat. But such decoration needs money and labour. In order to get money funds are raised in which Dalits of the village also contribute. Dalits have also to render services to make the decoration successful. For rendering these services, they do not get any payment. They serve in the name of mother Chhath.

On this occasion, in some villages Nautanki and drama are also staged. In other villages, only dance is staged. This involves additional expenditure and rendering of labour.

On this occasion Dalits have to play Dhol and Singha without any payment.

Exploitation in Celebration of Saraswati Puja

Mother Saraswati is Goddess of learning. This festival is festival of students of the village children of Dalits do not go to school regularly, but in the celebration of Saraswati puja, they are engaged actively. They are asked to bring subscription from their fathers like other children. Some have to take loan to pay subscription. They can take loan but don't want to displease the children. Not only this, they compel their fathers to play musical instrument and sing song at the time of worship.

Exploitation in Celebration of Ramnavami

Ramnavami is also big festival of Hindus on this day, the worship of Lord Hanuman's flag takes place. This day is also observed as the birth day of Lord Rama. This festival is also celebrated at the level of village in which each household takes part by contributing some cash as subscription. From the subscription a big flag of Lord Hanumana is prepared and worshipped amidst dance, song and prayer. Dalits have not only to contribute in the subscription, but they have to render labour without any payment. They have to offer Begar labour in the name of Gods and Goddesses. If they deny, they are threatened to be ousted socially from the village. From the threat of boycott, they can not dare to disobey the order of the villagers.

Exploitation in the Name of Pilgrimage

Visiting to the pilgrimage centres on different occasions is regarded as religious duty of every Hindu. It is related to the attainment. This belief is popularised among the masses by the pandas of different pilgrim centres. The pandas visit the villages to collect Dakshina and to maintain *jujmani* relation. The Dalits have to take loan to meet expenditure on pilgrimage. For pilgrimage they cannot obtain loan from the government. Naturally they have to go to Malik or Mahajan to take loan. The Mahajans do not refuse to pay loan. They provide loan on interest under some condition which is related to render services in the house of the Malik or Mahajan after return from the pilgrimage. Generally the aged persons like to go to pilgrimage. For them, their sons have to take loan from the Malik on condition to pay interest and to render service in the house of the Malik. So long as the loan is not paid back, he has to render service in the house of the same Malik. During this period he gets payment which is existing in the village for attached labour. They take loan nearly one thousand rupees. This big amount they have to repay from their wages. Being unable to repay, they have to work for the same Mahajan for many years. Some times, they have to sell their cattle wealth to repay loan in the hand of the same Malik from whom he had taken loan.

Here it will be better to quote some cases collected from the field in course of field investigation.

S.R. (40 yr.) a resident of village in Imamganj block of Gaya district informed that some 8 years ago his 60 years old father had expressed his desire to visit Mathura on the day of Yamdutia (2nd day of bright half of Kartic month). The bathing at Mathura on this occasion is believed to provide Moksha after death. Like previous years, pandaji of Mathura had come to meet their Jajmans and to collect Dakshina. He was also taking many pilgrims with him. His father expressed his desired to go to Mathura but he had no money. He went to Malik who belonged to Yadava caste. He requested him to pay a sum of Rs. 1000/- for the pilgrimage of his father. In the beginning he refused to pay such a big amount as loan. He told him to go to the Government to get loan. Because Government had prevented the practice of giving loan to a Dalit. But after much request he could be able to get loan at the rate of Rs.5 per cent interest. Besides interest on loan, another condition associated with loan was to render labour on existing wages till the total loan plus interest was not paid back. After one year compound rate of interest was charged on the loan.

He took loan and sent his father to the pilgrimage of Mathura along with other villagers. Since the very day of incurring loan, he became a labourer of the Malik. Now he had to perform work in the house of Malik. He tried to pay the loan back from the wages he earned. But he had to pay Rs. 600 interest in a year for principal amount. Each year he could be able to pay only the interest and the principal amount was left untouched. In this way he worked for six years in the house of Malik but could not be able to pay the principal amount of loan plus interest back. At last, he had to sell a cow, whom his family members had domesticated from childhood for milk. The cow was sold in the hand of same Mahajan. Then he could be able to free himself to work anywhere according to his wishes.

This is not only the case of R.M. but like him many Dalits are being exploited who incur loan from Malik to visit near or distant pilgrimage. They have to pay high interest and to mortgage their labour at the hand of Malik to obtain a loan either in cash or kind.

B.R. (45 year) a resident of a village in Bodh Gaya block of Gaya district has a similar story of exploitation in the name of pilgrimage to present before us. Nearly 4 years ago he had to take loan from a koeri Malik to sent his parents to Prayagraj for bathing in Triveni (confluence of Ganga, Yamuna and Saraswati) on the occasion of Magh purnima. His parents were old and it was their desire of oldhood to have to holybath at the Sangam of Triveni. B.R. wanted to fulfill this desire of parents any how. He had Rs. 200 with him but they required minimum a sum of Rs. 1000. To obtain Rs. 800 he visited the house of many Mahajans but no one was ready to pay loan. At last he went to the house of a Mahajan who belonged to a Koeri caste. He became ready to pay loan but on some condition. The first condition was that the rate of interest would be Rs. 6 per month per hundred, i.e. Rs. 72 per hundred per year. another condition was to mortgage the labour of any member to work on existing wages till the entire loan plus interest was paid back. The third condition was that after one year compound interest would be charged. He agreed to fulfill all the three conditions, then he could be able to obtain loan. Any way sent his parent to the pilgrimage and himself began to work for the Malik. He worked three years continuously for the Malik, but could not pay the loan and interest back. He is still working with the Mahajan. His family is domesticating a heifer. They are hopeful to become free from the loan of Mahajan when the heifer will become a cow. They will sell the cow in the market and pay the loan back to the Malik. In the meantime, each year they want to clear the interest on the loan. He has to pay a sum of Rs. 576 as interest for Rs. 800 every year.

L.R. (35 yr.) a resident of a village in Imamganj block of Gaya district informed that he had to take a loan from a Muslim Mahajan to take his old and blind mother at the pilgrimage of Haridwar. He had taken a loan of Rs. 1000 from the Mahajan by mortgaging his four Katha of land at the hand of the Malik. He had thought that he would be able to get the land free soon. But this could not happen. In five years he has not been able to get his land free. His land is situated in Diha. It is very suitable for the cultivation of vegetable crops. The Malik earns each year a sum of Rs. 2000 from the land. L.R. and his family members are struggling hard to get the land free. But each year the luck is not favouring them. Last year he had to spend a sum of Rs. 5000 at the time of delivery of his wife. Year before last, he had to spend a sum of Rs. 3000 on the treatment of T.B. of his 15 years old son. But they are hopeful that they would get their land back sooner or later. But will not sell their land at the hand of the Malik.

Exploitation in the Name of Akhanda Harikirtan

In the villages under study the Akhanda Harikirtan in the name of Lord Rama and Krishna is held in the form of prayer songs continuously for 24 hours, 48 hours or 72 hours, i.e., one day, two days or three days. An Akhanda Jyoti (continuous lamp), is kept lighting at the place where Akhanda Harikirtan takes place. This is done for the common welfare of the village. That is why all households of the village is expected to participate in it. Along with other castes Dalits are also involved in the performance of Harikirtan. It is believed that the performance of Harikirtan in a year makes the village disease free, brings peace and prosperity in the village and increases the harvest of the village. To perform Harikirtan the villagers set together to discuss the expenditure involved and to decide the rate of subscription per household. In case of Dalit, the rate is kept slightly less but they have to pay any how. If they do not obey the request of the villagers, they are threatened in different ways. They have to take loan to pay subscription of the Harikirtan. To repay the loan, they have to render labour in the house of person who provides them loan. Not only this, they have to render labour free of cost on this occasion. They have to render labour free of cost to clean the site, to erect stage, to sing prayer song and to carry Palaki of Lord Rama and Krishna at the time of procession in the village. They are taught that for rendering services free of cost on such only occasion is beneficial for this world as well as for world after death.

It will be in the fitness of the thing to present here case studies dealing with the exploitation of Dalits who refused to pay subscription and labour on the occasion of Harikirtan.

N.R. (25 yr.) is a resident of a village in Bodh Gaya block of Gaya district. Five years ago he refused to pay the amount of subscription and to render labour in Akhanda Harikirtan organised by the village. At that time he was just young and he did not believe in such religious activities. He earned wages to run his family. When villagers learnt that N.R. had disobeyed the decision of the village, they boycotted him. He was not given work in the village. To earn wages he had to go in other neighbouring villages. Nobody wanted to have discussion with him. Even Dalits of the village also did not want to have relation with him. His family members were not allowed to cut grasses in the field of the villages.

One night an incidence took place. He had a cow, the cow broke the rope and grazed the vegetable field of a Yadava Malik. The crops were ready for yield. The cow grazed and destroyed the entire vegetable field. In the morning, one of villagers saw this. He informed the Malik of the field. The Malik of the field caught the cow and brought her to his house. N.R. was called to be present there all villagers were also called. A panchayat of the villagers sat to decide the punishment. The Dalits of the village also took part. The cost of the crop was estimated Rs. 2000 and the cost of the cow was estimated Rs. 1200. Besides cow, Rs. 800 was still left. In order to pay the rest amount N.R. had to work 90 days in the house of the Malik without any payment.

The next day, when the time of Akhand Harikirtan arrived, N.R. had to pay the previous years subscription along with the present year only then he was included as the resident of the village. Now he does not dare to break the law of the village.

In different villages Akhanda Harikirtan takes place on different occasions in a year like Maghpurnima, Shivaratri day, Basant Panchami day, Janamasthmi day, Ramnawami day etc. If a villager runs shortage of money, his case is considered sympathetically. But if he refuses to pay subscription, he is boycotted socially.

EXPLOITATION IN PERFORMANCE OF YAGNA

In the area under study different types of yagna takes place. These yagna are performed by the Sadhus belonging to different religious cults. The performance of yagna takes time as well as money. The village where yagna takes place has to pay more in cash as well as in kind. The place for yagna is selected at the confluence of a river or on the bank of a big pond. In order to perform yagna, the Swamiji or Babaji pays a visit in the village. The villagers erect a hut for his stay. The arrangement of food is also made by the villagers. The chela of Swamiji prepares food and takes every care for him. The visit of Swamiji is popularised in the neighbouring areas. Swamiji gives preaching to the villagers for the one and quarter month. After preaching the Arati of Swamiji is held and prasad is distributed among the audience. The expenditure on the Swamiji's stay, Arati and prasad is shared by the villagers. The villager's contributed sun fried rice, gur, ghee, milk, curd, vegetables, etc. In the contribution of these items, Dalits also do not lag behind. They contributed gur, ghee, milk, vegetables etc. In the erection of hut they render labour without any wages. They participate in prayer songs in the morning and evening. After one and quarter, month the Swamiji announces the date and time of the performance of Yagna. Now the villagers sit and decide the rate of subscription to be contributed by each household. In case of Dalits, the rate is kept low but they are expected to perform various types of work related to the performance of Yagna like carrying goods from the villages, market, other village. They have to render labour in the erection of pandal where yagna is expected to take place. They have also to work to erect the stage where drama, dance, Rasleela, Krishnaleela, etc. takes place at night. They have also to work to prepare temporary road for the visitors of Yagna. For these works they do not get wages. But they receive breakfast and food from the managing committee of Yagna. From the day of visit of the Swamiji in the villages till the yagna is not over, the Dalits have to render various types to labour without wages. But they cannot become shrota of the rituals. They can remain present outside the Yagnashala to her and to see the rituals. In the ritual of Hawana, they are invited to take part along with ghee, oat, coconut, dhup, chandan, etc. In the last day of Yagna, the feast is given in the name of poor. But one finds the dominance of the rich at the time of feast. Many Dalits are left and do not get even prasad of the Yagna.

For Yagna, they work day and night on one leg to make it successful. But at the time of distribution of prasad they are neglected which hurt them very much.

6

POLITICAL AREA OF DALIT EXPLOITATION OF GAYA

In political area of Dalit exploitation an attempt has been made to discuss the exploitation of Dalits by those authorities who hold power. Due to possession of power in modern political and administrative system, they exploit the Dalits. The exploitation of Dalit by Choukidar, Dafadar, Mukhia, Sarpanch, Karmachari, Gram Sevak, Police thana, Block, court, etc. form the political area of Dalit exploitation. Now let us discuss the exploitation of Dalit by different political and administrative agencies.

Exploitation of Dalit by Choukidar

A Choukidar is an agent of thana. He is expected to provide news related to crime and administration to the thana police. Thus he is directly attached to thana police. The Choukidar moves from village to village collects information. He goes in Dalit tola and asks Dalit to render labour for his selfish purpose. If they deny, he threatens them to give their names to thana police as criminals. He employee Dalits as labour but does not pay them proper wages. In exploiting Dalits, the Choukidar takes side of the wealthy persons. He takes their chicks, goats, ducks, eggs etc. and does not pay the price. He takes them in the name of thana police.

The Choukidar get salary. From the saving of salary, they are purchasing land. They get land from the Malik to do share cropping. They give loan to landless poor and utilize their services at cheap wages.

It will be the fitness of the thing to present here one case study. S.D. (35 yr.) a resident of a village in Bodh Gaya block was exploited by the Choukidar of his panchayat. Nearly 10 years ago, he had a cow. His father was agriculture. He worked as attached labour in the house of a Rajput Malik. His father had made him free from agricultural work. He was asked to take care of a cow and few goats. As daily labourer, he worked to earn rice in wages. The Choukidar of his village was Yadav by caste. He owned land as well as money. Once the Choukidar approached his father and asked him to give S.D. for his domestic and agricultural work. His father refused completely. But the Choukidar took it ill. He made up his mind to punish S.D. and his family members for the refusal of the proposal. He was in search of such an occasion in which S.D. could be involved in cases. One day such an occasion reached S.D. left his cow and goats at road for grazing grasses and himself went to drink water at a *chappakal* situated nearby a school. His cow entered in the paddy crops of the Choukidar and damaged the crop. As soon as this news reached to the family of Choukidar, they rushed immediately to the field and tried to find out where S.D. was being terrified S.D. did not dare to appear before them. The cow was hurt ruthlessly and brought to the house of the Choukidar. The Choukidar was not at home there. He had gone to thana to meet the thana in-charge. He came back in the evening. He took a thick stick and went at the house of S.D. Reaching there he shouted angrily but S.D. did not come out of the house. His wife came out and she was abused badly. When his father and mother came out of house, they were also abused. They did not say anything. They thought that the anger of the choukidar would be cooled gradually. But he went on shouting and abusing them aloud. S.D. was young and energetic. He could not bear this insult any more. He took a stick in his hand and came out. He also started making verbal attach through abuses on the choukidar. Hearing the quarrel, the villagers gathered at the place. Some tried to mediate but in vain. The choukidar, who was also a muscle-man hit S.D. and his father with stick. They fell on the ground and started bleeding from their heads. Seeing them bleeding his anger cooled. He rushed to his village. He sent the cow to be sold at any price and himself went to thana to filed a case against S.D. and his family members when S.D. went to file a case, he was arrested. His case was not recorded in the register. His wife had to sell her ornaments and to take Rs. 500 loan to get S.D. released from the thana lock up. Neither doctor nor thana incharge took up his case. For loan he had to work on reduced wages in the house of another Yadav Malik.

Exploitation by Dafadar

To or three panchayats to gather had a Dafadar. A Dafadar possesses more power than the Choukidar is in direct contact with thana police. He is treated as reliable person for thana police. Whatever he says is taken as true by the thana police. Due to possession of such a power, he exploits and oppresses the Dalits. It will be better to quote one case study here to illustrate the phenomenon of exploitation by a Dafadar.

R.B. (50 yr) a resident of a village in Imamganj block reported that once he was exploited by the Dafadar whose effect can be even today. The Dafadar of his village was Brahmin by caste. He owned land as well as money. Thus, he was a resourceful person. He had approach to the authorities at different levels in the district administration. He exploited Dalits for his work. He did not pay proper wages to Dalits. He compelled them to do Begari for which he did not pay anything. On the 1st day of transplantation of paddy all Dalits had to perform work for him without any wages. On this day labourers were given no wages but only breakfast and midday meal. At the time of harvesting, each labourer of the village had to do one day work for the Dafadar only on midday food. On ceremonial and festive occasions, each Dalit labourer had to do Begari for him in carrying goods from different places.

Nearly 10 years ago, R.B. was ill and his wife was pregnant so they did not go to do Begari on the 1st day of transplantation of paddy seedlings. He took it ill and decided to take revenge at any time in near future. He was not ready to hear any excuse. He thought that R.B. was telling a lie.

One day R.B. was breaking dry small wood from a mango tree to prepare prasad for a worship. The tree belonged to the Dafadar, When Dafadar heard this, he called R.B. at his house. He was fined Rs. 200 to pay immediately or render labour for twenty days without any payment. R.B. requested many times to excuse but each time the fine went on increasing by Rs. 50. From Rs. 200. On several request, the fine shot up to Rs. 500 or to render labour for 50 days. At last he accepted to work. From next day, he had to render labour for 50 days only on breakfast and one end meal.

Exploitation by Mukhia

The Mukhia is the political head of the modern Gram Panchayat. The Mukhia is elected by the adult members of the villages falling under particular Gram Panchayat. Although he is Mukhia of the entire panchayat and he is expected to treat each member equally, but he, does not lag behind in exploiting and oppressing the Dalits. Some case studies presented below will clarify this statement as to how they are exploited.

K.B. (40 yr) a resident of Bodh Gaya block in Gaya district reported about his exploitation by the Mukhia of his panchayat. The Mukhia of his panchayat belonged to Yadav by caste. He owned 30 acres of land. He had many Bhuiyan as attached labour for work in agriculture. It was nearly

15 years ago that he went to Mukhia to mortgage his 10 Kathas of land which his family owned. This piece of land was situated in the middle of the 5 acre land of Mukhia. Mukhia was trying to own that land. But K.B. was not in a mood either to sell or to mortgage the land. But suddenly a bad occasion came on which he had to think to mortgage his only 10 kathas of land. His only son fell ill seriously. Suddenly he became unable to stand and walk. R.B. and his wife took the son to Gaya Medical College for treatment. The parents came to know that his son was suffering from paralytic attack. R.B. sold his goats and cows. The mother sold her silver ornaments, but they required still more money to meet expense on treatment. They were not in a position to earn wages because either husband or wife had to stay at hospital to take care of the sick child. Being disabled he decided to mortgage his land. He went to the house of many Malik but not one was ready to take his land on mortgage because it was only 10 Kathas and was situated in the middle of Mukhia's land. At last he went to the house of Mukhia and gave proposal to mortgage his land. Mukhia was also not ready to take the mortgage of the land externally. But he wanted to have the land internally. He was saying no just to pay less amount for the mortgage. He became ready to pay only Rs. 1000 for the mortgage of 10 kathas of land. This money was to be returned after three years.

Taking money K.B. went to hospital to take care of his son admitted in the hospital. He remained there for a month. His son was cured and he came back. He had spent all money but he was pleased to see his son well and cured. He and his wife began to struggle hard to get his land back by paying Rs. 1000 at the end of the 3rd year. His wife accepted the work of Dai in the house of Malik. He himself did not want to become absent from work. He wanted to earn more and more wages. They began to work from dawn to dusk. But their fate was not favouring. From little saving they purchased four goats and 10 chicks. But none of them could survive due to illness. They also bought a small calf for rearing. They had thought to earn money by selling the calf when it would become young. But the calf also could not survive.

In this way, the period of three years passed but they could not save money to get the mortgaged back. At the end of the 3rd year, the Mukhia compelled K.B. either to repay the money or finally to sell the land. K.B. requested the Malik to keep the land for another three years under mortgage. But the Malik was not ready. The Malik has made a plan to keep the land any how. He gave a time of one month more to pay the money back, if not the land was to be sold to the Malik. K.B. moved from door to door in the village and requested them to pay Rs. 1000 for the mortgage of his 10 kathas land. Mukhia had utilized his power. He had requested the villagers not to pay money to R.B. At last R.B. was compelled to sell his land only for Rs. 5000/-. In this way for a small amount the land of R.B. passed to the Mukhia for ever.

Now the only means of earning for R.B. and his family was wages. Mukhia assured him to provide work round the year. He also put a proposal to keep his son as herd boy so long as he would like. Now his son is working as a servant in the house of the Mukhia. R.B. and his wife are working as agricultural labour. They do not get minimum wages of the panchayat. He is judge for the whole panchayat but he too exploits and oppresses the Dalit. He, too, supports the resourceful persons in exploiting and oppressing the Dalits.

S.D. (38 yr) a resident of a village in Imamganj block of Gaya district reported that he was exploited by the Mukhia of his panchayat. The Mukhia of his panchayat was Muslim by caste. He owned 30 bighas of land. He had many Dalits as attached labour to perform agricultural work round the year.

Once a quarrel took place between him and another Dalit who was Chamar by caste. The quarrel occurred over a piece of land. The land was under his possession since his forefathers time. It was situated in front of the house of another Dalit, Dukha Chamar. Dukha Chamar worked in the house of Mukhia as attached labour. Dukha used to throw domestic waste in the land. He used to tie his cattle during day time. S.D. also threw waste product of house there. Since the land was barren, many Dalits kept their waste materials of houses to use as manures. S.D. never prohibited them. As a result, they began to think to use that land as their birth right. The marriage of the younger brother of S.D. was settled. Now he thought to erect a house for his brother. He asked all Dalits to stop using the land because he had to build a house for his brother. This pained them much. The users of the land made a plan to put S.D. in trouble. Dukha was a man of Mukhiaji. They asked Dukha to file a case in the panchayat against S.D. He was not aware of the development. Next day when he went to make preparation for the foundation of house, he also took his side. Mukhiaji prepared a false paper any how. Thus, the paper of Dukha became controversial. Mukhia, Sarpanch, Karmachari all sided with Dukha and S.D. was left alone. The panchayat gave the decision that it was a common land and S.D. was trying to take the land under his possession.

For capturing the common property, he was fined Rs. 500. In order to pay the fine, he had to serve for the Mukhiaji for 50 days only on breakfast and midday meal. Being poor he could not dare to move in lower court. In this way, there were many cases in which Mukhia had misused his position to exploit and oppress the Dalits.

Exploitation by Sarpanch

In modern Gram Panchayat System, the Sarpanch is the head of judiciary. Sarpanch makes hearing of criminal cases. Thus, he possesses huge power. The other powerful persons can challenge the sarpanch in court. But for poor Dalits do not have money to move in lower court. In order to show the exploitation made by the Sarpanch on the Dalits, few cases studies are being cited here.

D.C. (38 yr), a resident of a village in Bodh Gaya block informed about his exploitation by the Sarpanch in the following ways.

It was about 10 years ago that he was involved in a criminal case in panchayat by another Dalit who belonged to the same caste. The case was that S.C. had stolen a he goat of L.C. and had eaten up. Four Dalits of the village were witness in the case. They had not seen D.C. stealing the goat and killing it for eating. One had seen pieces of bones in the garbage of his house. One had seen his wife washing a dhoti with blood stains. One had heard that the meat was cooked very tasty. One had seen a member of the house going in the house of a neighbouring relative with pieces of meat. L.C. himself had seen the skin of goat being taken away by a dog.

First of all L.C. accused D.C. for stealing and killing his he goat for the purpose of eating. He asked him to pay the price of the goat, otherwise he would move in the court of panchayat. D.C. said as to why he was accusing him, he had not stolen his goat. He said that L.C. was making a false charge against him. He became angry to hear this news. In those days, meat was not cooked in his house. He said that he was not guilty. There might be some one else but he and his family members were not concerned with his goat. So he requested to not make such type of allegation. Actually he had not stolen the goat. The goat was stolen by a person of Bania caste who had killed the goat at a lonely place to eat the meat. He had put skin and bones of legs at the carbage of the D.C. The blood stain on Dhoti was of wound. One of his family members has visited the house of relative taking the rice of Sawan (a type of grass). All other Dalits were convinced that S.C. had stolen the goat.

At last, L.C. filed a case in the court of sarpanch. The court sat and heard the witness. The court arrived at conclusion that S.C. had killed the goat of L.C. for the purpose of eating, so, he was fined Rs. 500 to pay as compensation to the aggrieved party.

The compensation was to be paid within a period of one month from the date of decision. But he neither paid compensation nor moved in lower court against the decision of the court of sarpanch. When the period was over, he was called by the sarpanch. He asked him to pay now Rs. 1000, Rs. 500 to aggrieved party and Rs. 500 to the court to disobey the order.

A thumb impression on a plain paper along with stamp was taken on which the amount of punishment was raised up to Rs. 2000. He had nothing to pay in the fine. So he agreed to repay the fine by working as labour. He had to work in the house of sarpanch for a period of one year to repay the fine. The sarpanch utilized his labour without any wages, but he did not pay a single paise to aggrieved party.

R.B. (50 yr) a resident of a village in Imamganj block of Gaya district informed that he has a similar story of exploitation and oppression by the sarpanch of the panchayat.

Once a quarrel took place between his family and the family of the neighbour who belonged to the same caste. The matter of quarrel was related to sex. The daughter of neighbour was caught in illegal sex relation with one of the boy of his family. The neighbour, B.B. beaten the boy. The beating of boy had made his family member angry who also beat B.B. in return. As a result minor bleeding from the forehead took place in both sides. Both party filed cases in the court of the sarpanch. No outsider was witness in the case. Family members of both families were the witness. The Sarpanch belonged to Rajput by caste. He thought that it was a good chance to exploit both the parties. The court of sarpanch sat and heard the witness. The court accused both boy and girl. It was advised to get them married or to pay a fine of Rs. 1000 each to the court to violate the law of the village. Both were poor and unable to pay fine. Therefore, the thumb impression of both heads of the families was taken on a plain paper with stamp. They were given a time of one month for the payment. After a month, when they did not pay the fine, they were called again. They were asked to pay the fine immediately or they had to render services so long as the amount of fine was not paid back. They had to work for one full agricultural season only on breakfast and food. Then the amount of fine was paid.

Thus, the sarpanch utilized his position in exploiting the Dalit of the village.

Exploitation by Thana

The behaviour of thana police was very exploitative for any person because without bribe they don't write even the right thing. But for Dalits, they are more exploitative. Majority of Dalit are poor and illiterate. So police are confident that Dalits would not move in the court against their behaviour. When the name of Dalits come as criminal in the Thana, the thana police rush immediately to his house. They demand heavy money to get his name struck out. They took heavy money as Salami. They also took chicken and goats to eat. If he does not pay salami, chicken and goat are taken by force. If caught, they are beaten mercilessly. Few case studies in this regard are as follows :

A.B. (30 yr) a resident of village in Bodh Gaya block of the Gaya district informed that his father was exploited by the thana police. He was 15 years old at that time when one of the villagers had given his name in a dacoity case. The police has eaten his chicken and goat and had taken way the only cow. He had wept bitterly seeing the condition of his mother. He had to accept the work of a servant in the house of a Rajput Malik who had agreed to look into the case of his father. When caught, his father was beaten mercilessly. He was released on bail, but could not survive. His Malik has spent a sum of Rs. 1000 to get the bail of his father. His mother had to accept the work of Charwahin and Dai. She died working as Dai and Charwahin. He rendered services in the house of the Malik for 10 years only on breakfast and food to repay the loan.

E.L. (25 yr) a resident of village in Imamganj block of Gaya district disclosed about the exploitation made by thana police on Dalits. About 10 years ago his brother was exploited by the thana police. He used to sell vegetables on a bicycle. He did not like to work in the field. This was not taken good by the villagers. A case of theft was registered in thana against him. He was accused in stealing the potato from the potato field of a farmer. One villager caught him but was able to escape any how and run in his house along with the stolen potato in a sack. According to E.C. it was a false charge to harass his brother and his family members because he did not work for the Malik of the village.

The police came and heard the witness. He took Rs. 250 from the person who had gone to file the case as Salami. The police demanded Rs. 500 from the second party as Salami. G.B. the brother of E.C. had no-money to purchase clothes and medicine. How could he pay Rs. 500 as Salami. Non-payment of Salami made the police angry. The thanedar ordered the policemen to search the house of B.C. Three bags of potatoes, 2 bags of wheat, 3 cocks, 5 hens, 3 goats, and a heifer was there in the house of B.C. The police took the potato bags under his custody. They sold wheat bags to get cash. They took goats and cocks to eat. Then, they returned to thana. They had also beaten the children of the house and abused the women. Being poor and disable, they had to bear all such insults. Besides, these oppressive and exploitative behaviour, B.C. was sent to jail. Before sending jail, he was beaten in black and white. His wife had to take a loan of Rs. 1000/- from the house of a Malik to get B.C. released from jail. For that amount she had to work for the Malik as Dai for 15 years without any wages only for breakfast and meal.

Exploitation by Gram Sewak and Panchayat Sewak

Gram Sewak and panchayat sewak are part of block level administration. They mediate the programme of development between the villagers and the block development officer. They take contract of digging well for irrigation, installing *chappakal* for drinking water, preparing village roads, etc. They also make the villagers aware of the various types of programmes of development. In the work of digging well, constructing dam, making embankment of pond, sinking *chappakal*, constructing village roads, etc. the utilize the services of Dalits as labour. But they do not pay minimum wages fixed by the government. They convince the labourers that programme was approved some five or more years ago. When the rate of wages was same which they were receiving. But the fact remains some thing else. They make the old programme approoved in the new rate. Only then they take up the work. But in order to exploit the Dalits, they deny to pay the present rate of minimum wages. In this work, the labour inspector and block level officials get percentage share. But the maximum share goes in the hand of gram sewak and panchayat sewak.

Gram sewak and Panchayat sewak mediate between the bank officials and the beneficiaries of the programme who were Dalits. In order to get the loan sanctioned, the Gram Sewak, Panchayat Sewak and Bank officials take bribe. Only then the poor get the loan sanctioned. They give bribe in cash but do not receive loan in cash. They get in kind like oxen, cow, buffalo, sowing-machine, *thela*, rickshaw, etc.

Dalit have to take loan in cash to pay as bribe to Gramsewak, bank officials and block officials for loan they have to work on reduced wages. On payment of bribe, they are sanctioned loan. They get in kind equal to the value of loan. The value of thing is shown more by the officials.

Exploitation by Political Parties

Different political parties exploit the Dalits for their selfish purposes. Nowaday, it has become a fashion to organise rally and procession by different political parties to show the strength of their supporters.

The organisers of rally and the members of the political parties approach the poor and innocent Dalits and give them temptations of various kind to join the rally. The party workers say that they will be carried from the village to the place of rally by buses or train for which fare will be paid by the party. They will be given food, clothes, and money equivalent to the wages of a day for each day of rally. They also make false promise to take them at several visiting places at the time of return. The poor Dalits are attracted towards the false promise of the party workers. They join the workers to increase the number of crowds. At the time of going, the care is taken for the persons joining the rally. They are given some lunch packets as well. But when they reach the place of rally, they do not find any facilities. They are left uncared and hungry. They can be seen fighting among themselves for getting lunch packets, etc. In huge crowd, they are separated from the group. They are not only separated but left at their fate. They have to face great trouble in coming back home. They have to beg to come home back or they are forced to travel by train without ticket. They are promised but never get money equivalent to the wages.

B.R. (50 yr) reported that he had gone to Patna to join a rally organised by a political party. The workers of the party had approached his village for this purpose. They had made promise to carry them from village to Patna and back to the village.

They had promised to give breakfast, food and Rs. 20 per day. Being attracted towards these promises, he went to Patna along with the villagers. From village he was carried to Gaya Railway station by a metador. From Gaya he was carried to Patna by train. The persons participating in rally had travelled without any ticket. No authorities had dared to come to them to check the tickets. Any way, they reached at Patna Gandhi Maidan. This maidan was their shelter. In the evening, he inquired about the breakfast with other persons who had come to join rally, but did not find any trace. At night he had come to know about the distributors of food packets. But when he went there, he saw people fighting among themselves to get the packets. Suddenly it was heard that there was now shortage of packets. Due to shortage of food packets, they had to spend night without food. Fortunately, he had some *chura* and *sattu* with him. He ate *sattu*, slept in the maidan. In the next day, again many people did not get breakfast and lunch packets. They were hungry hut compelled to join rally. Being hungry many left the idea to join the rally. They tried first to eat something from the little money they had in their pockets. They came back to station. They came back Gaya without ticket. From Gaya they had spend their won money to reach the home. What to say about the money equivalent to wages, they did not get food and fare to come home back.

Exploitation by MLA and MP

MLA and MP are elected to make laws, certainly they make but they do not follow. They had made law to stop the exploitation and oppression of weaker sections in general and Dalits in particular. But they themselves exploit and oppress the Dalits. They utilize their services at low and nominal wages. The support the rich who exploit and oppress them. They favour the criminals who loot their votes. In election, they hire Goonda to loot the vote and booth of Dalits. They terrorise and even kill Dalits at the time of voting. Some of them give them some money for casting votes in their favour. When they win, they hire Dalits on little payment to organise rally and play musical instruments for the victory procession.

Exploitation by Local Sena

In the area under study there are different senas or armies who want to enter into national politics or state politics through organisation of sena.

Some senas claim that they fight against exploitation and oppression of the poor labourers. They enjoy support of the poor. Naxalite is one of such sena. Sangram Samiti, Indian Peoples Front, MCC also claim to fight against exploitation and oppression of the poor. They have their own sena. CPI (ML), JPF and MCC also fight elections to enter into state and national politics. These senas are aggressive. They want to bring revolution through violent means. They take revenge in such a terrible manner that terrorism spread in their names. They cut feet or head and called it Chhaw incha chota. They cut throat by *katta*. They hang the person on a tree with nail in chest. They insert bamboo nail in the stomach. They murder the person in terrible manner. These armies generally exploit and oppress the rich. On many occasions, they are involved in group murder. Sometimes the supporters of two such sena are involved in conflict among themselves. In such cases, many supporters of each sena are killed.

These senas collect money from the Dalit to run the organisation and to purchase modern arms. No Dalit can deny. Each family has to pay whatever is demanded in their name. If they deny, they are punished severely. The punishment goes from five in rupees to the murder. They have to take loan to pay money to these armies. The organisers utilize their services for selfish purposes. They take not only money but Begari as well. They have to carry goods at different places in the name of organisations. They have to contribute to hold meeting by the senas.

Whenever a quarrel takes place between two Dalit families or two Dalit communities or Dalits of two Tolas or villages, it is fought on the basis of Sena. If a sena supports one party, the other party seeks support of other sena. Some times over a piece of Garmaujarua land or fishing in a pond or Nala, the two sena come in front of each other with gun, rifles and bombs. They attack each with these arms. Due to such conflict, group murder takes place.

While these sena claim to enjoy the support of majority of Dalits to counter these senas some other senas have also come in to existence. They enjoy the support of caste or groups. For example, Kurmis have formed Bhumi Sena, Yadvas have formed Laurik Sena, Koeri have formed Kushwaha sena, Dalit have Thakur sena, Rajputs have Kunwar sena, etc. Besides these caste based senas, there are sena which enjoy the support of forward castes. These senas are known as Sawarna liberation front, Ranbir Sena, Sun Light sena etc. Muslims have also formed their sena which is called Safisena. The main aim of these senas is to curb the Naxal activities. These sena took law and order in their hand and are involved in exploitation, oppression and atrocities on Dalits. These sena collect money from their supporters and purchase guns, rifles and other modern arms. These senas have become a threat not only for the farmers and peace loving people but also for the administrators who run administration.

7

EXPLOITATION OF DALIT BY DALIT OF GAYA

A number of low status scheduled castes are termed Dalits. Among them some enjoy numerical dominance and reservation of status in political institutions. Numerically dominant Dalits have been able to get their share in Gram Panchayat, MLA and MP elections. After independence, Dalit have been benefited by educational programmes. They have been able to attain modern education and modern jobs in private and public sectors and in Government Institutions. As-a result of all these developed classes have emerged among the Dalits also. Some of them have reached the status of very rich, others are rich but majority of them are still poor. Thus, the exploitation of a poor and weak of status has also come to light. The exploitation of Dalit can be discussed under the three broad categories :

1. Exploitation of minor Dalit by major Dalit.
2. Exploitation of uneducated by educated Dalit.
3. Exploitation of the poor Dalit by the rich Dalit.

Exploitation of Minor Dalits by Major Dalits

In the area under study the Halalkhore, the Dom and the Dhobi belong to minor Dalit castes. The Halalkhore are Bhangies. They used to clean daily service latrine. They have their Yajmanika village. The Dhobis are washermen. They are kept to clean clothes at the time of death and at the time of birth in family. They have Yajmanika village. The Dhobi plays significant role on the 10th day of death of a person. He sits in the line of Gotia bhai at the time of eating us a feast. It is the Dhobi who shares first of all the feast, then Gotia bhai and other members start eating. The Dom are sacred specialist of death rites. They give fire at the time of cremation. They also provide soop for the performance of Chhath Vrata. Previously different types of baskets were supplied by the Dom. The Dom also have their Yajmanika village. They were regarded as the prestige of the village. That's why they were kept by the Zamindars and Malik of the village. Those Zamindars or Malik in whose Zamindari village, these were not found, the status of such villages were treated as inferior.

Again in the area under study the Chamar, the Dusadh, the Bhuiyan and the Pasi are the major Dalit communities. Their population is much more than the population of the Bhangi, the Dom and the Dhobi, Choukidar, Mukhia, Sarpanch, MLA, and M.P. can be seen from the major Dalit community. Not only in political sphere alone, even in villages minor Dalits are being exploited by the major Dalits. It will be in the fitness of the discussion to present here some case studies in this regard.

P.R. (45 yr) a resident of a village in Bodh Gaya Block of Gaya district reported about his exploitation by the Bhuiyas of the village. R.P. belongs to Dhobi by caste. Only one household of Dhobi resides in the village while 50 households of Bhuiya reside in the village. Besides these two Dalit castes, 300 households of the Rajput, the Brahmin, the Koeri, the Hajam also reside in the village. Dalits reside in a separate settlement called Dalit tola. Bhuiyas have numerical strength in the Dalit tola. They exploit and oppress P.R. because he does not have numerical strength in the village.

The Government like other Dalits of the village has given Parcha of homestead land to P.R. He has built a three-roomed house. The house is made up mud and is thatched with tiles. He has Yajmani relation with the High and Backward Hindu castes for which he gets in kind after the harvest of paddy and Rabi crops. He cleans the clothes of the villagers, besides cleaning dirty clothes of Chhathi and death rituals. As he is attached to high caste Hindus and Backward caste Hindus, he feels his status higher than the Bhuiyas of the village, who are agricultural labourer. This is the main reason for which he is exploited and oppressed by the Bhuiyas.

In front of his house, there is a land which belongs to him. He calls it as Bari land. He cultivates vegetable in this land. When vegetable crops are ready for the harvest, fruits are stolen by the Bhuiyas. They pluck fruits of the vegetables at night. In festive and ceremonial occasions, they pluck the vegetables forcibly. When he makes any complain, no one pays any attention to it. Even the aged do not listen to him. Being frustrated, they destroy the entire crops of the vegetables some time.

Three years ago, his cow was stolen at a dark night. He had reared the cow with great hope to get milk for the family members. Some young

Bhuiyas entered his house. R.P. woke to hear the sound. But he was attacked by lathi. He fell down and become unconscious. His wife and sons shouted, but no one came then to help them. By that time the thieves had gone with cow and his entire family had wept bitterly. He decided to file a case, but no one was ready to become a witness. The other matter was that he had no money to pay police to book a case. So weeping helplessly they released the burden of their heart and mind. They filed a case in the court of God by visiting the main temple of the village. They bowed their heads before the image of Goddess Bhagwati and made prayer to punish the guilty. They became satisfied and are hopeful that God will definitely punish them, some day.

Ten years ago, one Bhuiya of the village had captured his three feet homestead land. He made Mukhiaji of the village as Panch to look in to the matter. Mukhiaji was kind enough to take up his case. He found the Bhuiya as guilty. The Bhuiya had to leave the land immediately. R.P. made his own wall. Being defeated the Bhuiya thought to teach him a lesson. One dark night, he made a hole in the mud wall of his house. He stole boxes, ornaments, clothes and cooking utensils from his house, while R.P. and his family members were sleeping. In the morning, when they woke up, they found that there was nothing in their house everything, of the house was stolen. They had to purchase earthen pots from the potters to cook food. Even food grains were taken away by them. He had to take food grains as loan. He had to eat cooked food on leaf plate. He had taken a loan of Rs. 100 to purchase cooking utensils.

Last year paddy grains there stolen from the trashing ground. He had collected 100 bundles of paddy crop from his Yajmans. He thrashed and winnowed the paddy grains. Winnowing took place just before darkness of night, so he decided to carry the paddy grains next morning. He was sleeping by the side of the heap of the paddy grains. But Bhuiyas of neighbouring houses were waiting for his sleep. As soon as he fell asleep, paddy grains were stolen. When he woke up, he did not see the heap of paddy grains. But he could not do anything. He consoled himself in the name of his fate.

The Bhuiyas of the village ask P.K. to clean their clothes without any payment. They do not allow him to fetch water from the tube-well sunk in the tola by the Government. They call P.K. as to untouchables because he washes the clothes of other castes. Being vexed, he is planning to leave the village or to shift in another tola of the village. But no body wants to purchase his home and homestead land because it is situated in the Bhuiva

Tola. Other castes do not want to purchase land for house in that tola. Bhiya do not want to pay the price. They want to possess his house and homestead land without any price. Other castes of the village do not take interest because both belong to Dalit. No other castes want to involve themselves with the cases of Dalits.

In another case S.M. (36 yr), a resident in a village of Imamganj Block of Gaya district has been exploited and oppressed by the Dusadh of the village. S.M. belongs to the Mehtar caste. He used to subsist by cleaning the daily service latrine in the house of Zamindars and big landowners. But now daily service latrine have been converted into sulabh latrines. So he and his family members do not get work. Now his family members earn wages. Some female members do the work of cleaning safety tank latrine. There are two families of Mehtar in the village, while there are 5 households of the Dusadh in the village. Besides, these two Dalits Communities, other Hindu castes like the Rajput, the Brahmin, the Yadav, the Koeri, the Hajam and the Lohar, reside in the village. The Rajputs live in a separate tola. The Brahmins live in Brahman tola, the Yadavs, the Hajam, and the Lohar live in backward tola. The Mehtars do not form any strength because their number is very less. Due to their numerical dominance the Dusadhs exploit and oppress the Mehtar in many ways. Previously, he had good income from the Yajmani villages. From the savings, he had built a two story mud-house thatched with tiles. Some Dusadhs also had double-story house thatched with tiles. But majority of Dusadhs possessed mud house thatched with straw. That's why Dusadhs were jealous of him. They used to harass him in different ways. 20 years ago his house was set on fire by a Dusadh of the village. The reason was personal enmity. The Dusadh was stealing gram from the field of a Yadava. S.M. was coming from the village. He saw Dusadh boy stealing the gram crops which were ready for harvest. The Yadava has agreed to pay 1 maund of gram to S.M. for looking after the gram field. So, he snatched the gram crops and rushed to the house of Yadava. The Yadava took a lathi and gave a good beating to the boy of Dusadh. The Dusadhs of the village did not take it good. They decided to teach S.M. a lesson. The most easiest way was to set his house on fire. In one dark night, his house was set on fire. His family members were sleeping. The piece of burning wood fell on their bodies. They could come out of house hurriedly. The villages ran to put the fire out, but by that time his entire house was burnt to ashes, 6 pigs, 12 chicks, 2 goats were also burnt alive. Food grains and utensils were also burnt to ashes. Then his entire family members were on street. They took shelter below a Tamarind tree. The Rajputs and the Yadavs of the village made contributions to provide food grains to S.M. They also provided bamboos and straw to thatch the house. He took a loan of Rs. 150 to purchase cooking utensils. He did not file any case either in panchayat or in Thana. He left the case at the mercy of the God.

He decided to rear a heifer. He got a heifer at half share from the house of a Yadava. After the heifer grew a cow, the price of cow was to be evaluated by Malik and half of the price was to be received by S.M. His family members domesticated the heifer with great hope. Gradually, the heifer became a cow. Now his family members were confident to get a good price of the cow. But they were not aware of the evil desire of the Dusadh of the village. One dark night four/five Dusadhs came with arms and stole the cow. He was sleeping just by the side of the cow, but he could not woke up at the time of stealing. When he woke up and did not see cow, he understood that the cow was stolen. He rushed to the Malik and informed him about the theft of the cow. He and his Malik tried to find out the cow, but in vain. After a month, they left all the hope of getting the cow. This was record time that the Dusadhs tried to vex and exploit the family of S.M.

In an another exploitative and oppressive attempt, 15 maunds of paddy grains were stolen by the Dusadhs from his house. After thrashing, the paddy grain was stored in the courtyard of the house. R.M. had gone for the treatment of his son to Imamganj hospital. His old parents, wife and three small sons were in the house. They were anxious because R.M. had not returned from the hospital. The left the paddy in the courtyard and slept in the house. The door of the room was open. As soon as they fell asleep, some Dusadhs of the tola came and stole the paddy grains. In the morning the news of theft spread in the tola. Villagers came and saw the scene of theft. They criticised the thieves. All showed sympathy in abusing the thieves. After few hours of weeping and cursing the thieves, they compromised with their fate.

Very recently the Dusadhs have beaten his wives and 12 years old son mercilessly. The goats of a neighbouring Dusadh had destroyed the kitchen garden of S.M. S.M. had gone to earn wages. When 12 years old son of S.M. went with goats to make complaint, he was badly abused and threatened to be killed. When the mother of child came to hear noise, she was abused and beaten. This made the child angry he also beat one of Dusadhs. On this, many Dusadhs assembled and caught the boy. The boy was beaten till be became unconscious. When S.M. came back from work, he went to Chaukidar to report about the beating of his son. But as he was also a Dusadh so he did not listen to S.M. Next day he went to Thana, but his case was not registered because he did not pay any money to the Thanedar for registering his case. He had to take loan for the treatment of the son.

In an another exploitative and oppressive behaviour he was not given wages of 7 days by a Dusadh of the village. S.M. had worked in the construction of a house. The Dusadh had agreed to pay Rs. 15 without any breakfast and food. But after the completion of work he gave only Rs. 50 as wages. He requested for the wages several times but he was not given wages.

In the Dalit tola of village, S.M. is treated as a second grade citizen As his family members clean the tank of latrine, therefore, Dusadhs treat him and his family members as untouchable. His family members have to bring water from the chappakal of other tola. The Dalit tola has Government chappakal, but his family members are prohibited by the Dusadhs to take water from there.

Recently the state Government has built a three-roomed pucca house for S.M. He was selected on the basis of minor group. This has made the Dusadh of the Tola more jealous. They stole bricks and cement many times when the house was under construction. But the contractor was the Gram Sewak himself, so the house was constructed.

Thus, exploitation of minor Dalit by major Dalit community takes place. A Dalit exploits another Dalit. He becomes more exploitative and oppressive than the other castes.

Exploitation of Uneducated Dalit by Educated Dalit

Uneducated persons fall victims of exploitation very easily. They are simple and believe that educated persons are good. They do not tell a lie. They are honest and truthful. Therefore, whatever advice is given by the educated persons, that is taken as good. It is general observation that certain castes have enjoyed social, economic and educational status since centuries. They have exploited and oppressed the Dalits since centuries. But nowadays in our country exploitation of uneducated Dalit by educated Dalit has also become a unique future of our society.

After 50 years of independence of our country, and due to various educational programmes implemented by the Government for the development of Dalits, the educational status of Dalits has definitely gone up. They not only know to write their name and read and write letters, but some are non-matriculate, matriculate, graduate, post-graduate some of them also possess technical degree. These educated Dalits receive special regards and respects in their society. They act as leader. Uneducated Dalit come to seek their advice in different kinds of matter. But they exploit and oppress the Dalits in the same way as the others exploit. The educated Dalits utilize the services of uneducated Dalits for selfish purposes. The educated Dalits do not want to work as agricultural labour. They work as Metha (leader) of the leader. They do sharecropping. They lease in land for cultivation. They run shops. They are also engaged in service. Being educated, they are aware of the existing wages, but in payment of wages they take the side of other landowners who do not perform manual work. They think that they will also have to pay more wages if the wages is increased. They are also leading a life like other landowners of the villages.

As Metha of the labour, he takes side of the Malik or the contractor. He has pact with the Malik and contractor. For bringing labour collectively, he gets his share. At the time of work, the Malik contracts the Metha. The Metha assures the Malik to send the labour next day at the site of the work. For this work, he gets Rs. 1 for every labour. The Malik cuts Re one from the wages of the labour. In construction work, the contractor approaches the Metha. The Metha and contractor reach at an oral agreement regarding the mode of payment. For this work, the Metha gets share from the contractor as well as the labourers.

As sharecropper, he utilizes the services of uneducated Dalits, but do not pay the minimum wages fixed by the Government. He also pays the existing wages as paid by the other landowners of the village. Here he takes sides and supports the Malik of the villages. Because taking land on sharecropping from the Malik he also becomes Malik of the uneducated Dalits. He also prohibits the labourers from making any complaint before the officials.

They lease in land for cash cropping, but don't pay proper wages for the utilization of services of uneducated Dalit. Similarly service holders also exploit them. They also take Begari from the uneducated Dalit for which they pay nothing. They expect that as they provide suggestion to them, therefore, they should do Begari for them.

In the matter of quarrel, they exploit and oppress the Dalits in many ways. They do not want to settle the dispute in the village. But they bring them in Thana and court. They visit Thana or court for pairavi for which the expenditure is met by the persons concerned. The uneducated Dalits are unaware of pairavi and Dalali. But educated Dalits are veteran pairavikar and Dalal of Thana and court. By doing pairavi and Dalali, they show their importance in their society. It will be in fitness of the thing to present here some case studies dealing with the exploitation of uneducated Dalits by educated Dalits.

R.R. and S.R. are own brothers. They are resident of a village in Bodh Gaya block of Gaya district. Their father owned 5 kathas of home-stead land and 2 bighas of agricultural land. Their father had died when S.R. was only 12 years old. R.R. was the eldest brother. After the death of father, R.R. became the head of the family. After two years of father's death, their mother also passed away. Now it become the full responsibility to arrange marriage of S.R. with the help of his relatives, the marriage of R.R. was able to settle. For the marriage of S.R. took a loan of Rs. 2000/- for clothes, ornaments and other items of marriage. The marriage ceremony took place and both brothers began to live happily with their family. The only problem of R.R. was to pay the loan back. Both brothers did agriculture in own field and earned wages. As a result, the loan with interest was paid back. In next four five years, they were able to thatch their houses with tiles. They were also able to convert the house in double story. All villagers began to praise them for understanding and cooperation between R.R. and S.R. There were two matriculate Dalits in the village of the same caste. As they were educated, they did not like to render labour and earn wages. They were burden on the family. They lived on the wages earned by their wives. From the wages earned by wives, they liked to eat good food, wear good dress, chew tobacco and betel and drink Tari and Thara (locally prepared wine of Mahua). On these issues, they were seen quarrelling with their family members. They worked as Metha and Dalal and used to get money. Every people asked them to take lesson from R.R. and S.R. who were uneducated but handling the house peaceful and efficiently. They thought that their main enemy were R.R. and S.R. who were their classmate but could not continue his study due to death of his father. They began to meet S.R. and his wife regularly R.R. and his wife informed S.R. about the bad nature of both matriculates. The matriculate fellow did not stop meeting with them. They taught the wife of S.R. to separate his house and agricultural level. They taught that S.R. and his wife were working to feed seven children of R.R. and his wife. This hit the mind of S.R.'s wife. She asked her husband to make separation of the family. He also started quarrelling with R.R. and his wife. Thus, within few days, the house of R.R. and S.R. became battle-field, each day quarrel took place between the family of two brothers. To get rid of quarrel, R.R. decided to make separation. He called his maternal uncle as Pancha and made separation of house and agricultural fields. Grains, utensils etc. available in the house were divided into two parts.

The wife of S.R. had thought that she would become rich after separation. But this did not happen. S.R., his wife and children began to work hard for the development of the family. They did not like to sit even for a day without work. S.R. and his wife thought that they were only two therefore, they became idle. They did not want to work daily S.R. used to play card with his Matriculate fellow. He also began to chew tobacco and betal leaves. He used to take Tari and Tara. Now the three friends became famous for their antisocial activities. Gradually a day came, when the wife of S.R. had to face the situation of starvation. Now S.R. did not like to work in field and earn wages. Only his wife had to work for wage. One day she had not cooked food because there was no food grains in the house. Seeing no food in the house, S.R. began to beat his wife. As a result, blood began to flow from her forehead. Seeing blood he ran out of the house. The wife of R.R. came and provided first-aid with local medicine. They also gave food to eat her. In late night S.R. came drunken and demanded food. She said that there was not food grains in the house. Therefore, she did not cook any food. She asked here husband to bring food grains to cook food. This made him more furious. He started beating her. He went on beating till she became senseless. The news of her faint spread in the Tola. People ran towards her house. Her husband ran away leaving her senseless. The people brought her in the hospital. She remained admitted for a month. In order to meet expenses on treatment, S.R. had to mortgage his land for Rs. 1000 for three years. In three years he could not get his land back by paying Rs. 1000. His friends advised him to sell his land to establish shop in the village and to purchase a bicycle for carrying goods from the market. He sold his land for Rs. 1000. He purchased a bicycle and started a shop. But now, his shop has became failure. He has become landless by following the advice of his educated friends.

In an another incidence, S.C. and N.D. residents of a village in Imamganj block of Gaya district informed that they had been exploited by an educated fellow of their community. S.C. belonged to Chamar caste and N.D. belongs to Dusadh caste. 10 years ago, a quarrel took place between S.C. and N.D. families over a piece of land. In quarrel the members of both families used Lathi, Bhala, Grassa etc. Due to use of lethal weapons, bloodshed took place. Both families went to Thana and made a counter-criminal cases. As a result, they needed a Pairavikar to approach Thana and court. In their village there was a school teacher who belonged to

Dusadh and V.L.W. who belonged to Chamar. These two educated persons became the Pairavikar of their caste men. They began to take money from them in the name of Pairavi (approach). Both thought that it was the best time to exploit both families. They also had pact with each other. The case went from Thana to the court. They became middlemen between Thana, doctor and lawyer. The members of both families were Mudai as well as Mudalaya because there were counter cases. The case between two parties continued for a period of three years. During this period, both parties became economically weak. They took loan in the beginning to fight cases. In the beginning, they did not find trouble in getting loan. But as time passed on, they began to face trouble. They had to work on less payment according to the terms and conditions agreed upon for the loan. This made them more weak economically. Now they were not in a position to pay fees to lawyers and the Pairavikars, who were basically Dalal of Thana. Then they realised that their Pairavikars were virtually Dalal. They had earned Dalali from them. They withdrew their cases and became friends of each other. But they were badly exploited by the educated fellows of their community.

Exploitation of the Poor Dalit by Rich Dalit

Now all Dalits are not poor. It is beyond doubt that majority of them are poor. But now due to modern education and occupation, some are rich and some are very rich. They are no less than other castes so far as the money and property are concerned. From service and business, they have been able to purchase land and have emerged as other rich farmer of the village. They are like Malik. They own land but like other castes they do not cultivate land by their labour. Rendering manual labour in the field is not taken proper by their family members. For doing cultivation, they need labour. They employ other Dalit fellows as labour. Like landowners of other castes, they utilize the services of Dalit fellows in the same exploitative and oppressive manner. They want more and more work and pay less and less wages. They ask to do Begari. They send their children to school and employ the children of other Dalit family as herd boy and herd girl. The male and female of those families do not work like transplanting, weeding, harvesting, thrashing, winnowing etc. There is no harm in hiring labour if one can pay for it. Because if one is not able to do a work, he gets it done with the help of other labour. But the painful behaviour is non payment of wages properly. The poor have not sufficient to eat food without daily wages, that is why, they become ready to work even on less payment, than the prescribed minimum wages.

The rich Dalits are becoming richer day by day. Service holders give money to their father or brother to buy land. If not, they ask them to buy oxen for sharecropping. They also hire tractor for cultivation. Thus exploitation of Dalit labour by Dalit landowner have came to light. It will be meaningful to discuss here some case studies collected from the field in this regard.

L.R. (12 yr) a resident of a village in Bodh Gaya Block was found working as herd boy in the house of a Dalit landowner. The Dalit landowner owned 15 Bighas of land, 4 oxen, 2 buffaloes and 5 cows. In order to look after cattle he had employed a herd boy. The father of the boy had died when he was only five years old. He had three brothers, his mother was facing trouble in feeding the boy so he gave the child as herd boy in the house of a Dalit landowner who belonged to the same caste. In the beginning he was asked just to wash utensils and cattle shed. But now he has to clean shed, feed cattle and to bring them at the grazing ground. The Malik gives him 3 Maunds of paddy or wheat in a year. Besides this annual payment, he gets food of both ends and breakfast in the morning. He also gets clothes he does not go to school. His mother is happy that the child has learnt to lead life on the basis of his work. Now the child will not die of hunger. She sites example of other children of the village who go to school but do not render any kind of labour in the family. They are caught stealing mango, guava, paddy, wheat, sugar-cane etc. from the field. She is satisfied that her son is illiterate but laborious.

P.R. (45 yr) of a village in Imamganj block was an attached labour in the house of a Dalit landowner, who owned 10 bighas of land. a pair of oxen, 2 buffaloes and 6 cows. He had given 10 kathas of land to P.R. to render labour in his field round the year. He got 1.5 paddy per day as wages besides breakfast and midday meal. The yield of 10 kathas of land goes to P.R. He had to come in the early morning to feed the cattle and clean cattle shed. Then he had to go to field to work or he performed some domestic work. During off season, he was not given work nor was allowed to work in the field of other Mahajan. He could work only for the Malik or for himself.

He was serving in the house of this Malik for nearly 20 years. He came in agreement with this landowner to work as attached labour when he was 25 years old. At that time he had only one son. He was the only family member. His son had fallen ill. So he was in need of a loan of Rs. 100 for the treatment of the son. He got it from the Dalit landowner. Since then he is working in his house as an attached labour. He is getting the same wages as other attached labour of the village are getting. He does not like to change the Malik. He likes to work in the house of the same Malik.

S.K. (55 yr) of a village in Imamganj block of Gaya district is V.L.W. and one labour inspector in his family. He owns a good pucca house. He owns a tractor, 5 buffaloes and 10 cows. He owns a big cattleshed. He has herd boy to look after the cattle, attached labour to do agricultural works and domestic works, Dai to clean cattle-shed and prepare Goitha from the cowdung. He has a Gobar-gas plant. The members of his family do not render manual labour. They hire labour and give supervision to them. Though he belongs to Dalit and gets benefits of Dalit quota but he exploits and oppresses the Dalit in the same way as landowner of other castes. The poor Dalits call him Malik because he is man of means, property and wealth. He does not pay minimum wages to the labourers. He provides loan to the labourers at interest and utilizes their services on less wages. Thus, he is beneficial in double ways. He gives money at exorbitant rate of interest. Thus, he earns money from money. He utilizes their services at cheap rate of wages. Thus he is again in beneficial position. On the 1st day of transplanting, the Dalits have to do Begari in his field. On the occasion of marriage and feast, he gets Begari from the Dalit labour. He also works as Dalal of Thana and Block. He works as Pairavikar in Thana in cases of Dalit. He works as middlemen between block officials and the Dalit for which he gets Dalali. It is heard that he has illegal sex relation with many Dalit women of the village. Thus, he is also a great Gunda. But he enjoys respect and regards because he is a wealthy person.

Like S.K. many Dalit landowners have emerged who are involved in the exploitation and oppression of the Dalit.

Exploitation of Dalit by Service-Holder Dalit

Due to modern education and job reservation policy, many Dalit service holders have come into existence. They exploit the poor and uneducated Dalits for domestic works. They keep children of other Dalit family engaged as household servant. As servant, they have to perform such work as cleaning utensils, washing clothes, washing room, cooking, serving food, bringing vegetables, bringing goods from the shop etc. Some of the Dalit Maliks have cow. In this case, the domestic servant has to take care of the cow also.

If service holders do not get a boy as servant, they prefer to have a girl as servant. The girl servant has to perform the same function as a boy servant.

If they do not get a boy or a girl servant, they prefer to utilize the services of an aged female for such work. They call them as Dai. The Dai performs the household work. She also takes care of small children.

The Dalit service holders make promise to educate boy at the place of work. They also promise to pay money, and good dresses. Making these false promises, they bring the boy at the place of work. From the very day, the boy has to work at beck and call of the Malik. He takes rest and sleeps when the Malik desires. They are given food which are left in the plate after eating. Thus, the servant has to eat the Jutha of the Malik and their family members. They are given dress which are left by the children of the Malik. They never get a chance to go to school. They can see the children of their Malik going to school and reading in the house, but they have to work from morning till late night. If they do not work in proper manner they are beaten and sent back to home. In those cases, the parents do not get any payment. The child is blamed for negligence of duty.

The service holder Dalits behave with the poor Dalit in the same exploitative and oppressive manner as other rich Hindu castes. Let us go through same case studies in this regard.

N.B. (40 yr) of a village in Bodh Gaya block reported that his 10 years old son was exploited by S.R. of a service holder Dalit. S.R. was posted at Patna in a Government job. He resided at Patna with his family. The children were small so he needed a servant to assist his wife in household work. He approached N.B. when he came to enjoy puja vacation at the village. He requested to give his 10 years son to assists his wife in household work at Patna. He made promise to take every care of the child like his own son. He also agreed to send the child to school. Good food and dress plus expenditure on treatment were also agreed. Besides, these facilities Rs. 20 was decided as monthly salary.

N.B. sent his child with S.R. a Dalit officer, to perform household chores at Patna. The boy did not want to leave the parents convinced him that the Saheb would make him a worthy man by providing education and knowledge. The child went silently. The day he went Patna, he was asked to perform varieties of work. He had to get up early in the morning. He was not allowed to ease in the latrine of the flat. He had to go on road for natural call. He had to clean the rooms of the flat with broom. Then he had to wash the floor of the rooms with phenyle water. He had to clean the kitchen utensils and plates. He had to assist in cooking. He had to serve breakfast to the Saheb and Memsaheb. Around 12 noon he was given something as breakfast. Then he was asked to wash plates and cooking utensils again for cooking the lunch. After washing utensils, he had to wash clothes of entire family members. Finishing this work, he had to assist in cooking. At 3 p.m. he had to serve food to the family members. Around 4 p.m. he was given midday meal. After midday meal, he had to wash utensils again. He had to take care of the children. In the evening, he moved on roads taking children in lap or on shoulder. Around 7 p.m. he has to assist in cooking. At 9 p.m. he had to serve food to family members. At 10 p.m. he was given meal of the night. He used to go to bed for sleep at around 11 p.m. Thus, what to say about going to school, he did not get time to play and sleep sufficiently. His parents were informed that the child was quite well. Saheb used to go to village to meet his parents. Then he used to give some money to the parents of the child. In this way, the child served the saheb for two years. Suddenly he fell ill due to typhoied fever. The fever persisted for a month. The child became very weak. He become unable to walk and to sit on the bed. Now it was time to take proper care of the child. But he was ignored. He was asked to remain on fast and to take boiled water. Sometimes some medicines were given and some breads were given to eat. When the situation became beyond control, the boy was admitted in P.M.C.H. The parents of the child were informed. They came and stayed in the hospital with the boy. But saheb did not meet the expenditure. The expenditure was meet by the parents, who had Rs. 500 taking as loan. The child was cured. The parents brought him home. Now the child was very happy. He narrated the whole story of his exploitation to his parents. Now his parents were repenting on their decision. When they came to take the arrear salary of the child, they were not given. They were asked that many times more than salary amount were spent on the illness of the child.

In another case study S.K. of a village informed about the exploitation of his daughter as maid servant by a Dalit officer of the same village who was posted at Gaya. The wife of the officer remained ill. Therefore, he was trying to find such a maid servant who could take care of his children and house. He had come in the village. He approached to S.K. to give his daughter as maid servant. The daughter of S.K. was 14 years old S.K. was also distant relative of the officer. The saheb had agreed to treat the girl like his own daughter. He had agreed to give good food, good dress and amount of Rs. 5000 at the time of her marriage. The girl went there to work with saheb. She began to work like the family member. She took every care to the saheb. Memsaheb and the three kids, with her services, the illness of the Memsaheb was cured day by day. She worked for three years. Now the Memsaheb was quite well. This was a very happy news for the family. Now it was a time to give some extra money to the girl as prize. But when she desired to go to home, she was went in old dress. Even new dresses were not given to her. The Saheb did not give Rs. 5000 which was agreed for her marriage.

Exploitation of Dalit by Dalit Officers

Many Dalits have become officers nowadays by enjoying reservation policies. According to the Dalits of the villages under study, the Dalit officers and authorities are more exploitative and oppressive for them. They demand bribe openly. If bribe is not given, they take side of the other party. The Dalit officials posted in neighbouring areas demand chickens, goats, chura etc. from the Dalits. If they do not pay them, they are trapped in the name of crime. As criminals, they are sent to jail some case studies relating to the exploitation of Dalit by Dalit officials are as follows.

P.K. of a village in Bodh Gaya block informed that he was exploited by a Choukidar who belonged to Dalit (Dusadh). One of the Yadvas of the village had filed as false case against him. The case was relating to a theft of a buffalo. P.K. went to seek support from the Choukidar. He requested the Choukidar to tell the fact. The Choukidar demanded Rs. 500 or to work as attached his field on nominal wages. He did not pay any money. So the Choukidar took the side of the Yadava. Thus, P.K. was trapped in a criminal case. He had to fight a case for 10 years to prove his faultlessness.

S.P. (40 yr), of a village in the same block of Gaya district informed that he was exploited by a Dalit Sarpanch. A Rajput of the village had filed a case of stealing 20 bundles of paddy from the paddy field. Undoubtedly the bundle of paddy was stolen, but S.P. was not involved in it. It was the trick to get S.P. trapped in a criminal case. He asked the Rajput landowner to file a case before the Sarpanch. He did so. Thus, a criminal case against S.P. was instituted in the Gram Kachahari. The Sarpanch was a close friend of the Rajput landowner. He used to take money whenever necessary for the Rajpût landowner. There were no witness but even then the Sarpanch declared him as culprit. Then he want to file a case in the lower court. From lower court he won the case.

B.C. (35 yr) of a village in Imamganj block reported that his wife was exploited by the thana officials. One of the Gunda of the village had raped his wife. B.C. was not at the village. His wife went to file a case in the Thana. The thanedar was also a Dalit. He asked to the woman to stay for the night. At night she was exploited by the Thanedar and the police. Then the case of rape was registered. When B.C. came back, he came to know the entire story. But he thought to compromise with the situation. He advised his wife to forget about the rape. Because even protectors are destructors themselves or they take side of the wealthy persons. There is no one who could hear our voice. Only god will hear our voice. God will definitely punish the culprit.

M.D. (35 yr) of a village in the same block of Gaya district informed that Dalit Karamchari had taken a bribe of Rs. 500 for approaching the block officials to cover him under the Dalit Awas Yojna. He had taken loan in the name of the clerk of the Block. He demanded Rs. 500 more in the name of B.D.O. Then he was covered under the Awas Yojna. The house was constructed by a Dalit contractor who sold the bricks and cement. The quality of house built was very bad. The house fell down in the same rainy season. Thus, a bribe of Rs. 1000/- went in vain for the M.D. for this amount of bribe virtually M.D. got nothing.

C.C. (40 yr) of a village in Imamganj block of Gaya district informed that he was exploited by a Dalit Daroga of a Dalit Thana. Some one had stolen his bicycle from his house. He went to the Dalit Thana to file a case. The Thanedar was also a Dalit. The Thanedar heard the case. He demanded Rs. 500 to register the case. Hearing the amount of bribe, C.C. wanted to be trapped in another case, if he would not pay the money. C.C. had only Rs. 100 with him. He had to give this money to Darogaji to come out of the Thana.

B.B. (25 yr) of a village in Imamganj block of Gaya district informed us that he was exploited by the V.L.W. of the Panchayat who also belonged to Dalit community. He was interested in piggery. The V.L.W. approached him and informed about the programme of piggery. He thought that there was nothing harm in rearing pigs. He was getting pigs on subsidy. He became ready. He went in to the Block headquarters. He met the Karmachari, Gram Sewak and other clerical staff of the block. They asked him frankly to pay Rs. 500 as bribe only then he would be benefited by the scheme of piggery. He had no money in his pocket. He did not know about the bribe, otherwise he would have left the idea of initiating the programme of piggery. He came back home and decided not to do piggery. He began to earn wages as before. After about two months the Gram

Sewak again contracted him and asked him to give Rs. 300 not as bribe but as fare of the staff who goes to different places to buy the pigling. Although the staff who go to buy pigling they get T.A., D.A. from Government on this opinion B.B. was fully convinced. He went to the house of Malik and took a loan of Rs. 300 to give the Gram Sewak. Thus, he came in the trap of the Gram Sewak. He began to run to Block headquarters each time he was demanded more money as bribe. Even, Rs. 10 or Rs. 15 were taken from his pockets in the name of tea, and betal only then he was entertained. He has to give slowly more money than the subsidy. Virtually, he had to buy pigling from his own pockets.

S.K. (25 yr) of a village in Imamganj block informed that he was exploited by the labour inspector of the block who was also a Dalit. He had worked for a period of 45 days in road construction work. The work was being constructed under a contractor who belonged to Rajput caste. Contractor was not paying the wages for the work he had done in the road. this behaviour of contractor made him very much puzzled. After approaching and requesting many times he could get Rs. 360 which was @ Rs. 8 per day. The contractor had agreed to pay Rs. 15 per day. Thus, he was getting just about half of the wages agreed upon. This was really very painful for him. He was not begging from the contractor. He was demanding his proper wages for the work he had done. But the contractor was a great exploiter. He gave very little wages to the labourers, but used to show prescribed minimum wages in the register. He got thumb impression from some one else. Thus, he used to exploit and oppress the labourer.

S.K. decided to meet labour inspector and to make complaint against the exploitation made by the contractor in the payment of wages. He went one day but did not find him because he used to attend his duty from other place. But on the next visit he was able to meet the inspector. At the rate of Rs. 15 per day, the amount of wages was Rs. 45 x 15 = Rs. 675. He had received Rs. 360 only, thus Rs. 315 only was due. So the inspector asked S.K. to give Rs. 300 to him as bribe. Only then he was ready to lodge the complaint against the contractor. He was very much disappointed. He returned home hopelessly. He found out that there was link between inspector and Thickedar. The thickedar used to pay some money to inspector as bribe. The inspector used to finalise the payment on the register. Thus, the inspector and Theakedar. The Theakedar used to pay some money to inspector as bribe. The inspector used to finalise the payment on the register. Thus, the inspector and Theakedar exploited the poor S.K.

C.K. (26 yr) of a village in Bodh Gaya Block of Gaya district was exploited by the manager of Gramin Vikas Bank. C.K. was informed by the Karamchari and Gram Sewak about the availability of loan for buying buffalo. A buffalo equivalent to Rs. 5000 was to be given to Dalit family. Each family had to deposit Rs. 500 as security. C.K. made arrangement of Rs. 500 somehow and approached the bank situated in the block headquarters. The manager of the bank asked him to come with the Gram Sewak. He met with Gram Sewak and requested him to pay a visit to the manager. He demanded Rs. 300 for his visit to the manager. The manager demanded Rs. 500 for sanctioning the amount. He sold the ornaments of his mother and wife to pay bribe. He had to pay Rs. 800 as bribe to the officials and Rs. 500 as security money. Then the loan was sanctioned in his name. But he was not given cash in hand. The cash was given to the block official who were going to purchase buffaloes for distributing among Dalits. They made good money in T.A., D.A. They purchased old buffalo and showed the price very high. They were able to manage the receipt of price paid for the purchase of the buffaloes. Thus, virtually he was not in gain. Because he had to invest time in domesticating old buffalo which did not provide milk but only dung.

P.K. (22 yr) of a village in Imamganj block was also exploited by the manager of the Punjab National Bank. On the advice of the Gram Sewak, he was advised to approach the manager for the loan to buy a Rickshaw. The loan was to be obtained on the security of the block officials. He met the karmachari of the village to take his security. Karmachari took a bribe of Rs. 200 for this purpose. Then he along with karmachari went to meet manager. Manager took Rs. 500 as bribe to sanction the amount of loan, though he too was Dalit by caste.

D.R. (65 yr) of a village in Bodh Gaya block informed that he was exploited by the Bara Babu of the block in getting his Viradha Abastha pension. He used to get payment of Virdha Abastha Pension every month by post-office. Suddenly the amount of Pension was stopped. He approached the Bara Babuof the block. He informed that he would be sent money after receiving the fund from the Government. He remained silent for one year. After one year he informed D.R. to pay a visit to the block to receive the payment. Half of the amount was kept in bribe and only half was given to him. The Bara Babu was also a Dalit.

These case studies reveal clearly that Dalits are exploited by the Dalit officials, in the same way as the upper caste officials do. They have hardy any fellow feeling for the persons of their own community.

8

ATROCITIES ON DALIT OF GAYA

Atrocity may be defined as wicked or cruel acts committed by a person or a group of persons. The main aim behind the atrocity is to harm the person or group by wicked or cruel behaviour. Sometimes under the atrocity damage of property is made by such wicked behaviour as stealing cattle, foodgrains, money and ornaments from the house of a person. Stealing bundles from the paddy field and wheat field stealing bundles from the thrashing field, stealing paddy or wheat from the thrashing field etc. also come under the wicked behaviour associated with atrocities. The cruel behaviour associated with atrocities are beating mercilessly, breaking hands or feet, inserting wood nail in stomach, cutting the feet or hands, beheading, murder with gun, pistol, bomb etc. burning alive, burning the entire family members alive by setting the house on fire, mass killing etc. Rape and gang rape also form the part of atrocity.

From the wicked and cruel behaviour associated with atrocity one can divide the atrocity into following types.

Minor Atrocity

In minor atrocity, the affected persons are subjected to minor inhuman treatment. Beating mercilessly, putting fire on hand, putting chilli powder in eye, putting petrol at the anus, etc.

Major Atrocity

Under major atrocity the affected person or group is subjected to major inhuman treatment like cutting 6 inches from head or feet, murder, rape, gang-rape, etc.

Unplanned Atrocity

When atrocity takes place without any planning, it is called unplanned atrocity. For example, two persons suddenly made hot exchange and one broke the leg of the other.

Planned Atrocity

When atrocity takes place according to a previous planning, it is called planned atrocity. This is done to take revenge. For example, stealing property, murder, etc.

Organised Atrocity

When atrocity is committed by certain types of organisation, it may be called organised atrocities. For example, mass killing or mass rape by various violent organisations of local Senas.

The mass killing includes the killing of infants, kids, children and women, too.

Besides these types of atrocities, there are certain atrocities which are women specific, rape, mass rape, abortion by beating, cutting the breast, making the women naked etc. It is generally said that the poor are subjected to atrocities by the rich. But this does not hold true always, some times a poor person harasses and oppresses a rich person by his wicked and cruel behaviour. Nowadays, there are various organisations which claim the support of the poor. They commit atrocity on the rich persons.

Now let us see the pattern of Dalit atrocities in the villages under study.

TYPES OF DALIT ATROCITY

Beating Mercilessly

This type of atrocity is committed on Dalit children. Dalit children sometimes pluck mango, guava etc., from the tree which belong to others. They pull out gram crop, peacrop to eat gram and pea. They pull the sugar cane plant from the field. When they are seen, they are beaten mercilessly sometimes, they faint as a result of beating. It is true that majority of Dalits do not own fruit bearing trees due to lack of land. Seeing fruits in the tree, their children get tempted. Their parents ask them not to pluck fruits from the tree of others, but children forget this. They go near the tree of fruits and try to pluck fruits. When the owner of tree sees them, he beats them mercilessly, as punishment. Few case-studies in this regard are as follows :

S.M. (40 yr) of a village in Bodh Gaya Block reported that his 10 years old son was beaten by a Rajput Malik. The child was beaten so mercilessly that he got fainted at the place of beating. The child had gone to graze goats. Seeing no one he had attempted to pluck green mangoes from the tree which was owned by a Rajput Malik. The Rajput Malik saw the child from a distance. Hearing the voice of Malik, the child came down from the tree and ran towards his house. The Malik of the tree also followed to catch the boy. The Malik was tired of running. This made him more angry. He thought to teach the boy a lesson. On next day he was sitting at a place nearby the tree. He had hidden himself. The boy came to graze the goats. Suddenly he appeared and caught the boy. He began to beat the boy mercilessly. He continued beating till the boy got fainted. When he saw the boy fainted, he brought water from a pit to put it in his mouth. In the meantime his parents also reached there. They brought the boy to house. The called local doctor for the treatment. They had to spend Rs. 200 on the treatment of the child. When the Malik heard about the treatment, he went to see the child and met the cost of treatment.

B.R. (38 yr) of another village of Bodh Gaya Block informed that his 12 years old son was beaten in black and white when he was trying to pull out gram crops to eat green gram. He had entered the field to up-root the crops, in the meantime some children of Yadava community saw him. The plot of gram crop belonged to a Yadava. The children of Yadavas community started beating the child. They tortured him physically till blood began to flow from his nose and mouth. Seeing the drops of blood they left beating. The child was carried before the adult members. His father B.K. was called. He was informed about the theft of gram crops committed by his child. They showered abusive words on him. He went on bearing all such insults because his son had committed mistake of visiting the field of Malik. No one was showing pity on the child and his father. Atlast they allowed him to go to his house on a bond of Rs. 100 as a fine. The bond was taken on a plain paper on which his thumb impression and the amount were written.

P.B. (45 yr) of a village in Imamganj Block of Gaya district informed that his 15 year old son was beaten badly by the children of Koeri caste. His son had committed a mistake of uprooting a sugar cane plant from a plot which belonged to a Koeri. The children of the Koeri had gone to see their crops. They saw the child coming out of the plot with a sugar cane in his hand. They encircled the child and took sugar cane from his hand. The boy told that he had not broken sugar cane from the field. He had asked it from a Malik. He was just coming through the field. But the children of Koeri did not believe him. They thought that the child was telling a lie. They began to beat the child with the sugar cane. As a result, the back and hand of the child were torn here and there. His forehead had become blackish. The child cried a loud but no one could come to save him and he fell on the ground and fainted. Seeing the child fainted, the children ran away. The news reached to the parents of the child. The child was brought home. A local doctor was called for treatment. The cost of the treatment reached up to Rs. 250. He was unable to pay such an amount, so he approached the father of children who had beaten the child. They gave the cost of treatment but asked him to keep the child in control.

The Theft of Cattle

This is a wicked act by which a Dalit family is put in economic hardship. The Dalits domesticate heifer and calf to supplement their income. They purchase a calf or a heifer from the market and domesticate them. When they become cow, they sell them to get money. Some Dalit family domesticate cow to get milk. They sell milk and earn money. They also domesticate goat, chicken and ducks, they get cattle from the Government for the purpose. They also get calf or heifer from the Malik to domesticate on half share. To put a Dalit in economic hardship, the evil persons make theft of the cattle during night. Dalits do not have sufficient house. They keep cattle in open place thatched with straw.

R.R. (55 yr) of a village in Imamganj block of Gaya district informed that his cow worth Rs. 3000 was stolen by the young men of the village who belonged to high caste. They had came to his house to purchase the cow R.R. had demanded Rs. 4000 but they were ready to pay Rs. 2000. At last R.R. said that he would not sell the cow for less than Rs. 3000. This version of R.R. pained the young men of the village. They decided to teach him lesson by stealing his cow. One dark night, they came with arms and took away the cow and calf of R.R. tried to shout but seeing gun and pistol in their hands he could not shout. When they went away with cow and calf, he shouted. The neighbours and villagers came to know the incidence some of them suggested to file a case, while other suggested to keep quiet. He remained silent did not file any case.

P.K. (36 yr) of the same village informed that his buffalo worth Rs. 10,000 was stolen by a Yadava of the village. One of relatives of the Yadava had come to purchase the buffalo. He had put the price of the buffalo as Rs. 12,000 but they were ready to pay only Rs. 8000, P.K. lowered the price to Rs. 10000 but they did not go above Rs. 8000. An another trader of buffalo came and was paying Rs. 9000 but he did not sell. His buffalo became the subject of discussions among the villagers. Few young Yadavas of the village decided to steal the buffalo. One dark night they came with gun and took away the buffalo. When P.K. got up in the early morning went to cattle-shade, he did not find the buffalo with calf. He understood that his buffalo was stolen. His family members began to accuse him because he had not sold the buffalo even for Rs. 9000. He had to hear criticism even by his relatives and friends. He was very much shocked with this evil act because buffalo was a heavy source of income for him. He consoled his family members and himself. He knew well about the persons involved in the theft of the buffalo but he did not fild any case. He left it upon the mercy of the God to punish the culprit.

B.D. (25 yr) of another village of the same block informed that his he-goat worth Rs. 500 was stolen by the Muslims of the village. They had come to purchase the goat for meat to be cooked in a marriage ceremony. They were paying Rs. 300 only. But B.D. was not ready to sell the he-goat for less than Rs. 500. Even in the name of marriage of girl, he did not reduce the price of the goat. This behaviour of B.D. pained them very much. They decided to hurt the ego of B.D. by stealing the goat. One night they entered his house and took away the goat by force. B.D. went on shouting but they carried away the goat from his house. Some villagers came to hear shouting but by that time they had gone far off. They brought the goat to the house of a relative and asked him to hide the goat. They asked him that they would kill the goat on marriage day. B.D. tried to find out the goat but he did not succeed. On the day of marriage, the goat was killed in the house of relative and from there meat was brought for the Barat Party and Sarat Party. B.D. came to know about all such news but he remained silent. He did not file any case. He went in the temple of the village and prayed to punish the guilty.

D.P. (31 yr), a resident of a village in Bodh Gaya block of Gaya district reported us that his 5 cocks were stolen by a young boy of Bhumihar caste. He was posted in air force. He had come in the village to enjoy holiday. D.P. has 10 cocks and hens. The boy had come to purchase cocks but he refused to sell them. This made the boy angry. He did not say anything. He left the place silently. At midnight, he came with other young boys and took away five cocks. When he got up in the morning, he did not find his cocks. They were missing. Soon he understood what had happened. He made the villagers aware of the theft of cocks.

Such types of wicked acts are done on the Dalit not only by non-Dalits but some stronger Dalits also commit such wicked acts on weaker Dalits.

Taking away Cattle by Force

Sometimes the cattle from the house of a Dalit are taken away forcefully.

Dalits are poor. They have to take loan from the Malik. The Malik provides them loan at exorbitant rate on one hand and utilize their services at cheap wage on the other hand. When due to some unavoidable reason they become unable to pay the loan and interest back, the Malik tries to recover the money forcefully from their property. He sends his men, who may be the Dalit attached to him as labour to bring the ornaments of wife of the man who had taken loan or to bring cow, goats, cocks etc. from his house. If they try to prohibit, the men of Malik beat them sometimes for a small amount of loan, a goat, or cow or calf is taken away forcibly.

C.B. (30 yr) of a village in Bodh Gaya Block informed that his calf worth Rs. 1500 was taken away by a Yadava for Rs. 300 he has taken Rs. 300 as loan three years ago. During three years, the loan plus interest became Rs. 1500. So he came one day took the calf to his own house. He sold the calf in the local market at Rs. 1500. Such type of incidences were reported from different Dalit families residing in different villages of the study area.

Confiscation of Property

Sometimes it so happens that being unable to pay the loan and interest of the Malik, a Dalit decides to leave the village for ever. Suddenly he leaves the village without informing anybody. In such as the Malik who had given loan to him took the land and house under his possession. He gives the house or land on lease to other Dalits. The Malik manages some how the paper of land and house in his name.

S.B (21 yr) a resident of a village in Imamganj block reported that the house of his brother was taken away by a Rajput under his possession because his brother had taken a loan from the Malik. He did not know the amount of loan and the rate of interest. But he was well aware of the fact that the Malik was compelling him again to repay the loan. He was vexing his brother in different ways. Being vexed his brother left the village for ever. He settled permanently in the village of his father-in-law. When the Malik came to know about the escape of his brother, he took the house under his possession. He had taken Rs. 1500 from another Dalit to dispose off the house. He has been able to manage the paper from the block headquarters somehow.

Taking Away Bundles of Crop from the Field

This a very common wicked act by which a Dalit is put in economic hardship. Some Dalits have land and do cultivation. Some do cultivation on Bataidari or on Manidari. Some are attached labour. The attached labours get 10 kathas or 15 kathas of land by the Malik for the purpose of cultivation. The Malik also gives plough, seed and fertilizer. Somebody who have any kind of enemily with a Dalit commits theft of bundles of crops from the harvesting field. This is not always that a non-Dalit commits theft of bundles of crops, but a Dalit also does such type of wicked act against another Dalit. The purpose is to harass the man economically.

S.P. (25 yr) a resident of a village under Imamganj block reported that a Koeri had stolen 25 bundles of paddy crop from his field. He had done farming on Bataidari system. Previously the Koeri used to do Bataidari on the same plot. But being disqualified the Malik had given to plot to S.P. to do Bataidari. The paddy crop was very good. For this work he was appreciated by everybody of the village. Gradually the crop became ready for harvesting. He harvested the crops and left few days for drying the stalk. After few days, he made bundles of the crop. He could not be able to carry all the bundles to the thrashing ground. 25 bundles were left in the field. At night, they were stolen by the family members of the Koeri.

Taking Away Grains from the Thrashing Ground

After harvesting bundles are carried to the thrashing ground where the work related to thrashing is done. After thrashing winnowing is done. After winnowing grains are stored in the thrashing ground. Then it is weighed and carried to the house. Sometimes, in order to vex a Dalit, non-Dalit makes theft of grains from the thrashing ground sometimes they steal the grains and sometimes they take away forcefully with arms.

C.P. (30 yr) a resident of Bodh Gaya Block reported that five years ago his 15 Maunds of paddy were stolen from the thrashing ground. He was a Bataidar. The day was spent in weighing and sending the grains in the house of the Malik. His share was left in the thrashing ground. He decided to carry them the next morning. He was sleeping by the side of the heap of the grain, but 15 men came with arms and sacks. They asked him to remain silent. His mouth was closed with clothes. They filled up the sacks with grains and took them away. In the morning when people came they saw him tied and his mouth was closed. He was set free and then narrated the whole story.

Some times a Dalit also commits such acts to harass another Dalits.

Theft and Docoity of Boxes from the House

Each Dalit family has some boxes in their house in which they keep their clothes and ornaments made up of gold and silver. In order to harm the Dalits, some non-Dalits plan to steal the boxes. Majority of Dalits have only Tali to close the door or the entrance of the house. Sometimes boxes are stolen at night or sometimes they take away the boxes forcefully with arms. Sometimes the boxes of a Dalit is also stolen by another Dalit.

C.B. (25 yr) a resident of a village in Imamganj block informed that the boxes of his family members were stolen forcibly by some antisocial elements of the village who belonged to Dalits and non-Dalit both the communities. There was a marriage in his family. Many relatives were invited to participate. Female relatives and come with their boxes. There were 12 boxes kept in a room. They were full of dresses and ornaments. The marriage of his brother was over. A day after the visit of bride, a special feast was organised in honour of the guests and relatives. A pig was killed and its meat was cooked. Locally prepared liquor were brought. Men, women and children took liquor and ate meat. Then they went to sleep. Male members were sleeping outside the door, while female and children were inside the door. At mid night 10 to 15 persons came with arms and carried away all the boxes. Boxes and ornaments of bride were also looted.

To Set the Thrashing Ground on Fire

This is also a wicked act by which Dalit are put into troubles. The bundles of the crops after harvesting are placed in the thrashing ground. The thrashing ground works as the storage of bundles and grains. In order to harass Dalits, the entire thrashing field is set on fire so that all bundles of crops with grains could be burnt to ashes.

R.P. (37 yr) a resident of a village in Imamganj block informed that five years ago his entire thrashing ground was set on fire. He owned 5 bighas of land. He had own well and diesel machine for irrigation. He was a good producer of wheat and vegetables. For these two crops, he was known in the village. That year, he had 350 bundles of pea and gram. His development was not taken good by the non-Dalits who were Koeri by caste. One dark-night the thrashing ground was set on fire. The people ran to save the bundles of the crop, but they could not succeed because there was no water. Thus, all bundles were burnt to ashes.

Setting the House on Fire

In order to put Dalits in trouble, their house is set on fire. The fire in house damages the life and property. As no one sees the person who sets the fire, no case can be booked against any one. This is a very sad and cruel act to arm a person or a group of persons.

P.R. (50 yr) a resident of a village in Imamganj block of Gaya district informed that nearly 10 years ago his house was set on fire. He owned a double storied house thatched with wood bamboo and tiles. He used to do sharecropping. He was of good economic position. That is why some Dalits and non-Dalits were jealous of him. In order to harass him, one night his house was set on fire. His family members were sleeping inside the house. When the burnt wood and tiles fell on their body, they got up. All family members were able to come out of the house, but his one cow, two calves, 5 goats, 12 chickens, grains, dresses, bed, utensils etc. were burnt to ashes. Thus, there was a hug damage of lives and property. He rushed to the block to seek some financial help to repair the houses. He got some subsidy for this purpose and took some loan from his relatives. Thus, he could be able to thatch the house with tiles again.

Demolishing the House

This is an evil act by which Dalits are put in to trouble by powerful persons. Nowadays, the population Dalits is increasing. They are trying to capture the Governments land or Gairmaujarua land for construction of the house. But even the Gairmujarua land belong under the possession of powerful persons. Some how if they are able to construct the house, the house is demolished at the level of to updation or before the work of thatching. The work of demolishing is done forcefully during day time or silently during night time.

L.B. (26 yr) a resident of a village in Bodh Gaya Block reported that his house was demolished by the young man of the village who were non-Dalits. L.B. had constructed a house on a Gairmujarua land through which people used to go and come for various purposes. Building of house by L.B. on that plot was a painful development for the entire villagers who were non-Dalits. A young Yadava had joined the service of the police. He took initiative to hold a meeting in the village. The villagers agreed to demolish the house. From the place of meeting, the villagers went to the place where he was constructing the house. He was asked to stop the construction work. In the meantime, the mob demolished the house. Thus, his effort to construct the house went in vain.

Not Allow to Move Through the Field

When there is crop in the fields. Dalits are not allowed to move through the road between the two fields. It is assumed that they can steal the grains from the crops. This continues till the harvesting is done. He can go in the field to work with the Malik, but they are not expected to move alone. If they do not obey this rule they are punished.

S.B. (25 yr) a resident of a village in Imamganj block informed that once he had violated the rule to call in a local doctor, he was punished by the villagers. He was fined Rs. 50 for this act. He had to pay the fine immediately.

Not Allow to Cut Grasses on the Boundary of the Field

Dalits domesticate cows, calves, goats etc. they need grasses to feed them. But they don't own their field. They have to move boundary to boundary of the fields to cut grasses. But when crops are not harvested, they are not allowed to cut grasses. The Dalits working as attached labour enjoy this right. They are free to cut grasses on the boundaries belonging to the fields of his Malik. Those Dalits who do not obey this rule, they are punished. In case of male, the punishment may go up to Rs. 100. But in case of female even the rape may take place.

S.P. (22 yrs) reported that he had to pay a fine of Rs. 100 because he had dared to cut grasses on the boundary of a paddy field of Koeri. He had gone there to cut grasses with other attached labour. He did not work as attached labour. So he was caught and brought to the house of the Malik with the bundle of grasses. The bundle of grass was taken and a fine of Rs. 100 was made for the dare he had done to disobey the rule of the village.

Not Allowed to Pluck Edible Herbs

The herbs of gram, Khesari pea, mustered etc. are edible. Generally Dalit women rush to the field of Rabi crops to pluck edible herbs. But only the women of attached labour are allowed to pluck the edible herbs in the field of their respective Malik. While other women are not expected to visit the field when they are caught they are put to punishment. The rape of women also takes place when they are caught in the field. Dalits are poor. They can not purchase the edible herbs daily. So they dare to visit the field of Malik to pluck edible herbs and shrubs for which they are abused and have to pay fine.

Not Allowed to Fish in Pond and Nala

Each village has some pond and Nala. They contain fishes. The fishes of the pond and Nala are caught by any one because they are treated as common property. But the powerful person of the village possess the ownership of pond and Nala, though they are the common source of irrigation. The enjoy the right to catch fish from pond/Nala. Nowadays young Dalits also want to fish in this conflicted pound but one has to pay for this.

B.R. (18 yr) of a village in Bodh Gaya Block informed that he was beaten badly by the Malik of the village, who were Pathan, because he had attempted to fish in a Nala flowing through the village. He was not only beaten, but he was fined also Rs. 100 so that he might not dare to fish in future.

Not Allowed to Play in Common Ground

The children of Dalits are not expected to play in the common play ground. They are kept of a distance. They can see the play but are not allowed to play football.

R.R. (18 yr) a resident of a village in Bodh Gaya Block informed that once his brother had dared to play football with the other children of the village. In course of playing football he quarreled with a Yadava boy. The Yadava boy fell on the ground. Hearing this news, the father of the boy came and tortured his brother physically. He also fined Rs. 100. Now no children of Dalit tola dare to visit the common play ground.

Not Allow the Cattle to Graze in Common Field

Every village has some common grazing ground. But Dalits are not expected to utilize the grazing ground because the possession is hold by the powerful community of the village.

K.R. (32 yr) a resident of a village in Bodh Gaya Block reported that he had to pay a fine of Rs. 100 for the mistake he had done to graze his cattle in the common ground. Though it was a common grazing ground but the Yadavas had their possession. He took his cow in the field. His cow began to quarrel with another. In the quarrel the horn of another cow was broken. That cow belonged to Yadava. Hearing this news, he came and abused K.R. in many ways. He fined Rs. 100. He had to pay the fine immediately.

Not Allow to Defecate in the Field

The Dalits reside generally in a separate tola. Majority of them have only homestead land. They have to visit in the field of other for defecation. When the field is barren, they are allowed to ease. But when seeds or crops are cultivated they are stopped to ease in the field. If they are caught, they are abused, when they do not stop, a fine is also imposed.

M.R. (26 yr) of a village in Imamganj Block informed that he was fined Rs. 100 by the Malik because his son was found defecating in the field in which mustard was sown.

S.R. of another village of the same block informed that a Dalit woman was raped by a young Yadava when she was easing in the field of the Yadava.

Stealing of Diesel Machine

Dalit farmers have been given diesel machine on subsidy by the Government to do agriculture. This has become a painful development for the non-Dalits of the village. To put the Dalit in trouble, the diesel machine is stolen.

B.K. (45 yr) of a resident of village in Bodh Gaya Block informed that he had taken a diesel machine from the Government on subsidy to do irrigation. He was able to do cultivation in a good manner. But this development made other Dalits and non-Dalits of the village jealous of him. He had kept diesel machine outside the house. One night the machine was stolen and sold in other village.

Filling up the Well

Dalits have been benefited by the programme of digging up a well for the purpose of irrigation. They fetch water of the well with the help of diesel machine. In order to vex them, the well is filled up with the grasses, rocks, bricks, straw etc.

S.P. (26 yr) informed that the well situated in his tola was filled up with leaves, grasses, bricks etc. by the Muslims of the village, who are the Malik of the village.

Destruction of Vegetable Field

Some Dalits have been motivated towards the cultivation of the vegetables. They grow brinjal, tomato, gourd, potato, lady's fingers etc. In order to put them in trouble, the non Dalit destroy the entire vegetable crops. They not only pluck the fruits, but destroy them as well. They uproot the crops besides breaking the fruits.

N.R. (35 yr) of a village in Imamganj block informed that his 5 kathas of vegetable field was destroyed by the non-Dalits because they wanted to put him in economic hardship.

M.K. (26 yr) of another village of the same block informed that his 5 kathas of potato was uprooted from the field.

L.P. (26 yr) of a village in Bodh Gaya Block informed that he was put in trouble by the non-Dalits who had destroyed their 3 kathas of onion crops. They had also destroyed five kathas of wheat crop by beating with sticks.

Physical Punishment in Group

Sometimes the entire family members belonging to Dalit are punished physically with a group of non-Dalits. This situation arises when Dalits try to possess some Gairmaujarua land lying mixed with the plot of non-Dalit. In order to teach a lesson, the other villagers attack the Dalits. In this attack, male members are caught and brought before the villagers. They are asked to remain kneel down for two or three hours. If they stand up before the expiry period, they are beaten physically.

M.B. (47 yr) a resident of a village in Bodh Gaya Block informed that five Dalit families of the village were allotted five piece of land by the Government. Those plots were the Gairmaujarua land. The Yadavas were the landowners of the village. They were able to get the possession of the Gairmaujarua land from the Tekariraj. When Dalits went to capture the land, they were prohibited. 12 Dalits were caught in group. They were brought under a banyan tree. Their hands were tied and then they were asked to kneel down for two hours. There were children, young, adult, and aged. All had to go through the same treatment. When they tried to stand up, they were beaten with the stick. In this way, they were tortured physically. From the same day, they were prohibited to ease in the field of landowner, to cut grasses on the boundary, to graze cattle in their fields, to walk through their fields etc. They were not given work. When they surrendered completely and promised not to do any such behaviour in future, they were accepted as the members of the village.

Setting the House of Entire Dalit Community of Fire

This is an organised cruel behaviour on Dalits by a group of non-Dalits. When Dalits behave in such a way which is very painful for the non-Dalits. Then Dalits are subjected to such cruel punishment in group by the group of non-Dalits.

L.B. (28 yr) a resident of a village in Imamganj block informed that the house of 13 Dalits were burnt by a group of Pathans, who were the landowners of the village. A Pathan was abusing a Dalit women when she had gone to cut grasses. In the mean time two young Dalits saw him abusing the women. They ran and gave a good beating to him. The Pathan of the village organised themselves and hatched out a plan to demolish their houses. They waited for a month. Suddenly one dark night, they came in group and set the houses on fire. They also had fire arms. The male members had gone to a Barat. Only females and children were there. Seeing fire, they ran towards the village but nobody could come to see them. When male members came back, they saw their houses burnt to ashes. They rushed to thana to file a case. The Thanedar asked him a huge amount to admit the case. When they did not give money, the Thanedar took money from the Pathans and disposed of case in their favour.

Murder

This is a very cruel act by which a Dalit is put to death. Now Dalits do not behave in traditional way. The young generations are not submissive. They are rather aggressive. They give reply to Maliks of the village. They do not obey the Malik. They live in their own way. They organise themselves to fight against the exploitation and oppression. When Maliks are put to trouble by a Dalit, who acts as the leader, they decide to murder the leader. Within a well hatched plan, the leader is murdered.

L.P. (36 yr) a resident of a village in Imamganj block informed that his brother was murdered because he had stopped the agricultural work in the village. The landowners were facing great problems. So they decided to murder him. One evening he was returning home, when he was murdered. A criminal case was filed against the Rajput landowners. But in absence of any witness, they did not get punishment.

Group Murder

This is recent phenomenon in which Dalits are killed in group by the a group of non-Dalits. Such type of cruel behaviour is done by the local Senas. The Dalits also have their local Sena, while non-Dalits also have their Senas. Sometimes, Dalit Senas commit murder of non-Dalit Senas. To take revenge, non Dalit Senas also commit murder of the Dalit Senas. In this way, group killing from both sides takes place. In Imamganj and Bodh Gaya there are different types of Sena, but the incidence of group killing has not taken place as yet. But in other parts of district, such incidence has occured till recently.

ATROCITY ON DALIT WOMAN

Dalit women are worst victim of atrocity. They are subjected to atrocity by wealthy and powerful men of the society. Rape and gang rape are the two wicked act by which Dalit women are subjected to atrocity. They have to work as Charwahin, Dai, Kamin, etc. in the house and in the field of Malik. They have to go out to ease in the field of Malik. They go for defecation in early morning and in late evening. They have to go to cut grasses on the boundary of paddy field, sugar cane, field or Arhar field. They have to go to graze cattle away from the village. They have to collect dry leaves for fuel from the tree to the Malik. They have to collect dry dung from the field of the Malik. In such places, Dalit women go either in group or alone. Some young and adults of the village, who are Gundas, wait their presence in such lonely places. When they found such women alone, they attack on them to establish illegal sex relation with them. They close their mouth with Gaurachha or towel so that they may not shout.

The rape of Dalit women is very common phenomenon in the villages under study. These women are submissive and do not want to disclose their cases of rape. They know well that they would be beaten in their house, if they would disclose the fact. Sometimes, non-Dalit Gundas pay them money do close their mouth. Getting money in hand, they become pleased and forget their rape.

Sometimes, the group of women caught such Gunda and brought them before their parents. They threat them to kill in future. Sometimes, women have been able to get rid of Gunda by attacking with sickles or by biting.

Sometimes a group of men rape the same women or a group of men rape a group of women. In both cases, women are subjected to immoral wicked and cruel act. It is not that a Dalit women is always raped by a non-Dalit men. Some times Dalit women is raped by a Dalit Gunda. Muslim also do not lag behind in raping Dalit women. Let us see some case studies in this regard.

Case No. 1 Rape by a Yadava Gunda

S.D. (38) a resident of a village in Bodh Gaya Block informed that she was raped by a non-Dalit Gunda who belonged to Yadava by caste. She had gone to cut grassess on the boundary of sugar cane field. The Yadava had also gone to look after his sugar cane field. Seeing a woman on the boundary inside a sugar can field, the sex hunger of Yadava increased. He was famous for the rape of Dalit women. No Dalit women dared a face him alone. She wanted to go out of the field, but he caught hold her hands with one hand and closed the mouth with another hand. He took her aimed the sugar cane plants, where she was raped. She never disclosed this fact before her family members. But some persons who had seen S.D. and Yadav coming out of sugar can field had disclosed the fact. She was badly beaten by her husband. She was not allowed to go out of house for cutting grasses of collecting fuels for a pretty long time.

Case No. 2 Rape by a Koeri Gunda

M.D. (25 yr) a resident of a village in Bodh Gaya Block was raped by a Koeri Gunda, when she had gone to defecate in late evening. She was defecating in a potato field. He was also know as the hero of the village. He saw a women defecating alone in his field. As soon as the woman stood up, he put her on his shoulder and brought her in the building of a school. She tried to get rid of him, but she could not succeed. She was raped in the school building when she was freed, she wanted to shout. But she did not shout because she was looted. She did not disclose her rape. She told that in their community no one believes her. they do not believe in the rape forcefully. They believe that the affected girl or woman might have invited the man for getting money. When the fact is disclosed, the affected woman is beaten badly by her family members.

Case No. 3 Rape by a Pathan Gunda

R.D. (20 yr) a resident of a village in Imamganj block was raped by a pathan Gunda. The Pathans are the land owners of the village. She worked as a maid servant in the house of Pathan. She had to remain in the house of the Pathan some times for he whole night. Once there were no family members in his house. The Pathan took advantage of this occasion. He forced R.D. to surrender her self before him for his sexual satisfaction. She was surrendered forcefully. Thereafter, the Pathan began to exploit her sexually. She wanted to disclose the fact before her husband. But she thought that she would be beaten by her husband. At last, she decided to leave the job of maidservant in the house of Pathan. She gradually took her previous wages and left the work in his house. The Pathan waited for her presence anywhere in the field. One day, she had gone to a local mela. It was evening and darkness spread. Suddenly she show a big shadow infront of her. It was Pathan took her forcefully in a dry pit, where she was raped. Some visitors of the fair saw them conjugating. This became a news for the villagers. When her husband knew this news, he cut her hairs and put fire on her palm.

Case No. 4 Rape by a Rajput Gunda

B.D. (18 yr) a resident of a village in Imamganj block was raped by a Rajput Gunda, who was very young and hero of the village. B.D. had gone to collect dry leaves for fuel. She saw a field of gram. She saw around and did not find any one. So he entered the field and began to cut edible herbs. It was the field of the same Rajput Hero. He saw her cutting edible herbs.

He reached there silently. He asked her to give the edible herb. She gave them in no time. Then he asked him to surrender herself for his sexual satisfaction. She did not surrender herself. She ran for safety. But the young man caught hold her. The young man closed her mouth and brought her in a bush, where she was raped. Many people of the village saw her in that condition but no one could come to help her. In this way, her chastity was looted. The news spread like fire in the entire village. Her husband came and began to beat her on the spot. She had to hear abuses from her community members. But no one was ready to go to the house of Gunda to make a complaint to his parents. She herself went to make complaint. The parents of the Gunda showed sympathy with her. They assured to punish the boy. They gave her a new dress, because her dresses were torn in struggle. They also gave some money for the treatment. When the boy returned home, his parents did not serve any food. They asked him to leave the village. He was sent in the house of Nana to settle there permanently. Because, his Nana (grand father) had no son.

Case No. 5 Rape by a Dusadh Gunda

M.D. (23 yr) a resident of a village in Bodh Gaya informed that she was raped by a young hero who belonged to Dusadh caste. M.D. belonged to Nat caste. 5 Nat families had come in the village. They had erected a temporary hut on a barren land which was used for going and coming by the villagers. This place was nearby the settlement of Dusadh community. The young Dusadh used to come to their temporary settlement regularly. He used to make funs with them. He also helped them in many ways. They though that he was a good boy. They did not prohibit the boy from visiting their Dera. One night M.D. had gone to defecate. It was a very dark night. He went to defecate below a tamarindus tree. While she was defecting, the young Dusadh also went there silently. When she began to return, the Dusadh attached on her. She got fainted temporarily. When she opened her eye, she found her away from her Dera. The Dusadh was there. He asked her to surrender completely seeing no other way. She had to surrender herself for the sexual gratification.

Case No. 6 Rape by a Karmachari

P.D. (27 yr) a resident of a village in Bodh Gaya Block of Gaya district reported about her rape by a Karmachari. The name of Karamachari was N.R. He was nearly 50 years old. P.D. was Chamar by caste. N.R. also belonged to the same caste. He was in need of a room to live in the village P.D. had a separate room. So she gave that room to N.R. He began to reside there. He used to take help from her in cooking. One day, he was cooking chicken. He asked P.D. to prepare masala. He made promise to pay some cooked chicken. The cooking of chicken was finished at around 10.30 p.m. by that time all family members had fallen asleep only P.D. and N.R. were awaking. N.R. asked P.D. to serve boiled rice and chickens. He also asked her to eat there. She first of all refused but on many request she also all there in a separate plate. When the eating was over, P.D. made preparation for going in side his house. In the mean time N.R. cutout the lamp. He caught hold her hand and raped her. N.D. was not ready for such type of treatment. She had high regards for N.R. she did not like to shout and make the people aware of this fact. Because it was totally her fault that she was with him till late night she abused and accused the N.R. for his behaviour. She asked her to leave the house in the morning.

Case No. 7 : Rape by Gram Sewak

L.D. (36 yr) a resident of village in Imamganj block was raped by the Gram Sewak, who was incharge of Dalit Awas Yojna. One day at the site of the Awas Yojna, he raped S.D. S.D. had come to get her wages. The Gram Sewak asked him to stay till evening. She waited till evening. When darkness began to spread, she requested the Gram Sewak shape to make payment. The Gram Sewak brought here in a lonely room, where she was raped. After rape, the Gram Sewak gave her more than the wages. But she did not understand this. She remained silent because he thought that nobody would help her, rather they would laugh at her.

Case No. 8 Rape by a Lower School Teacher

K.D. (20 yr) a resident of a village in Imamganj block informed that she was raped by the teacher of the school. It was a Dalit village. There was a lower school. A Dalit teacher came there to teach the students. He used to stay in the school. Suddenly he asked the husband of K.D. to send her to assist in her cooking. For this purpose he agreed to pay Rs. 100 per month. The teacher was also her distant relative. The husband of K.D. allowed her to work for the master saheb. She used to cook food for the master saheb. One night the husband of K.D. had gone the village of a relative. K.D. was alone. So, she asked master saheb to come to her house. His food was cooked there. Master saheb came but he had bad intension. After eating, when K.D. was raising the plate, the master saheb caught her waist and spread her over the cot. He was behaving like an animal. He came quite after raping her. This was such a wicked at, which she did not like to disclose. Because nobody would help her. Rather the people would-laugh at her. She tore the shirt and dhoti of master saheb and asked him to go out immediately. Since then, she never went at school to cook food for master saheb.

Case No. 9 Rape by a Shopkeeper

A Bania of another village had come to establish a shop in the village of C.D. (30 yr) which was under.the Bodh Gaya Block. The Bania was able to get a piece of land on which he built a Kachaha house. He began to run a shop in the house. The villagers used to buy materials of day to day consumption. He lived alone in the village. At night he used to go to his own village by a bicycle. His original village was situated at a distance of 1 K.M. one night he decided to stay in the shop. He also decided to cook chicken. He bought a cock in the house of C.D. she sold the cock for Rs. 50/-. The Bania asked her to come to share chicken. She came and helped the shopkeeper in cooking chicken and boiled rice. It became 10 p.m. in cooking. As it was almost mid night only the shopkeeper and C.D. were left there. The Shopkeeper took Mahua liquor and gave some liquor to C.D. also. Then they shared chicken. After sharing food C.D. wanted to go to his house which was very close to the shop. The shopkeeper caught her and forced to lay over the ground. She tried to get rid of the shopkeeper, but she could not succeed. She became the victim of rape. Then she understood why the shopkeeper had invited her to share the chicken. She herself had come in the trap of the Bania, so she did not disclose this fact to her family members.

Case No. 10 Rape by a Cattle Merchant

D.D. (23 yr) a resident of a village in Bodh Gaya Block informed that she was raped by a Paikar (Cattle Merchant) who had come to sell oxen in the village. He had 160 oxen. He remained in the village for a month. D.D. used to go there to collect cow dung. She also helped the Paikar in cooking, and cleaned the utensils, etc. she used to give Goitha (dry dung), for fuel. In this way D.D. and Paikar came in close contact of each other.

One night it was raining. It took time in cooking. All people went to sleep. Only D.D. and Paikar were there. The Paikar though that it was the fine time to rape D.D. when she began to go to her house, the Paikar took her waist in his arm and pulled her towards his bed. He made her to surrender for his sexual gratification. She had no alternative but only to surrender. Thus, she was raped by the Paikar.

Case No. 11 Gang Rape

E.D. (46 yr) a resident of a village in Imamganj block informed that she was raped by a gang of 12 youngmen of the village. It was the time of Holi. The youngmen had drunk liquor. They had gone to defecate. E.D. also went there for defecation seeing a women, there sex for hunger increased. They attacked the woman and brought her in a sugar cane field. There she was raped one by one all men. When she fainted, she was brought in the house. It was told that she was lying on the road. Thus, they won the sympathy of her family members. When she became conscious, she knew the story was something else.

Case No. 12 Rape by Police

G.D. (31 yr), a resident of village in Bodh Gaya Block informed that she was raped by the police. Once on the request of the Mukhia, a police camp was established in his village to provide protection to the Dalits, who were agitating for the payment of minimum wages. The police ~~camp~~ remained there for six months. The house of G.D. was close to the police camp. The police used to come to her house to take Goitha, fire, fuel and other things. She used to help them. One day, her only son fell ill. Her husband took the boy to the block head quarters for the treatment. He could not return by evening. So in the evening, she became very sad. She was waiting for her husband and son sitting at her door. The police came to know this news. One police man came to her and consoled her that they would be coming tomorrow. When deep darkness spread over, she closed her door went inside the house. Suddenly her door was knocked. She opened the door with a hope to see her husband and son. But she saw a police man standing at her door. The policeman entered her room and closed the door forcibly. She could not understand as to why the police man was behaving in that manner. She did not know as to why the police man had come and what he wanted from her. The police man said that the camp incharge had saint him to take care of her. She said that she was quite well and did not want any help from the police. She allowed to police to take rest at the door of her house. But this was a great mistake on her part. The police had bad intension. Suddenly the police man attacked her and compelled her to surrender for his sexual gratification. In this way, she became prey of the police. She wanted to make the news public, but she thought that everybody would blame her. So, she never disclosed this news before her family members. She disclosed this news before the informant.

Case No. 13 Dalit Women as Kept

The information obtained from the study villages reveal that some Dalit women have to lead a life of kept of some wealthy and powerful persons of the village The life of kept begins from the rape. Such women live in their houses with their husband and children, but when the man pay visit in her house, she has to please him. Such women get financial support from the man with whom she becomes attached as kept. She also bears children from the man but her real husband is called as the father of the children let us see some case studies as the father of the children let us see some case studies as to how these women become kept and please her husband as well as the man whose kept she is.

P.D. (38 yr), a resident of a village in Imamganj Block informed that she was leading a life as kept of the Mukhia of the village who belonged to Rajput caste. She was 14 years old, when her marriage with S.K. (40 yr) took place. After 4 years her Gauna effective marriage took place. She came to her husbands house. After a month she had to go to collect fuel, to cut grasses and to work in the field. She was a gay girl at that time. Her husband was an attached labour in the house of the R.K. Singh, who was not Mukhia at that time, but he was the richest landowner of the village. S.K. P.D. were happy that they were attached as labour in the house of the big landowner of the village P.K. used to pay visit on the field to supervise the work of agriculture. He saw P.D. and became attracted at her beauty. He began to see a chance to establish, illegal, sex relation with P.D. One day he went to see his field of Arahar. He saw P.D. cutting grasses amidst the Arhar plants. He first of all made some fun with her. She responded the fun with smiling face. He saw in and around the field and become convinced that there was no other person nearby the field. He attacked on P.D. who was not ready to counter such evil activities. Amidst quarrel, she was raped.

She had very high regard for his Malik. But seeing his such behaviour, her attitude towards the respect and regards of Malik was changed. After rape, she was offered a note of Rs. 100. This was the price of her hastily. She threw the note with spit on the mouth of the Malik. She took grass on her head came back home in sad mood. She wanted to tell this news to her husband. But she thought he would not take it good. Rather he would beat her. Therefore She did not tell this to her husband.

From that day, her Malik began to get her any time. When ever he used see her, he used to offer a note of Rs. 100. But she did not turn towards his offer. But one day, in broad day light she was again raped by the Malik amidst bushes. She had gone to cut grasses. Other women of the village were also cutting the grasses. So, she was feeling herself in safe position. But peacefully and silently, her Malik came and took her in his hand. He brought her amidst bushes and satisfied his hunger of sex forcefully. This news spread in the village like fire, but her family members did not become aggressive. They remained submissive because it was the act of their Malik whose help they were taking since years. Her husband did not accuse her, but he accused his fate because it was not a serious matter for the rich of the village. Like Mukhiajee, there were many rich persons of the village who were entangled with Dalit women. For them, Dalit women were like things to be consumed in the manner they liked.

From that day P.D. began to live with Mukhiajee. Mukhiajee used her in the manner he liked. Now neither she, nor her husband, nor any villagers criticise their meeting in front of them. But villagers criticise them in their absent. With the financial supper of Mukhiajee, P.D. has been able to build a pucca house. She has purchased two bigha of land. Her husband domesticate two cows and a buffalo. She uses the tractor of Mukhiajee for the purpose of cultivation for which no fare is charged. She has two sons and a daughter. They resemble very much with the Mukhia. The villagers call them a Dogala. But not body dares to tell them Dogala in presence of P.D. or S.K., though everybody knows that P.D. is a kept of Mukhiajee.

Like P.D. there were many more women who were leading a life of kept of males of not only forward Hindu Castes, but backward Hindu castes like Yadava, Koeri, Kurmi, Naua and even Pathan. Some were leading a life of kept of Dalit males of the same castes or of different caste. These Dalit male were men of means.

Kept of Dalit Activists

Dalit women are raped even by Dalit activists who want to bring change in the society through violence. Undoubtedly, they have been able to organise these rural masses. With their efforts, the Dalit in general and Dalit women in particular have been able to lead a prestigious life. But the Dalit women have become prey of some activities, who come to organise them and they are accepted as their leader. But after his acceptance, some of them established, illegal sex relation with the Dalit women, which begins with rape and ends in kept.

PART II – DARBHANGA

9

DESCRIPTION OF SAMPLE VILLAGE OF DARBHANGA

The Universe of the study was Darbhanga district of North Bihar. For the purpose of study two Block namely Darbhanga urban and Bahadurpur were selected purposively on the basis of concentration of Dalit population. From each Block, 20 villages were selected randomly. Now it will be the fitness the thing to present here the description of the sample villages.

DARBHANGA URBAN BLOCK

Family and Family Size

In the villages, the village population is distributed into family or household. The family size differs from family to family. The average size of family suggests whether the fertility is high or less.

Table 9.1 : Distribution of Village Population According to Family Size

Sl. No.	*Name of Village*	*Total Population*	*Total No. of Household*	*Family Size*
1.	Adalpur	5170	850	6
2.	Amdhare	2598	630	6
3.	Atihar	1420	240	6
4.	Bela	744	122	6
5.	Bhalpatti	7643	1241	6
6.	Dulalpur	2206	367	6
7.	Mabbi Belauna	1602	267	6

(Contd.)

(Contd.)

Sl. No.	*Name of Village*	*Total Population*	*Total No. of Household*	*Family Size*
8.	Padari	1914	621	6
9.	Sarafazil	1332	222	6
10.	Siso	7242	1207	6
11.	Sonaki	1538	256	6
12.	Ruchaul	2078	346	6
13.	Harpur	889	148	6
14.	Alinagar (Ward No. 1)	3562	572	6
15.	Sunderpur (Ward No. 2)	5141	857	6
16.	Shivdhara (Ward No. 3)	4495	749	6
17.	Katahalbari (Ward No. 7)	4734	789	6
18.	Lakshmisagar (Ward No. 9)	6819	1136	6
19.	Lalbag (Ward.No. 12)	5046	741	6
20.	Hospital Area (Ward No. 25)	7100	1200	6
	Total	73283	12651	6

The average family size in the study village was observed as 6. Parents were also included in the family size. Thus, the average number of children in the family was seen as 4.

Sex Group and Sex Ratio

The study of Sex group and Sex ratio is important from the fertility point of view. The sex balance is essential for the society otherwise it leads to various practice related to sex imbalance. Let us see the sex ratio in the study villages.

Table 9.2 : Distribution of population According to sex ratio

Sl. No.	*Name of Villages*	*Male*	*Female*	*Total*	*Sex Ratio*
1.	Adalpur	2570 (47.77)	2600 (52.23)	5170 (100.00)	1011
2.	Amdhare	1250 (48.11)	1348 (51.89)	2598 (100.00)	1080
3.	Atihar	720 (51.55)	700 (48.45)	1420 (100.00)	972
4.	Bela	372 (50.00)	372 (50.00)	744 (100.00)	1000
5.	Bhalpatti	3840 (51.55)	3803 (48.45)	7643 (100.00)	990
6.	Dulalpur	1000 (45.33)	1206 (59.67)	2206 (100.00)	1206
7.	Mabbi Belauna	850 (53.06)	752 (46.94)	1602 (100.00	861
8.	Padari	900 (47.00)	1014 (52.98)	1914 (100.00)	1126
9.	Sarafazil	700 (53.30)	632 (46.70)	1332 (100.00)	902
10.	Siso	3642 (50.29)	3600 (49.71)	7242 (100.00)	988
11.	Sonaki	800 (52.08)	738 (47.92)	1538 (100.00)	922
12.	Ruchaul	1000 (48.12)	1078 (51.88)	2078 (100.00)	1078
13.	Harpur	499 (49.94)	450 (50.06)	899 (100.00)	1002
14.	Alinagar (Ward No. 1)	1862 (52.27)	1700 (47.73)	3562 (100.00)	913
15.	Sunderpur (Ward No. 2)	3041 (59.15)	2100 (41.85)	5141 (100.00)	690
16.	Shivdhara (Ward No. 3)	2295 (51.06)	2200 (48.94)	4495 (100.00)	958
17.	Katahalbari (Ward No. 7)	2350 (47.53)	2384 (52.47)	4734 (100.00)	1014
18.	Lakshmisagar (Ward No: 9)	3419 (50.88)	3400 (49.12)	6819 (100.00)	994
19.	Lalbag (Ward No. 12)	2546 (50.40)	2500 (49.60)	5046 (100.00)	978
20.	Hospital Area (Ward No. 25)	3500 (49.29)	3600 (50.71)	1100 (100.00)	1024
	Total	37106 (50.05)	36177 (49.95)	.73283 (100.00)	975

In the study villages the number of male was slightly greater than the female. The male constituted 50.05 per cent population, whereas female represented 49.95 per cent population. The sex ratio was 975, i.e., there were 975 female for every thousand males. The percentage of 'male' female and sex ratio was different for different villages.

Table 9.3 : Ethnic Group of Populations

Sl. No.	*Ethnic Group*	*No. of Households*
1.	Maithil Brahma	1500
2.	Bhumihar Brahman	500
3.	Rajput	1000
4.	Yadav	2500
5.	Koeri	1500
6.	Kurami	500
7.	Barahi	50
8.	Bania	150
9.	Kumahar	50
10.	Naua	50
11.	Dhanuk	50
12.	Dusadh	960
13.	Chamar	1000
14.	Musahar	1000
15.	Pasi	10
16.	Bhangi	10
17.	Dhobi	10
18.	Dom	10
19.	Muslim	1651
	Total	12651

Altogether, there were 12,651 households in all 20 villages of Darbhanga Urban block. Among them, 1500 households belonged to

Maithil Brahman, 500 households to Bhumihar Brahman, 100 households of Rajput. There were 2500 households of Yadavas, 1500 of Koeri, 500 households of Kurami, 50 households of Barahi, 150 households of Bania, 50 households of Kumahar, Naua, Dhanuk each. There were 960 households of Dusadh, 1000 households of Chamar and Musahar each. There were 10 households of Pasi, Bhangi, Dhobi and Dom each. Besides these Hindus, there were 1651 households of Muslims in the study villages.

Political Ethnic Group

Nowadays, our government has created political ethnic groups for the purpose of bringing some groups under reservation policy. These political ethnic groups are (i) Forward castes which include Brahman, Bhumihar, Rajput and Kayasthas or Lala; (ii) Backward castes which include Yadava, Koeri, Kurami, Barahi, Kumahar, Lohar, Naua, Dhanuk, etc. and (iii) Lower castes or scheduled castes which include Dalits.

Table 9.4 : Distribution of Households According to Political Ethnic Groups

	Political Ethnic Group	*No. of Households*
1.	Forward castes	3000
2.	Backward castes	5000
3.	Scheduled castes	3000
4.	Muslim castes	1651
	Total	12651

This ethnic classification by the government is based on the heirarchical position prevalent in traditional India. In traditional caste system, the high caste Hindus have been placed under the ethnic category Forward or Upper castes. The castes occupying middle position in heirarchy have been placed under the ethnic category Backward Castes. The caste occupying lower position caste heirarchy have been scheduled by our honourable President. That is why, they are called scheduled castes. The Muslims occupy a separate ethnic group, although within Muslims heirarchical order like Hindus can be observed. For example, Shekh, Saiyad, Pathan are upper Muslim caste, Darjee, Dhumiya are middle Muslim castes. Halalkhor etc. occupy the inferior most position in the society. Each Muslim section practice endogamy to maintain its racial purity.

Education

After independence, the government has started educational programmes. Within this programme lower primary schools have been established in almost all villages, Middle and High schools have also been started in neighbouring villages. Nowadays +2 school or Intermediate college are available at Block headquarters. These efforts of governments have brought change in the educational status of the persons. The table below presents the facts regarding the educational status of the population under the study village.

Table 9.5 : Educational status of Populations

Educational Status	*Number*	*Percentage*
Illiterate	40000	54.18
Just literate	10000	13.54
Upto Lower School	5000	6.76
Upto Middle School	6500	8.87
Upto High School	4500	6.14
Upto Intermediate	3000	4.09
Graduation	2000	2.72
Post-graduation	1000	1.36
Technical	1283	1.75
Total	73283	99.01

Of total 73283 population of village under study, 54.18 per cent were illiterate among literate, 13.54 per cent were just literate. They knew to write their names, 6.76 per cent possessed education upto Primary School level. 8.87 per cent population possessed education upto Middle School level. 6.14 per cent population had education upto High School level. 4.09 per cent were Intermediate etc., 2.72 per cent were graduates, 1.36 per cent were post-graduates and 1.75 per cent were technical degree holders.

Economy

The economy of the village understudy is namely based on agriculture. The agriculture economy has three basic components :-

(1) The landowner, (2) The labourer and (3) Artisan castes bound to landowner and labourer through *jujmani* relation.

The landowners : The landowners are locally known as Malik or Babu.

The labourers : The labourers are known by the term Kam a, Jana, etc.

The Artisan Castes : The artisan castes are known locally as Pawania. They supply materials related to agriculture and domestic uses to landowners as well as labourers.

The distribution of land is not same in all villages. It differs from village to village. Again in a village, land is not distributed equally among all families. Some are big landowners, some are medium landowners and small farmers. Some are landless and possess only homestead land.

Table 9.6 : Distribution of Land According to Village

Sl. No.	*Name of Village*	*Land in Hectare*
1.	Adalpur	466.60
2.	Amdhare	271.54
3.	Atihar	180.49
4.	Bela	78.51
5.	Bhalpatti	811.70
6.	Dulalpur	499.38
7.	Mabbi Belauna	129.09
8.	Padari	126.69
9.	Sarafazil	63.63
10.	Siso	547.13
11.	Sonaki	219.34
12.	Ruchaul	114.12
13.	Harpur	104.00
14.	Alinagar (Ward No. 1)	98.08

(Contd.)

(Contd.)

Sl. No.	*Name of Village*	*Land in Hectare*
15.	Sunderpur (Ward No. 2)	60.75
16.	Shivdhara (Ward No. 3)	80.95
17.	Katahalbari (Ward No. 7)	70.89
18.	Lakshmisagar (Ward No. 9)	60.78
19.	Lalbag (Ward No. 12)	40.60
20.	Hospital Area (Ward No. 25)	30.37

Table 9.7 : Caste Wise Distribution of Land

Land in Acre	*Caste group*			
	F.C. No. of Household	*B.C. No. of Household*	*S.C. No. of Household*	*Muslim No. of Household*
Only homestead land	-	20	2000	700
Upto 1 Acre	500	1480	500	700
1 – 2.5 Acre	1000	2000	300	100
2.5 – 5 Acre	500	1000	100	50
5 – 7.5 Acre	550	700	50	50
7.5 – 10 Acre	250	200	35	36
Above 10 Acre	200	100	15	15
Total	3000	5000	3000	1651

The above table reveals that no Two family in F.C. possessed only homestead land. Few B.C. family (20) possessed only homestead land. In case of S.C. 2000 households possessed only homestead and in Muslims the number of households possessing only homestead land was 700.

In F.C. 500 households possessed land upto 1 Acre. Whereas in B.C. 1480 households possessed land upto 1 acre. In S.C. 500 households possessed land upto 1 acre, while in Muslims 700 households belonged to this category of land owner.

1000 households of F.C. possessed land 1 acre to 2.5 acre, whereas in B.C. 2000 households belonged to this category of landowner. In S.C. 100 households possessed land upto category, whereas in Muslims only 50 households belonged to this category of landowner.

500 F.C. families possessed land in between 2.5 A to 5 A, whereas 1000 B.C. families belonged to this category of landowners. In S.C. 100 households possessed land upto 5 Acre, in Muslim also 50 households possessed land upto 5 Acre.

550 households of F.C. possessed land in between 5A to 7.5 A, whereas 700 B.C. families belonged to this category of landowners. In S.C. 50 households belonged to this category and in Muslims 50 households belonged to this type of landowners.

250 families of F.C. possessed land in between 7.5 Acre to 10 Acre, whereas in B.C. 200 households has this category of landowners. In S.C. 35 families possessed land between 7.5 A to 10 A, while in Muslims 36 households belonged to this category.

In F.C. 200 households possessed land above 10 acre and in B.C. the number of this category of landowners was 100. In S.C. only 15 families belonged to this category landowners which similar was the number with Muslims.

Now due to various land reforms measures and distribution of land in each generation, the acreage of land to each family has gone down. Joint family is breaking rapidly. As a result, the acreage of land in the hand of forward caste has gone down. Forward caste are selling their land. These lands are being purchased by B.C. and S.C. Thus today in each caste group, small farmer middle farmer, big farmers etc. can be seen. Now really the B.C.'s are purchasing land more and more. They have now become medium and big category of farmers. Among B.C.'s Yadavas, Koeri, Kurami occupy top positions in land possession.

The soil : The soil is fertile. It is sandy and kewal, all type of crops can be obtained from the soil.

Crops sown : Four types of crops are sown in the villages under study. These crops are as follows : Maize.

Bhodoi crops : These include Marua, Kodo, Seraha, Sathi, (lowers variety of paddy). These crops are sown in the month of Asarh and get ready for harvesting in the month of Bhado.

Agahani crops : These crops include HVV of paddy. Which are transplanted in Shrawan month and get ready for harvesting in the month of Agahan.

Rabbi crops : These include wheat and pulses which are sown in Agahan and gets ready in Chait, Baisakh month.

Grama crops : These include some variety of paddy, moong, maize, etc. These are cultivated in February or Magh-Phalgun and become ready in the month of Jyestha-Asarh.

Vegetable crops : Besides these cereals and pulses, vegetables are grown round the year in each season vegetables like bean, tomato, potato, bringal, papaya, katahal, cucumber, lady's finger, gound, etc. are sown time to time.

Table 9.8 : Occupational Status of the Families Under Study Villages

Occupational Status	*No. of Households*
Agriculture	5000
Sharecropping	1651
Agriculture labour	2500
Casual labour	1500
Small business	250
Shopowner	150
Contractor	1000
Service	1000
Other	500
Total	12651

The above table reveals that 5000 households were engaged in agriculture households had adopted share cropping. 2500 and 1500 households were agricultural labour and casual labour respectively 150 household were engaged in shopkeeping and 250 households were carrying on business. 100 household were engaged as contractor in different types of works. 100 household's occupation was different types of service. 500 households were engaged in other types of works like Rickshaw, Tanga, Collie, Thela, Dairy, Poultry, Fishery, etc.

Means of Irrigation

Agriculture is solely dependent upon means of irrigation. Previously agriculture were dependent upon rainfall. Only good rainfall used to bring good harvest. But nowadays, the farmers are not only dependent on rainfall. They have ponds, tank, nala, well, boring diesel machine, etc. For the purpose of irrigation. In the purpose of irrigation with the help of boring, electric pump, well and diesel machine.

Table 9.9 : The Means of Irrigation in the Study Villages

Sl. No.	*Name of Village*	*Means of Irrigation*					
		No. of Ponds	*No. of Nala*	*No. of Tubewell*	*No. of Wells*	*No. of Diesel Machine*	*Rehat Tube-well*
1.	Adalpur	5	2	10	10	18	5
2.	Amdhare	6	—	8	7	15	4
3.	Atihar	4	—	5	6	11	3
4.	Bela	3	1	7	6	8	4
5.	Bhalpatti	21	3	16	13	21	6
6.	Dulalpur	9	2	7	5	16	2
7.	Mabbi Belauna	3	—	3	2	8	1
8.	Padari	8	1	9	10	3	4
9.	Sarafazil	15	3	16	10	8	4
10.	Siso	21	5	25	20	11	6
11.	Sonaki	7	3	4	6	2	3
12.	Ruchaul	9	6	5	4	3	2
13.	Harpur	3	2	4	10	3	2
14.	Alinagar	21	2	5	4	4	1
15.	Sunderpur	3	2	6	5	2	—
16.	Shivdhara	4	1	7	8	5	—
17.	Katahalbari	3	1	5	3	2	—
18.	Lakshmisagar	2	—	3	2	2	—
19.	Lalbag	3	1	2	3	2	—
20.	Hospital Area	2	—	2	2	2	—

Table 9.10 : The Vehicle Types in the Study Village

Sl. No.	*Name of Village*	*Vehicle Type*						
		Cycle	*Rickshaw*	*Tanga*	*Bullock Cart*	*Buffalo Cart*	*Tractor*	*Scooter*
1.	Adalpur	50	4	1	3	3	2	3
2.	Amdhare	20	6	3	1	1	—	2
3.	Atihar	15	3	—	1	1	—	—
4.	Bela	17	—	1	1	—	1	1
5.	Bhalpatti	65	—	2	—	1	—	—
6.	Dulalpur	41	3	1	1	1	1	—
7.	Mabbi Belauna	19	7	2	—	1	2	—
8.	Padari	27	6	—	1	1	33	-
9.	Sarafazil	36	—	—	—	1	1	1
10.	Siso	32	5	1	1	—	—	2
11.	Sonaki	45	3	3	1	1	1	3

(Contd.)

(Contd.)

Sl. No.	*Name of Village*	*Vehicle Type*						
		Cycle	*Rickshaw*	*Tanga*	*Bullock Cart*	*Buffalo Cart*	*Tractor*	*Scooter*
12.	Ruchaul	47	2	2	1	1	--	4
13.	Harpur	21	—	1	1	1	1	1
14.	Alinagar	17	6	2	1	1	2	2
15.	Sunderpur	22	9	3	1	—	3	3
16.	Shivdhara	24	7	1	1	—	1	1
17.	Katahalbari	17	5	—	—	—	2	2
18.	Lakshmisagar	18	10	1	—	—	—	4
19.	Lalbag	19	13	1	—	—	—	5
20.	Hospital Area	21	12	—	—	—	—	1

Vehicle Type

The study of vehicle type is essential, because it provides the mode of transportation of passengers and goods.

Religions Festivals

The villagers enjoy the religious festivals by wearing new dresses, cooking tasty food and worshiping Gods and Goddesses. Although Hindus are divided into different castes and class, but they celebrate festivals at the level of village, for this purpose all households of the village contributed cash or kind to meet expenses on the festivals. The expenses includes the establishment of image, items of worship, parsad and stage of drama, Nautankee, Natak, Ramleela, Krishnaleela, dance of Bhikhari Thakur etc. In the contributing of cash or kind, the economic status of the household is taken into account. The big landowner contributes more than others. According to the possession of the acreage, the subscription for the celebration of festival is raised. Those who are not in a position to pay in cash, they are free to give in kind like rice, wheat, maize, ghee, etc. The landless labourers also contribute from the wages they earn. For them, the rate of subscription is kept minimum. The service holders have to pay more than the others. The celebration of festival reveals religious unity in the village. In the celebration of festivals Muslims also take part. They join the religious procession. They are also engaged in selling goods in fair organised on the occasion of festivals. On the occasion of Muslim festivals, Hindus also join the procession.

Gods and Goddesses

In Hindus villages one finds many religious spots in the name of Gods and Goddesses. These are Satisthan, Bhagwatisthan, Shivasthan, Brahmastha, Dihawarsthan, Goraiyasthan etc. In each family and on each screed place, there is a flag of Lord Hanumana and a plant of Basil (Tulsi). In each family, there is a room dedicated to family deity who are ancestors of the family. They are offered worship on various occasion. The major Hindu festivals are celebrated at village level. These festivals are Holi, Ramnawami, Janamasthami, Durgapuja, Lakshmipuja, Saraswatipuja, etc.

There are some festivals which are celebrated by particular caste, but all people of the village are invited to participate. For example, Govardhan Puja is celebrated by the Yadava, Vishwa Karma Puja by the Lohar and the Barahi.

Due to conflict and tension, the religious unity of the village has come under threat in some village. In some village due to caste conflict and tension, the village divides into two or more groups. Each group establishes images of Goddess Durga and every festival is celebrated at the level or group.

Political Institutions

Previously each village had a traditional Panchayat system. In this panchayat system, each head of the households participated. The Panchayat sat either or a scred place, i.e., Shivasthan, Devisthan, under peepal tree or on the out door of the biggest landowner, where social status was regarded as very high. The Panchayat sat to discuss the village level matter and matter related to peace and prosperity of the village. In village, each caste had its own caste Panchayat to settle their problem through Jati Panchayat. Jati Panchayat was limited only for a particular caste. But intra-village and inter-village problems were solved by the village Panchayat. If caste Panchayat failed to reach a decision, the problem was brought in village Panchayat. The village Panchayat tried to solve the problem. Nowadays, the traditional village Panchayat and Jati Panchayat are in existence but its decision is not binding on the individuals. Because being dissatisfied with the decision of traditional Panchayat, now individuals move in modern political system institution like court, police, etc.

In modern political institutions, there is modern Gram Panchayat. Mukhia, Sarpancha and their executives are elected through elections. In traditional Panchayat, the member of high caste enjoyed high status, but in modern Gram Panchayat, Mukhia and Sarpancha are elected on the basis of number. As a result, now Mukhia and Sarpancha come on the basis of numerical dominance of castes and alliance between castes. Now Dalits and backwards are winning elections of Mukhia and Sarpancha because they have numerical strength in the village.

The villagers take part in the elections of MLA and MP. In these elections polarisation votes takes place on the basic of castes. But sometimes, the personality of the candidate is also take into consideration.

In these areas, there are certain political parties which claim the support of the poor in general and Dalits in particular. These parties are Janta Dal and C.P.I. But activists political parties like CPI (ML), IPF, MCC etc. do not have ground as yet. Some caste of the area are aggressive like Yadava, Rajput, Koeri, Kurami etc, but local senas like in central Bihar have not come in to existence. The impact of Naxalism is also negligible in the area in comparison to central Bihar.

Play, Games and Sports

In villages children play with toy made up of soil, wood, leaves etc. The play like Lukachhipi, Bagh-Bakari, Barahgharawa, Chorsipahi etc. are played by the children. The young play games like playing cards, ludo. The vollyball, football, cricket are also played on festive occasions like Ramnawami, Gadaka, Lathi, Mugadar, Talwar, Bhala etc. are played. These constitute folk sports. In folk sports members of all communities take part.

Means of Entertainment

The children entertain by listening to stories, riddles, proverbs, idioms from the aged persons, generally Dada – Dadi or Nana – Nani. The young entertain themselves by taking part in Bhajan and Kirtan, Natak, Ramleela, Rasleela, Krishanaleela, dance etc, are stage on festival occasions. Religious Bhajan and Kirtan are organised in the temples. Besides, these traditional means of entertainment, the villagers now have modern means of entertainment. Among modern means, the radio is most popular. Radio is found almost in every houses.

BAHADURPUR BLOCK

Family and Family Size

Table 9.11 : Distribution of Village Population According to Family Size

Sl. No.	*Name of Villages*	*Total Population*	*Total No. of Households*	*Family Size*
1.	Bahadurpur	1112	186	6
2.	Basatpur	1723	287	6
3.	Bhairavpatti	1470	245	6
4.	Chintamanpur	380	63	6
5.	Darhar	2082	347	6
6.	Dekuli	2638	439	6
7.	Gangapatti	1084	181	6
8.	Govindpur	1523	253	6
9.	Jogiara	2199	366	6

(Contd.)

(Contd.)

Sl. No.	Name of Villages	Total Population	Total No. of Households	Family Size
10.	Madhuban	1906	317	6
11.	Maniari	1333	222	6
12.	Ojhaul	2654	462	6
13.	Pingi	988	164	6
14.	Pirari	2040	340	6
15.	Pokhar-Bhinda	414	69	6
16.	Raghaipura	789	131	6
17.	Rambhadrapur	1686	261	6
18.	Rashalpurkhurd	442	73	6
19.	Taralahi	3703	617	6
20.	Ughra	7351	1225	6
	Total	37917	6249	6

The family size in sample villages was observed as 6. Thus, there were average four children in each household.

Sex and Sex Ratio

Table 9.12 : Distribution of Population According to Sex Group and Sex Ratio

Sl. No.	Name of Villages	Male	Female	Total	Sex Ratio
1	Bahadurpur	600 (53.48)	512 (46.52)	1112 (100.00)	853
2	Basatpur	823 (47.70)	900 (52.30)	1723 (100.00)	1091
3	Bhairavpatti	735 (50.00)	735 (50.00)	1470 (100.00)	1000
4	Chintamanpur	150 (42.10)	190 (57.90)	380	1266
5	Darhar	1000 (48.03)	1682 (51.97)	2082 (100.00)	1084
6	Dekuli	1300 (47.00)	1338 (53.00)	2638 (100.00)	1028
7	Gangapatti	500 (46.12)	584 (53.80)	1084 (100.00)	1178

(Contd.)

(Contd.)

Sl. No.	*Name of Villages*	*Male*	*Female*	*Total*	*Sex Ratio*
8	Govindpur	800 (52.52)	723 (47.48)	1523 (100.00)	903
9	Jogiara	1100 (50.20)	1099 (49.30)	2199 (100.00)	999
10	Madhuban	906 (47.53)	1000 (52.47)	1906 (100.00)	1210
11	Maniari	633 (47.48)	700 (52.52)	1333 (100.00)	1120
12	Ojhaul	1327 (50.00)	1327 (50.00)	2624 (100.00)	1000
13	Pingi	500 (50.50)	488 (49.50)	988 (100.00)	976
14	Pirari	1000 (49.01)	1040 (50.99)	2040	1004
15	Pokhar-Bhinda	200 (48.30)	214 (51.70)	414 (100.00)	1070
16	Reghaipura	400 (50.70)	389 (49.30)	789 (100.00)	972
17	Rambhadrapur	800 (47.47)	886 (52.53)	1686 (100.00)	1107
18	Rashalpurkhurd	200 (45.25)	242 (54.75)	442 (100.00)	1210
19	Taralahi	180 (48.77)	1900 (51.23)	3703 (100.00)	1053
20	Ughra	3700 (50.33)	3651 (49.67)	7351 (100.00)	987
	Total	18477 (48.73)	19440 (51.27)	37917 (100.00)	1052

In the village under study the percentage of female was greater than the males. The females constituted 31.27 per cent and males constituted 48.73 per cent. The sex ratio was observed as 1052, i.e., there were 1052 females for every thousand males.

Ethnic Group

In village under study caste was an important ethnic group. Every caste was maintaining its ethnicity on the basis of practicing caste endogamy. Within each caste clan exogamy was stricitly followed.

Brahman, Bhumihar, Rajput have been placed under forward castes. Yadava, Bania, Koeri, Kurami, Barahi, Lohar, Naua, Dhanuk, Kumahar have been placed in backward castes. Dusadh Chamar, Musahar, Dhobi, Dom, Mehalar, have been placed in lower castes or scheduled castes. Muslim have been placed in a separate category.

Table 9.13 : Distribution of Households by Ethnic Group

Sl. No.	*Ethnic group*	*No. of Households*
1.	Maithil Brahman	500
2.	Bhumihar Brahman	200
3.	Rajput	300
4.	Yadava	500
5.	Bania	50
6.	Koeri	200
7.	Kurami	50
8.	Darahi	20
9.	Kumhar	20
10.	Lohar	20
11.	Dhanuk	20
12.	Naua	20
13.	Dusadh	300
14.	Chamar	1200
15.	Musahar	900
16.	Dhobi	33
17.	Mehalar	50
18.	Dom	17
19.	Muslim	1249
	Total	6249

Table 9.14 : Political Ethnic Groups

Political Ethnic Group	*No. of Households*
Forward Castes	1000
Backward Castes	1000
Lower Castes	3000
Muslims Castes	1249
Total	6249

Education

After independence inputs related to education has been facilated in villages. As a result, literacy level has gone up, but still there are illiterate. Certain section of society like women and scheduled castes, are still more sufferer. The table below will present the literacy level of population under study.

Table 9.15 : Distribution of Population According to Educational Status

Educational Status	*Number*	*Percentage*
Illiterate	13000	47.47
Just literature	8000	21.09
Upto Primary	3000	7.90
Upto Middle	4000	10.54
Upto Metric	2000	5.27
Upto Intermediate	1000	2.63
Upto Graduation	500	1.31
Upto Post-graduation	400	1.05
Technical	1017	2.68
Total	37917	99.94

The above table reveals that in village under study 47.47 per cent people were illiterate. 21.09 per cent people were just-literate, they knew only to put their signature. 7.90 per cent people possessed educations upto primary level. They knew to read and write letter. 10.54 per cent people possessed education upto middle school level and 5.27 per cent people had education upto metric level and 1.31 per cent had education upto graduation level. 1.05 per cent population possessed education upto post graduation level and 2.68 per cent population had technical education.

It was further observed that among literate, the percentage of males was greater than females. Again it was found that among Dalits, the percentage of illiteracy was greater than other communities.

Occupation

The table below presents the occupational status of the households under study.

Table 9.16 : Occupational Status of the Households

Occupational Status	*No. of Households*	*Percentage*
Agriculture	2000	32.04
Shareeropping	500	8.00
Agriculture labour	2000	32.04
Casual labour	500	8.00
Contractor	200	3.20
Business	100	1.60
Shopkeeper	100	1.60
Service	300	4.80
Other	549	8.80
Total	6279	100.08

The above table reveals that 32.04 per cent households were carrying on occupation of agriculture. 8.00 per cent households were doing occupation sharecropping. 32.04 per cent households occupation was agriculture labour. 8.00 per cent households occupation was contractor. 1.60 per cent households were engaged in business and 1.60 per cent in shopkeeping. 4.80 per cent households occupation was service. 8.80 per cent households were engaged in traditional occupation, rickshaw puling, Thela pulling, Tam-Tam driving, Feriwala, etc.

It was further observed that majority of forward castes were in agriculture, service and business. Similarly, backward castes in majority were engaged in agriculture, business and service. Very few Dalits were agriculturists and service holders. Majority of them were engaged as agriculture labour, casual labour and other occupations.

Land

The quality of land is fertile. The colour is brown. Each village has its own land which is demarcated by boundary. The boundary demarcates the land between two village. In each village the land is distributed in to households. Each households possess khatiyani land, which they inhert from the ancestors. Besides, the sale and purchase of land also takes place. Due to sale and purchase the acreage of household decreases or increases. Each household has three types of land. These are homestead land, Bariland, and agriculture land. The level of homestead land is generally high in comparison to other types of land. The people construct houses, therefore, they select such a land which level is high or if they construct house on an agriculture land, they make the level high. The agriculture land situated nearby the village is called Diha. Its value remains very high. The Dalits generally own homestead land and some Bariland. Previously, they did not own homestead land. They were given land by the Jamindar or Jagirdar to construct of house. They were known as the *Jana* or *Adami* of the Jamindars or Jagirdars who gave them land to settle. For the land of house, they had to work for the Jamindar life long. Their sons also had to render labour in the house of Jamindars. But after independence, the government has made the Dalits free from the clutches of the Jamindars. The parcha of homestead land have been given to them. Any type of loan and bondedness have been made free. As a result now Dalits are free to lead independent life and to work where they like. During 50 years of independence, some Dalits have emerged as rich. They are purchasing land from the landowners, whose ancestors were Jamindars or Jagirdars.

The Crop Sown

In villages crops are sown round the year. The crops are termed by different names according to the harvest time and season. The common names for varieties of crops are as follows :

Bhadai crops : These crops are sown in Asarh month and are barvested in the month of Bhado. These include coarse variety of paddy like seraha, sathi, teni, etc., and marua, makeya, kodo, kurathi.

Agahani crops : These include high yielding varieties of paddy. These varieties of paddy became ready for harvestation in the month of Agahan. These include Mansuri, Ganga Kaveri, IR8, Sita, etc. These crops require proper maintenance of seed, manure, fertilizer and pesticides.

Rabi crops : These include cereals like wheat, oat, barely and cereals like gram, masur, pea, khesari etc. They become ready for harvesting in the month of Vaishakh (March and April).

Garama crops : These include cereals like paddy. Rabi crops are sown in the fields were after the harvesting of the Bhadai and Agahani crops. Garama crops are sown after the Rabi crops. In order to maintain the fertility of soil, the field is left barren during summer season. Only in limited area, the Garama crops are cultivated.

The table below presents the villages is distributions of land.

Table 9.17 : Distribution of Land According to Village

Sl. No.	*Name of Village*	*Land in Hectare*
1.	Bahadurpur	103.60
2.	Basatpur	231.48
3.	Bhairavpatti	95.50
4.	Chintamanpur	12.95
5.	Darhar	190.00
6.	Dekuli	159.85
7.	Gangapatti	53.82
8.	Govindpur	69.39
9.	Jogiara	156.21
10.	Madhuban	251.71
11.	Maniari	146.90
12.	Ojhaul	143.66
13.	Pingi	157.83
14.	Pirari	277.21
15.	Pokhar-Bhinda	171.99
16.	Reghaipura	46.13
17.	Rambhadrapur	151.35
18.	Rashalpurkhurd	42.06
19.	Taralahi	6135.35
20.	Ughra	1193.81

Besides these cereals and pulses, the vegetables is cultivated round the year. Majority of people cultivate vegetables to get money by selling them in the market.

Table 9.13 : Distribution of Land in Households

Size of Land	*Number of Households*	*Percentage*
Only household	1500	24.07
Upto 1 Acre	1500	24.07
1 – 2.5 Acre	1000	16.02
2.5 – 5 Acre	900	14.40
5 – 7.5 Acre	600	9.63
7.5 – 10 Acre	500	8.00
Above 10 Acre	249	4.00
Total	6249	99.19

The above table reveals that like other villages of Bihar, the village under study show unequal distribution of land. Some possess only homestead land. Some are near landless because they own some land but not sufficient for cultivation. Some are small farmers, some are medium farmers and some are big farmers.

24.07 per cent households possessed only homestead land and 24.07 per cent households possessed land upto only 1 Acre. 16.02 per cent people had land in between 1 Acre to 2.5 Acre. 14.02 per cent households possessed land in between 2.5 Acre to 5 Acre. 9.63 per cent households had land between 5 Acre to 7.5 Acre. 8 per cent households had land between 7.5 Acre to 10.00 Acre. Only 4.00 per cent households possessed land above 10 Acre.

Some castes like Dalits were landless since centuries. Some castes were engaged as artisans and they owned some land. While other caste owned land. Some of the were Jamindars. But division of land in each generation has resulted in decrease in acreage per household.

Means of Irrigation

Irrigation is essential for the cultivation of crops. In absence of proper means of irrigation good yield cannot be obtained. Previously villagers were fully dependent upon rainfall. Good rainfall used to bring good harvest. It is still true of majority of villages. But nowadays, there are electric pump, open boring-well and diesel machine etc. By these means

Table 9.19 : Distribution of Village According to Means of Irrigation

Sl No.	*Name of Villages*	*Electric pump*	*Open Boring*	*Well*	*Diesel Machine*	*Rehat*	*Nala*	*River*	*Canal*
1.	Bahadurpur	07	03	16	5	1	1	1	—
2.	Basatpur	11	05	15	6	2	1	1	—
3.	Bhairavpatti	06	02	03	2	1	—	1	—
4.	Chintamanpur	02	01	02	3	—	—	1	—
5.	Darhar	08	06	03	6	1	—	—	—
6.	Dekuli	14	10	07	7	1	1	1	—
7.	Gangapatti	05	03	02	2	1	—	—	—
8.	Govindpur	07	04	03	4	1	1	1	—
9.	Jogiara	15	11	08	6	2	—	—	—
10.	Madhuban	21	08	06	7	3	—	—	—
11.	Maniari	14	06	12	8	1	1	—	—
12.	Ojhaul	17	07	05	6	2	—	1	—

(Contd.)

(Contd.)

Sl No.	*Name of Villages*	*Electric Pump*	*Open Boring*	*Well*	*Diesel Machine*	*Rehat*	*Nala*	*River*	*Canal*
13.	Pingi	13	3	3	5	3	—	—	—
14.	Pirari	22	13	06	04	01	1	—	—
15.	Pokhar-Bhinda	14	02	08	11	02	—	—	—
16.	Reghaipura	03	—	05	02	01	—	—	—
17.	Rambhadrapur	10	02	03	01	03	1	1	—
18.	Rashalpurkhurd	02	—	02	03	06	—	—	—
19.	Taralahi	25	03	11	17	08	1	—	—
20.	Ughra	35	16	37	24	10	—	—	—

Table 9.20 : Distribution of Village According to Vehicle Type

Sl. No.	*Name of Villages*	*Cycle*	*Rick-shaw*	*Tamtam*	*Bullock Cart*	*Buffalo Cart*	*Scooter*	*Tractor*	*Tempo*
1.	Bahadurpur	15	3	—	1	1	1	1	—
2.	Basatpur	17	2	—	1	1	—	2	—
3.	Bhairavpatti	16	2	—	1	1	—	—	—
4.	Chintamanpur	12	2	—	1	1	—	—	1
5.	Darhar	13	3	—	2	1	1	1	—
6.	Dekuli	20	2	1	3	2	—	—	—
7.	Gangapatti	27	—	—	1	1	—	—	—
8.	Govindpur	16	—	—	1	2	1	2	—
9.	Jogiara	18	—	—	1	1	—	1	—
10.	Madhuban	20	2	2	2	2	—	—	—
11.	Maniari	25	—	—	1	1	—	—	—
12.	Ojhaul	16	1	1	1	1	3	1	1

(Contd.)

(Contd.)

Sl. No.	Name of Villages	Cycle	Rick-shaw	Tamtam	Bullock Cart	Buffalo Cart	Scooter	Tractor	Tempo
13.	Pingi	17	2	2	1	2	1	—	2
14.	Pirari	18	—	—	2	1	2	—	1
15.	Pokhar-Bhinda	20	1	—	1	1	1	1	1
16.	Reghaipura	21	3	—	1	2	1	—	2
17.	Rambhadrapur	22	5	—	1	1	—	1	1
18.	Rashalpurkhurd	16	6	1	1	1	1	2	1
19.	Taralahi	25	2	—	1	2	1	3	1
20.	Ughra	35	17	—	1	1	1	5	—

people try to utilize underground water or water of neighbouring rivers for the purpose of irrigation.

Religion

Religion is an important aspect of the village. The behaviour of villagers are guided by religious beliefs and attitudes. In villages under study, majority of villages are inhabited by Hindus. Some villages are inhabited by only Muslims. Some by Hindus and Muslims. Very few villages are inhabited by only Muslims. Hindus and Muslims celebrate their own festivals. Among Hindus there are many common festivals. But there are some festivals which are caste specific. Important common festivals are Ramnawami, Krishnasthmi, Durgapuja, Deepawali, Holi, etc. Caste specific festivals are Govrdhanpuja by Yadava, Vishkarma Puja by Lohar, Barahi and Kumar, Dawatpuja by Kayastha. Some festivals are meant for brother and sister for example Rakshabandhan and Bhaiduj. Some festivals are meant for husband and offspring's, for example, Tij and Jitia.

The great common festivals are celebrated at the level of village. This purpose found is raised in which all heads of the households contribute in cash or in kind. From the fund raised, image of Gods and Goddesses are established, Bhajan, Kirtan and Satsanga are held, musical instruments are hired and drama is staged.

In some villages festival is celebrated on the basis of tola. Each tola of a village celebrates festival independently, but they take out procession commonly. In the festival of Hindus, Muslims also take part. They play musical instruments, take part in drama and play Lathi, Bhala, Gadaka, Talwar, etc, at the time of religious procession. Similarly, in the festival of Muslims, Hindus also take part. They take part in religious procession and play Lathi, Bhala, Talwar, etc.

Each village has some common village deity like Dihawarbaba, Brahmababa, Satisthan, Shivasthan, Bhagwatisthan. In each religious place, one finds a flag dedicated to Lord Hanumana. In each Hindu household, one can see the flag of Lord Hanumana and cultivation of Tulsi plant. Each family of the village has its own family deity named Kuladevata. Religious performance in the house takes the place before the Kuladevata, hereby the flag of the lord hanumana and Tulsi plant. In order to unload a Manauti, religious performances take place in Dihawarsthan, Brahmasthan, Shivasthan or Bhagwatisthan. For the welfare of the village some religious performances take place before the village deity commonly.

Political System

The villages under study have traditional political system as well as modern political system. Under traditional political system, one finds the existence of Village Panchayat and Jati Panchayat. Jati level problem is solved by Jati Panchayat, where as village level problem is solved by village Panchayat. In village Panchayat, each head of the households takes part. In Jati Panchayat, only the heads of a particular caste families takes part. They may be of same villages or of different villages. The decisions of Jati Panchayat is limited to only a particular jati. Other caste of the village are not affects by the decision of the Jati Panchayat. The decision of the village Panchayat is obeyed by all. The Jati Panchayat is related to intra Jati problems, whereas village Panchayat is related to inter-Jati, inter-Tola, inter village problems. Thus, the scope of village Panchayat is wider than the Jati Panchayat.

In modern political system, one finds the existence of modern Gram Panchayat. The election of Mukhia, Sarpancha and their executives takes place. Mukhia looks after the development works of the villages under Gram Panchayat, whereas Sarpancha cames for the law and order problems of the villages under a particular Gram Panchayat. Many cases are solved through Gram Panchayat. Each Panchayat has a Panchayat Bhavan, where Panchayat site for any decision. If one does not get justice through Panchayat, he is free to go to thana and court. Besides, people take part in the election of MLA and MP. People are well aware of the different political parties. The members who attain 18 years of age, become entitled to cast vote in election. In villages votes are casted on the basis of castes and political parties. Sometimes, the whole villages takes a decision to cast vote in favour of a particular party. Sometimes, the supporters of two political parties are found quarrelling among themselves. Sometimes, some antisocial elements try to capture the booth. They fire the gun to frighten the people.

Means of Entertainment

Entertainment is essential for every individual. In villages, family is the first recreational institution. In family one finds joking relations. through this relation, two kins make fun with each other. Joking relation is extended for the entire village because Devar-Bhabhi relationship exists for the whole village. Husband-wife also make joke with each other. The children generally prefer to spend their time with grand parents. The grand parents tell story, riddles, idiom etc. to children and, thus, they entertain. Sometimes, children and grand parents make joke with each other.

On festive and ceremonial occasion, females sing Geet in a separate group and males sing Bhajan-Kirtan in a separate group. They play musical instruments at the time of singing.

On festive and entertainment occasions, dance, drama, play, Leela etc., are organised for the purpose of entertainment. Nowaday, the people have modern means of recreation. The modern means of recreation includes listening radio, seeing TV, reading newspaper etc. with these means, people entertain in the houses. Some indoor games like playing cards, Chess, Cairam, Ludo, etc. are also played. Children and young play football, volleyball, cricket, etc.

10

STATUS OF DALIT OF DARBHANGA TODAY

STATUS OF DALIT TODAY

The status of Dalit today is not the same as was in the past. Literature available reveals that in past Dalits did not occupy any status. They were treated as inferior and low grade castes. As they were associated with unclean occupation. They were treated as untouchables. Being untouchables, other Dalits did not have food, water and sitting relation with them. In villages, they lived in a separate tola. They were not invited to participate in marriage and death feasts of other castes, but they were expected to come for food like beggars. They were treated so as their survival dependent upon other castes.

Dalits did not receive such treatment during early Vedic period, when the Hindu civilization was established. In order to maintain structural and functional order in the Hindu society, the system of varnavyavastha was established. Varnavyavastha was related to Karma (work) not Janma (birth). On the basis of Karma, and individual gets membership in a particular varna. The food, water and marriage relation between different varnas were maintained. No verna was superior and no varna was inferior, because they were structurally and functionally interdependent and interrelated to maintain the whole Hindu civilization.

In course of time varnayavastha was changed into Jativyavastha. In Jativyavastha birth began to play significant role. The membership of Jati was given on the basis of Janma and not on Karma. In order to maintain the ethnicity of Jati, endogamy began to be practiced and each caste appeared as an endogamous group. To exchange daughter within the caste group, the system of clan exogamy came into existence, and inter-caste marriage was tabooed. Inter-caste marriage was not taken good and the offspring's from such marriages were treated as *Dogala* (Mongerel). They were abused frequently.

In Jati vyavastha, different castes were functionally, structurally and economically related through Jajmani vyavastha. Through these vyavastha all castes were structurally and functionally interrelated and interdependent to maintain the whole. The food and water relation within the caste was maintained through Kachcha food (rice, pulse, vegetable, etc.). But the food relation between different castes was maintained through Pucca food (puri, vegetable, curd, milk, etc.). The food and water of untouchables were not accepted but untouchables accepted Kachcha and Pucca food before the house of other castes.

During Mughal period, feudalism was established. Feudalism subjected untouchables to exploitation and oppression by feudal lords and their musclemen. The similar was the case during Zamindari system established during British rule. Zamindar provided land to depressed castes to establish house. They were called as their own men. They used them for their selfish purposes. They had to do *Begari* for the Zamindars.

After independence, the things have changed. Our Constitution has provided them all facilities. Slavery, Begari, bonded labour and untouchability have been abolished. Education has been made free. Provision for reservation in jobs and politics has been made on account of all such efforts the present day status of Dalits is not the same as before independence. Various legislative, protective, rehabilitative measures have certainly brought transformations in the status of Dalits. Now among Dalits some are well educated. They have food, water and invitation relationship with other Hindu castes. Some occupy responsible posts in government jobs. They are Mukhia, Sarpancha, MLA, MP, etc. Now let us see the empirical reality of the status of Dalits today.

Social Status of Dalit Today

Untouchability was derogatory to the social status of Dalits. On account of untouchability, they were allowed to settle in a separate Tola in the village. Food, water and sitting relationship were tabooed for them. They were not given invitation but they visited as beggars in the house of other Hindus on festive and ceremonial occasions for food. For eating, they were not allowed to go in the courtyard of the house. They were given food outside of the house. They used to quarrel among themselves for food. But now due to ban on untouchability and general awareness, they do not visit the house of other Hindus for food on festive and ceremonial occasions. They visit only on receiving oral invitation. Some educated Dalits occupying responsible posts in local administration or government bodies, maintain invitation relationship through cards.

Table 10.1 : Opinion of Heads of Dalits Households on Food, Water and Invitation Relationship

Opinion	Response		
	Yes	No	Total
1. Do you have food and water relationship with other Hindus ?	400 (100.00)	— —	400 (100.00)
2. Do other Hindus have food water relation with you ?	100 (25.00)	300 (75.00)	400 (100.00)
3. Do you visit to take food without invitation ?	100 (25.00)	300 (75.00)	400 (100.00)
4. Do you get oral invitation for participation in the feast ?	200 (50.00)	200 (50.00)	400 (100.00)
5. Do you get card for participation in feast ?	100 (25.00)	300 (75.00)	400 (100.00)

When 400 heads belonging to 40 villages under study in Darbhanga district were asked to opine on food, water and invitation relationship, their responses were as follows :

They all opined that they had food and water relationship with other Hindu communities. But only 25 per cent opined that other Hindus had food and water relationship with them. This shows that untouchability is still going on in majority of cases. In majority of cases, food and water relationship was one way. Those who opined that other Hindus had food and water relationship with them, were school teachers, Karamchari, Mukhia, Sarpancha, V.L.W., etc. The status of these Dalits was seen higher than Dalits working as labour on the fields of landowners. Majority of labourers opined that they got rice, wheat, pulses vegetables etc. from the house of landowners as Newata in whose houses, they worked regularly. But they did not want to take their *Dharma* by compelling them to share food with them. They sent Newata in our houses and invite us to participate in the function.

75 per cent heads informed that they did not opt for food without invitation, while 25 per cent heads informed that they went for food without any invitation. These were Musahars, Dom, Nat. They visit to take food on the occasion of Shradha feast or marriage feast without any invitation.

As soon as thus heard about the Shardha in any village, they reach there for food.

The Dalits residing in the same village receive oral invitation for participation in the feast. They are communicated orally by the barbers on behalf of the owner of the house to participate in the feast. Dalits occupying responsible posts in local administration and politics receive card for participation in the feast.

Table 10.2 : Opinion of Heads of Dalits Households on Sitting Arrangement

Opinion on Sitting Arrangement		*Response*	
	Yes	*No*	*Total*
1. Do you visit to the House of owner ?	400 (100.00)	—	400 (100.00)
2. Do owners visit to your house ?	400 (100.00)	—	400 (100.00)
3. Do you sit on cot before the owner ?	—	400 (100.00)	400 (100.00)
4. Do you sit on chouki or bench before the owner ?	300 (75.00)	100 (25.00)	400 (100.00)
5. Do you go in courtyard of the owner to participate in feast ?	300 75.00)	100 (25.00)	400 (100.00)
6. Do you sit in the same line at the time of feast ?	75 (18.75)	325 (81.25)	400 (100.00)
7. Do you carry your patal after eating ?	375 (83.75)	25 (16.25)	400 (100.00)
8. Do you stand Upto see your owner passing through your street ?	400 (100.00)	— —	400 (100.00)

All heads informed that they visited the house of owners frequently for any kind of work. They informed that owners also visited when they needed our work. They informed that they did not sit on cot before the owner. But 75 per cent heads informed that they could sit on chouki or bench or on land before the owner. 75 per cent head reported that they went in the courtyard of owner to participate in the feast. Only 18.75 per cent informed that they could sit in the same line at the time of feast. While majority of them informed that they sat in a separate line, 83.75 per cent heads reported that they had to carry their patal after the feast. All heads informed that they stood Upto see owners at their house.

Table 10.3 : Opinion of Heads of Dalits Households on Sitting Arrangement on Public Place

Opinion	*Response*		
	Yes	*No*	*Total*
1. Do you sit with your owner or other Hindus in train ?	400 (100.00)	—	400 (100.00)
2. Do you sit with your owner or other Hindus in Bus ?	400 (100.00)	—	400 (100.00)
3. Do you sit with other Hindus on tea shop ?	400 (100.00)	—	400 (100.00)
4. Do you sit with other Hindus in hotel?	400 (100.00)	—	400 (100.00)
5. Do you sit with other Hindus on a place of public meeting ?	400 (100.00)	—	400 (100.00)
6. Do you stay with other Hindus in a waiting hall or Bus stand ?	400 (100.00)	—	400 (100.00)
7. Do you see drama, dance, etc. with other Hindus ?	400 (100.00)	—	400 (100.00)
8. Do you visit fair with other Hindus ?	400 (100.00)	—	400 (100.00)
9. Do you sell articles in fair ?	400 (100.00)	—	400 (100.00)
10. Do other Hindus purchase articles from your shop ?	400 (100.00)	—	400 (100.00)

According to responses obtained from the heads of the Dalits households, untouchability does not exist on public places. Nowadays they travel in bus and train with other Hindus. They stay in bus stand, dharmasala, waiting hall, etc. with other Hindus. They take tea with other Hindus from the same shop. They visit in hostel with other Hindus. They attend social meeting with Hindus. They visit fair together. They see drama, dance, cinema, etc. together. They purchase article from the same shop. They establish shop in fair from where all Hindus purchase articles.

Table 10.4 : Opinion of Heads of Dalits Households on Acceptance of Food, Water and Other Articles at Public Place

Opinion	*Response*		
	Yes	*No*	*Total*
1. Do your community members work as servant in hotel ?	400 (100.00)	—	400 (100.00)
2. Does your community member cook food in hotel ?	400 (100.00)	—	400 (100.00)
3. Does your community member clean utensils in hotel ?	400 (100.00)	—	400 (100.00)
4. Do they serve food in hotel ?	400 (100.00)	—	400 (100.00)
5. Do they serve water in hotel ?	400 (100.00)	—	400 (100.00)
6. Do member of your community open tea shop ?	400 (100.00)	—	400 (100.00)
7. Do other Hindus take tea there ?	400 (100.00)	—	400 (100.00)
8. Do member of your community do job like feriwala for selling articles, vegetables, and other items of daily use ?	400 (100.00)	—	400 (100.00)
9. Do all Hindus purchase articles from them ?	400 (100.00)	—	400 (100.00)

According to heads of the Dalits households untouchability on food, water and articles does not exist at places like tea shop, betel shop, tobacco shop, hotel, etc. On these shops, Dalits work as servant or they own their own shop. these shops are visited by all Hindus. Dalit cook tea, breakfast and food. They serve food and water. They clean utensils. Everybody gladly accepts food and water from them. Some Dalits work as feriwala. They sell toffee, sweat, vegetables, cosmetics, etc. Other Hindus purchase these articles from those Dalits feriwala. Not only this, other Hindus purchase fish, meat of goat, chicken, eggs etc. from the houses of Dalits. In sell and purchase of these items, no untouchability exists.

Nowadays, Dalits keep cows and buffaloes for milk. Other Hindus purchase milk, ghee, etc, from the houses of Dalits. Thus, modern occupation has brought change in the social status of Dalits.

Educational Status of Dalit Today

Literature available reveals about taboo on education of untouchables in pre-independent India. But after independence things have changed. The government of free India made educations compulsory for all citizens of the country beyond any caste, creed, religion etc., primary schools were established in the entire country. Now almost all villages have primary schools. There were middle and high schools within the boundary of 2 to 5 kms. Education Upto school has been made free. Dalit students receive books, dress and scholarship. Now in primary school, they get midday food as well. During 50 years of independence, the educational status of Dalits has gone under modifications. Now Dalits are literate. Some of them are well educated and well placed in government jobs. Seeing their casteman well placed in jobs, each Dalit heads have become conscious towards the education of children. Previously, they used their boys and girls as means of income. They did not send their children to school. They sent them in the house of Zamindars to work as *Charwaha* or *Charwahin.* For their work, they got food, cloths and some quantity of paddy agreed on annual basis. This was also fact that they did not own their homestead land. Zamindars used to provide them a piece of land for house. As they did not own their land for house, they were known as the men of the Zamindars. Zamindars did not like to see the children of untouchables reading in school. Another reason was that they received very low wages. They were kept always thinking that their survival was dependent upon Zamindars. How could they think of education in this situation.

After independence, parcha of homestead land was given to Dalits by the government, untouchability, slavery, bonded labour etc were banned. Any type of ban given by Zamindars was made free and non-recoverable. Protective legislations were made prohibitive and rehabilitative steps were taken up. As a result Dalits became independent to select occupation other than attached or bonded labour. They were given assistance to construct houses, to purchase cows, buffaloes, goats, pigs, etc. They were given loan to establish small shops or do work like Feriwala. They were given cycle and rickshaw. Now, they are not under the clutches of the landowners. They send their children to school. During fifty years of independence, majority of them are literate. Some are matriculate, graduate and even post graduate. Some have received technical education. Some of them have received government job like school teacher, Gram Sewak, Karamchari, Barababu, police, clerk, etc.

Table 10.5 : Educational Status of the Heads of the Dalit Households

Educational Status	*Number*	*Percentage*
Illiterate	100	25.00
Just literate	100	25.00
Upto lower	50	12.50
Upto primary	50	12.50
Upto middle	30	7.50
Upto high school	30	7.50
Upto Intermediate	20	5.00
Upto graduate	10	2.50
Upto post-graduate	5	1.25
Upto Technical	5	1.25
Total	400	100.00

The above table reveals that 25.00 per cent Dalits heads were illiterate and 25.00 per cent were just literate. They knew to write their signature and count bundles of crops. 12.50 per cent heads possessed education Upto primary level. 7.5 per cent had education Upto high school. 5.00 per cent heads were intermediate. 2.5 per cent heads were graduates. 1.25 per cent heads were post-graduates and 1.25 per cent heads possessed technical education.

Table 10.6 : Opinion of Heads on the Education of Children

Level of Education of Children	*Number*	*Percentage*
Upto primary	100	25.00
Upto middle	100	25.00
Upto high school	70	17.00
Upto intermediate	50	12.50
Upto graduate	30	7.50
Upto post-graduate	20	5.00
Technical	30	7.50
Total	400	100.00

To above table reveals that 25.00 per cent heads wanted to provide educational to their children Upto primary school. They were very poor but wanted to see their children well literate. 25.00 per cent heads provided education to their children Upto middle school. 17.50 per cent heads wanted to see their children educated up to high school. 12.50 per cent heads wanted to provide education to their children Upto intermediate level. 7.50 per cent heads wanted to educate their children Upto graduate level. 5.00 per cent heads wanted to educate their children Upto post-graduate level. 7.50 per cent heads wanted to educate their children Upto technical level like Medical, Engineering, Law, etc.

Table 10.7 : Opinion of Heads on the Job of their Sons

Jobs of Boys	*Number*	*Percentage*
Choukidar	70	17.50
Police	60	15.00
Chaprasi	70	17.50
Clerk	70	17.50
Teacher	80	20.00
B.D.O.	25	6.25
Professor	10	2.50
Doctor	5	1.25
Engineer	5	1.25
Lawyer	5	1.25
Total	400	100.00

The Table 10.6 reveals clearly about the awareness of heads towards the education of their children.

The Table 10.7 reveals that 17.50 per cent heads wanted to see their sons as Choukidar. 15.00 per cent heads wanted to see their sons as police. 17.50 per cent heads wanted to see their sons as Chaprasi in any government institution. 17.50 per cent heads wanted to see their sons as clerk in office. 20.00 per cent heads desired to see their sons as school teachers. 6.25 per cent heads liked to make their sons as B.D.O. 2.50 per cent heads liked to see their sons as professor. 1.25 per cent heads wanted to see their sons as doctor. Similar was the percentage for engineer and lawyer.

Table 10.8 : Opinion of Heads on the Job of Daughters

Job of Daughters	*Number*	*Percentage*
Chaprasi	100	25.00
Nurse	80	20.00
Clerk	60	15.00
Teacher	50	12.50
Police	30	7.50
B.D.O.	15	3.75
Professor	15	3.75
Doctor	20	5.00
Engineer	15	3.75
Lawyer	15	3.75
Total	400	100.00

The above table reveals the opinion of heads on the job of daughters. 25.00 per cent heads wanted to see their daughters as Chaprasi. 20.00 per cent heads wanted to see them as nurse. 15.00 per cent heads wanted to see their girls as clerk. 12.50 per cent heads desired to see their girls as teacher. 7.50 per cent heads wanted to see their girls as police. 3.75 per cent heads liked to make their girls as B.D.O. Regarding the professor, the percentage of heads was same 3.76. 5.00 per cent heads liked to see their daughters as doctor. 3.75 per cent heads wanted to see their girls as engineer and lawyer each.

Table 10.9 : Opinion of Heads in the Efforts for Education of Children

Efforts for Education of Children	*Number*	*Percentage*
Send children school regularly	400	100.00
Have private teacher for tuition	200	50.00
Saving money to spend after matriculation	200	50.00
Send the child in the Dera of relatives for the study	100	25.00

All heads informed that they sent their children to school regularly. 50 per cent heads informed that they had employed private teacher for tuition. 50.00 per cent heads informed that they were saving money to spend on the education of children after matriculation. 25.00 per cent heads had decided to send the children in the Dera of relatives for higher education.

Education Status of Dalit Today

Literature available reveals that Dalits did not enjoy economic rights during pre-independence India. They did not own right to have property of any kind. They were treated like property. Like property they were sold and mortgaged. But after independence the economic status of Dalits has undergone considerable change. Now, they own their own homestead land. Majority of them are owners of same cultivable land. Now their houses are made up of Pucca or made up of soil thatched with tiles. They own cattle like oxen, cow, buffaloes, goats, etc. Now they are not only agriculture labour. Some of them do cultivation on their own lands. Some are sharecroppers. Some have established small shops. Some are rickshaw owners, some are cart owners and some are Tanga owners. Some are tempo owners also. Some work as driver of tractor, truck, or bus. Some earn as coolie while some are engaged in the work of Feriwala. Some are in jobs. Thus, now they are not dependent upon the landowners for their livelihoods and survival.

Table 10.10 : Distribution of Heads According to the Type if House

Type of House	*Number*	*Percentage*
Madeup of soil thatched with straw	150	37.50
Madeup of soil thatched with tiles	150	37.50
Madeup of brick thatched with tiles	50	12.50
Madeup of brick and cement with lintel	50	12.50
Total	400	100.00

37.50 per cent heads informed that they owned house made up of soil thatched with straw. 37.50 per cent heads informed that they owned house thatched made up of soil but thatched with tiles. 12.50 per cent heads informed that they owned house made up of brick thatched with tiles. 12.50 per cent head informed that their houses were made up of brick and cement, and thatched with lintel.

Table : 10.11 : Distribution of Heads According to the Type of Land

Type of Land	*Number*	*Percentage*
Only homestead	100	25.00
Homestead + Bariland	100	25.00
Homestead + Bariland + Cultivable land	200	50.00
Total	400	100.00

25.00 per cent heads owned only homestead land, while another 25.00 per cent heads informed that they owned homestead land and Bariland. 50.00 per cent heads informed that they owned cultivable land also along with homestead land and Bari land.

The Table 10.12 reveals that 25.00 per cent heads owned only homestead land and thus, they were put under landless category. Again another 25.00 per cent heads belonged to near landless category. They owned land upto one acre. 21.25 per cent heads owned land upto 2.5 acres. 18.75 per cent heads owned land upto 5 acres. 5.00 per cent heads owned land upto 7.5 acres. 3.75 per cent heads possessed land upto 10 acre and only 1.25 per cent heads possessed land above 10 acres.

Table 10.12 : Distribution of Heads According to Acreage of Land

Acreage of Land	*Number*	*Percentage*
Landless	100	25.00
Upto 1 Acre	100	25.00
1 Acre to 2.5 Acre	85	21.25
2.5 Acre to 5 Acre	75	18.75
5 Acre to 7.5 Acre	20	5.00
7.5 Acre to 10 Acre	15	3.75
Above 10 Acre	5	1.25
Total	400	100.00

Table 10.13 : Distribution of Heads According to Primary Occupation

Primary Occupation	*Number*	*Percentage*
Labour	120	30.00
Bataidar	60	15.00
Manidar	20	5.00
Own farming	30	7.50
Small shop / business	30	7.50
Rickshaw-wala	40	10.00
Tanga-wala	10	2.50
Gariwala / Thelawala	5	1.25
Feriwala	25	6.25
Coolie	20	5.00
Service	30	7.50
Contractor	10	2.50
Total	400	100.00

The Table 10.13 reveals the distribution of heads according to primary occupations. The table indicates that the primary occupation of 30 per cent heads was labour. These families subsisted as agriculture labour, brick kiln labour, contract labour, etc. The primary occupation of 15.00 per cent heads was Bataidar. They took land from the owners for doing sharecropping. They had to pay half share to the owners of the land. The primary occupation of 5.00 per cent heads was Manidari. They leased in land from the owners on the basis of agreement either in case or in kind. They generally cultivated cash crops like vegetables, tobacco, potato, etc. The primary occupation of 7.50 per cent heads was own farming. They owned sufficient cultivable land for doing own farming. Again 7.50 per cent heads were engaged in small shop or business. 10.00 per cent heads primary occupation was Rickshaw driving. 2.50 per cent heads were

Table 10.14 : Distribution of Heads According to Secondary Occupation

Secondary Occupation	*Number*	*Percentage*
Seasonal labour	100	25.00
Harvesting	100	25.00
Cow/Buffalo rearing	40	10.00
Goat rearing	30	7.50
Pig rearing	20	5.00
Chicks rearing	10	2.50
Sharecropping	20	5.00
Tractor driving	15	3.75
Rickshaw driving	10	2.50
Bullock cart driving	5	1.25
Vegetable selling	20	5.00
Toy selling	18	4.50
Cloth selling	10	2.50
Quota shop	2	0.50
Total	400	100.00

engaged on Tanga driving and 1.25 per cent head primary occupation was bullock cart driving and Thela driving. The primary occupation of 6.25 per cent heads was Feriwala. The primary occupation of 5.00 per cent heads was as coolie. The primary occupation of 7.50 per cent heads was service in private or government jobs. The primary occupation of 2.50 per cent heads was as contractor of soil cutting, land tilling, house construction, etc.

The Table 10.14 shows that secondary occupation of 25.00 per cent heads was seasonal labour again secondary occupation of 25.00 per cent heads was harvesting. The secondary occupation of 10.00 per cent heads was cow/buffalo rearing. The secondary occupation of 7.50 per cent heads was goat rearing. The secondary occupation of 5.00 per cent heads was pig rearing and 2.50 per cent heads was chicks rearing. The secondary occupation 5.00 per cent heads was share cropping and 3.75 per cent heads was tractor driving. The secondary occupation of 2.50 per cent heads was rickshaw driving and 1.25 per cent heads was cart driving. The primary occupation of 1.25 per cent heads was vegetable selling and 2.50 per cent head was toy selling. The secondary occupation of 2.50 per cent heads was cloth selling and 0.50 per cent heads was Quota Shop.

Table 10.15 : Distribution of Heads by Annual Income

Annual Income (in Rs.)	*Number*	*Percentage*
Below 5000	60	15.00
5,000 – 10,000	80	20.00
10,000 – 15,000	90	22.50
15,000 – 20,000	70	17.50
20,000 – 25,000	40	10.00
25,000 – 30,000	35	8.75
Above 30,000	25	6.25
Total	400	100.00

The above table reveals the annual income of heads of Dalit households. The table shows that the annual income of 15.00 per cent heads was below Rs. 5,000 to Rs. 10,000. The annual income of 22.50 to 17.50 per cent heads was between Rs. 15,000 to Rs. 20,000. The annual income of 10,000 per cent heads was in between Rs. 20,000 to Rs. 25,000. The annual income of 8.75 per cent heads was in between Rs. 25,000 to Rs. 35,000 and the annual income of 6.25 per cent heads was above Rs. 30,000.

Table 10.16 : Distribution of Heads by Annual Expenditure

Annual Expenditure in Rs.	*Number*	*Percentage*
Below 5000	80	20.00
5,000 – 10,000	90	22.50
10,000 – 15,000	100	25.00
15,000 – 20,000	80	20.00
20,000 – 25,000	25	6.25
25,000 – 30,000	15	3.75
Above 30,000	10	2.50
Total	400	100.00

The annual expenditure of 20.00 per cent head was below Rs. 5,000. The annual expenditure of 22.50 per cent head was 5,000 to 10,000. The annual expenditure of 25.00 per cent head was 10,000 to 15,000. The annual expenditure of 20.00 per cent head was 15,000 to 20,000. The annual expenditure of 6.25 per cent head was seen between Rs. 20,000 to 25,000. The annual expenditure of 3.75 per cent head was between 25,000 to 30,000 and the annual expenditure of 2.50 per cent head was above 30,000.

Table 10.17 : The Distribution of Heads by Saving

Saving	*Number*	*Percentage*
Yes	125	31.25
No	175	68.75
Total	400	100.00

31.25 per cent heads reported about saving during the year when survey was conducted. 68.75 per cent heads reported that they were under debt.

Table 10.18 : Distribution of Heads by Amount of Loan

Amount of loan in Rs.	*Number*	*Percentage*
Below 1000	10	5.71
1,000 – 5,000	50	28.57
5,000 – 10,000	40	22.85
10,000 – 15,000	30	17.14
15,000 – 20,000	25	14.28
Above 20,000	20	11.42
Total	175	99.97

5.71 per cent head were under debt of Rs. less than 1,000. 28.57 per cent heads had taken loan in between Rs.1,000 to 5,000. 22.85 per cent

Table 10.19 : Distribution of Heads by Purchase from Loan

Purpose of Loan	Number	Percentage
To purchase Cow/Buffalo	15	8.37
To purchase Goats	20	11.42
To purchase Chicks	10	5.71
To purchase Pigs	15	8.57
To purchase Cycle	15	8.57
To purchase Thela/cart	10	5.71
To purchase Tanga	10	5.71
To establish Shop	20	11.42
To establish Gumati	15	8.57
To erect house	10	5.71
To meet expenditure on marriage	15	11.42
To meet expenditure on treatment	10	5.71
To meet expenditure on higher education	8	4.57
To fight case	2	1.14
Total	175	100.80

heads had taken loan in between Rs. 5,000 to 10,000. 17.14 per cent heads had taken loan in between Rs. 10,000. 14.28 per cent heads had taken loan in between Rs.15,000 to 20,000. 11.42 per cent heads had taken loan of above Rs.20,000.

The Table 10.19 reveals the purpose for which heads of the households had taken loan. The table reveals that 8.57 per cent heads had taken loan to purchase cow/buffalo. 11.42 per cent heads had taken loan to purchase goats. The percentages of households for taking loan to purchase chicks and pigs were 5.71 and 8.57 respective. 8.75, 5.71 and 5.71 per cent heads had taken loan to purchase cycle, Thela and Tanga respectively. 11.42, 8.57 and 5.71 per cent heads had taken loan to establish shop, Gumati and to create houses respectively. 11.42, 5.71 and 4.57 per cent heads had taken loan for children respectively. 1.14 per cent heads had taken loan to fight cases.

Table 10.20 : Distribution of Heads by Source of Loan

Source of Loan	*Number*	*Percentage*
Government Bank	100	57.14
Friend	10	5.71
Relative	15	8.57
Mahajan	50	28.57
Total	175	99.99

The above table reveals sources from where heads had taken loan. The table shows that 57.14 per cent heads had taken loan from government bank. 5.71 per cent heads had taken loan from friend and 8.57 per cent heads had taken loan from the relatives. 28.57 per cent heads had from the Mahajan.

The Table 10.21 show that 57.14 per cent heads had taken loan at 14% per year rate of interest. 5.71 per cent heads had taken loan at 36 per cent per annum rate of interest. 8.57 per cent heads had taken loan at 48 per cent annual rate of interest. 20.00 per cent heads had taken loan at 60 per cent per year rate of interest. 8.57 per cent heads able to get interest free loan.

Table 10.21 : Distribution of Heads by Rate of Interest

Rate of Interest : Annual	*Number*	*Percentage*
14%	100	57.14
36%	10	5.71
48%	15	8.57
60%	35	20.00
No Interest	15	8.57
Total	175	99.99

Religious Status of Dalit Today

Literature available on pre-independence period reveals that Dalits did not enjoy any status religiously. They were untouchable, so they were not allowed to enter into temple, to visit pilgrimage centres, to perform religious rites and rituals. Undoubtedly, there were some Dalit saints or sadhus and even great religious preachers. In independent India secular constitution was adopted. Untouchability was banned. Attempts were made to integrate Dalits with Hindu community. Abolishment of untouchability enhance the religious status of Dalits. Their visit to temple, pilgrim centre

Table 10.22 : Opinion of Heads on Visit to Religious Places

Opinion on Visit to Religious Place	*Response*		
	Yes	*No*	*Total*
1. Do you visit freely in the temples of the village ?	400 (100.00)	—	400 (100.00)
2. Do you visit in the temples of neighbouring village ?	400 (100.00)	—	400 (100.00)
3. Do you visit the pilgrim centres of local level ?	400 (100.00)	—	400 (100.00)
4. Do you visit pilgrim centres of regional level ?	400 (100.00)	—	400 (100.00)
5. Do you visit pilgrim centres of national and international level situated in the country ?	400 (100.00)	—	400 (100.00)

and religious places is welcomed. They participate in great Hindu festivals and worship. They take part in religious rites and rituals. Now let us see the empirical reality of religious status of Dalits.

The Table 10.22 reveals clearly that Dalits today are free to offer worship in temples situated anywhere in the country. The table indicates that they freely visit in temples of villages, neighbouring village, pilgrim centres of local, regional, national and international importance.

Table 10.23 : Opinion of Heads on Bathing Rituals in Different Ponds, Wells and Rivers

Opinion on Bathing Rituals	*Response*		
	Yes	*No*	*Total*
1. Do you perform the ritual of bathing is scared well of the village ?	400 (100.00)	—	400 (100.00)
2. Do you bath freely in scared pond of the village ?	400 (100.00)	—	400 (100.00)
3. Do you bath freely in sacred rivers situated nearby the village ?	400 (100.00)	—	400 (100.00)
4. Do you perform the ritual of bathing at various places of Tirtha ?	400 (100.00)	—	400 (100.00)

The above table reveals that no untouchability exists today in the performance of bathing rituals in sacred wells, ponds, rivers or confluence of rivers. Dalits perform the ritual of bathing on all these sacred wells, ponds and rivers.

The Table 10.24 reveals that Dalits participate fully in the great village level festivals like Ramnawami, Janamasthmi, Durga Puja, Deepawali, Holi, etc.

Table 10.24 : Opinion of Heads on Participation in Religious Festival

Participation in Religious Festival		*Response*	
	Yes	*No*	*Total*
Do you participate in village level Ramnawami festival ?	400 (100.00)	—	400 (100.00)
Do you participate in village level Janamasthmi festival ?	400 (100.00)	—	400 (100.00)
Do you participate in village level Durga Puja festival ?	400 (100.00)	—	400 (100.00)
Do you participate in village level Deepawali festival ?	400 (100.00)	—	400 (100.00)
Do you participate in village level Holi festival ?	400 (100.00)	—	400 (100.00)

Table 10.25 : Opinion of Heads on Participation in Great Religious Rituals

Participation in Village Level Religious Rituals		*Response*	
	Yes	*No*	*Total*
Great Akhanda	400 (100.00)	—	400 (100.00)
Great Hawana	400 (100.00)	—	400 (100.00)
Great Shrota	400 (100.00)	—	400 (100.00)
Great Yagya	400 (100.00)	—	400 (100.00)

The above table reveals that Dalits today participate in great village level religious ritual like Akhanda, Hawana, Shrota and Yagya.

Table 10.26 : Opinion of Head on Visit to Sacred Specialist

Visit to Scared Specialist	*Response*		
	Yes	*No*	*Total*
Do you visit to Brahman Priest ?	400 (100.00)	—	400 (100.00)
Does Brahman Priest visit to your house to tell Satyanarayan Katha ?	400 (100.00)	—	400 (100.00)
Does the village Priest visit your house to perform marriage rituals ?	400 (100.00)	—	400 (100.00)
Does the Priest visit to perform Kuldevata Puja ?	400 (100.00)	—	400 (100.00)

The above table reveals clearly that today the village priest visit in the house of Dalits to perform Satyanarayan Swami Katha, to perform marriage rituals and to perform Kuldevata Puja.

Table 10.27 : Opinion of Heads on Acceptance of Prasad

Opinion on Acceptance of Prasad	*Response*		
	Yes	*No*	*Total*
Does the Priest accept the Prasad of your house ?	400 (100.00)	—	400 (100.00)
Do the High caste Hindus accept Prasad of your house ?	400 (100.00)	—	400 (100.00)
Do the backward caste Hindus accept Prasad of your house ?	400 (100.00)	—	400 (100.00)
Do other Dalit castes accept Prasad of your house ?	400 (100.00)	—	400 (100.00)

The above table reveals clearly that the Prasad of Dalits houses is accepted now by all castes residing in a village community.

Table 10.28 : Opinion of Heads on Acceptance of Items of Worship

Acceptance of Items of Worship		*Response*	
	Yes	*No*	*Total*
Do the sun-fried rice of your house are accepted for worship ?	400 (100.00)	—	400 (100.00)
Do Dhup and Agarbatti of your house are accepted for worship ?	400 (100.00)	—	400 (100.00)
Do milk, ghee and curd of your house are accepted for worship ?	400 (100.00)	—	400 (100.00)
Do fruits of your houses are accepted for worship ?	400 (100.00)	—	400 (100.00)
Do Tikari and Thenkua, Kasar etc, of your house are accepted for worship ?	400 (100.00)	—	400 (100.00)

The above table reveals clearly that items of worship like sun-fried rice, milk, ghee, curd, fruits, thenkua, tikari, kasar, etc., are accepted from the house of Dalits at the time of great village level religious rituals.

Political Status of Dalit Today

Literature available reveals that Dalits did not enjoy any political status in pre-independence era. However, they had their own caste panchayat. But at village level or inter-village level politics they did not enjoy any status. The decision of majority was binding on them. They had to accept the decision otherwise they were subjected to exploitation and oppression. But after independence, the political status of Dalits have gone under change. Now Dalits have got voting right. They can fight election and cast vote in election of Gram Panchayat, member of legislative assembly and member of Parliament. In the election of MLA and MP, reservation of seats for scheduled castes have been made. From these reserved seats only Dalits candidates of different political parties fight elections. In this way, they have become part and parcel of modern political system.

Table 10.29 : Opinion of Heads on Participation in Election

Participation in Election	*Response*		
	Yes	*No*	*Total*
Do you cast vote in election of Gram Panchayat ?	400 (100.00)	—	400 (100.00)
Do you cast your vote in election of MLA ?	400 (100.00)	—	400 (100.00)
Do you cast your vote in election of MP ?	400 (100.00)	—	400 (100.00)
Do your community member flight election of Gram Panchayat ?	400 (100.00)	—	400 (100.00)
Do your community member fight election of MLA ?	400 (100.00)	—	400 (100.00)
Do your community member fight election of MP ?	400 (100.00)	—	400 (100.00)

The above table reveals that the Dalits of today participate in modern political system. They cast their vote and fight election as well. Sometimes, when situation at both becomes worst and criminals capture the booth, then they do not resist. They do not want to fight with the criminals. But when situation is normal, they participate fully in the election system.

Table 10.30 : Distribution of Heads According to Supporter of Political Parties

Supporter of Political Parties	*Number*	*percentage*
Janata Dal	50	12.50
Congress	25	6.25
C.P.I.	30	7.50
B.J.P.	95	23.75
C.P.I. (ML)	60	15.00
I.P.F.	70	17.00
Samajwadi Party	10	2.50
Samata Party	60	15.00
Total	400	100.00

12.50 per cent head were supporter of Janata Dal and 6.25 per cent heads were supporter of Congress Party. 7.50 per cent heads were supporter of C.P.I., 23.75 per cent head, were supporter of B.J.P., 15.00 per cent head were supporter of CPI (ML), 17.50 per cent head were supporter of IPF, 2.50 per cent heads were supporter of Samajwadi party and 15.00 per cent heads were supporter of Samata Party.

Table 10.31 : Distribution of Heads According to Membership of Political Parties

Membership of Political Parties	*Number*	*Percentage*
Janata Dal	35	8.75
Congress	25	6.25
C.P.I.	40	10.00
B.J.P.	80	20.00
C.P.I. (ML)	40	10.00
I.P.F.	60	15.00
Samajwadi Party	10	2.50
Samata Party	10	2.50
No membering	100	25.00
Total	400	100.00

The heads of Dalit households were not only supporter of political parties but they were members of political parties. 8.75 per cent heads

Table 10.32 : Awareness of Heads about Regional Political Parties

Regional Political Parties	*Yes*	*No*	*Total*
Asam Gana Sangram Parishad	200 (50.00)	200 (50.00)	400 (100.00)
Manila Congress	100 (25.00)	300 (75.00)	400 (100.00)
Shiva Sena	300 (75.00)	100 (25.00)	400 (100.00)
Telagu Desam	200 (50.00)	200 (50.00)	400 (100.00)

were member of Janata Dal and 6.25 per cent heads were member of Congress. 10 per cent heads were member of CPI and CPI (ML) each. 15.00 per cent heads were member of B.J.P., 2.50 per cent heads were member of Samata Party and Samajwadi Party respectively. 25.00 per cent heads did not possess membership of any political parties.

The Table 10.32 reveals that 50.00 per cent heads knew about Asam Gana Sangram Parishad. 25.00 per cent heads knew about Manila Congress, 75.00 per cent heads knew about Shiva Sena and 50.00 per cent heads knew about Telagu Desam.

Table 10.33 : Awareness of Heads About Symbols of National Political Parties

Symbols of National Political Parties	*Yes*	*No*	*Total*
B.J.P.	400 (100.00)	—	400 (100.00)
Janata Dal	400 (100.00)	—	400 (100.00)
Congress I	400 (100.00)	—	400 (100.00)
C.P.I.	400 (100.00)	—	400 (100.00)
C.P.I. (ML)	400 (100.00)	—	400 (100.00)
I.P.F.	400 (100.00)	—	400 (100.00)
Samata Party	400 (100.00)	—	400 (100.00)
Samajwadi Party	400 (100.00)	—	400 (100.00)

11

SOCIAL AREA OF DALITS EXPLOITATION OF DARBHANGA

In the social area, three sections of Dalits are worst victims of exploitation. These are children, women and aged. Now let us see as to how these sections of Dalits are exploited in the society.

Exploitation of Dalit Children

Children are the future of a society. They are the backbone of a nation. The development of a society or nation cannot be imagined without the development of children. Today every country is trying its best to develop the children. Various developmental inputs are being given to bring qualitative and quantitative change in the life of children. But our country is such where one finds clear cut disparity between 'haves' and 'havenots'. Dalits have to suffer from various kinds of disabilities since centuries. They belong to the category of 'havenots'. After independence attempts have been made to develop the Dalits. But success in this regards is not very promising. Undoubtedly status of Dalits has changed and some have emerged as rich. But still many Dalits belong to the category of poor. They are struggling hard to maintain their survival. Being very poor, they are struggling hard to maintain their existence. These families are not in a position to take advantages of various types of development schemes meant for the development of children. They send their children to school. Their children are admitted in school. But due to household work or to earn little wages from the children, non-attendance and drop-outs can be seen. Thus, those children remain uneducated. They are kept busy in various works during the time when they are supposed to attend school situated in the village. For them bread because more important than education.

The exploitation of children starts from the family, poor parents from early childhood keep them engaged in household chores. The girl has to cooperate her mother. She has to clean stoves, courtyards, room, etc. She has to bring water from *chapakal*, well or pond. She has to assist in cooking. She has to serve food to the parents and other small children. She has to look after the kids. She also assists parents in agriculture fields. During late childhood, she has to assist in domestic as well as agricultural works. She has to look after cattle. The poor parents give them to landowners for works, when they are unable to provide foods and cloths to them. In the house of land unable to provide food and cloths to them. In the house of landowners, they are engaged as domestic servants. They have to clean cattleshed and prepare Goitha (fuel from cowdung). The landowner provides her food, cloths and some wages at annual basis. Sometimes the parents of girls take loan from the landowner and give the girl to work in the house of landowner. To get more wages, the girl is compelled to work in the house of more than one landowners. Sometimes, parents also assist them in completion of works. Thus, being poor, the girls are not kept engaged only in family works, but they are compelled to work for little wages to supplement the income of the family.

Not only girls but boys of poor Dalit families have to meet the same fate. During early childhood, they are kept engaged in family work. They clean cattle and look after cattle. They bring fuel and fodder from the barren fields. They graze cattle during late childhood, he has to assist parents in work either at home or in agriculture fields. Thus, they are kept engaged in work. When parents find that their boys can earn wages, they send the boy to work in house of landowners for wages. Sometimes, the parents take heavy loan from the landowner and give the boy to the landowner to work as *charwaha* (herd boy). As *charwaha* he has to stay in the house of landowner 24 hours. He receives food, cloth and some payment on annual basis.

So long as loan is not paid back, he has to work as *charwaha* in the house of the Malik. Thus, Dalit children are exploited as charwaha or charwahin by the landowners. During peak agricultural season they are exploited as child labour. During harvesting period, they are engaged in harvesting by the parents because they get one bundle out of every 12 bundles of harvested crops.

Exploitation as Charwaha

When a Dalit boys is kept to look after the cattle in the house of landowners, he is termed as charwaha. The parents of the boy take loan from the landowner and give the boy as charwaha in the house of landowner. According to the term and conditions related to charwaha, the boy has to work as charwaha for one complete year. The initiation starts in the month of Asarh and continuous till full moon day of the month of Jyestha. The landowner agrees to pay food, clothes and some fixed quantity of paddy. The landowner also provides loan to the parents of charwaha either in cash or in kind. The owner provide loan at interest or without interest or sometimes partly on interest and partly interest free. In the month of Jyestha, when our national calendar is expected to end, the parents of charwaha pay all loan taken from the owner and the owner pays wages agreed at the time of initiation. When owner and the parents of charwaha pay the dues of each other, the terms and conditions of charwaha meet an end. Now the owner becomes free to employ another boy as charwaha and a charwaha also becomes free to works anywhere. But when the parents of a charwaha become unable to pay the loan till full moon day of Jyestha, the charwaha has to work for the next year. He may request to his owner to increase the wages. Sometimes, the parents of a charwaha incur a fresh loan and the child has to work as charwaha in the house of the same owner. Sometimes the parents take loan from another owner and pays the loan to previous owner and the child has to work as charwaha in the house of another owner. To get a charwaha has become difficult because no parents want to send their boys as charwaha in the house of owners, unless their survival comes under threat. Therefore, a competition among the owners has been to have a charwaha. In this situation the parents of charwaha can bargain the amount of loan, rate of interest and the wages. Those who agree to pay more loan interest free and more wages become successful in getting a charwaha.

A charwaha has to work from dawn to dusk. He gets up early in the morning. He puts the cattle out of shed. He provides fodder to them. Then he cleans the shed. He takes the oxen to the field for plonghing. He prepares Goita from cowdung and carries breakfast and food to labourers at the field. He has to take cows and buffaloes in the grazing ground. He has to bring the cattle from grazing ground and field to shed in the evening. He has to provide fodder to them. At night he has to sleep in the shed to look after them. He has to assist the owner in watching the fields and thrashing floor. He has to assist in household work. It will be the fitness of the thing to present a case study to show the exploitations of a Dalit boy as charwaha.

S.R. (13 yrs) was found working as a charwaha in the house of a landowner. From early childhood he was very playful. He was admitted to school but could not complete the study of primary school. During peak agricultural season he was kept engaged in household work. So he did not attend school properly. In school he felt nervousness among the teachers and children belonging to other castes of the village. He did not feel well in school. Gradually he left the school for ever. Thus, he remained illiterate for ever. Now he does not know to put signature, nor to read letters or count the bundle of paddy crops. His parents never encouraged him to attend school. When he was seven years old, his father was in need of money. He could be able to obtain loan from a landowner but he had to give S.R., his son as charwaha in the house of landowner. The landowner had given him a loan of Rs. 500 only.

Exploitation as Domestic Servant

Some well-to-do Dalit families and service holder Dalit families employ the children of poor Dalit families of the same community as domestic servants. These families send their own children to school but need some helping hand to assist in household works and agricultural works. So, they employ domestic servant. They give some loan in cash or in kind to the parents of the child. The loan may be interest free or partly interest free and partly on interest. Some service holders belonging to Dalits exploit the children of Dalits as domestic servant. Besides, some government officials residing in local areas exploit the children of Dalits as servant. The parents of the children get loan from the owner or saheb and send their children to perform household work. These servants get breakfast, food and very little payment may be Rs. 20 or 25 per month. Some may get upto Rs. 50. The domestic servants working in the house of owners belonging to the same villages or neighbouring villages or in neighbouring towns get chance to meet their parents. But domestic servants who are brought to distant towns for work do not get such chance. They come in the village with their masters occasionally.

The children of the owners receive regards in the family. They go to school. But the children of poor Dalit families work in their house as servants. They do not receive regards and proper treatment. They are not given proper to eat and good clothes to wear. When they commit some mistakes in performing works, they are abused and physically tortured. Sometimes they are beaten badly. When they leave the work, they do not get any payment. Their parents are compelled to repay loan immediately. If they do not pay the loan back, their cows, calf, goats, etc are brought and compensated against the amount by loan. Under such exploitative and oppressive situations the children of poor Dalit families have to work as domestic servants for very little payment. They remain illiterate and miss their childhood for virtually getting nothing or for very little payment.

Exploitation as Hotel Servants

The children of poor Dalit families are exploited as hotel servants. The hotel owners of neighbouring areas approach the Dalit families of local areas and try to get their children to work as hotel servants. As hotel servants, they get Rs. 30 to 50 per month depending upon the age and satisfactory performance of work in the hotels. The hotel owners agree to pay breakfast, food, cloths besides monthly payment. They also give some advance loan which they compensate in the monthly payment. They assure to provide good treatment to the children working as servant. In order to get servant, the hotel owners give various temptations to the parents of the children. They agree to pay more payment than the landowners of the village. When parents of poor children come under the trap of the hotel owners, they provide their children to work as servants. The children are brought to the place of hotel. As hotel servants, they have to perform work round the day and night. When there are no customers, they get chance to take rest, but even during these homes, they have to clean the floor and benches, table etc. They have to clean utensil of cooking and serving food and breakfast. They have to clean oven and put coal in the oven. They have to bring vegetable in the hotel from the local market. They have to cut vegetable for cooking. They have to clean rice for cooking. They have to prepare flour for making bread. They have to serve breakfast, tea, meals and water to customers.

They have to clean the plates left after eating. They have to fetch water. The initiation of S.R. as charwaha took place in the month of Asarh and he had to work as charwaha till the month of Jyestha which is the last month of our national calendar year. The owner has agreed to pay breakfast, both-end meal and clothes on festive occasions or whenever needed when S.R. joined his work. He took the cattle to grazing field after breakfast. He had to come early morning to clean the shed. He had to graze cattle for the whole day. He had to bring cattle in the shed during evening. After evening meal he returned to his house. The owner had agreed to pay 5 maunds of paddy after completion of year. The year came to end but his parents could not pay the loan plus interest back. This compelled S.R. to work for another year as charwaha. But the next year, too, his parents could not pay the entire loan back. In this way, he remained working as charwaha in the house of the owner. At the time of survey he was working as charwaha at the same payment which was initially agreed. He was bound to work till the loan plus interest was not paid back.

Exploitation as Charwaha

The girls of Dalit are exploited as charwahin. The term charwahin is opposite gender of the term charwaha. The process of initiation and the terms and conditions of works are similar to a charwaha. A charwahin has to come early in the morning to clean cattle shed, to make goitha from the dung and to provide fodder to the cattle before going to work. Then, she gets breakfast. After breakfast she is expected to assist the females in household chores. She has to bring the cattle to grazing ground. She comes for midday meal and again goes in the grazing ground. She returns with cattle in the evening. She provides some fodder to the cattle. She takes the meal of night and then returns her house. In this way, she has to work for the whole year. Besides food and clothes, she gets a fixed annual payment in kind may be 3 maunds, 5 maunds, 7 maunds, 9 maunds etc., depending upon the age of the charwahin and quality of work. The parents of charwahin enjoy loan facilities in the house of landowners. They can take loan anytime from the house of owner either in cash or in kind. The mother of charwahin also assist her in the performance of works. Like a charwaha, a charwahin has to work round the year in the house of the same owner. She cannot work for the another owner at the same time.

Exploitation as Farm Servant

Dalit boys belonging to 10 to 18 years of age are exploited as farm servant. As farm servant they have to work more than a charwaha. So, they enjoy more loan facilities and more payment. Their payment varies from 15 maunds to 25 maunds in a year. They have to remain at the house of owner for 24 hours. They have to perform work from dawn to dusk. At night, they have to stay at the shed of the owner. On very specific occasion, they are allowed to go home to meet their family members. But they are free to meet their family members for some time whenever they need.

These servants have to get up early in the morning. They have to clean shed and prepare Goitha for fuel. Then they have to provide fodder to the cattle. They have to drive oxen to the place of work and to bring them back in the evening. After breakfast, they have to bring fodder and fuel from the fields, from grazing grounds and garden. After mid day meal, they have to bring cattle to the grazing ground. They bring cattle in the shed before sunset. They have to provide fodder at night. After meal, they have to sleep in the cattle shed to look after them at night. They have to assist in household work like bringing fuel, boiling paddy, drying paddy, cleaning other grains, bringing wheat to mill for flour, bringing boiled and dry paddy at mill for rice. They have to take breakfast and fetch water from chapakal, wells, ponds, etc. For cooking, drinking and washing utensils. As they have to work with water, the fingers get rotten. But even then they are compelled to perform work. They are brought before the doctor for treatment, but amount spent on treatment is adjusted against the payment. They have to clean the clothes of owners and rub oil on their body during night.

Exploitation as Khatal Servants

Nowadays, the business of Khatal is gaining popularity. Not only Yadavas castes, who are traditionally equipped in the business of Khatal, but other castes occupying high status in society are also engaged in this business. Khatal is a feature of urban areas, but nowadays, Khatal are being established in the rural areas, too. With increasing number of Khatals, the demand for Khatal servants is also increasing. In order to get a Khatal servant, the Khatal owners approach the poor Dalit families to get their children to work as Khatal servants. Boys above 10 year are most preferred for the Khatal servants.

The Khatal owners who generally belong to the same village or of neighbouring villages give some cash as advance to the parents of the servants. The amount of advance varies from Rs. 500 to 1000. They agree to compensate the amount advanced against the payment of the servant. Khatal servants get payment of Rs. 50 to 100 per month depending upon the age and dedication towards works. They get breakfast, both end meal and clothes on festive occasion.

As Khatal servants, they have to get up early in the morning. They have to clean dung from the Khatal. They have to assist the owner in milking the cows or buffaloes. They have to supply milk in the house of customers in the morning. Then they are to provide fodder to cows/buffaloes. After breakfast, they have to prepare Goitha from the dung. Goithas are used for fuel. In midday, they wash cow/buffalo. They bring fodder. In the evening, they have to assist the owner in milking. Again they have to supply milk in the houses of customers after that they have to clean the shed and provide fodder. At night, they remain in the Khatal to look after the cattle.

Besides the works related to Khatal the Khatal servants have to perform the household work of the Khatal owners during rest hours. They have to fetch water for cooking and washing purposes. They have to bring vegetables from the local market. They have to bring materials from the shops. They remain at the disposal of the owners twentyfour hours. Thus, they remain actively engaged.

The payment of the Khatal servants present very poor picture. They receive very little payment in comparison to work. They remain twenty-four hours at the disposal of masters but they get only Rs. 50 to 100 in cash and breakfast, food and clothes. Whatever they get, that is their saving. Because they do not have to spend on food and clothes.

Exploitation as Garage Servants

The owners of the Garage need some servants to perform various types of work. For Garage servants children between 10 to 20 years are preferred because they work actively on less wages. The Garage owners of neighbouring towns approach the parents of poor families residing in the village. The want to attract them by various temptations. They promise to pay more wages. They make promise to make regular payment and provide some leave in a month. They also agree to pay some advance already given. They also agree to give breakfast, food and cloths. The payment of these Garage owners are not proper. They receive Rs. 30 to 50 per month.

As Garage servants, they have to works during day as well as in night. They get chance to take rest when there is no work. When there is work, they have to work for the whole night in the light of electricity or generators. These servants are seen working wearing very dirty clothes. It is because they have to clean and repair the parts of machine which run by diesel or petrol. The diesel, petrol, mobile etc. make their cloths very dirty. Again, they have to open parts of machine, bus, truck, tractor of laying on the ground, therefore, their clothes remain always dirty. They work, eat and sleep wearing the same dirty dresses. In spite of hard work, they are abused and sometimes, beaten by the owners for negligence of duty. They receive proper treatment till the loan given is adjusted against their payment. When payment exceeds, the behaviour of owner is also changed. When the payment of servants become more than Rs. 500 to 1000, the owner of Garage starts behaving in more oppressive manner. The servant is not given proper food and breakfast. When they go to take rest, they are abused in the name of negligence of duty. When they demand oil to message on the body and soap to clean body and cloths, they are again abused. They ultimately get but have to bear abusive words. When father or guardian of the servants come to meet them, they receive good treatment. They get good breakfast and food. Some payment of monthly salary is made to them. They receive complaints of the negligence of duty.

When the boys make complaints, their guardians or parents do not believe them. They rather ask the boy to perform duty sincerely. Sometimes, they are beaten mercilessly so that they may leave the Garage for ever. When they leave the Garage, they are lodged complaints in thana of run away stealing money and motor parts from the Garage. The police reach their village and oppress the child and parents in various ways.

Exploitation as Khalasi

The children of poor family are exploited as Khalasi of bus, minibus, truck, matador, etc. As Khalasi the boys are preferred because they perform their duties very efficiently on little payment. They receive little payment but perform more than a young and adult. They wash the bus, truck with water. They help the driver and conductors. They have to work at back and call of driver and conductors. They receive breakfast, food and cloths. They have to perform day and night duty on the bus or truck. Sometimes, they are misbehaved, abused and beaten for negligence of duty. As payment, they receive Rs. 30 to 40 per month. For this little payment and food, they have to perform duty day and night.

Exploitation as Contract Labour

Sometimes, the parents of the children taken contract to finish a work like cutting soil, uprooting seedling, transplanting a particular field etc. On a fixed payment. They want to complete the work as early as possible. To complete the work at earliest, they utilize the services of the children. Harvestation is also done on contract basis. Here also the service of children is utilized for selfish purposes.

In the work of house construction, road construction, dam construction, digging ponds, making embankment, the services of the children is utilized by the contractors.

Exploitation by Factory Owners

The owners of the small factory utilizes the services of children for the work in factories : In the local factories of carpet, blanket, shoes, loaf, sugar etc. the service of Dalit children are utilized. For very little payment, these children have to perform work for the benefit of the factory owners. In rice mills, flour mills, chura mills, the services of children are utilized for the performance of work.

EXPLOITATION OF DALIT WOMAN

Men, women, agreed and children are the features of population of a community. About the exploitation of children we have seen previous pages. Here, let us see the exploitation of Dalit women. Dalit women are exploited in the following ways :

Exploitation as Gobarkadanee

A woman employed for cleaning shed is called Gobarkadanee in local term. In villages owners of land have own cattle to plough field and to get milk. In order to clean the dung from the shed and to prepare Goitha from the dung, they employ a Dalit woman, who is known as Gobarkadanee. As the name indicates, the main function of a Gobarkadanee is to clean the dung from cattle shed and to clean the ope4n space where cattle are kept. Her another important function is to prepare goitha from the dung for the purpose of cooking. In villages, animal dung provide fuel for cooking in 90 per cent cases. For this work, she gets annual payment which depend upon the number of cattle available in the house of owners. She gets half maund of paddy per cattle per annum. Besides, she gets cooked food at every weak end and on festive and ceremonial occasions, she gets food for entire family member. She also gets clothes on the occasion of Holi and Durgapuja.

A Gobarkadanee is employed for a period of one year which begins in the first month of our national calendar year and ends in the last month of our national calendar year, i.e., from Asharh month to Jyestha month. At the time of initiation the owner and the women concerned have to accept the terms and conditions of each other. A Gobarkadanee demands money as loan which may be interest free or partly interest free and partly on existing rate of interest. She demands annual wages. On loan and annual wages a Gobarkadanee tries to bargain her labour with the owners. When she find that owner is not ready to pay loan and wages which she demands she may reduce her demands and accepts the term and conditions of the owner.

According to the condition of owner, she has to perform work regularly. On absent and illness, she has to send her family members on works. She has to prepare Goitha and put them in the store. She has to show sincerity in work. She has to replay the loan before the full moon day of Jyestha month. If she does not reply the loan, she has to continue her work for the next year also.

In order to earn more wages, a Gobarkadanee accepts work in the house of two or three owners. From each house, she takes some advance as loan. She has to adjust the loan against her annual payment. For very little wages, she has to perform work round the year. When she does not come to work and does not send any family member to work, she is treated as absent. For absence, she has to work in the next day or her payment is not given for the number of days of absence. If she does not perform her work properly, she is scolded and abused, too. If she accepts the terms and conditions of Gobarkadanee, she has to perform work even during pregnancy period.

Exploitation as Charwahin

Generally for a charwahin, girls are preferred, but if a girl is not available then a women is employed as charwahin. As charwahin her duty is to bring the cattle back to shed during evening. Sometimes the same women performs the work as charwahin who performs the work as Gobarkadanee. Generally cattle are bring for grazing after 10 o'clock. By that time the concerned women accomplishes her household and other types of work.

A woman charwahin is paid annually on the basis of number of cattle. Generally she receives half maunds of paddy or other grains per cattle per annum. In order to earn more and more wages, she accepts the work of charwahin in the house of four five owners.

As charwahin she gets mid-day meal from the house of any one owner, she gets this meal turn-wise. She gets one sari from the house of each owner. She gets meal of entire family member on festive and ceremonial occasion. She gets old clothes whenever she demands for her children. As a charwahin she enjoys loan facilities in the house of the owner.

A charwahin is not expected to be absent because her absence creates trouble in the house of different owners. Therefore, on illness or visit to another places, she has to send her family members. If family members are not available, she seeks pardon from the owner and inform them in advance about her absence. In this situation, the owners make some other arrangement.

As charwahin she is not expected only to bring cattle in grazing field and to bring them back in the shed during evening, but she has to see that they may not graze the crops of any one else. She has also to see that they may not fight among themselves. Because fighting creates breaking of feet, horns and abortion of expectant cow/buffaloes. On these issues, she has to remain careful. If she shows negligence in such duties she is thrown out and no payment is made.

Exploitation as Dai

Dalit woman belonging to Chamar caste are exploited as Dai. As Dai, she has to assist the expectant woman and nursing mother. Traditionally these woman are expert in delivery. So, they are employed Dai in the house of owners where there are expectant mothers. She massages M.Oil in the body of expectant woman and cleans her clothes. She goes with her in the hospital. After delivery she stays with her in the hospital and in the house when the mother and child come back home. If she is not brought in the hospital, it is duty of the dai to get the deliverly done successfully by traditional method. In this case, she stays with the women and children in delivery room. She cleans the delivery room on the 6th day of birth of the child. She cleans the clothes of mother and the child. She massages oil in the body of mother and the child. She stays with mother so long as the women requires her assistance. She remains day and night in the house of the owner. For this work, she receives breakfast, food and 1 k.g. grain per day. She also gets clothes, rice and rupees in Neg on the day of *chhathi*. She also receives ornaments of gold and silver in rare cases.

Exploitation as Maid Servant

In the house of the big landowners, there is always need of a woman assistant to perform domestic works other than cooking. These works include oven making, grainery making, cleaning paddy for chura and making rice, boiling paddy for preparing rice, drying boiled paddy, cleaning wheat, washing of rape seed, washing and drying them for making oil. Similarly cleaning, washing and drying gram, masure, mung, etc. for making pulses. Such works exist in the house of owners round the year. For the performance of such works a Dalit woman is kept as a maid servant. She actually works as an assistant of malkin in cleaning, washing, drying and storing grains for household consumption and selling.

These Dalit woman as maid servant receive annual payment which varies from 10 to 15 maunds of grain per annum. Besides, they get breakfast and mid-day meal. They do not get the meal of night. They receive sari on the occasion of Holi and Durgapuja and food on all festive and ceremonial occasions.

They enjoy loan facility in the house of the owner. They can get loan any time in cash and in kind from the house of the owner in off season, they also enjoy leave facilities for few days.

Nowaday, some officials residing in local urban areas and in rural areas are employing a Dalit woman as maidservant for bringing water, cleaning, cooking and eating utensils and for cooking as well. These officials do not believe in untouchability and they want to get cooked food because they do not have time to cook. So, they have Dalit woman as maid servant to cook the food. They pay Rs. 30 to 50 per month. They also give midday meal and sometimes clothes.

Exploitation of Kamin or Baniharin

The wife of a kamia or Banihar, is known as kamin or Baniharin. A kamia works as an attached labour in the house of a landowner for a period of one year. After one year, he may work in the house of the same owner or he may change his owner. The initiation begins in the month of Asarh and continues for a period of one complete year with a kamia, his wife is also attached with the owner. The Kamia works like Kalwaha, Kudalwaha, Kabaria (one who uproots the paddy seedling, etc. The Kamin does the work of Ropani transplanter of paddy seedlings. This work is done specially by the Dalit women who are expert is the art of transplanting. In harvesting and threshing the work of kamia and kamin both are required and both perform these works efficiently. For these works they receive payment but their payment is less in comparison to males.

Exploitation as Ropani

Women folk belonging to Dalit community are exploited by landowners as Ropani. This particular work is done especially by women. During transplantation period, more and more number of Ropani is required. Women who are widow, divorced or whose husbands go to work in towns and cities, cannot get work as Baniharin. They can get work only as Ropani and Katniharin. A Ropani transplants paddy seedlings and a Kataniharin harvests the crops. A woman without husband attached herself with the owner of the land to perform the work related to transplantation, weeding and harvesting. For transplantation, they receive one part payment less than the wages of a male labour. Sometimes, they receive half the payment of a male labour. It is because they come late on the work and work less than male labours, for harvesting they get equally. But again for thrashing, they receive less than male labours. The pregnant and expectant woman go to earn wages, but they receive less than their male counterparts.

Exploitation as Reja

The term Reja is given for those women who work as contract labour on truck, in road construction, in house constructions, in dam construction, digging ponds, cutting soil of upland field, in brick kiln. The services of Dalit women are utilized in these works, but they receive less payment for the same hours of work. Now let us see as to how Rejas are exploited.

(a) *Exploitation of Reja as Truck Labour* : For construction work, soil, cement, rod, chips, etc. are carried by trucks from one place to another. For loading and unloading the truck, labours etc. are required. The truck owners and drivers utilize the services of Dalit women for these works. Sometimes, few male labours also remain with women labours. These women are called Reja. The work of these Reja is to load the truck with soil, sand, brick, cement and to unload them at the place where materials are required. For these works, the truck owners pay some fixed wages at the rate of per truck. The rat of loading is more than the rate of unloading. For loading a small truck with soil, it is Rs. 20 per truck and for unloading, it is Rs. 15 per truck. For loading bricks, it is Rs. 20 per truck and for unloading it is Rs. 15 per truck. They receiving the same rate for loading and unloading. Each truck has five to seven Rejas to do the works of loading and unloading. The truck owners and even truck drivers exploit and oppress the Rejas in different ways.

(b) *Exploitation of Reja in Road Construction* : Rejas are exploited in road construction, first of all the level of the proposed road is made up in comparison to the existing level of soil. For this purpose the soil is cut and the level of road is made up. The work of soil cutting and filling up the road is done by Reja. The male labours of the group cut soil and put the soil in a bamboo made basket called Deli. The Reja put the load of soil on there head and throws it on the road. For cutting the soil, the rate is fixed or agreed between the contractors and the leader of the Reja group. The contractors pay much reduced rate than the finalize rate in the proposal. For these works, the Rejas remain at the site of work day and night by erecting temporary huts or tents. They fill the road with soil and then make levelling. Each Reja group has to complete this work for a particular distance already demarcated by some symbols. Men, women and children stay there for completing work. They are supposed to get payment on each day but they have to request many time to finalise their payment. Sometimes, they have to go back without receiving final payment because contractors promise them to pay after availability of fund.

(c) *Exploitation of Reja in Bridge Construction* : Bridge is an important aspect related to road and railwyline. In railway line and roads brides have to be constructed either on rivers or places where there are Nala, Baha, etc. At the site of bridge construction, Rejas have to stay with the leader of the group. They erect a temporary hut with bricks as straw or stay simply in a tent with plastics, old cloths and tripal. They keep their little children and belongings in that temporary hut and start working for the construction of bridge. They perform work of soil cutting for the foundation of the bridge. They work in the erection of walls and perspiration of lintel. They cut soil and put them at the ends of the bridge to connect it with the road. The poor Rejas work efficiently without caring for their children, husbands and even their health but they do not receive proper payment. They receive less wages than the prescribed minimum wages. Sometimes, they are exploited sexually by the contractors or his watch men for the little amount. Sometimes some Rejas have to please the officials who visit to provide supervision works. They are given meals, local made liquor, some amount of costly dresses and are exploited in the manner the contractors like. The leader of the group also help the contractor or his men to do such act.

(d) Exploitation of Reja in Dam Construction : Sometimes dams are constructed to make hydro electric and dig canals or to provide irrigation to the villages. Again in these types of work the services of Reja is utilized. The Rajas visit place of site with their group leader and erect temporary hut. They start working to construct dam. The construction work continues for years. The work is stopped during rainy season. Rejas work day and night they do not take care for their children, husbands and even their health. They work for the constructions. But for sincere work, they do not get their payment properly and regularly. They get less than a male labour. They get much less than the prescribed minimum wages. They have to request again and again to receive payment. During rainy season they have to come back without taking final payment. They have to visit again the next year to accomplish work. Some of them are exploited sexually too.

(e) Exploitation of Reja in Digging Ponds : To provide irrigation facility the government is trying to dig the old ponds and to make its embankment. In these works the services of Rejas are utilized by the contractors. The mode of exploitation and oppression of Rejas is same like other works done by the contractors.

(f) Exploitation of Rejas in Making Pucca Embankment : Sometimes, the bank of rivers, big pokhara or canal have to be made pucca to provide protection against the flood. Banks are made pucca by bricks, sand and cement. For this purpose stone bricks are used. In carrying bricks, cement, sand, chips, etc. services of Rejas are utilized. Again in construction works, the services of Reja is required. The entire work is

completed by the Rejas but their payment presents exploitative and oppressive pictures. They get less than the male counterparts. They get much less than the prescribed minimum wages. They have to request again and again to receive payment. Sometimes, they are behaved in such a way that they have to come back without receiving final payments. Sometimes, some of them also fall victim of sexual exploitation for petty amount of loan.

(g) Exploitation of Reja in Brick-kiln : For preparation of kucha bricks making khewals of kucha bricks, putting kucha bricks in kiln, pulling out the pucca bricks, loading and unloading the pucca bricks, the services of Rejas is required. The owner of the bricks kiln visits the village of the Rejas, give them some advance for meeting expenditure on travel. He also agrees to pay the existing wages for different types of work in kiln. The owners provide them brick to erect temporary house to stay. He provides them rice, pulse, vegetables and other things. The loan is adjusted against the payment. These things are provided by the owners at high rate so that more and more amount could be made from the articles and grain supplied. They receive different payment for different works like preparing bricks, preparing Bhatta, preparing khewals, loading and unloading trucks or tractors, arranging bricks according to quality. For day and night work, their payment reveals exploitative picture.

Exploitation as Migrant Labour

Woman with their husband or relatives migrate in other neighbouring states like U.P., Haryana and Punjab to work in farm. They receive more wages than existing in their areas. But they have to perform 16 hours work including day and night. The owner of the farm gives them rice, wheat, milk, curd, matha and have facility of electricity. In the light of electricity they work even during night and in early morning. For performing work 16 to 18 hours in a day, they receive Rs. 30 to 40 per day. They are given mutha and curd free. They also get milk for tea free of cost. When the owner of the farm becomes pleased they pay the fare of returning home. But the labours have to invest money from his own pocked for going there. As soon as they go there, they become bonded labour of the farm owners. They cannot stop working without the permission of the owner. They cannot sleep without the permission of the owner. For any thing they become dependent upon the owner. They cannot go back without the permission of the owner. Intoxicants are given to male and female labours to get more and more work. If cash or kind is given in advance, that is adjusted against the payment of wages. Thus, as migrant labour their per day wages is certainly more, they have to work generally 16 to 18 hours in a day and night.

EXPLOITATION OF AGED

Individuals above 60 years of age are called aged. The exploitation of aged Dalits start in the family. Those aged who are able to work, receive work in the house of landowners, but those aged who are unable to work due to physical defect become dependent upon the sons. Dalits are poor, so they do not meet the liability of aged in proper manner. Such aged are seen moving door to door of owners for food. Physically able aged receive work but at reduced wages than an adult labourer. Aged are exploited by the landowners for the following purposes :

Exploitation of Aged as Halwaha

Like adults aged male Dalits are exploited as Halwaha. The man who ploughs the field with oxen is called Halwaha in local term. Physically fit aged Dalit are experienced in the work of Halwaha. So they get work easily as Halwahas during the season of cultivation of Vadai, Agahani and Rabi crops. Another reason is that the owner has to pay less wags to an aged labour. So some owners like aged Dalit as Halwaha. They work slowly but steadily. They work not less than an adult labour. The young Halwaha learns the art of ploughing from the aged Halwaha. When an aged Halwaha approaches the owner of land for work, the owner agrees to provide him work but at a reduced rate of wage than the adult Halwaha. Unemployment, age and lack of alternative arrangement compels the aged Halwaha to accept work at reduced rate.

As Halwaha, he is expected to perform work not less than 8 hours in a day. Some times he has to work for 9 to 10 hours to plough a particular field because the owner asks him to complete the work of ploughing of that plot the same day. For this extra work, he gets some food and intoxication materials like Biri, Tobacco and local made liquor.

Exploitation of Aged as Kudalwaha

The man who works with the kudal (spade) to make the boundary of the paddy field for the storage of water is called kudalwaha. A kudalwaha is employed only during the season of transplantation of paddy. For transplantation of paddy, the boundary of the field is repaired every year so that water can remain in the field. The paddy field requires 7 inch water every time for the proper growth. Every labour is not expert in this art. So, she aged labours also get work as kudalwaha. They perform work slowly undoubtedly, but they perform work in better manner. The unfortunate thing is that they get payment less than the adult because they are aged. They accept to work at reduced wages because they need work and wages to survive. The economic condition of their sons are not so strong enough to provide them food and clothes without work. That is why they accept work gladly even at reduced wages.

Exploitation of Aged as Kamia

Dalit aged are also exploited as kamia, they take some loan from the owner and accept to perform work round the year. He has to work as Halwaha, Kudalwaha, Kabria, Katnihar and other kinds as work in the house of owner. He can work for another owner. He is given leave to perform his own work but at any circumstances he is not expected to work for other owner without the permission of the own owner. Along with a kamia his wife called kamin has to work for the owner. Kamia gets leads wages than the other casual or free labours. But he gets work round the year and a small piece of land for the cultivation. The yield of that plot goes in the house of the kamia. The aged kamia does not get piece of land.

They get midday meal and reduced wages. As kamia, they have to work at beck and call of the owner. They are not expected to be absent on work. On festive and ceremonial occasion, they receive food for the entire members. They can avail loan facilities in the house of the owner.

Exploitation of Aged as Barahil

Barahil is a highest status given to a labour by the owner. Most faithful, obedient and confidential labour attains the status of Barahil. The aged remains attached with the owner since years. So they became Barahil of the owner. A Barahil is made incharge of the agricultural work. The owner gives him power to take his own decision related to agriculture. The other laboured have to obey the Barahil because whatever he says is taken as the voice of the owner. On critical issues, the Barahil approaches the owner and communicates the decision of the owner to the other labours. As Barahil, he has to stay at the house of the owner even during night. He moves plot to plot to see the crops. He is available at the time of ploughing, uprouting seedlings, transplanting seedlings, harvesting paddy, sowing Rabi crops, and harvesting Rabi crops. He also remains in charge of the thrashing field. He has also to see the cattle. He has also to assist in some domestic work. Thus, he becomes the special man of the milk. The Barahil gets food round the year and cloths on all festive occasions. Besides, he gets a plot to do cultivation. The yield of the plot goes in the house of the Barahil. Thus, a Barahil becomes more or less a family member of the owners house.

Exploitation as Watchman of House

The big landowners require a watchman of the house. The watchman looks after the house and the cattle during night. The aged Dalits are exploited for this purpose. That get food, clothes round the year but have to stay at the Darwaja of the owner at night. They are given a bed, a torch, a blanket and a lantern for this purpose. Sometimes, they employed as watchman to see the materials at the time of construction of a new house. But for this work only those Dalit aged are employed who are physically well and who have been loyal and faithful of the owner during adulthood.

Exploitations as Watchman of the Agriculture Field

Some agricultural fields require watching during day and night. During day, birds, squirrels damages the sugarcane fields, potato fields and other vegetable cultivated fields which require constant watching. For this purpose, the aged are suited. The aged get breakfast, food till they work as watchman. They are also given cloths and blanket during winter season. They are given torch or lantern at night. For doing the work obediently they also get a little share in the yield.

Exploitation as Watchman of the Thrashing Field

The aged Dalits are also exploited at the thrashing field. The harvest paddy bundles are deposited in a thrashing field. The thrashing fields are watched during night. A temporary hut is erected in which the each man of the thrashing field reside at night. Not all labours get opportunity to work as watchman of the thrashing field. Only very faithful man is engaged as watchman of the thrashing field. In thrashing field, the thrashing of the harvesting crops is done. Grains are then brought in the house to store. If a faithful watchman is not available, the thrashing field is watched by the owner himself. For watching the thrashing field during night the watchman gets food at night and some wages too.

Exploitation as Watchman of the Diesel/Electric Pump

For the purpose of looking after the electric pump/diesel machine, a watchman is required. For this work a physically fit Dalit aged is employed. The aged Dalit becomes ready to such type of work. They go to the site of pumping set after taking the meal at night. The meal of night is given by the owner. Besides meal, some nominal payment in kind is also made. They have to guard the pumping set. The owner of the pump also makes visit at the site time to time.

Exploitation as Watchman of the Pond

In the area under study, the ponds play economic role. In the ponds fishes are reared and Singhara fruits are grown. When fruits become ready and fishes become big in size, the watching of ponds become a must. The owner does not have sufficient time to watch the pond during day and night. So they employ a watchman for certain periods. For the watchman of ponds, the services of aged Dalit are exploited for watching the ponds, they receive food during night and some nominal wages in the form of Singhara fruits and fishes.

Exploitation as Watchman of the Garden

The area under study have gardens of mango, guava, jamun, etc. The owners of the garden require watchman to look after the fruits of mangoes, guava, lichi, jamun, etc. To watch these gardens, the services of aged Dalits is utilized. the gardens have to be watched during day and night. The watchman of the garden receives food during day and some nominal shares in the fruits.

Exploitation as Seasonal Labour

During the time of transplantation and harvesting the services of aged Dalits are taken as seasonal labour. They get work during these seasons in the houses of owners. But for the same kind of work an aged labourer receives less payment than the adult labour.

Exploitation as Contract Labour

The services of aged Dalits are also utilized as contract labour. They perform work on contract basis under the supervision of a contractor. They perform, work contract labour in road construction, house construction, bridge construction, dam construction, embankment etc. As contract labour, they are exploited by the contractor in getting proper payment. They receive less wages even by governments contractors.

Exploitation of Aged Women

The exploitation of aged women have been covered under the topic of exploitation of women. Therefore, it is not necessary to discusses here in detail about the exploitation of aged women. The only differences is that aged women receive less wages than the adult woman for the same kind of work.

12

ECONOMIC AREA OF DALIT EXPLOITATION OF DARBHANGA

In economic areas, the exploitation of Dalits take place as different types of labour such as agricultural labour, contract labour, brick kiln labour. In each category, there are child labour, woman labour and aged labour. The mode of payment of different types of labour is different. Again Dalits are exploited as migrated labour. They are exploited by the contractors, brick kiln owner, factory owners, etc. They are exploited by middlemen, businessman, block officials, bank officials etc. In economic area, one thing is clear, that they are exploited by different agencies on less wages. Now, let us see as to how Dalits are exploited economically.

EXPLOITATION OF DALITS AS AGRICULTURE LABOUR

Dalits constitute the major work force for the agriculture. As majority of them are still landless or near landless, therefore, wage is the only means for their survival. Nowadays, they get work in non-agriculture setting, but they get employment more in agriculture. The landowners employ Dalits for agriculture and domestic work. For agriculture, various types of labour are exploited.

Exploitation of Dalits as Kamia or Jana or Banihar

A Dalit labour who accepts the terms and conditions of a landowner to work in house for a period of one complete year, i.e., round the year is called as Kamia, or Jana or Banihar. As soon as a Dalit labour accepts the terms and conditions of a Kamia, he is known as the special labour of a particular landowner. He is also known as attached labour because he attaches himself with a particular landowner for a period of one year.

The initiation takes place in the month of Asarh. In the month of Asarh a landowner approaches a Dalit labour to be his Kamia. If the labour agrees, he puts his certain conditions before the owner. The conditions are related to the amount of loan as advance and the rate of interest. At the time of initiation, he demands loan up to Rs. 1000/- and 5 Maunds of rice or wheat. He demands loan interest-free. The landowner does not agree to pay the same amount as demands by the labour. He agrees to pay Rs. 500

Table 12.1 : Wages of a Kamia for Different Kinds of Work

Types of Works	*Wages*	*Other Facilities*	
		Plot of Land	*Loan*
Ploughing	1.5 kg. rice and breakfast	10 kathas of land	Loan up to Rs. 100.00
Spading	— do —	for one complete	any time. Same amount interest
Uprooting seeding	— do —	year, seed, fertile	free and same
Carrying bundle of seedling	— do —	year, irrigation	on interest
Harvesting	one bundles out of every 16 bundles	are provided	
Thrashing		on festive and ceremony	Loan
Winnowing	1.5 kg. rice or wheat + breakfast	occasional food	kind in also
Carrying grain in the house	— do —	is given to entire family members clothes	given only
For any other work	— do —	are also given on festive and	time a kamia
For performing work at night on some occa-ssion.	only meal of the night and some drink.	ceremonial occa-ssions.	needs.

or 600. He agrees to pay partly amount on interest free and partly amount on existing rate of interest in the village. Kamia is given a plot of land to cultivate for a year. At the time of initiation, the labour has liberty to select the plot. When a labour as Kamia came first day on work, he received good food to eat. Now a Kamia has to work at back and call of the landowner. He has to come everyday on work. If there is no work in the house of the landowner, he is not supposed to earn wages by working in the house of another landowner. He can work for his family or in the plot which he receives from the landowner.

Along with a Kamia his wife also becomes attached with a particular landowner. She also has to perform work round the year for the landowner. She performs work like transplanting, weeding, thrashing, etc. The main purpose behind exploiting a labour as Kamia is to get assured labour round the year and at cheap rate. A Kamia receives less wages than a free labour or casual labour. But he avails food facilities in the house of the Mahajan but he does not receive wages equal to a free labour. This is because he gets loan interest free and a plot of land to cultivate, the seed, fertilizer, irrigation to that plot are provided by the landowner. But the owner adjusts them in the wages of the Kamia.

Table 12.2 : The Wages of a Kamia (Wife of Kamia)

Type of Work	*Wages*
Transplanting	1 kg. wheat or rice + breakfast
Weeding	do
Thrashing	do
Carrying grains in the house	do
Harvesting	One bundle out of every 16 bundles. The bundle has to be carried to the Thrashing field.

A kamia can change his owner in next Asarh month or he may continue in the house of same owner. But he has to clear all previous dues and loans before the last day of Jyestha month. The owner also makes the payment of wage of Kamia clear before this date. Sometimes a Kamia takes, loan from another owner to repay the loan of previous owner. Now he becomes Kamia of another owner. But there are many kamia who thinks that the terms and conditions related to kamia are same in the house of different owners. Therefore, it is useless to change the owner. They take fresh loan and continues as Kamia in the house of same owner. In course of field work, same Kamias appeared who had worked in the house of same landowner for the whole life. Now they were working as watchman of agricultural fields, garden, thrashing field, pump etc. in the house of the same owner. But when relation between the owner and the Kamia became bitter due to same reason in that case the owner and the Kamia both want change.

Bonded Labour

This is another kind of attached labour in which a landowner takes heavy loan from the landowner and enters into an agreement to work for the owner so long as the loan plus interest is not paid back. A kamia is bonded labour for one year. But for bonded labour the time is not fixed. If a labourer repays loan in one year, he becomes free but, if he does not repay the loan he has to work for another year. He takes such a heavy loan on interest that he goes on working for years but he does not become able to pay the loan plus interest back. An attached labour or a kamia can bargain at the time of initiation, but for a bonded labour bargaining capacity is comletely surrendered. He does not put any condition for the rate of interest and for the payment. He has to accept the rate of interest and the mode of payment as given by the owner. There is no fixed time for the initiation of bonded labour. If a labourer became unable to receive heavy loan from any other sources, he approaches an owner and takes loan on all the conditions of bonded labour. As bonded labour, he looses freedom of every kind. He cannot move freely for going anywhere, he has to seek permission of the owner. He cannot work for another Mahajan. He cannot remain absent without the prior information of the owner. During peak agricultural reason, he is not given any kind of leave. He has to come everyday to enquiry about the work. When there is no work, he is engaged in some minor work for which he receives no payment but receives only breakfast or food. Sometime, he is sent is the house of gotia bhai or relatives to work on some nominal wages. But he cannot refuse to go there or to work. He has to work as the owner desires.

The loan is given at high rate of interest and the wages is given less, so he remains always under bondage. Sometimes he has to work for the whole life, but the entire loan is not paid. When he becomes physically unable to work, he requests his owner to make him free so that he can die freely, if he dies suddenly, his sons have to repay the loan. If he escape, from the village, his property is captured by the owner. Sometimes, his sons have to repay the loan by taking loan from yet another owner.

A bonded labour has to perform work even during night. He has to watch the cattle shed, house, crops, thrashing fields, pumps etc. of the owner at night. For this work he receives only meal of night and extra payment is made for the work.

Table 12.3 : Type of Work and Payment of a Bonded Labour

Types of Work	*Payment*	*5 other facilities*
Ploughing	1 kg paddy/wheat + break fast and midday meal.	5 Katthas of land
Spading	— do —	for cultivation loan up to 3000.00
Uprooting the paddy seedling	— do —	at any time the labourer needs.
Carrying and spreading the bundles of seed-ling in the field.	— do —	
Thrashing	— do —	
Winnowing	— do —	
Carrying grain in the house	— do —	
For any work at Night	only meal of night	
Harvesting	one out of every 16 bundles for cutting and carrying up to khalihan.	

Table 12.4 : Type of Work and Mode of Payment of Wife of Bonded Labour

Type of Work	*Mode of Payment*
Transplanting	1 kg paddy or wheat + breakfast and midday meal
Weeding	— do —
Thrashing	— do —
Winnowing	— do —
Carrying grains to the house	— do —
Harvesting	one bundle out of 16 bundles.

Along with a bonded labour, his wife also becomes bonded labour of the owner. She also performs work in the house and in the field of the owner. She also receives the same wages.

Daily Wage Labour or Casual Labour

A daily wage labour is free labour. He is not attached to a particular owner. He can work in the house of any owners for wages. He gets more wages than kamia and bonded labour or any kind of work a daily labour receives the same payment. Children, women, aged and adults are employed as daily wage labour. Sometimes, a daily labour works in the house of the same owner till the work is not completed. He receives wages according to the number of days. If a particular work is finished in the house of a particular owner, he receives the payment of all days and from next days he seeks work in the house of another owner.

Table 12.5 : Mode of Payment of Daily Wage Labour

Type of Work	*Payment of Daily Wage Labour*			
	Child Labour	*Woman Labour*	*Aged Labour*	*Adult Labour*
1	*2*	*3*	*4*	*5*
1. Phoughing	Do not do	Do not do	1.5 kg rice/ wheat + breakfast	2 kg rice/ wheat + breakfast
2. Spading	Do not do	Do not do	— do —	— do —
3. Uprooting the paddy seedling	1.5 kg rice/wheat + breakfast	1.5 kg rice/ wheat + breakfast	— do —	— do —
4. Making bundles, carrying and spreading the seedlings in the field.	— do —	— do —	— do —	
5. Transplanting	do not do	— do —	Do not do	Do not do
6. Weeding	1.5 kg rice/ wheat + breakfast	— do —	1.5 kg rice/ wheat + breakfast	1.5 kg rice/ wheat

1	*2*	*3*	*4*	*5*
7. Harvesting	1 bundle out of 16 bundles	1 bundle in every 16 bundles	1 bundle in every 16 bundles	1 bundle in every 16 bundles
8. Thrashing	1.5 kg rice/ wheat + breakfast	1.5 kg wheat /rice + breakfast	1.5 kg wheat/ rice + breakfast	2 kg wheat/ rice + breakfast
9. Winnowing	— do —	— do —	— do —	— do —
10. Carrying grains in house	— do —	— do —	— do —	— do —
11. Manuring	— do —	— do —	— do —	— do —
12. For any other work	— do —	— do —	— do —	— do —

Agricultural Contract Labour

In agriculture, some works are performed by contract labour as uprooting seedlings, transplanting, harvesting, thrashing, winnowing, etc. The payment of contract labour for various agricultural works are as follows :

Table 12.6 : Mode of Payment of Agricultural Contract Labour

Type of Work	*Mode of Payment*
1. Ploughing per bigha	For 1 thrice time Rs. 60 with oxen and Rs. 40 without oxen.
2. Spading per bigha	Rs. 15
3. Uprooting paddy seedling per katha	10 kg of rice or wheat
4. Spreading the paddy seedlings in the field per bigha	5 kg of rice or wheat
5. Transplanting per bigha	12 kg of rice/wheat
6. Weeding per bigha	5 kg of rice/wheat
7. Thrashing and winnowing	10 maunds in every hundred maunds
8. Harvesting	10 bundles in every 16 bundles.

Non-Agricultural Contract Labour

Harvesting labours have to perform work on contract basis in road construction, bridge construction, house construction, etc. They enter into contract with the contractor to perform work till the work is over. They also agree to work at certain fixed rate.

Table 12.7 : Mode of Payment of Non-agricultural Contract Labour

Type of Work	*Mode of Payment*			
	Child	*Woman*	*Aged*	*Adult*
1. Cutting	Rs. 50 for every 100 maunds of soil	Rs. 50 for every 100 maunds	Rs. 50 for every 100 maunds	Rs. 50 for every 100 maunds
2. Loading trucks	Rs. 20	Rs. 20	Rs. 20	Rs. 20
3. Unloading trucks	Rs. 20	Rs. 20	Rs. 20	Rs. 20
4. Daily labour	Rs. 20	Rs. 20	Rs. 20	Rs. 20

6. Exploitation as bricks kiln labour

Some labourers are expert in the art of making mud bricks and making bricks Bhatha. In these work they take help of their children and women. In bricks kiln every work is done at contract. The mode of payment of labourers in bricks kiln is as follows :

Table 12.8 : Mode of Payment of Brick Kiln Labour

Type of Work	*Mode of Payment*
1. For preparing mud bricks	Rs. 60 per thousand in Khewal form
2. For making bhatha	Rs. 40 per thousand
3. For putting coal	Rs. 4 per maunds
4. For taking out pucca bricks and making Khewals	Rs. 40 thousand in Khewal form
5. For loading truck	Rs. 20 per day
6. For unloading truck	Rs. 20 per day

Migrant Labour

Some Dalits labour migrate to other neighbouring states like U.P., Punjab to work as labour in the farm. They may go there along with their wives and children. Some of them visit Delhi to work in local factories as casual labour. They get a hut to live. They are also given some advance in cash to purchase the materials of daily use. The have to go with their own money but they come back by the money of the owner of the farm or factory. Mode of payment of migrant labour is as follows.

Table 12.8 : Payment of Migrant Labour

Type of Work	*Mode of Payment*	*Hours of Work*
Ploughing	Rs. 30 + breakfast and midday meal	12 hours
Spading	— do —	— do —
Uprooting paddy seedlings	— do —	— do —
Transplanting	— do —	— do —
Weeding	— do —	— do —
Harvesting	— do —	16 hours
Sowing rabi	— do —	— do —
Thrashing paddy	— do —	— do —
Winnowing	— do —	— do —
Storing grains	— do —	— do —
Thrashing wheat	— do —	— do —
Storing grains/hey	— do —	— do —
Manuring the field	— do —	— do —
Spreading fertilizer and pesticide	— do —	— do —
As casual labour in factory	Rs. 40 per day	14 to 16 hours

Exploitations of Bataidar

Some Dalits have emerged as rich in comparison to other Dalits. They have land and money. But land is not sufficient so take land from the owner to do cultivation on share basis. As they become shareholder of the owner. So they are termed locally as Bataider and their occupation is called Bataidari. The Bataidar has to approach the owner to get a particular plot of land to do sharecropping. The Bataidar has to give half share to the owner and half share goes in his house. The status of a Bataidar becomes high in comparison to agricultural labour. The Bataidar has to invest his own seed, plough, oxen, fertilizer and half share of irrigation.

Table 12.9 : Share of a Bataidar in Bataidari System

Item	*Share of Malik*	*Share of Bataidar*
Seed	No share	All share
Fertilizer	Half	Half
Ploughing	No	All
Spading	No	All
Uprooting paddy seeding	No	All
Weeding	No	All
Harvesting	No	All
Thrashing	No	All
Winnowing	No	All
Carrying grains in the house	No	All
Yield	Half Share	Half Share
Straw and hey	Half Share	Half Share

If a Bataidar does not give good yield, he is not given land next year. The next year, the land is given to another Bataidar or is cultivated by the owner himself. So a Bataidar has to be very careful in cultivating the field timely so that good yield can be obtained from the land. He fears of not getting land next year if he shows not good yield in the crop.

Exploitation of Manidar

The man who takes land paying cash in advance or agrees to pay a fixed quantity of grains at the time of taking plot is called Manidar. If a Manidar agree to pay the amount in cash agreed, he has to pay the amount in advance in the month of Asarh. But if he agrees to pay Mani in kind, then he has to make promise to pay a fixed quantity of grains after the harvest. The Manidar lease the land from the owner for one complete year. By paying cash in advance he becomes free to do cultivation like his own field. He can cultivate crops whatever is more paying. He can cultivate cash crops or anything's. But if he leases in land by making promise to pay paddy or wheat, he has to pay the same quantity of paddy after the harvest.

Table 12.10 : Share of Manidar and Malik in Manidari System

Item	*Share of Malik*	*Share of Manidari*
Ploughing	No	All Share
Spading	No	All Share
Seed	No	All Share
Fertilizer	No	All Share
Uprooting paddy seedlings	No	All Share
Weeding	No	All Share
Harvesting	No	All Share
Thrashing	No	All Share
Winnowing	No	All Share
Carrying grains to house	No	All Share
Yield	As per agreement	Remaining goes in the share of Manidar.
Straw / hey	No Share	All Share
Irrigation rent	No Share	All Share

After one year, a Manidar has to approach the owner again for the plot of land. Both the Malik and the Manidar enters in a fresh agreement. The leasing in and leasing out of land takes place in the month of Asarh. The agreement continues for the Jyestha month. If no agreement is reached, the Malik is free to given land to some other Manidar and Manidar also tries to seek land from some other Malik.

Exploitation by Shops Owners

The shop owners of the villages exploit the Dalit in different ways. The shopowners have M. Oil, K. Oil, Sugar, Gur, etc. for all these a Dalit consumer has to visit shop. They do not have cash so they generally purchase these items by kind. The shop owners give articles at a high price and takes profit in both ways. They bring articles not of good quality. They keep two number good but they are sold at the rate of one number goods or even more than that. The shop owner makes bungling in weighing the articles. He does not have goods balance and weight. Sometimes they are given goods as loan for certain periods. The shop owner increases the amount of loan. If they do not repay the loan in time, he compels them to do some work in interest. Thus, exploitation of Dalits labourers is a common feature in villages. They do not purchase goods of daily use in huge amount. they visit shop daily to purchase goods of daily use in huge amount. They visit shop daily to purchase materials of their requirements.

Exploitation by Traders/Middlemen

Dalits are exploited by traders or middlemen. They do not get due price of commodities produces by them. They earn wages in kind. They harvest paddy and wheat. Thus, they have paddy and wheat to seed. The traders do net purchase the grains from their house at the same rate. He gets more grains in the house of owner. So They pay more price to their grains. Dalits have to sell in little quantity, therefore, they receive less. The rate differs from Rs. 10 to 15 per maund. Some Dalits are engaged in cultivating cash crops particularly vegetables. To purchase vegetables at reduced rate. Similarly, the middlemen purchase the milk from Dalit at reduced rate and they sell in the market at high rate. Thus, the profit goes in the hands of middlemen.

Exploitation by Money Lender

The local moneylenders are known by the term Mahajan. They may be a landowner, a Bania or a businessman. They give loan in cash to any person who needs loan. The poor Dalits are always in need of money. So, they approach frequently the house of Mahajan to get loan. For short duration loan, the rate of interest is more but for long duration loan, the rate of interest is slightly less. Sometimes, they have to put the ornaments as Bandhak to receive loan. At the time of repayment of loan the ornaments are returned. Sometimes, they have to give goats, chickens, or cows and buffaloes to the Mahajan to get free from the loan of the Mahajan. The government has banned on the loan to Dalits. But some Mahajans have license and they are recognised moneylenders. They have power to get the loan back. So, they provide loan to Dalits. For short duration loan, the rate of interest is Rs. 6 per hundred per month. After one year, the interest becomes the principal amount and interest is charged at compound rate.

Exploitation by Official

In order to receive loan from government agencies for seed, fertilizer, oxen, cow, buffalo, rickshaw, cart, thela, tamtom, gumati, etc. Dalits have to approach the block officials and bank officials. These officials demand bribe from the poor Dalits. They take bribe first and then sanction loan. Sometimes, they have to pay such a huge amount as bribe that they virtually get nothing. They have to pay as bribe whatever they receive. The VLW and Karamachari act as middlemen between the Dalits and the bank officials. For this act, they get share. Sometimes, they become stirred that they decide to give the idea of taking subsidy or loan.

13

RELIGIOUS AREA OF DALIT EXPLOITATION OF DARBHANGA

Dalits have been treated as untouchable since centuries, but they have been an integra l part of Hindu religion since time memorial. On account of untouchability, they are now enjoying the performance of religious rites and rituals. In the name of religion, Dalits are exploited even to-day. Their service is utilized in the society for religious purposes for which they virtually get nothing or very nominal payment. On many occasions, they have to perform Begari at the time of performance of religious rites and rituals. The service of Dalits is utilized in the performance of following type of religious activities as :

1. Exploitation of Dalit in the erection of temples.
2. Exploitation of Dalit in digging a sacred pond or pokhara.
3. Exploitation of Dalit in digging a sacred well.
4. Exploitation of Dalit in religious preaching.
5. Exploitation of Dalit in the performance of Akhanda Harikirtan.
6. Exploitation of Dalit in the performance of Yagya.
7. Exploitation of Dalit in the celebration of Durgapuja.
8. Exploitation of Dalit in the celebration of Lakshmipuja.
9. Exploitation of Dalit in the celebration of Ramnawami.
10. Exploitation of Dalit in the celebration of Janamasthami.
11. Exploitation of Dalit in the celebration of Chhatpuja.

Now let us discuss about each type one by one.

Exploitation of Dalit in Erection of Temple

Each Hindu village is characterized by the existence of temples of

Hindu Gods and Goddesses like temple of Lord Shiva, temple of Goddess Bhagwati temple of Lord Hanumana, temple of Radha-Krishna and temple of Rama-Janaki, etc. In the erection of temple the big landowners and some great saint take initiative. The saint pays a visit in the villages. He requests the villagers to assemble at a common place. He puts his proposal regarding the erection of a temple. He makes the villagers aware that the God had appeared before him in dream. The erection of the temple was the desire of the God. In the name of erection of temple, every villager supports the great saint. The saint asks a big landLord to provide land for this purpose or he asks anybody to provide land for this purpose. Only those lands are considered for this purpose, which are located nearby the village. The land for this purpose is taken free of cost. If one landowner is not ready to provide such a big acreage of land, then two or three landowners of the neighbouring plots are requested for this purpose. If a Gairmaujarua of government land is available, then a common decision is taken to erect temple at that place.

When the problem of land is solved, under the chairmanship of the big landowners of the village, a temple erection committee is constituted by the Great saint. The great saint acts as a supervisor of the committee. The members of committee are assigned different tasks. First of all, the villagers are requested to stand up one by one and to make announcement about the subscription or donation they want to give for the erection of temple. On a register, the name of the head of the household and subscription to be paid is noted one by one. Dalits are also included in the committee. Heads of the Dalit households are also requested to pay subscription. Now condition is put for the amount they are requested to pay as much as they like. At the time of foundation and erection of temple, Dalits are requested to perform *Shramadan* (labour donation). As they pay little subscription as cash or kind, so they are requested to pay Shramadan at least for two days by each member. After Shramadan, they are requested to work on nominal wages at least for one day by each family. Thereafter, they are requested to work at the existing rate of wages. They are never given wages according to Minimum Wages Act. Nobody dare to disobey the order of the temple erection committee. It is because, they fear God. Another point is that if anybody disobeys the request of the temple erection committee, he is socially ousted. Every villager breaks relationship with him. Thus, he and his family members have to live in isolation. In the erection of temple, the services of children, woman and aged are also utilized. The head of the house can send his child son or daughter, wife or his aged father or mother to do *Shramadan.* It will be the fitness of thing to present here one case study in this regard.

M.R. (45) of a village in Darbhanga district informed that he was exploited badly in the erection of temple of Lord Shiva by the villagers. A great saint of Hardwar had come in the village. It was the time of Kartik Purnima. He requested the villagers to assemble below a pipal tree situated nearby the village. The request of the Sadhuji was taken as divine order and everybody, at least head of the households, went there. Sadhuji expressed his happiness over the pressure of villagers on this request. He, then, disclosed the divine order before the people. He came before him in dream and asked him to take initiative for the erection of temple dedicated in his name. He presented the matter in such a manner that the villages welcomed the move and formed committee for the erection of temple. The biggest landowner of the village was made president of the committee. Then the name of Secretary, treasures and member were announced. Care was taken to involve at least one member of every caste of the village as the active member of the committee. Then head of each household were asked to come before Sadhuji and disclose the amount which they wanted to subscribe in the name of erection of temple. Then Dalit members were requested to give 2 day Shramadan and one day work at reduced wages. Therefore, they were requested to work at the existing wages in the village. Some members of the committee were made incharge to raise fund from the neighbouring villages for the erection of temple.

Sadhuji stayed in the village till the Magn Purnima. A hut was made for the stay of Sadhuji by the initiative of the villagers. The landowners provided the materials and the Dalit made the hut with their labour. In the evening, the villagers assembled before the hut of Sadhuji. Sadhuji used to preach the villagers. Some prayer songs, bhajan and kirtan were sung. At last Arti songs were held then people dispersed towards their houses. The villagers were very happy by the presence and proposal of Sadhuji. Villager paid sun-fried rice, flour, vegetable, gur, ghee, milk, curd etc. For the bhoga of Sadhuji and his disciples. Rice, pulse, vegetables, ghee, milk etc. of Dalits were also accepted by the Sadhuji. On the day of foundation, entire villagers, men women and children were present. Bhajan, song dedicated to Lord Shiva, Goddess Bhagwati, Lord Ganesh etc., were sung. Some Vedic mantras were also sung by the Sadhuji, his disciples and Brahmans of the village and neighbouring villages. Every people of the neighbouring villagers became aware of the foundation of the temple. From the next day of foundation, the work began. The villagers began to come to perform Shramadan. It was the duty of the committee to request 10 heads to come to perform Shramadan for the construction of the temple. Along with Dalits some heads of the other castes were also requested to come to make Shramadan and to supervise the work. Sadhuji also remained there to provide supervision. Thus, under the care of Sadhuji and committee the work began. One day M.R. was also requested, but due to illness of his son and wife he could not go there. In the evening he was asked to be present before the committee. He went there and pardon for his absence. The committee asked him to perform one day more Shramadan for the reason he had disobeyed the request of the committee. He promised to do Shramadan for three days instead of two days. He performed Shramadan for two days but could not do on 3rd day. This made the members of the committee angry. They decided to teach a lesson to M.R. for disobeying the request in near future. One day such an occasions came. M.R. had a cow and few goats. One night they came out of house and destroyed one Katha of brinjal and tomato. The owner of the field requested the villagers to take part in the village Panchayat. M.R. informed the villagers that he had kept the cow and goats in the house but there was no Tati. He had closed the gate of house by some bamboo peace. These pieces were broken by the bull who had entered the house suddenly. Cow and goats got feared seeing a bull in the house. They broke the rope and came out of house and destroyed the vegetable field. The village Panchayat decided that M.R. should pay Rs. 500 as fine. He requested the members of the village Panchayat to reduce the fine but they did not consider the request. A plain paper was brought and his thumb impression was taken. The amount of fine was written and the members of the village Panchayat put their signature as witness. It was given to the owner of the field. M.R. had to sell the cow to pay the fine.

An another informant S.R. of a village in Bahadurpur Block of Darbhanga district informed that he was exploited badly by the villagers in the name of construction of temple dedicated to goddess Bhagwati. S.R. had to pay Rs. 20 and perform two days Shramadan and two days work at nominal wages, i.e., breakfast, food and one seer of wheat. He paid Rs. 20 and performed two days Shramadan but he could not be able to perform work at nominal wages. On that day, he went to work in road construction. The members of the temple committee took it ill and decided to exploit S.R. in some other way on any occasion in near future. One day such an occasion was brought by 10 years old son of S.R. The child was plucking mangoes from free of owner. Suddenly, he was caught. The child was beaten badly and kept at the door of owner. In the evening, the parants of the child were called when they returned from construction work. They were asked to pay a fine of Rs. 250 immediately. If not, the owner threatened to send the child to Jail by the police. S.R. had received payment in the same evening. He brought money from the house and got the child free.

It is not only the cases of M.R. and S.R., but like them many Dalits are exploited in the name of construction of the temple. When the temple is constructed, it becomes the property of the landowners and the Brahman priest. Dalits do not visit temple daily. They visit temple on festive and ceremonial occasion to seek blessing of Gods and Goddesses. But for utilizing their labour as beggar at cheap rate in the name of religion, they are integrated in the scheme of temple construction.

Exploitation of Dalit in Digging a Sacred Pond/Pokhara

Every temple is accompanied by a sacred pond/pokhara. When the work of construction of temple is completed, everybody expresses desire for a pond dedicated in the name of Gods or Goddesses. On the day of *Pranpratistha* (ritual of giving life in the images of Gods or Goddesses), every villager pay a visit to the temple, Kirtan and Bhajans are held, Ramleela and Krishnaleela are also staged to provide recreation to the villagers. When this ritual is over, the committee makes promise to dig a sacred pond in the name of God or Goddess. The committee makes the members of the village aware of this decision. Now again funds are raised in the name of pond dedicated to a God. Each head of households has to pay subscription again. Dalit are also no exception. They have to pay subscription, perform Shramadan, and to work at reduced wages in the name of digging of sacred pond. Nobody can dare to disobey or deny the decision of the committee. However, the suggestions for a change in the decision is always welcomed. Valuable suggestions ore incorporated in the main decision. The foundation of digging a sacred pond is laid on any religious day by a senior members of the village but work is started when agricultural season is off. In off agricultural season labourers are easily available to perform Shramadan or to work on wages. The help of funds and labour is sought from the neighbouring Hindu villages. The decision of the committee is not binding for the another neighbouring Hindu villages. But in his own village the decision of the committee is taken seriously. The period of Shramadan is kept two hours in the morning and two hours in the evening so that a labourer can earn casual wages anywhere. Two days of Shramadan is counted as equivalent to one day work. For nominal wages, they have to work for 8 hours a day. They are given breakfast and midday meal plus 1 kg wheat or rice. As a casual labour, they receive what wages are paid to a casual labour in the village. Wages is paid from the subscription received in the name of digging the sacred pond. If there is sufficient fund, work is completed in few months. But when there is lack of fund, work is completed in few years. When the pond is dug completely, a *Jatha* is erected in the middle of the pond. Through this Jatha, Goddess Ganges is supposed to appear on the earth to serve Gods, Goddesses and devotees. On the day of erection of Jatha some rituals are performed and the spirit of ponds is requested to take abode on the Jathi when the work is completed, a great worship is organised at village level and the water of pond is allowed to use for the purpose of worship.

Sometimes, a temple is constructed on the bank of a pond but the shape of the pond is deshaped due to deposition of soil during each rainy season. The villagers take a decision to give the shape of the old pond again. They want to renovate the pond. For this purpose they dig the pond and make the bank high so that more and more water can remain stored even during the summer season. The work of renovation is done with the help of villagers. The villagers have to pay subscription, Shramadan and labour at nominal wages. Dalits are poor. They do not pay sufficient money but they have to pay Shramadan and labour at nominal and reduced wages. If any Dalits deny to offer labour or subscriptions, they are oppressed and harassed in different ways. They have only homestead land. Thin cows, goats, etc. They have to go in the fields of the landowners for various purposes. If they disobey the village level decision, they are put to hardship.

Sometimes, the villagers take decision to make the bank of the pond pucca. For this purpose government officials are also approached. The government officials give some fund for this work. Funds are also raised by the villagers. From the funds bricks, cement, sands etc. are purchased and the payment of labourers are made. The brick owner, cement-owner, tractor-owner, mason and labourers are requested to work at reduced rate of payment in the name of sacred pond. The labourers belonging to Dalits are worst affected. They are compelled to do Shramadan and work on reduced wages. They have to work as per the decision of the village. They cannot deny. If they dare to do so, they are harassed and oppressed in different ways. As a member of the village, they have to obey the decision of the village. The decision about such religious activities is taken by the big landowners and great sage, but all the villagers have to co-operate them by money and labour. At the time of rituals, Dalits have to do Begari. They have to play their musical instruments and sing songs. They also perform dance on this occasion.

Exploitation of Dalits in Digging Sacred Well

The small ponds become drys during summer season. Besides, some sage and visitors come to offer worship in the temple. They need water for the purpose of worship and drinking. Therefore, traditionally a well is preferred. The work of digging well is done at the level of village. The villagers have to pay subscription for this purpose and offer Shramadan. The Dalits have to dig well. They have to make Shramadan and to work on wages. Digging well is a difficult work. All labourers cannot do this work. But there are certain labourers who are well expert in digging well. They dig the well. But some labourers are required to pull the digging soil outside. For this kind of work many labourer is required. For this type of work, the labourers of the village are engaged. They pull the soil dug out and put them slightly away from the well. The expert is paid full payment but other labourers are paid a reduced wages in the name of religion. Sometimes, the expert is also requested to take less payment in the name of religion. The experts have to consider the request of the villagers.

When the well is dug out, the Kucha well is made Pucca. A wheel of wood made up to the wood of Jammu is placed at the bottom of the well. The well is made pucca from all sides. The wall is made one feet above the ground surface. In all these works the services of Dalits residing in the villages is utilized. For these religious work, they virtually get nothing. They have to perform Begar labour, Shramadan and work at nominal or very less wages in comparison to causal labourers of the village. They are subjected to such treatment in the name of religious and community property. As a member of the village community, they too participate injoys and sorrows of the village's community. They have to obey the decision of village Panchayat of which they are also members. If they deny, they are harassed, oppressed and exploited on many occasions in future.

Exploitation of Dalits in Religious Preaching

Once or twice in a year some great religious saint pays a visit to the village. They decide to stay in the village for a month or more. Their visit is taken good and fortunate by the villagers. For such a long stay a Kutia of Sadhuji is required. The Dalits of the village are called and asked to do the job of building a good Kutia. They are asked to bring straw hey, branches of trees and bamboos from different place. For these works, they are paid only breakfast and meal by the owners. They build the house on the basis of Shramadan. They have to prepare three or four roomed Kutia. In one room Sadhuji makes his stay. In another room, his disciples stay. In one room food is cooked and one room is made store. A big and slightly high platform of bamboo is made to sit the Sadhuji at the time of preaching the public. They have also to clean ground available nearby the Kutia. In performing these works, they have to do Begari or Shramadan in refined terminology of the exploiters.

When the entire arrangement regarding the long stay of Sadhuji is made, Sadhuji starts his religious discourse. He preaches the public daily in the evening. The preaching is over by singing Bhajan, kirtan and Arti by the villagers. The Dalits of the village are requested to wash the preaching ground. Thus, in the religious preaching the services of Dalits is utilized for selfish purpose. Dalits are requested to bring milk, vegetables, gur, etc. from their houses for the items of Prasad shared by the Sadhuji and his disciples. One the last day the ritual of Chadawa is made at the feet of the Sadhuji. Women, children and men visit the place of Kutia and offer money, grains, cloths, etc. at the sacred feet of the Sadhuji. From this income Sadhuji runs Bari at Prayagraj, Kanshi, Ayodhya, Haridwar, etc.

Exploitation of Dalit in Performance of Akhanda Harikirtan

To bring prosperity, peace and wealth in the village and to keep the villagers away from various kind of calamity, Akhanda Harikirtan is performed in the village. To perform Akhanda Harikirtan fund is raised at village level. Dalits of the village also have to pay the amount of subscriptions fixed by the Akhanda Harikirtan Samiti. The amount of subscription per household of landowners is fixed on the basis of acreage and the amount of subscription per Dalit households is fixed seeing the income of the family. If the head of the household pays amount less than fixation of the committee, that is accepted hearing the request of the head of the family. But if a head of family does not pay any amount of subscription that is not taken well at the level of the village. If he does not pay, it is believed that he does not want village. If he does not pay, it is believed that he does not want common peace and prosperity in the village. He is treated as enemy of the village. He is boycotted socially and is compelled to live in isolation. Thus, from the fear of social boycott, no heads of the Dalits households dare to refuse the payment of amount of subscription. In the performance of Akhanda, first of all a sacred place is selected. This place may be in front of a temple dedicated to any deity. The days and date of the performance of Akhanda is fixed. This date may be Ramnawami, Janamasthami, Magh Purnima, Kartik Purnima, Shivaratri etc. Before the initiation of the ritual, the place is cleaned properly. Thorns and bushes are cut. The place is washed with cow dung and water. A big vedi of mud is prepared where all Gods and Goddesses are supposed to take abode to bless the villagers with peace, prosperity, wealth, good health and good yield. Around the Principal Vedi, few small Vedis are made where Nawagraha are supported to take place. At all four corners, four small Vedis are made Gods of direction and corner takes abode to keep guard on the entrance of evil spirits. Then a tent is erected and the space around the corner Gods is covered with coloured clothes outside the Akhandashala, a big flag of Lord Hanumana in a big bamboo pole is erected. The erection of temporary Akhandashala, preparation of Vedi, cleaning and washing of place require manual labour. For the performance of manual labour on such occasions Dalits are requested. If they do not hear the request they are forced to perform these works in the name of religion and welfare of the village.

In Akhanda, when the rituals relating to taking abode of Gods and Goddesses are over. A Chaumukhi dwip (four faced earthen lamp) is kept lighted in ghee of cow for twenty-four hours or 48 hours or 72 hours, depending upon the duration of Akhanda for one, two or three days and nights. The name of Lord Rama and Krishna are recited alternatively for entire period. The name of these Gods are recited in prayer song form amidst playing of musical instrument. The *Shrota* (one who is associated with the ritual of hearing) and *Vakta* (the village priest who tells) sit in front of Choumukhidip taking beads of *Tulsi* in hands. There are two or three Shrota and two or three Vakta. They sit one by one. Again singing songs, require labour. For singing prayers and playing musical instruments Dalits are requested. For these works, they are paid nothing but they are supposed to be benefited by God. When the ritual of Akhanda is accomplished, the ritual of Hawana is made and all Gods and Goddesses are requested to go back to their respective Lok (abode). The procession of Akhanda visits door to door singing prayer songs amidst musical instruments and band partly. In singing prayer songs and paying musical instruments like Jhal, Dholak, Kartal, etc., the services of Dalits are utilized. Dalits have band party. They are requested to play band on such occasion. They are paid nothing, but as a member of the village community, they are supposed to obey the decision. Again, they are taught that for playing musical instruments and bands, they will be benefited by Almighty God.

Exploitation of Dalit in the Performance of Yagya

Great Hindu Sages belonging to different cults like Vaishnava, Shiva and Shatuta visits in villages to perform Yagya (great worship) in the name of God to which cult they belong. For performing Yagya, they selected a village situated at the bank of a river or nearby confluence of rivers. In Yagya, lakhs and lakhs of devotees pay a visit on all days of Yagya, which continues for a week, 11 days or two weeks. For this purpose the consent of villagers is sought by the Sadhuji. Villagers are guided by the religious beliefs. When the sage communicates them that Gods and Goddesses have selected this pious piece of land to take abode for the performance of Yagya, they become glad and accept the decision happily. When the villagers accept the proposal of Sadhuji, a village level or sometimes, inter village level meeting is held where Sadhuji makes his stay. Different committees are constituted for different activities, for instance Pravachan committee, recreation committee, Prasad distribution committee, finance committee, subscription collection committee, feast committee, administration committee, light committee, marketing committee. Each committee has a chairman and five members to assist him.

First of all an Ashram of Kash, Phoos, Bamboo etc. is erected for the permanent stay of the Sadhuji. He stays in the Ashram for four months before the performance of Yagya. Ashram is erected with the Shramadan. The big landowners provide the materials and the labourers belonging to Dalits do the work of preparing Ashram. Generally such an Ashram has three rooms, one room is four the worship and stay of Sadhuji. In another room disciples and guests of the Sadhuji take shelter. The 3rd room is used as storage of Prasad and food grains. In the evening, Sadhuji makes religious speech before the villagers. He tells varieties of Katha Goddesses and Gods approach before a devotee to help him, when he is in trouble. He feels about the benefits achieved by the devotees in religious performance like Puja-path, Akhanda & Kirtan, Bhajan, Satsanga, Yagya etc. People are benefited by the speech of Sadhuji. Gradually, people from neighbouring villages start coming to get benefit from his speech. When the speech is over, the ritual of *Arti* is held. The ritual of Arti is accomplished by the singing of prayer songs by the disciples of Sadhuji and the villagers. In Arti some coins are put. From these amount items of Prasad like Mishri, Rori, Gari, Chhuhara, Kismis etc. and ghee for Arti is purchased for daily religious discourse.

Sadhuji invites some other Sadhus to come over the place and to make speech. Thus, daily three-four Sadhus come to make speech.

Children, women and men of the neighbouring villages take part in the religious preaching. At the time of departure, they put coins in the pot containing Arti. This continues for three months. By this time the villages situated nearby become well aware of the performance of Yagya. The Chanda Sangraha Samiti visit each village and makes few persons of the village to collect subscription in cash and kind and to send them at the place of Sadhuji. Thus funds from more and more villages are collected and villagers are requests to participate in Yagya. Thus, lakhs and lakhs of rupees are collected in the name of performance of Yagya. The Yagya starts in the bright half of 4th month. By this time, every arrangement for the performance of Yagya is completed. A beautiful Yagyashala is prepared in which materials are supplied by Yagya Samiti and the labour is rendered by the Dalits belonging to neighbouring villages. For preparing Yagyashala, they do not receive payment. They do it in the name of Yagya and in the name of Shramadan. Arrangement of light is made on temporary basis. Stages are made for religious speech and the performance of Ramleela and Rasleela. Tents are erected in the entire space available for the Yagya. Shops are established on both sides of road leading to the place of Yagya. In these works the service of local Dalits are involved in the committee and through committee they are asked to volunteer their services. They have also to render labour to carry the goods back after the Yagya is over. Thus, right from the stay of Sadhuji up to the entire period of Yagya, the services of local Dalits is utilized for different purposes for which no payment is made. They are exploited in the name of religious, Shramadan, Volunteer etc. Not only this, even in distribution of Prasad and in feast, they are isolated. They do not receive proper treatment.

Exploitation in the Performance of Durgapuja

Durgapuja is regarded as very popular worship prevalent at national level. In rural areas also this worship is celebrated with great enthusiasm. This worship is held at village level. For the performance of Durgapuja, a Durgapuja Samiti is constituted at the level of the village. Attempts are made to incorporate members of all castes of the village in the Samiti. The Samiti decides the rate of subscriptions for each households. For this purpose the expected expenditure is taken in to consideration on the basis of expected expenditure the role of subscription for land owners is decided per Bigha land. Thus, those who have more bigha of land have to pay more subscription in the name of Durgapuja. For landless, it is fixed equal to the wages of a day. Thus, each heads of the Dalit households has to pay subscription equal to the ways of a person earned in a day. Besides, this little subscription, they are requested to do Shramadan and to volunteer labour on this occasion for various types of work. They have to clean the place where images of Goddess Durga is to be established. They have to wash it with soil, cow dung and water. They have to prepare a stage for the installation of the image and for the performance of drama and dance during night. A temporary Pandal is also erected in the space available for the stage of image and dance and drama. A tent is erected for the visitors to come and see drama and dance. They have to bring images from the town on their shoulders. They have to collect wood of mangoes tree for the performance of the ritual of Hawana. They have to carry images on shoulders at the time of procession. They have to sing Bhajans and Kirtan. They have to play musical instruments and Baja. For these works, they get nothing but they are expected to perform these works as the member of the village community. When the worship is over, they have to send back the materials and goods used in the erection of stage pandal and tent to their respective owner. Thus, for the performance of Durgapuja, the services of Dalits are utilized without any payment. They work more and more on this occasion, but in the distribution of Prasad they do not find proper place.

Exploitation of Dalit in Celebration of Lakshmipuja

Goddess Lakshmi is the Goddess of wealth. She is wife of Lord Vishnu. She does not make her stay in the house of a person for long duration. On the day of Dipawali she is expected to pay visit in every household where her worship is performed. Dipawali is celebrated in each household. But the worship of Goddess Lakshmi is held at village level. For this purpose fund is raised, a meeting of villagers take place in which all heads of the households participate. A Lakshmipuja Samiti is constituted unanimously. The committee is empowered to decide the rate of subscription to be paid by each household. The committee first of all explores all the probable expenditure related to Lakshmipuja. Then the rate is decided per Bigha of land. It may be Rs. 5, 7, 10, 15 etc. Per Bigha of land owned by the landowners. For labourers, it is equal to the wages of a day of a person per household. Chanda collection committee visits door to door of households made the heads to pay subscription soon so that work related to Lakshmipuja could be started.

Besides, the payment of subscription, Dalits are expected to perform labour for erecting stage, carrying images from the town to the village, carrying images at the time of procession, erecting tents and Pandals. They have to carry the materials of tent and pandals back to the owners. Thus, they are kept engaged for manual work but are given nothing as wages. As a member of the village, such works are expected from the Dalits.

The worship of Lakshmipuja takes place at midnight. At that time men, women and children come to see and offer worship. Goddess is worshipped to bring wealth in each family of the village. After worship, they sing prayer song round the night. Next day, they take part in the ritual of procession. They carry the image of Goddess Lakshmi door to door so that all family members of the village could worship. Prasad is given in each to share keeping the member of the family members in view.

Exploitation of Dalit in Celebration of Ramnawami

Ramnawami is also a great festival of Hindu. On this very day, Lord Rama was born. It was 9th day of bright half of Chaita month, the first month of our national calendar year. That is why in each year, this day is celebrated as Ramnawami. Some villages have temple dedicated to Rama, Lakshmana and Janaki. A great worship is performed in the temple. Fund is raised for decoration, drama and dance. The temple is decorated in beautiful manner. Tents and Pandals are erected. Prayer songs are sung. Ramleela and dance are performed. From each household *Pakwans* are brought to offer as Prasad, besides Prasad offered by Ramnawami celebration committee. If the village has no temple dedicated to Rama, the worship of Lord Hanumana, a great devotee of Rama is made. The temple of Lord Hanumana is beautifully decorated. A big flag of Lord Hanumana is prepared and erected with the help of a big bamboo. Prasad is offered to Hanumana by the committee and from each family *Pakwans* are offered as Prasad. Lathi, Bhala, Mugadar etc. are played and prayer songs are sung. The procession of Ramnawami visits the entire village in which all villagers take part. On this festive occasion, Dalits have not only to pay subscription but they are expected to perform manual work in bringing materials related to the worship, tent, Pandal, Dance etc. They have to bring those materials back to the owners. For these works they are not given any payment by the committee. Those who deny are forced to perform such works. If not, they are exploited and oppressed in future.

Exploitation of Dalit in Celebration of Janamasthmi

Janamasthmi is regarded as the birth day of Lord Krishna. On this very day Lord Krishna was born to Devaki, while she was in Jail with her husband Vashudeva. It was the 8thday of dark half of Vado month. That is why this is celebrated each year as the birth day of Lord Krishna. To celebrate Janamasthmi, funds are raised by subscription in which Dalits also have to contribute. Besides contribution of subscription, Dalit have to perform manual work to bring materials releted to decoration, drama, dance and worship from different places. They have to bring them back again to the owners. They have to sing Bhajan and Kirtan. They have to take part in procession.

Exploitation of Dalit in Celebration of Chhatpuja

Chhathpuja is regarded as very pious Puja for the Hindus. Chhath mai and Lord Surya are the chief deity of this worship. The total duration of Chhathpuja is of four days. The 1st day is called Barauna, the second day is known as Lohar, the 3rd day is called Upawash and the 4th are final day is called Paran. On each day some rituals are performed. Chhath Vrata takes place twice in a year. In the month of Chaita and in the month of Kartik. In both months the Vrata begins on 4th bright half and ends on 7th bright half.

The river banks, ponds, sun temple with big tanks are cleaned and decorated beautifully. The streets leading to the Ghats are also cleaned and decorated. The Ghats where Arghya is offered, are also decorated. In cleaning and decorating the streets and Ghats to offer worship, the services of Dalits are exploited. They are forced to pay subscription, to perform Shramadan and to volunteer their services.

14

POLITICAL AREA OF DALIT EXPLOITATION OF DARBHANGA

Dalits are victim of exploitation by the heads and officials of different political and administrative institutions. They are exploited and oppressed by caste Panchayat, village Panchayat, inter-village Panchayat, modern Gram Panchayat, Choukidar, Dafadar, Thanedar, and lawyers. They are subject to exploitations and oppressions by School Teacher, Karamachari, Gram Sewak, Barababu and other officials of the Block and Bank. Thus, Dalits are victim of exploitation and oppression not only by landowners belonging to different castes and community, but political and administrative officials also do not lag behind in exploiting the Dalits. Elites, leaders and some social workers also exploit Dalits. Now let us discuss about each type, one by one.

1. EXPLOITATION OF DALIT IN INTRAVILLAGE PANCHAYAT

Each village has traditionally a village Panchayat is which every heads of the households are expected to be its member. The Panchayat sits to settle the quarrel or to punish the culprit. In this Panchayat, there is dominance of landowners. When a case against a Dalit comes in the Panchayat, all landowners make up mind to punish him, whether he is guilty or not. But as a member of the village, he has to obey the decision of the Panchayat. Now let us quote some case studies to substantiate such type of exploitation by the traditional village Panchayat.

H.R. (38) of village in Bahadurpur Block of Darbhanga district informed that he was exploited by the decision of traditional village Panchayat. It was the summer season and the fruits of mangoes were hanging in the trees of the village. His 10 years old son had gone to ease. He had a small plastic container full of water in his hand. To ease quickly, he entered in the garden of a Yadava owner. He was crossing the garden to ease, in the mean time one of boys of Yadava family saw him. When he reached nearby the garden, he saw the body sitting for defecation. He thought he was trying to deceive him by his such act. When he came, he was caught and beaten by the Yadava boy. He was brought at the door of Yadava house. The Yadava boy told that the boy was trying to pluck mangoes. He had thrown few *dela* (piece of brick, bolder or soil) to pluck mangoes. When he became unsuccessful, he climbed the tree. Few mangoes were also found in his container. Hearing the noise, neighbours and other villagers also came there. Suddenly, there was a huge crowd of villagers before the door of Yadava. The village Panchayat was requested to sit to decide the fine for the crime committed by the Dalit child. all heads of the households residing in the village assembled on the door of the Yadava. The members heard the nature of crime done by the Dalit boy from the mouth of the Yadava boy. Then Dalit boy was also given chance to speak. Seeing the crowd Dalit boy got nervous. He remained silent for sometime. The members of the Panchayat thought that the child hand done evil act because he was speaking nothing to save himself. Then the father of the child came forward and took the child to his place. He asked the boy to tell the fact. Then he told slowly that he had gone to defecate. He had crossed through the garden but he had not made any attempt to pluck mangoes. The fact told by the Dalit boy was entirely opposed to the fact presented by the Yadava boy. Now question arose in the Panchayat as to who was correct. After much inquiry, the fact revealed by Yadava boy was considered as true. No other Dalit or any other boys were caught and brought for punishment. This was the strongest proof for the Yadava boy. The boy was fined Rs. 50 for making evil act of plucking mango and Rs. 50 for telling lie before the member of the Panchayat. To repay the fine, the father of the child had to work for the Yadava owner for ten days without wages. He was given only breakfast.

In another case study, H.R. (50) of a village in Darbhanga block of Darbhanga district informed that he was exploited by the decision of the village Panchayat. Her 8 years old daughter had gone to bring dry leaves for fuel. She saw a gram field and entered the field to cut *Sag* (herbal leaf). It was the field of a landowner belonging to Koeri caste. The son of the owner had gone to watch the field. He saw the girl cutting *Sag*. The girl was brought at the door. The village Panchayat was called to decide the fine for this evil act. The girl accepted her fault. The father of the girl was asked to pay Rs. 50 as fine. For paying fine, the father of girl had to sell a goat in the hand of another landowner of the same caste. Thus, even for minor mistakes, Dalits are exploited by the decision of the village Panchayat.

Exploitation of Dalit in Inter Village Panchayat

The boundaries of neighbouring villages meet with each other. Dalit boys and girls go to herd the cattle. They herd the cattle and play. Sometimes, their cattle inter the field of other villages and destroy the crops. Sometimes, the children cut *sag* or uproot, pea, gram crops to eat. When they are caught, they are beaten mercilessly. An inter village Panchayat sits to decide the amount of fine so that they might not do such evil act in future. E.R. (36) of a village in Darbhanga block of Darbhanga district informed that he was badly exploited by the decision of inter village Panchayat. He had ten goats. His 10 years old son used to herd them. The grazing ground was situated at the boundaries of three villages. It was the place where herd boys came to graze cattle and goats. They used to play elic small ball of grass, Kabaddi, Bagh-bakari etc. While his son saw Khesari. It was the field of a landowner belonging to Kurami caste. Suddenly, the herd boy of the landowner also reached there. He saw that the field of Khesari crop of his master was destroyed by the goats of E.R., while his son was engaged in playing. He told this news to his master. Next day, master of the field came to see his field. He saw that crop of the field was badly damaged. He sat there and was waiting for the arrival of heard boys of different villages. The child with goats also came there. The child was called and beaten by the owner of the field. Then the child and the goats were brought at the door of the owner. The owner called an inter village Panchayat to decide the amount of fine. The Panchayat sat and E.R. was fined Rs. 150 for this evil act. He had to sell three goats immediately to repay the fine to the owner of the field.

S.R. (40) of a village in Bahadurpur Block of Darbhanga district informed that he was exploited by the decision of an inter village Panchayat. His 14 years old son had plucked a sugarcane from the field of a landowner belonging to Koeri caste.

An another landowner the child threw the sugarcane and ran away. The owner came back to his village and informed the owner of the field that some Dalit boys of the neighbouring village are destroying the crops of sugarcane. All landowners of the village decided to teach those boys and their parents a lesson. Next day the owner of the field were sitting inside the field. From outside nobody was visible. The boy came again and entered the field to pluck sugarcane. As soon as he entered in the field he was caught. He was beaten badly and brought at the house. A inter village Panchayat was called in which landowners of the neighbouring village participated. The father of the child was also called to participate.

Some sugarcane and the child were brought in the Panchayat. The Panchayat fined Rs. 200 for this evil act. To repay the fine, the child had to render labour as herd boy in the house of the landowner for one year on nominal wages.

Exploitation of Dalit by Mukhia of Modern Gram Panchayat

The Mukhia of modern Gram Panchayat also does not lag behind in exploiting and oppressing the Dalits. Dalits approach Mukhiaji to solve problems. On many occasions he took side of landowners, not of the poor Dalits. Sometimes, for this selfish purpose, he utilizes the services of poor Dalits.

G.R. (48) of a village in Bahadurpur Block of Darbhanga district informed that he was exploited by the decision of the Mukhiaji of his Gram Panchayat. Once, he was asked to perform works in the house of Mukhiaji, but as he was going to market, so he refused to work. Mukhiaji had taken ill of it, on one more occasion Mukhiaji wanted to send him to the house of one his relatives along with some goods, but this time also he could not do the work of Mukhiaji. Mukhiaji wanted to teach him lesson. Once, his son and the son of a Banihar of Mukhiaji made quarrel in which hands of the son of Banihar of Mukhiaji was broken. Mukhiaji called G.R. and asked him to pay Rs. 1000 immediately for plaster and other works, otherwise both father and son would be sent to jail. He had no money at that time. Rs. 1000 was a big amount. Nobody wanted to pay such a huge amount. At least G.R. requested Mukhiaji to pay Rs. 1000 as loan. He also agreed to work in his house as Kamia. He had to work continuously for five years to repay this heavy amount.

L.R. (28) of a village in Darbhanga Block of Darbhanga district informed that he was exploited by the Mukhiaji in Jawahar Rozgar Yojna. Under this Yojna, village street, dams and roads are made Pucca. The Mukhiaji was incharge of this Yojna. First of all, the drains and street of the village were made Pucca. Dalits of the village were engaged in this work. As it was off season, so he asked his Kamia to go to earn wages. L.R. was a Kamia of Mukhiaji. He worked in this scheme along with other labourers for one month. When he went to seek wages, he was asked to come next day. Other labourers were paid 2 kg. of rice per day, but he was paid only 1 and ½ kg. of rice per day. He was given the same wages, he received as Kamia,

Exploitation by Sarpanch of Modern Gram Panchayat

Dalits are exploited by the Sarpanch of modern Gram Panchayat.

Sarpanch is head of criminal cases. Whenever, a case against Dalits come in the Panchayat, he takes side of the other. Not only this, he also exploits Dalits in different ways. Being political authority, he exploits and oppresses Dalits even for minor mistakes or faults. He wants to exploit the services of Dalit labour at cheap rate.

M.D. (45) of a village in Bahadurpur Block of Darbhanga district informed that he was exploited by the Sarpanch in a case. One of the landowners of the village had filed a criminal case against him in the Panchayat. A Muslim labourer, who was living in the house of Sarpanch had made allegation that M.D. had stolen a cock of one kg. to eat, legs, feathers, bones were seen in his Bariland. Two Muslims were witness of the case. They had seen M.D. cutting and cooking cock in his Bari. M.D. was not ready to accept it. He told the Panchayat members that he has cooked cock, no doubt, but he had bought it from the house of an another Dalit. Two Dalits were the witness from his side. The Panchayat under the chairmanship of Sarpanch did not accept the witness and statement of M.D. and M.D. was fined Rs. 300 for this criminal case. He was verbally threatened not to go to court against the decision of Sarpanch. He had no money to pay fine. Sarpanch gave him money on loan. He had to work in the house of Sarpanch at reduced wages to pay the loan back. C.P. (25) of a village in Darbhanga Block of Darbhanga district informed that he was exploited by the Sarpanch of his Panchayat. Sarpanch belonged to his village. A landowner had placed a case against C.P. in the court of Sarpanch. The case was related to the theft of potato from the field. At midnight C.P. was digging potato from the field. Just then owners of other field came to watch the field. They saw a man stealing potato. Hearing the voice, the thief ran away with bag on his head but his chappals were left. The owner filed a case in which three other owners were witness. C.P. made statement before the court that he was absent on that day because he had gone to the house of a relative. His relative was witness in the case. The Sarpanch heard the plea of both parties and C.P. was accused. He was fined Rs. 300 to pay within a week. He had to pay this fine to sell a calf.

Exploitation by Choukidar

A Choukidar is a part of Thana police. He makes the Thanedar aware of the day to day criminal activity in the villages. He puts truth before the Thanedar. Each Panchayat at least has one Choukidar whenever a crime takes place in the villages, he goes to Thana to inform the Thanedar about the crime. As he is attached to Thana, he is supposed to have power. On the basis of this power he tries to exploit and oppress the poor Dalits. He goes to Dalit Tola and asks Dalits to perform work in his field. The Choukidar pays themselves wages. If they deny, they are harassed in different ways. In the name of protection, he takes eggs, cocks and sometimes, goats from the Dalits. In the name of Thana police, he collects ghee and vegetables from the house of Dalits. If Dalits deny the order of Choukidar, he threatens them to teach a lesson by the Thana police. Sometimes, a false criminal case is registered against some young Dalits.

L.C. (30) of a village Bahadurpur Block of Darbhanga district informed that he was exploited by the Choukidar of the village, who belonged to Yadava by caste. The Choukidar had asked to give his 10 years old son to work as herd boy. L.C. had denied. The Choukidar had made up his mind to teach lesson. A dacoity took place in the neighbouring village. The Choukidar put the name of L.C. under suspicion. Now, he had to go to Thana to give daily attendance or whenever called. Now he was under the clutch of Choukidar. The Choukidar asked him to go in Thana with four-five cocks. He did so. Again the Choukidar asked him to go there with a he-goat. Cocks and he-goats were consumed by the Thana police, but the case of L.C. was not finalised. He was unable to work properly due his daily attendance before Thanedar. At last, the Choukidar asked him to pay a sum of Rs. 1000 to get his name cut from the case. He had no money. The Choukidar gave him money as loan. Not only this he and his son had to work in the house of Choukidar to pay the loan back. They received nominal wages. They had to work for five years to pay loan back.

P.B. (36) of a village in Darbhanga Block of Darbhanga district informed that he was exploited and oppressed by the Choukidar who belonged to Koeri by caste. The Choukidar had come to the house of P.B. to buy his cow. P.B. had a cow. P.B. wanted to sell the cow. The Choukidar had come to purchase the cow. He was ready to pay Rs. 800 but P.B. did not agree. He was not ready to sell the cow on less than Rs. 1000. The Choukidar went back but he decided to teach P.B. a lesson. Once a dacoity had taken place in the house of a Halawai. The name P.B. was included by the Choukidar in this dacoity case. Thus, he was put to trouble. Now, he had to sell his 10 Kathas of land to pay bribe and to get rid of the dacoity case.

Exploitation of Dalit by Dafadar

A Dafadar is more powerful than the Choukidar. He is also a part of law, order and administrations. The Dafadar exploits and oppresses the

Dalits in many ways. He has link with Thana and district administration. The Dafadar utilizes the services of Dalits at cheap rate. He say that he is the protector of Dalits and so they should perform labour for him at less rate. If they deny, the Dafadar teaches them lesson by introducing their names in cases of theft, dacoity, etc.

D.C. (35) of a village in Bahadurpur Block of Darbhanga district told that he was exploited by the Dafadar, who belonged to the same village. The Dafadar owned 10 Bighas of land. He asked cow and a buffalo besides two oxen to cultivate the land. He had asked D.C. to become his Kamia but he had refused. Again he asked D.C. to given his 12 years old son as herd boy in his house, but D.C. did not agree. This behaviour of D.C. made the Dafadar angry. He thought to teach lesson to D.C. in future. One day such an occasion came. A dacoity took place in the house of a landowner. The name of D.C. was included in this Dacoity case by the police. He had take a loan of Rs. 3000 from the Dafadar to pay bribe in Thana and to get his name cut from the case. To repay the loan, he had to accept the terms and conditions of Kamia in the house of Dafadar. His son had to accept the work of herd boy in the house of the Dafadar. They had to work for six years on less wages to repay the loan of Dafadar Sahib.

L.M. (36) of a village in Darbhanga Block of Darbhanga district informed that he was exploited by the Dafadar Sahib of his village. A theft of buffalo in the house of a landowner had taken place. In this case L.M. was made accused. Now L.M. approached to Dafadar Sahib to help him. The Dafadar Sahib said that he would help him only when he would accept to work as Kamia in his house. L.M. accepted the conditions of Dafadar Sahib. The Dafadar told that he would have to pay bribe to save him. He went in the Thana and settled the case. His name was taken back. When Dafadar Sahib returned from the Thana, he told L.M. that he had to pay Rs. 2000 as bribe to save him, For this amount, he had to work as Kamia for ten years. Only then, loan plus interest was paid back.

Exploitation of Dalit by Thana-Police

The Thana-Police exploits and oppresses the Dalits in many ways. Sometimes Thana-Police make trip at night in the rural area to supervise law and order. In this trip, the suspected persons are contracted. If some one are caught committing any type of evil act or criminal act, he is put under custody for investigation. Poor Dalits are subject to exploitation and oppression. The police enters the Dalits Basti in the name of supervision law and order. If the police finds some Dalits quarreling, some taking liquor etc. these behaviours provide the ground for the exploitation and oppressions of Dalit by the police. The police takes, eggs, chickens, goats, ghee etc. from the Dalits. In several cases, they are asked to pay heavy amount as bribe.

P.M. (36) of a village in Bahadurpur Block of Darbhanga district informed that he was exploited by the Thana-Police. One night, his wife had fallen ill suddenly. He had to go to consult a doctor of the neighbouring village. His son was also with him. They were coming taking some medicine from the doctor. In the mean time, police jeep came. The wire from the electricity pole was fallen down on the earth. The police caught them in the crime of cutting electric wire. P.M. requested again and again but they were not left. They were brought to the Thana. A criminal case was instituted against them. The Choukidar informed his family members. His wife had gone to Thana to tell the truth. But nobody was ready to hear her voice. At last, she approached to her brother who was driver of a lawyer in the district. With her attempt, P.M. and his son were left on bail. Later on they were also declared innocent by the court.

D.R. (39) of a village in Darbhanga Block of Darbhanga district informed that he was subject to exploitation and oppression by Thana-Police. One day, he had gone to market, but could not return to the village in time. Till late evening he remained marketing. It became nlight in the market. He had bicycle, so he decided to come back his house. He put goods on the carrier of the bicycle and set out for the village. His village was situated 10 kms away from the market. It was winter season. The police jeep was on tour on the same road. Seeing the light of the jeep, D.R. stopped his bicycle. He came down and started urinating. Sighting the bicycle and man sitting to urinate, the police stopped the jeep. One of police caught the man and began to make various inquiry. Police also searched the cloth bag put on the carrier of the bicycle. The police found some polythene of local made liquor along with other goods. He had purchased liquor to serve among his relatives who were coming to participate in the Samskar of Gauna of his daughter. But police suspected that he was a liquor seller in the village. He was caught and brought to the Thana. The next day, Choukidar informed the family member of D.R. The wife of D.R. took Rs. 500 on loan from a Yadava landowner. She went to Thana. She gave Rs. 500 to Darogaji, then D.R. was set free from the police custody.

Exploitation of Dalit by Lawyer

Dalits are exploited by the lawyers. Dalits have to approach the lawyer in different court cases. The lawyers know well that Dalits are poor and illiterate. So, they demand huge amount as fee to fight their cases. If they do not pay fee, they deny to take up their case.

L.M. (50) of a village in Bahadurpur Block of Darbhanga district informed that he was exploited badly by the lawyer in a court case. His 20 years old son was arrested and sent to jail by the police in a dacoity case which took place in the house of a big landowner of a neighbouring village. The owner of the house had not given any name but one of the criminal, caught by the police mentioned his name. For the bail of his son, L.M. approached a lawyer with the help of a landowner of the village.

The lawyer demanded Rs. 500 as fee. He gave Rs. 250 immediately, and Rs. 250 was due. The next day, L.M. could not manage this amount, the lawyer refused to take up his case. Then with the help of his relative, he approached another lawyer. The lawyer demanded Rs. 300 as fees. He told about his poverty before the lawyer, so he left Rs. 100. Then he had to pay Rs. 100.

J.R. (55) of village in Darbhanga urban block of Darbhanga district informed that he was exploited by the lawyer in a land case. His 5 Kathas of land was captured by his uncle who was not ready to return it. He called his relatives and requested the uncle to leave his land. When his uncle refused, he filed a case in the court. He approached a layer for this purpose. The lawyer demanded a fee of Rs. 500. He agreed and paid the fee immediately. The lawyer saw all paper and convened him about his victory. The case started. On each date both parties had to go. This was also a costly affair. The final hearing was made by the magistrate and the Judgment was reserved for 15 days. I.R. was contacted and Rs. 2000 was demanded to pay as bribe to the Magistrate. This was a common practice. I.R. could not manage such a big amount but the next party paid Rs. 2000 through its lawyer. Thus, Judgement went in his favour.

Exploitation of Dalit by VLW

VLW is servant of the villages. That is why is called as Gram-Sewak. It is duty of the Gram-Sewak to make the people aware of various development programmes. He is connecting link between the block and the villages. There are various schemes of development which are especially meant for the Dalits. He also makes the villagers aware of the new seed and fertilizer. He also take contact work for irrigation, road construction, etc.

J.C. (32) of village in Bahadurpur Block of Darbhanga district informed that he was exploited badly by the Gram-Sewak of the village. Gram-Sewak asked J.C. to apply for loan to buy a Rickshaw. He assured him that he would get a sum of Rs. 5000 for this purpose. Gram-Sewak said openly that for such a big amount he will have to pay some bribe to the officials related to this scheme. He demanded a sum of Rs. 1000 for this purpose. After few months Gram-Sewak demanded Rs. 500 more. Any way, J.C. could manage this amount and he paid Rs. 1500 in the hand of Gram-Sewak. At the time of payment, Rs. 500 more was demanded. Thus, to got a loan of Rs. 5000, he had to give Rs. 2000 as bribe. He had to visit many times to block and banks.

M.R. (28) of a village in Darbhanga urban block of Darbhanga district informed that he was exploited by the Gram-Sewak of the village in obtaining loan for a Gumati. Gram-Sewak asked M.R. to establish a Gumati to run shop. For this purpose government is paying a loan of Rs. 2000. But to get this amount some bribe is to be given to the Block officials. M.R. managed to pay Rs. 500 as bribe. At the time of payment he had to pay Rs. 200 again.

Exploitation by Karamachari

A Karamachari is in charge of revenue collection from the villages. He runs villages to villages to collect revenue of land possessed by the landowners. The Parcha of land among the villages is also distributed through the Karamachari. Karamachari takes revenue and gives receipt for the same. After the death of father, the land is divided among the sons. To make the land in the name of son, Karamachari takes bribe.

N.R. (46) of a village in Bahadurpur Block of Darbhanga district informed that he was exploited by the Karamachari in the allotment of Parcha of the homestead land. It was the decision of the government to provide Parcha of homestead land on which Dalits had their houses erected. This was a welcome worth decision of the government. Because they were exploited and oppressed by the landowners on whose land their house belonged. But at the time of distribution, Dalits were exploited by the Karamachari who was in charge of allotting Parcha to the land. The Karamachari of the Block approached to the Dalit Tolas to see the actual position of the possession of area of land. He open by demanded bribe from the Dalit to allot the land and to increase the area of the land to be allotted. To increase the area under allotment scheme, Dalits began to approach the Karamachari who lived in the house of a Yadava landowner. He took Rs. 500 to 1000 for this purpose. Those who could not manage the amount were allotted very small area of land or they were left the amount were allotted very small area of land or they were left knowingly.

M.R. (41) of a village in Darbhanga urban Block of Darbhanga district informed that he was exploited and oppressed by Karamachari. His uncle had no sons. So, he made a registry of the land in his name. In the revenue collection register, the name of his uncle was continuing. After his death, he approached the Karamachari to get this work done. Karamachari demanded bribe of Rs. 300 for this work. He had to sell a calf to manage this amount of bribe. Besides Rs. 300 he had to serve a cock to Karamachari.

Exploitation of Dalit by Barababu of the Block

The head clerk of the block exploits the Dalits in various development schemes. For various purposes Dalits have to approach the Block headquarters, to obtain diesel or pumping set, sewing machine seed, fertilizer, etc. Barababu of the block demands bribe which varies from Rs. 100 to 1000 depending upon the price of the goods to be given. Sometimes, some goods are given to Dalits on the subsidy which are not refundable. In this case Barababu and the V.L.W. takes nearly half the amount of the subsidy to be given.

O.P.R. (37) of a village in Bahadurpur Block of Darbhanga district informed that he was exploited by the head clear Bahadurpur of the block. A scheme to provide diesel pumping set to Dalits was launched. This scheme was partly on subsidy and partly on loan. The price value of diesel pumping set was Rs. 3000 at that time. So Rs. 1500 was a subsidy and Rs. 1500 was as loan. The Barababu demanded Rs. 1000 from Dalits to provide diesel pumping set. Dalits were not ready to give a bribe of such a huge amount. A bargaining took place and at last Dalits agree to pay Rs. 700. The amount was to be submitted to V.L.W. whose share was Rs. 200. They submitted the amount to V.L.W. and got pumping set with diesel machine.

O.C. (31) of a village in Darbhanga Block of Darbhanga district informed that he was exploited by the Barababu of the block in obtaining a sewing machine under TRYSEM scheme. The value of sewing machine was Rs. 2000 at that time, Rs. 1000 was subsidy and Rs. 1000 was as loan. The Barababu demanded Rs. 800 as bribe but he was not ready to buy such a big bribe. So Barababu became ready to reduce the rate of bribe. He agreed to pay Rs. 500. He received the machine on the payment of Rs. 500 as bribe.

Exploitation of Dalit by Bank Official

Manager of the bank exploits the Dalits in sanctioning loans under various development schemes. Once a scheme of providing cows, buffaloes, oxen, goat, chick and pigs was launched by the government. These scheme were launched on the basis of loan facilities. Banks were directed to provide loans to Dalits to start dairy, poultry, goatery, piggery, etc. So that they might increase their income through these scheme. In sanctioning loan, the manager of the bank took bribe from the Dalits. Dalits were approached by the VLW. They were brought to block headquarters. Barababu provided the form to apply. Barababu disclosed the rate of bribe to be given to the manager of the bank.

P.RC (34) of a village in Bahadurpur district informed that he was exploited by the manager of the bank in sanctioning loan of a buffalo. He was brought by the VLW. He received form from the Barababu of the Block. The form was sent to the manager of the Bank for sanctioning loan. The VLW took Rs. 50 and Barababu Rs. 100 as bribe. The manager of the bank took Rs. 350 per beneficiary. Receiving bribe, the manager sanctioned the loan.

P.S. (36) of village in Darbhanga Urban Block of Darbhanga district informed that he was exploited by the manager of the bank in receiving loan for piggery. He had to pay Rs. 50 to VLW, Rs. 100 to Barababu and Rs. 350 to manager to receive the loan.

Exploitation of Dalit by Village Leaders

Each village had some village leaders. These village leader have contact in Thana, block and district. They utilize the service of Dalits for their selfish purpose. They take contract of village street, damas, well, and exploit Dalits. They take money to make *Pairavi* in the case of Dalits. They exploit Dalits at the time of election.

S.RC (27) of a village in Bahadurpur Block of Darbhanga district informed that he was exploited by a village leader who belonged to Barber by caste. He had good contact with the Thana and Block officials. The name of S.R. was given by the police in a dacoity committed recently. Thana-Police were demanding Rs. 2000 to get his name cut of from the list of dacoits. S.R. was not in a position to pay such a huge amount as bribe. S.R. was absconding but his father had sent the village leader Thakurji to look in to the mater. Thakurji informed that Thanedarji was demanding Rs. 2000. His father again requested Thakurji to get reduced the amount of bribe from the Thanedar. Thakurji met the Thanedar and asked him to take some hard step so that the amount of bribe could be obtained easily.

Thakurji, thus, became the *Dalal* of Thana. He came to his village back. He said to the father of S.R. that Thanedar Sahib was not ready to reduce the amount. He asked him to manage the amount to send to the Thanedar. At mid night police came suddenly to arrest the criminal but he was not available. The people of Dalits Tola approached to the Thakurji to do something. Thakurji came and asked Jamadar Sahib and police to come and take rest at his residence. Butter, Mishri (a kind of sweat), Dalmot and tea were served to them. the two cocks were cooked to serve Jamadar Sahib and Police. Rs. 200 was given as Salami to the police. All costs on Jamadar Sahib and police were met by the father of S.R. Thakurji assured them that the amount of bribe would be sent soon. His father took loan from Yadava and paid Thakurji to pay the Thanedar. He paid Rs. 1500 to Darogaji and took Rs. 500 in his pocket. He had also taken Rs. 100 twice to visit the Thana.

S.B. (25) of a village in Darbhanga Urban Block of district informed that he was exploited by a village leader who belonged to Yadava by caste. His Mausa was minister in Bihar cabinet. C.B. was matriculate. He wanted a job.

Yadavji was able to manage the job of police for his brother and nephews. S.R. thought to take help of Yadavji. He approached at the door of Yadavji. He wished Yadavji in well manners saying Malik, and sat on the ground nearby the feet of Yadavji. Then he requested him to manage the job of police for him. Yadavji kept mum for sometimes. He asked S.B. to meet some other day because he was planning to go to Patna. S.B. went back and after a week he came again to meet Yadavji. Yadavji told that it was very difficult to manage the job this time. But he assured S.B. to manage his job anyhow. He told openly that a sum of Rs. 5000 would be needed to pay bribe. This amount would be refundable if he would not qualify in running. Because pairavi is done at higher line and not at the stage of running. He also said that some more amount would also be needed at various stages. S.B. agreed. His father had a buffalo. He sold the buffalo at Rs. 8000 and gave Rs. 5000 in the hand of Yadavji. Yadavji went Patna to do his Pairavi. After a week he returned and said S.B. to make preparations to get success in running. He started making preparation. He used to run 15 kms daily in the morning and also in the evening. He succeeded in the test of running. He was very much hopeful because he had given bribe through Yadavji. But when final list was published his name was not there. He came to meet Yadavji. Yadavji told that he would go to Patna to look into the matter. On return, he told that he was rejected on the ground of physical fitness. The doctor who had taken bribe was changed suddenly. S.B. asked about his money. Yadavji told that money of bribe is very difficult to get back. But if possible, he would try best to repay him. S.B. told that five years had gone, but he could not get his money back. As Yadavji is powerful, he now does not dare to demand his money.

Exploitation of Dalit by MLA

MLA are elected by the public but after victory they do not behave as public servant. They behave with public like a servant. They do not come to meet public, rather public have to go to meet them. Dalits become victim of MLA easily. At the time of election, the candidates provide money, liquor and money for votes. Candidate makes commitment to help them any time. But when Dalit dares to meet them, he is not allowed to enter the Bangalow of MLA Sahib. He contact them through via-media.

T.RC (26) of a village in Bahadurpur Block of Darbhanga district informed that he was exploited by his MLA when he had gone to take his help for a job as a Chaprasi in Secretariat. MLA Sahib made him promise to extend full cooperation and help. He had worked for the victory of MLA Sahib. He had attracted Dalit voters in his favour when he met job for secretariat, he was asked to take seat by his P.A. He was served tea. Then MLA Sahib came out to meet him. He was asked to contact his son for further action. T.R. visited the residence of MLA Sahib four-five times and contacted his son who resided in his village. The son of MLA Sahib informed that in Secretariat appointment is made on the basis of bribe. He will have to pay Rs. 5000 to get the ob. He could be able to manage this amount to pay bribe for job. T.R. was told to get information of appointment. He could not hear any thing. So, he again approached to the son of MLA Sahib who informed that the price of bribe had gone up to Rs. 10,000. That is why his appointment was not made. When T.R. asked about his money, he was informed that his money was with appointing authorities. The money will be repaid on receiving from them. Till now he has not received his money.

T.C. (23) of a village in Darbhanga urban block of Darbhanga district informed that he was exploited by his MLA who was Yadava by caste. The MLA Sahib had taken a sum of Rs. 10,000 from T.C. to get him appointed in Daroga. the amount of bribe was taken through the Sala (wife's brother) of MLA Sahib. But his appointment was not made. He wanted to take his money back, but he was told that the amount was not with MLA, but it was given to the appointing authorities. Who have betrayed

MLA Sahib. They neither returned the money would be returned on receiving from them. Till the time of survey. T.C. had not received his money back.

Exploited of Dalit by M.P.

M.P. is also a public representative. He is elected by the public. But public are exploited by the M.P. for various purposes. His muscle men try to purchase the vote of Dalits. If not, the booth of Dalit villages are looted. Dalits are terrorised and their booths are captured.

A.R. (26) of a village in Bahadurpur Block of Darbhanga district informed that he was exploited by the M.P. his residence in Darbhanga to get the problem solved. A.R. met the son of M.P. Sahib expressed his desire to get a job. The son of M.O. assured him to get appointment in Railway, but he would have to pay Rs. 10,000 as bribe. A.R. said that it was the matter of life. So, he would try to manage this the money was paid but job was not given.

Exploitation of Dalit by Political Parties

Political parties exploit the Dalits for their selfish purposes. They collected Dalits for their participation in rallies organised by them. For this purpose, they also distributed some money to attract the men, women and children belonging to Dalit communities. In rallies, they are assured of free journey, free food and free stay. But as soon as they approach at the place of rally, they are left at their fate. They have to quarrel to seek breakfast, food and seat to sleep in the open field. At the time of return journey, some of them are left. For rally, they give two days time, but virtually they get nothing.

U.C. (23) of a village in Bahadurpur of Darbhanga district informed that he was badly exploited by a political party which had organised a rally at Patna to show public strength in his support. The followers of the party approached Dalits villagers. They attracted the Dalits by making various promises like free up and down journey, free breakfast and food and a pair of Dhoti or Sari. The workers of the party assured them that they would be given time to visit different places of Patna. Many men, women, and children were attracted. U.C. was also one of them. In the morning of the day of rally, a minibus came to carry them to Patna and from Patna to the village. People were more than the number of seats. So only women and aged were asked to take seat. Children were told to remain standing. Young men were asked to go on roof of the bus. In this situation, they had to travel. In the bus, there was no one except driver and Khalasi to take care of them for breakfast, food and tea. They reached Patna at around 12 a.m. They were badly hungry. They wandered here and there to seek the arrangement of food and water. They did not see any proper arrangement of food and water. At one place, they saw a huge line to receive lunch packet. But they could not get lunch packet due to shortage. Some of them had Chura, Bhunja and Sattu. They took them as launch. Just then they were asked to participate in rally. The rally was over at 6 p.m. and they were asked to take seats in their respective buses for return journey. What to say about Sari or Dhoti, they could not receive breakfast and food. U.C. was left at the time of return because the owner of the bus was not ready to wait for him. He had to come by train without a ticket.

U.S.R. (24) of a village in Darbhanga urban block of Darbhanga district informed that he was participated in a Rally organised by the party to show his support and strength. His villagers were brought on the promise of free journey, free food, free breakfast. They were also promised to get Rs. 10 per individual. He with his Dalits villagers went Patna by a truck. They had to make journey at late night. They reached Patna in morning. From morning till 12 p.m. a small lunch pocket per individual was served. They had to made 10 kms in Rally. They were sent back by the same truck. They did not receive Rs. 10 per individuals.

15

EXPLOITATION OF DALIT BY DALIT

The status of Dalit today is not same as it had in the past. Now Dalits are educated, officers, leaders, administrators and rich also. Thus, exploitation of Dalit by Dalit has come into existence. For our purpose of research we may discuss the exploitation of Dalit by Dalit under the following headings:

1. Exploitation of minor Dalit by major Dalit.
2. Exploitation of uneducated Dalit by educated Dalit.
3. Exploitation of poor Dalit by rich Dalit.
4. Exploitation of Dalit by Dalit Officials.
5. Exploitation of Dalit by Dalit Leaders
6. Exploitation of Dalit by Dalit Shopkeeper.
7. Exploitation of Dalit by Dalit Middlemen.
8. Exploitation of Dalit by Dalit Contractor.

Exploitation of Minor Dalit by Major Dalit

There are some Dalit group whose population is very less in comparison to other Dalit groups. They are found in one or two houses in some villages. For example, the Dhobi, the dom, the Halkhor, etc. These Dalit castes are numerically less. But the Chamar, the Dusadh, the Pasi and the Musahar are numerically dominant. Again in village structure, numerical strength is decided on the basis of number of houses. The Dhobi, the Dom, the Master etc. were part of Jajmani system. One or two families of these castes were brought to settle at a place in the village to obtain their service. The Dhobis are traditionally associated with cleaning on birth, death and other occasions. The Dom are associated with Agnisanskar and supplying bamboo baskets on the occasion of birth, marriage, death etc. the Mahtar are associated with Agnisanskar and supplying bamboo baskets on the occasion of birth, marriage, death etc. the Mehtar are associated with cleaning daily service latrine of landlords. The use of safety tank latrine has reduced this occupation nowadays. In village structure, one finds a Dalit Tola where different Dalit castes reside. In this Tola, there is supremacy of those Dalit castes whose number of houses is more. For this Tola, they are dominant caste. They exploit and oppress the minor Dalit castes. Some case studies in this regard are as follows :

S.B. (50) of a village in Bahadurpur block of Darbhanga district informed that he has been exploited by the Dusadh of the Dalit Tola. His numerical strength in the village is very less because there is only one family of Dhobi. 15 houses of Dusadh are in the village. As they are numerically more, they exploit the Dhobi whose strength is very less. Being Dhobi S.B. is directly related to the economically well-to-do families of the village. He cleans clothes of rich family. He provides service of birth and death. On the feast of 10th day of death, he is sacred specialist. He gets regard and respect among the members of high castes and backward castes of the village. He serves only to forward castes and backward castes. He does not clean the clothes of Dalit castes. Sometimes, he make iron on shirts and pants of Dalit castes for which he demands cash immediately. Such behaviour of the Dhobi makes the Dusadh of the village angry. They consider themself as a Kshetriya. But Dhobi does not consider them as a Kshetriya. For this reason, they try to put the Dhobi under trouble of various kind.

S.B. informed that his family is residing in this village since the time of his grand father who was brought here by the Rajput landlords of the village. They had given three-roomed big house to him. The house was erected with mud and thatched with tiles. His grandfather had to provide services under Jajmani system. He father also carried the same occupation and he is also carrying the same occupation but in slightly modified form. Now he has established a laundry. He washes Dhoti, Kurta, Paijama, Pasnt, Shirt and irons them. He provides services to Rajput landowners under Jajmani system and earns some cash from the laundry. This was also a matter of iealousy for the other Dalits of the village. His house was set on fire in which his 3 year's old daughter was burnt-alive. Besides, one cow, three goats and 6 chicks were also burnt alive. He did not file any case. He moved door to door of his Jajmans and collected money and grains in the name of repairing house. Within a month, he got his house repaired.

He had collected some bundles of crops from the field of landowners. He had put them outside the house to thrash. One dark night, bundles were carried away and thrown in to an old well. He had an ass. He kept ass in a small hut made for his stay. The ass was stolen and sold in market far away from the village. On festive and ceremonial occasions, the young Dusadh asked him to clean the pant-shirt or paijama-kurta and to iron them. He cleaned them but when he asked for money, they told him to pay in future. He also told them that their clothes would also be given in future. This made the Dusadh boys angry. They paid the money but made up their mind to teach the Dhobi a lesson. One dark night, they made a hole in his house and stole boxes, utensils, grains etc. Now he went to Thanedar and registered a case of theft in which the names of five Dusadh boys were given. Police came and took witness and asked the villagers. The villagers told the story of his exploitation. The police arrested them and brought them to Thana. They were beaten mercilessly. Their names were included in many dacoity committed in neighbouring areas. They had to spend money and stayed in Jail. Since then S.B. is staying peacefully in the village.

T.M. (45) of a village in Darbhanga urban block of Darbhanga district informed that he was exploited by the Dusadh of the village. Only one house of Musahar was there, while there were 30 houses of Dusadh in the Dalit Tola of the village. Thus, Dusadh enjoyed numerical dominance among the Dalit of the village, the services of T.M. was utilized by the Dusadh of the village. He did not accept pucca food from the house of Dusadh. So, Kucha foodgrains were given for food. Once, he had worked for a month to erect house of a Dusadh who was a primary school teacher in a neighbouring school. He had agreed to pay 1.5 kg rice as wages and 0.1 kg rice for his breakfast and Rs. 2 per day for Biri-Khaini was to be given because the landowners of the village used to pay him. Dusadh gave him wage but adjusted Rs. 60 in the wages which he had received for Biri-Khaini.

T.M. owned 5 Kathas of homestead land. He had erected house in one Katha and four Kathas were used as Bari land. He had erected a boundary of thorn and bushes. There was a tati to enter in to it. He used to cultivate potato, brinjal, tomato etc. He used to exchange them with paddy. He exchanged nearly 20 maunds of paddy from the vegetables. Seeing the progress of T.M., Dusadh became jealous of him. To put T.M. in trouble, they, once destroyed the potato, brinjal, tomato, bean plants. Thus, they put him in the loss of nearly 20 maunds of paddy. They vexed them so that he might sell his house and leave the village.

Exploitation of uneducated Dalit by educated Dalit

Now, among Dalit there are some educated, while remaining are uneducated. Uneducated Dalit exploit uneducated Dalit. Uneducated Dalits approach to educated Dalits for the solution of some problems like litigation of land, criminal cases, education of children, marriage of daughter, treatment etc. Educated Dalits exploit them for performing such works.

H.R. (36) of village informed that he was exploited by his educated brother. Once his wife had fallen ill. He had only daughters. There was no male member in the family. So he requested his cousin brother to help him in the treatment of wife. His brother went with him. He had to stay five days at Darbhanga hospital. The expenditure on stay of brother was met by H.R. In this period, daughters of H.R. used to graze and feed the cattle of their uncle. When he returned, he demand Rs. 100 more which was spent at his stay at Darbhanga. H.R. had to pay the amount by taking loan.

In the litigation of a plot of land, H.R. had also taken the help of his brother, but he was proved to be a Dalal of Thana and lawyer. Whenever any Dalit asked him to help, he took money for going, coming and refreshment. He also took Dalali for these work. He utilized the services of Dalits for selfish purposes.

I.C. (38) of a village in Darbhanga urban block informed that he was put into trouble by an educated Dalit, who was also his brother in distant relation. He had taken a loan of Rs. 100 from him for a month, but at the time of repayment he told that he had given Rs. 300 and I.C. had to pay.

Once I.C. sent him to receive seeds and fertilizer. He received in the name of I.C. but sold in the hand of one of his relatives. When I.C. asked about the seed and fertilizer he told innocently that they were not available. When he asked about money, his educated brother told him that they were spent on breakfast and food. He promised to return in near future. But I.C. did not get his money back from his educated brother.

Exploitation of Poor Dalit by Rich Dalit

Nowadays, some Dalits have entered into the category of rich. They have earned money from different sources and have become rich. They have purchased land from their Malik for whom their forefathers used to work as kamia. Thus, now some Dalits have become big-landowners. Big acreage of land requires labour. In order to meet the demand of labour, these Dalits utilize the services of other Dalits. Who are still poor. The poor Dalits have to perform work in the house and in the field of the rich Dalits. The rich Dalits are termed as Malik like other landowners of the village. They exploit the poor Dalits in the same way as other landowners belonging to forward and backward castes. They want to exploit their labour at cheap rate. They pay much less wages than the wages prescribed under Minimum Wages Act. They give loan to poor Dalit labourers but charge more interest like the Mahajan of the village. In fact, they do not behave properly with their poor Dalit brothers. Let us quote some case studies collected from the field in this regard.

M.P. (36) of a village in Bahadurpur block of Darbhanga district informed that he was exploited by his cousin brother who had become rich. He worked in coal field area. He also run a Khatal. He earned lot of money and gradually purchased 10 Bighas of land in the village from a Rajput landowner. He had also built a beautiful cemented house. Previously, he hand given land to his brother for doing cultivation. But after retirement he with family members came to settle in the village. He purchased two oxen, one cow and one buffalo. He started cultivation himself. But he required a regular labour for this purpose. He was in search of such a man who could perform work like a Kamia in his house and field. M.P. was badly in need of money to meet expenses on treatment of his wife. But nobody was ready to pay him loan due to his poor condition. At last, he approached to his rich brother, who gave him Rs. 1000 as loan immediately. He made promise to pay the amount by selling his cow. His rich brother did not say anything. He advised M.P. to go immediately at Darbhanga for the treatment. After three days, he again came back for money as loan Rs. 1000 was spent in three days. He was again in need of Rs. 1000. He went to his brother and requested again for loan. His brother took pity and gave him money from a local bank. Now he came back with good health of his wife. Both husband and wife were indebted to his brother. they were praising him for his kindness. But after a month, both husband and wife were called. He asked as to how they would repay such a big loan. They had only a small cow which was worth not more than Rs. 1000. But for another Rs. 1000 there was nothing. Therefore, the rich brother put a proposal for work as Kamia. This hurt their ego but due to inability, they were compelled to accept the terms and conditions of Kamia. A plot of 10 Katha was given to them to cultivate. They received 1½ kg. rice and midday meal Rs. 1000 was made interest free and Rs. 1000 was at the rate of 36 per hundred per year.

M.P. sold his cow to repay the loan and paid Rs. 1100 to him. But Rs. 900 plus interest was still with him. He worked for 10 years continuously but inability to repay loan compelled him to work for another year. In 11th year, he was able to repay his loan and then he became free. He informed that as Kamia, he was not treated well with his brother and brother's wife. He was not given good breakfast and food. He got neither proper wages nor proper treatment.

B.C. (28) of a village in Darbhanga urban block of Darbhanga district informed that he was exploited as kamia by his uncle who was owner of 8 Bighas of land. B.C. was landless. He had only house and some goats and chicks.

His father had expired, when he was 10 years. His mother thought that it would be better to give B.C. as herd boy in the house of his uncle. The uncle also became pleased with this behaviour. He had given loan to spend at the illness of his father. After the death of his father, the uncle disclosed that he was spent a sum of Rs. 1000 from his pocket. His mother accepted him. He gave B.C. as herd boy to compensate loan in his wages. He worked for ten years as herd boy. Then the loan was repaid. Then he was married in a neighbouring village. His mother again took Rs. 2000 loan for his marriage on a condition that the couple would work as kamia till the repayment of loan plus interest. B.C. informed that he had to work with his wife and mother for his uncle till 7 years more. Then loan plus interest was paid back. At the tiem of Survey he was working as daily casual labour. As Kamia, he had to perform work received by other type of labour. He received only 1 ½ kg rice per day as wage, plus mid day meal. He did not work for another landowner. He worked only for his uncle.

EXPLOITATION OF DALIT BY DALIT OFFICIALS

Exploitation by Dalit Choukidar

S.M. (46) of a village in Bahadurpur Block of Darbhanga district informed that he was exploited by the Choukidar, who was also a Dalit. Once a theft was committed in his house. He recognised the thief but he ran way. He belonged to Dusadh caste. The Choukidar was also Dusadh by caste. The Choukidar asked S.M. to go to Thana to file a case and he himself went to Thana before him. He made the Thanedar aware of the fact that S.M. was coming to file a case. A theft had been committed in his house. He recognised the thief but could not catch him. The thief had stolen ornaments and clothes from his house. S.M. reached at Thana and filed a case against a Dusadh of the village. His wife, son and daughters were the witness. The case was registered. Next day police came to verify the fact. They met the villagers and collected facts. The Choukidar asked him to pay Rs. 300 as Salami to Jamadar Sahib. Then the police reached at the house of Jamadar with Salami. The choukidar was Dusadh and the

Chor (thief) was also Dusadh, So, Choukidar took the side of the accused. The Choukidar asked the accused person to give Rs. 2000 for final rejection of the case. He gave the amount and became free. Thus, in cases, Choukidar exploited both party by taking the amount as bribe.

P.P. (38) of village in Darbhanga urban of Darbhanga district informed that he was exploited by the Choukidar who belonged to his own caste. He had a he-goat worth Rs. 300. One day the Choukidar came and purchased the goat at Rs. 300 but he did not pay the amount. He promised to pay the amount after returning from home. He again, promised to give the money. In today and tomorrow one month passed, but P.P. did not get his money. One day his son was seriously ill, so he went to the house of Choukidar to take money. The Choukidar gave him Rs. 200 and promised to pay Rs. 100 on some other day. But that money was no given till the time of survey. P.P. has given up his all hopes. He now does not go to ask for money.

Exploitation by Dalit Mukhia

S.C. (48) of a village in Bahadurpur block of Darbhanga district informed that he was exploited by the Mukhia of his Panchayat. The Mukhia also belonged to his own caste. His Mukhia had constructed a village road under food for work programme. S.C. had worked in this programme for a period of one month. Mukhia had assured that a payment of 3 kg of wheat or rice would be made for a labourer as a wages of one day. This assurance had attracted more and more labourers of the village to work in road construction. This wages was double the wages received by a casual labourer in a day. But at the time of payment, Mukhia made announcement that due to shortage of grains received by the Panchayat it was not possible of pay 3 kg wheat/rice per day as wages of labourer. But now the payment would be made 2 kg wheat/rice per day per labour. Due to shortage of grains, some labourers could get only half payment. They were promised to get payment in near future, but till the time of survey, they were not able to receive their payment.

M.P. (38) of a village of Darbhanga urban block informed that he was exploited by the Mukhia of the Panchayat. He had brought Mukhia to settle a dispute over a plot of land. Mukhiaji came and did not provide him justice. So, he went to court for justice. Mukhiaji took ill of it because he had disobeyed the decision of Mukhiaji.

Once the son of M.P. was herding his buffalo on the bank of road. He was playing as well. In play he became so busy that buffalo entered the plot of Mukhiaji and destroyed the crop. This news reached to Mukhiaji.

He called M.P. and his son and fixed Rs. 500 for this M.P. had no money, so he requested Mukhiaji to allow him to work as daily wage earner. The wages were to be adjusted against the amount of fine. He has to render labour for two months to repay the fine.

Exploitation by Dalit Sarpanch

Sarpanch is important authority of modern Gram Panchayat. He looks after the criminal cases. As he owns power he exploits and oppresses the Dalits. At the time of exploitation and oppression, he behaves like other castes of the village.

Once the Sarpanch had asked to S.P. (25) of a village of Bahadurpur block of Darbhanga district to sell his cow in his hand. According to S.P., the cow was worth of Rs. 1500. The Sarpanch was ready to pay Rs. 1200. So, S.P. did not sell his cow to Sarpanch. Another person of a village came and brought the cow at Rs. 1500. The Sarpanch decided to teach S.P. a lesson by exploiting and oppressing him.

Once, his son had gone to herd his another cow. A cow of an other neighbouring village came and began to fight, the horn of another cow got broken. When the cow returned in the evening, the owner saw cow hornless. He also saw blood over head. At night, the cow delivered calf untimely. This, his all hopes of getting milk in future went in vain. He began to repent as to why he had left the cow uncared, this happening made him angry. He began to try to find out as to how the incidence took place. Some herd boys of his village disclosed the name of owner of the cow and son of S.P. The owner of the cow filed a case in the court of Sarpanch. He bought two herd boys as witness who were present when the incidence had occurred. In this case, the son of S.P. was accused for beating the cow mercilessly. The Sarpanch also heard the statement of the son of S.P. who refused to accept it. There was no one as witness from the side of S.P. The Sarpanch and his panch found the son of S.P. as accused. For this criminal behaviour, S.P. has to pay a sum of Rs. 1000 as fine. In absence of money, S.P. had to make agreement with the owner of the cow to serve him till the amount of fine was not paid back.

Exploitation by Dalit Thana

The government has established Dalit Thana to look into the cases of Dalit. In this Thana, Dalits can approach for justice. But the fact remains that these Dalit Thanas also do not lag behind in exploiting the Dalits. Let us see some case studies in this regard.

S.K. (39) of a village in Bahadurpur block of Darbhanga district informed that he was exploited by the Thanedar of a Dalit Thana. Once a dacoity was committed in his house on the occasion of marriage of his son. Clothes, ornaments and cash were looted at pistol point. The ornaments of his relative were also looted. He went to lodge complaint regarding the concurrence of dacoity in his house. The Thanedar noted the case on a separate paper. He made promise to come next day for verification. Next day police came on a jeep. They asked about the materials looted. They made a list on a piece of paper. They also asked from the villagers. He did not give the name of any person as dacoits. At the time of departure the police sent the Choukidar to pay Rs. 300 as Salami for the visit of police. He managed Rs. 300 from somewhere and gave it to the police. Thereafter, he did not dare to go to Thana for verification.

A.C. (36) of a village in Darbhanga urban block informed that he was exploited by the same Dalit Thana, here he had gone to file a case against a crime committed by a person of the village who had broken his forhead. The Thanedar demanded Rs. 200 to register his case. He gave Rs. 100 and promised to pay Rs. 100 in near future. He went to the doctor of the block. He asked certificate from the doctor. The doctor assured him to give it tomorrow.

In the mean time the pairbikar of the accused person reached the Thana. They paid Rs. 500 to Thanedar. They also paid Rs. 500 to doctor. The Thanedar changed the report and the doctor also gave unfavourable report to A.P. Thus, his case became weak. Thereafter, he did not dare to move in Thana and court.

Exploitation by Dalit Barababu

The Barababu of Block exploits the oppresses the Dalits, whether the Barababu belongs to the same community or not.

B.C. (28) of a village in Bahadurpur block of Darbhanga district informed that he was exploited by the Barababu in receiving his Bekari Bhatta. He was matriculate but could not get any job. His name was selected for Bekari Bhatta. In this scheme, Rs. 50 per month was to be given to him. This was to be sent to the beneficiary through the post office. He received the amount for some month through the post office but suddenly the amount was stopped. He went in the block for inquiry. Barababu informed him that he would send the amount on receiving from the government. He used to go to inquire the matter at least thrice or four times in a month. Thus, he visited block for six months. One day, Barababu told that the amount had come and he would receive Rs. 300 together. He asked him to come tomorrow. He went tomorrow. Barababu asked for Rs.

50.00 as bribe which he paid from the amount of Bekari Bhatta. Now, this scheme is not going on.

S.Devi (60) of a village in Darbhanga urban block of Darbhanga district informed that she was exploited by the Barababu of the block in receiving old age pension (Bridha Bhatta). She was selected for this scheme because she was widow and lived alone from her sons. Her pension was sent initially through the post office. But suddenly, the pension was stopped due to non-availability of fund from the government. After 8 months, she heard that the money of pension had come. The Barababu was also Dalit by caste. But he took Rs. 50 as brike, then he paid the amount of pension. She had no money with her. So she was paid Rs. 50 less than the actual amount of pension.

Exploitation by Dalit VLW

Gram Sewak is the Sewak of the village but he exploit Dalits in various ways. Even the Dalit VLW also exploits the Dalit.

C.P. (36) of a village in Bahadurpur block of Darbhanga district informed that he was exploited by the VLW who also belonged to Dalit. The VLW had come to inform the villagers particularly Dalits for various types of development schemes. Housing scheme was also one of them. Under this scheme a sum of Rs. 5000 was being given to erect house under own supervision. C.P. went to apply for it. VLW took Rs. 50 for giving the form and filling it. Whenever, he came in the village he took eggs and chicks from his house in the name of pairavi. At the time of final payment, he had to pay Rs. 700 as bribe. This amount was distributed among bank managers, and block officials.

D.K. (32) of a village in Darbhanga block informed that he was also exploited by a Dalit VLW. On the advice of VLW he applied for a buffalo. The cost of buffalo was estimated Rs. 2500 at that time. In order to receive this amount, he had to give 2 cocks to VLW and Rs. 500 as bribe. Then he was able to obtain a buffalo. He did not receive the amount. But a buffalo was purchase by the block official.

Exploitation by Dalit Karamchari

Dalit Karamchari of the block also exploits the Dalit when they come to make a survey for distribution of Parcha of homestead land among the Dalits. For this purpose, he demands bribe from the Dalits. To get favour Dalits have to pay bribe.

P.M. (51) of a village in Bahadurpur Block informed about his exploitation by Dalit Karamchari of the block. The Karamchari had come to distribute Parcha of the homestead land. For this purpose, he made a survey of the actual possession of land by each Dalit family. Then he put his proposal to meet again for this purpose. At night he stayed in the village. He asked Dalit of the village to cook cock for him. He shared the cooked cook. In the morning he took Rs. 100 from each Dalit family for the allotment of Parcha of house. For allotting more land, some Dalits gave him bribe up to Rs. 500.

S.M. (53) of the same village informed that he had purchased a land from his brother. To get the receipt cut by the Karamchari of the purchase land, he had to pay a bribe of the Rs. 200.

D.P. (46) of a village in Bahadurpur block was exploited by the doctor of the block who was also a Dalit. She was admitted in the block hospital for delivery. Lady doctor was not there. Only nurses were available. The doctor asked his husband to pay Rs. 500 as fees and Rs. 500 for medicine. He had only 500 with him. He promised to pay the amount next day. At night delivery took place in normal way. But doctor sahib took Rs. 500 in pocket. He also demanded another 500 which he had spent on medicine.

These cases reveal that here is no caste of officials. They are above caste is exploiting and oppressing a person.

Exploitation of Dalit by Dalit Leaders

Each Dalit village has some Dalit leaders. These leaders have contact with block officials, Thana, police, bank officials etc. These leaders own some cultivable land. In the name of pairavi for jobs etc. they take money from the poor Dalits. These leaders exploit the poor Dalits for selfish purpose.

S.K. (26) informed that in his village there is a Dalit leader. He has contact with some outside people and officials. He has also contact with some outside M.P. He owns five Bighas of land but does not cultivate them himself. He exploits the Dalits in water, rent etc. but takes half share of the yield in both crops for pairavi. In Pairvi he gets Dalali from the Dalits and the officials with whom he has contact. He visits Thana and block regularly. For going and coming, he charges fare and expenditure on food, breakfast, tea etc.

R.P. (30) of a village in Darbhanga urban block of Darbhanga district informed that he was exploited by a Dalit leader in the name of doing a Pairvi, for allotment of Gairmanfarua land, which belonged to a Yadava landowner. He had taken a sum of Rs. 500 from him for his purpose. But till the time of Survey, the land was not allotted to him. He demanded his money back from the leader, but the leader has not given money back to him. He says that the leader has not given bribe to the officer, but he was transferred, and went with money. From where I would pay the money back to R.P.

Exploitation of Dalit by Dalit Shopkeeper

Nowadays, some Dalits in village are running small shops in which they keep commodities of day to day use. These shopkeepers exploit the Dalits. They give commodities at high rate but take commodities at reduced rate. Thus, they exploit the poor Dalits in both way – in selling as well as buying. They provide commodities as loan for which they charge heavy interest. They also manipulate the register of loan. The poor and illiterate Dalits have to pay them.

R.R. (32) of a village in Bahadurpur Block of Darbhanga district informed that he was exploited by a Dalit shopkeeper of the village who runs a small shop of essential commodities. It was the month of Bhado and R.R. had no money or grain to buy oil, salt, spices etc. So he approached the Dalit shopkeeper. He requested the shopkeeper to provide mustard oil and other things on loan. He promised to pay the loan in a month. The total loan was Rs. 150. He had taken a Kuccha receipt of the amount to be paid back. After a month, he came to pay the loan back. The shopkeeper opened his register and showed him that Rs. 250 was due on him. R.R. said that he had taken only articles worth 150 and how it became Rs. 250 in the shopkeeper told that he had taken more which he had forgotten. At last, R.R. had to pay Rs. 250.

S.C. (38) of a village in Darbhanga urbán block of Darbhanga district informed that he was exploited by the Dalit shopkeeper of the village on the occasion of Gauna of his daughter, S.C. had taken oil, spices, soap, surf etc. from the shopkeeper. The value of item was Rs. 450.

After a month S.C. went to pay the loan back. He had Rs. 450 in his pocket. The shopkeeper opened the register. On register, it was written Rs. 650. S.C. became worried to hear the amount because he had brought Rs. 450 which was the due. He asked as to how the amount increased from Rs. 450 to Rs. 650. The shopkeeper told that he had forgotten about the money. S.C. paid Rs. 450 immediately. He also paid the remaining amount after a month.

Exploitation of Dalit by Dalit Middlemen

Some Dalits have established good relationship with the big traders of the block level market. They work as middlemen. They are connecting link between the trader and the villagers. They purchase paddy, wheat, rice etc. from villagers and brought them in the Gola of the big traders. For this purpose, they got commission from the traders. Dalits have very little rice, paddy or wheat to sell. That is why they do not get proper rate from the middlemen and trader. Their commodities are purchased at much reduced rate than the big farmer who sell more and more grain at a time and, they get full amount from the traders.

C.R. (36) of a village in Bahadurpur block of Darbhanga district informed that he was exploited by the Dalit middle-men at the time of selling 4 maunds of wheat. The Dalit middle men approached him to buy wheat. He asked about the rate. The middle men became ready to buy the wheat at Rs. 200 per quintal, though just a day before he had purchased wheat at Rs. 250 per quintal from a big landowner. C.R. disclosed the fact but the Dalit middlemen did not agree to pay the price more than Rs. 200 because for such a small quantity he would have to pay more transportation cost.

Exploitation of Dalit by Dalit Contractor

Some Dalits work as contractor. They take work on contract for cutting soil from a higher land, for filling a ditch, etc. They also take contract of drain construction, street construction, house construction, well construction, installing chapakal etc. The government had taken a decision to provide work on contract to a Dalit. The leader type Dalit were selected as contractor. These Dalit contractor also exploit the Dalit labourer.

L.R. (26) of village in Bahadurpur block of Darbhanga district informed that he was exploited by a Dalit contractor who had taken a work of constructing drain and street in the village as a contractor from the government. He had used Dalits as labourers. He had agreed to pay Rs. 20 per labour per day as wages. On this promise 5 Dalit labourers worked continuously to complete the work of drain and street construction in the village. When the work was completed, labourers demanded their wages. They were paid at the rate of Rs. 15 per day per labour and Rs. 5 for officials to get the fund released.

The above studies reveal that nowadays exploitation of Dalit by Dalit has also come in the existence. Dalits are being exploited and oppressed by their follow Dalits also.

16

ATROCITY ON DALITS OF DARBHANGA

Atrocity is evil or criminal act by which a person or group put other person or group into various kind of trouble. Dalits have been poor and weaker since centuries. Therefore, they have been subjected to atrocity more than the other group. The change in the status of Dalits due to adoption of democratic secular Constitution after independence has become a painful development for those groups who used to utilized the services of Dalits at a cheap rate for selfish purposes. The change in behaviour of Dalits is unbearable for them. These rich and powerful groups commit following types of atrocities on Dalit :

1. Physical and mental torture as well as beating mercilessly.
2. Not allow to move on the boundary of cultivated fields.
3. Not allow to cut grasses on the boundary of cultivated fields.
4. Not allow to defecate in cultivated field.
5. Not allow to pick Mahua under Mahua tree.
6. Not allow to enter the garden of mango or other fruits.
7. Not allow to collect dry leaves as fuel.
8. Not allow to fishing in the pond and Nala.
9. Not allow to cut sag.
10. Stealing cocks, eggs, goat, etc.
11. Stealing cattle.
12. Stealing grains, box, ornaments from the house.
13. Stealing bundle of crops.
14. Setting the thrashing field on fire.

15. Setting the house on fire.
16. Committing dacoity.
17. Rape.
18. Gang rape.
19. Dalit women as kept.

These are the areas where atrocity on Dalit had taken place. Now let us see atrocity in these areas through case studies.

Physical and Mental Torture as Well as Beating Mercilessly

This type of atrocity is committed most on Dalit children who commit some such mistake which make the landowners angry. They abuse and heat the Dalit children. Sometime, they beat them mercilessly.

P.R. (36) of a village in Bahadurpur block of Darbhanga district informed that his 15 years old child was beaten mercilessly by a Yadava landowner. His son had gone to herd his cow in a grazing field. His cow entered the field of the landowner. The field was situated by the side of the road. It was a potato field. The landowner was coming from somewhere. He saw the cow in the field; seeing this, he became very angry. He immediately rushed to the field and started beating the cow. Then he saw the boy. He started beating the boy mercilessly. They boy began to weep bitterly but no one came to help him.

In another case study K.C. (38) of a village in Darbhanga in urban block of Darbhanga district also informed about the beating of his 12 years only son mercilessly. K.C. had given his son as herd boy in the house of a Kurami landowner. One day, the horns of a cow were broken in quarrel with another cow. Seeing the horns of the cow broken, the owner became out of control. He began to beat the child mercilessly. He began to weep bitterly but he went on beating. After good beating he was removed from the service. He did not pay anything for the six months service of the boy as herd boy. The boy and his parents remained quite silent. They did not dare to ask for the wages.

Not Allow to Move on the Boundary of Cultivated Fields

Dalits are not allowed to move through the boundaries of cultivated fields particularly when crops are ready to harvest. If they are found moving through the boundaries of the fields, they are abused. They are sometimes beaten or fined through the village Panchayat. Only those Dalit are allowed to move on the boundary of fields who are Kamia or Banihar.

A.P. (31) of a village in Bahadurpur block of Darbhanga district informed that his 15 years old son was abused and beaten by a landowner of the village for going through the boundary of his fields. It was the field of gram crop which was ready for cultivation. He was going to see a fair. He tried to catch the other villagers through the gram field. The owner saw him and cried to stop him. The child was stopped. Reaching the field, the owner showered the abusive words and started beating with hands. The child could not understand as to why the owner was beating him. After beating the anger of owner came down and he allowed the child to go. He warned the child not to pass through the boundary of the cultivated crop.

S.D. (36) of a village in Darbhanga urban block also reported about the atrocity treatment of the owner of the fields for passing though the boundary of the cultivated crops. She was going for the treatment of her 12 years old son to a quack who resided in a neighbouring village. To reach the residence of quack, quickly, she decided to pass through a short cut way. She used the boundary of the field of green pea. The child pulled out one crop. The owner of the field saw him from a distance. It was the field of a Koeri. He started abusing the mother and child from a distance. He showered abusive words on them. On reaching the field, he beat the child with hand. He did not consider the request of the mother about the illness of the child.

Not Allow to Cut Grasses on the Boundary of Cultivated Fields

Dalits, who are not Kamia or Banihar of a landowner, are not allowed to cut grasses on the boundaries of the field by the landowners. If any one of them does so, he or she is oppressed.

B.C. (26) of a village in Bahadurpur block of Darbhanga district informed that he was oppressed by a Muslim landowner for cutting use to bring grasses from anywhere. He reached at the boundary of there. He abused B.C. and beat with hands on his chicks and back. He asked B.C. to bring grasses at his house. B.C. had to obey his order. His sickle and lathi were taken by the landowner. B.C. was told not to cut grasses on the boundary of cultivated crops, otherwise a fine would be taken from him. B.C. had to hear abuses and was subjected to physical torture for cutting grasses on the boundary of fields of landowners.

B.D. (28) of a village in Darbhanga urban block of Darbhanga district informed that she was abused by a Yadava landowner for cutting grasses on the boundary of his field in which Khesari was cultivated. She was widow and had a cow. She used to sell milk. The cow was a means of income for her. Before and after working as Dai in market. She came late, and did not find fodder to feed the cow. She thought that she would collect some from nearby field and would ask pardon from the owner of the field if prevented to collect. She was busy in cutting grasses. Suddenly the owner of the field came and saw her in the field. He took grasses and sickle from her and broke her basket. She became terrified to see his behaviour. She ran away immediately towards her house.

Not Allow to Defecate in Cultivated Field

This is the most painful aspect that Dalits are not allowed to ease in the cultivated field by the landowners. Even children and women are not allowed for it. When caught, they are beaten with *Della* (small piece of dry soil) and are abused.

C.D. (26) of a village in Bahadurpur block of Darbhanga district informed that she was abused and her 7 years old child was beaten with *Della* by the landowners who belonged to Koeri caste. Just in front of there house, the landowner possessed a plot of land in which mustard seeds were sown. Just by the side of this plot, there was a field of potato. The owner of the field was coming to see the potato and the mustard in his field. Her child was easing in the mustard field and the mother was standing at the boundary. Seeking this the owner became angry. He began to shower abusive words on the mother. The owner threw Della to beat the child. The mother of the child was also beaten by the Della. Both ran to see such behaviour of the owner of the land.

D.D. (28) of a village in Darbhanga urban block informed that Dalits are not allowed to defecate in the field of landowner. For this purpose, they have to visit to government land. Once it was evening and her 12 years daughter expressed her desire to ease. Both mother and daughter could not go at a distant place for this purpose. They sat in the field of Khesari to ease. Suddenly the owner of the land came and started abusing them from distance. The landowner beat them with Della. They had to hear insult and beating from her natural call.

Not Allow to Enter in to Garden

In village, the landowners have their garden in which there are trees of Mango, Lichi, Jamun, Ber, Bel etc. In these garden Dalits are not allowed to enter particularly during the season of fruit. If anyone is caught, he or she is abused, oppressed and finally fined.

P.R. (38) of a village in Bahadurpur block of Darbhanga district informed that his 20 years old son was abused and beaten when he entered the garden of a landowner to collect guava fruits cut by parrots were lying on the ground of the garden. Seeing guava fruits, his mouth began to salivate. He entered the garden and began to collect the fallen guava fruits. Suddenly the owner of the garden reached there. He saw the Dalit boy in the garden. Seeing the boy in the garden his anger grew up. He ran using abusive words. He carried the boy to remain stand up as punishment. The boy requested that he had collected only fallen guava which were half eaten by the parrots. But the owner started beating him for the reason he had entered the garden. The boy received beating silently, because he had done wrong by entering in garden without the permission of the owner.

L.D. (28) of a village in Darbhanga urban block of Darbhanga district also presented a similar fact regarding the atrocity on Dalits boy. His 15 years old son had committed a mistake of entering in to the garden of a Koeri owner. It was the season of Jamun fruits. Dalit boys used to wander from tree to tree collect ripe Jamun which were falling upon the ground. There was a Jamun tree in the garden of an owner. The garden had many other trees of fruits. Generally, nobody wanted to enter the garden without seeking permission from Jamun fruits owner, another boy went to the owner and told about the boy in the garden. This made the owner angry. He ran towards the garden abusing the boy and his parents. The boy heard the cry of the owner and became terrified. His feet began to shake. Jamun fruits fell on the ground. But the owner did not take pity on him. He started beating the child with shoe. There was no one to save the boy. He received beating silently. When the owner got tired of beating, he allowed the boy to go to his home.

Not Allow to Collect Fuel from Garden and Fields

Dalit women and children collect cow dung from the fields of the owner. They also collect dry leaves and wood from the garden of the owner. But for such work only those Dalits are allowed who are Kamia. Dalits working as casual labour are not allowed. If they are caught, they are abused and beaten.

C.R. (29) of a village in Bahadurpur block of Darbhanga district informed about the abuse and beating of Dalit women and children in collection of fuel. When the fields are barren, cattle are allowed to graze in the fields. In fields, they give dung. The owners ask their Kamia to collect fuel. Kamir give half fuel to owner and half fuel goes to his house.

C.R. was a free labourer. One day his wife and children went to collect cowdung from the government land. They saw cowdung in the field of an owner. They collected the dung from the field. A Kamia saw it. He informed the owner about it. Next day the owner was sitting in the way. His wife and children were coming. They were not aware of the owner. When they reached near the owner, he started abusing the woman. He pulled basket from her head and broke it. He gave a good beating to the boy with shoe. Their all baskets were broken. They were subjected to such treatment because they had dared to collect cow dung from the field of owner.

L.D. (46) of a village in Darbhanga urban block of Darbhanga district informed that she was subjected to atrocity by the owner of a garden. In this garden there were trees of Sisam, Siris, Kahua, Gular etc. These all trees were of wood value, they were not fruit giving trees. During the period of autumn, the old leaves of the tree fall down and new leaves come up. The fallen leaves are dried. These leaves are used as fuel for cooking by the poor Dalit families. They collect these leaves and stored them at a place near the house. They used them for cooking. For this purpose, they have to seek permission from the owner of the tree. However, a Kamia is allowed to collect these leaves even without permission of the owner. But other Dalits are not supposed to do this work without the prior permission of the owner. L.D. did not seek permission of the owner of the garden. She thought she would seek permission of the owner at the time of bringing them to house. 20 years old son of the owner saw her collecting dry leaves. He went there and asked whether she had taken the permission from his father. She said that she would seek after making heap of leaves. This made the boy of owner angry. He started abusing her. He took her broom, spread the leaves on the ground and tore the cloth which she had brought to carry the leaves. He also threw *Della* to beat her. In this abusive and oppressive manner she was thrown out of the garden.

Not Allow to Fishing in the Pond and Nala

Each village was some Pond and Nala in which fishes are found. After rainy season, fishes are caught, in ponds and Nala, the landowners of the village possess right and ownership. Dalits are not allowed to fish in these ponds and Nala without the permission of the landowner. If any one makes attempt, he or she is subjected to oppressive treatment.

P.R. (48) of a village in Bahadurpur block of Darbhanga district informed that he and his 12 years old grand son were beaten by the landowner for fishing in a government Nala. The Nala was flowing in the Gairmanjua land of the government. By the side of Nala, the landowners possessed their land both sides. They used the water of Nala for the purpose of irrigation. After rainy season, the water went down at the bottom, then fishing was started. First of all, the landowners sent their men to fish; when they got tired of fishing, they left the Nala open for fishing, but only for their Kamia. P.K. was not kamia of any landowner. When Nala was made free for all to fish, he with his grand son went there. They were fishing, using a piece of cloth as Net. Fortunately, they were able to fish nearly 3 kg. of fish and he was still fishing. He got tempted to see the fish. He thought to take the fish anyhow. He asked as to why he was fishing in his Nala, P.K. did not give replay. He started abusing them. He compelled them to come out of Nala. He took fishes from them. He threatened them to take fine for doing such daring work without the permission of the landowner.

C.D. (24) of a village in Darbhanga urban block Darbhanga district also presented the similar fact. In his village there was a big pond located in Gairmanjarua land of the government. The landowners of the village possessed right and ownership over the pond. After rainy season, the landowners tried to catch the fishes for eating. For this purpose, they used to send their own men. When they got tired off fishing, they asked their Kamia for fishing. Kamia had to bring half fishes in the house of owner. When there was no probability of getting fish, the pond was made open for the public. This was the general rule of fishing in the village.

One day C.D. also went to fishing when Kamias of landowners were fishing. He thought that he would also pay the half fish to the owner. With this view in mind he also began to fish. Fortunately, he was able to fish nearly 5 kg of fish. This made the other Kamias jealous. One of Kamias went in the villages and informed about fishing in the pond by C.D. without the permission of the landowners. This made the landowners angry. The landowners sent his men to bring C.D. at the house. C.D. was coming with fish to give half share to the landowners. When he reached, the landowners began to fire on them with abusive words. They took all fishes from him and fined him Rs. 100 for violating the rule of fishing in the village.

Not Allow to Cut Sag

Sag is herbal leaves used as an item of vegetable. The sag of Gram, Khesari, Pea, Mustard, Bathua, Karami etc. are eaten by the people. Dalits do not have their own fields to grow gram, Khesari, Pea, Mustard etc. But they want to eat sag. The sag saves expenditure on vegetable. Generally, women do this work. The women belonging to the family of Kamia are allowed to cut sag in the field of their respective landowners. But other Dalits are not allowed. If any such person is caught, he or she is subjected to oppressive treatment.

L.D. (28) of a village in Bahadurpur block of Darbhanga district informed that she was subjected to atrocity by the landowner when she had gone to cut sag from his field. Her fault was that she had not taken permission from the landowner to cut the sag. One day some relative came in her house. They expressed their desire to eat sag. L.D. went to cut sag in the field of a landowner. She had worked in his field as casual labour. She had also done the harvesting of paddy crop in his field. She had thought to seek pardon from the landowner, if she was caught. She was busy in cutting sag. Soon the landowner reached there. He asked as to who had told her to cut sag. She could not speak anything. He again repeated his question. But she did not tell anything. He understood that she was cutting sag without seeking permission from the landowner. He took sag from her. He also took sickle from her hand. He broke her basket. She requested to give sickle. This made the him angry. He started abusing her and throwing Della on her. She was beaten with Della. She had to go back hearing abusive words.

S.D. (49) of a village in Darbhanga urban block of Darbhanga block informed that she was subjected to atrocity by the landowner for cutting sag in his field. Her son was herd boy in the house of the landowner. With this right, she was cutting sag of Gram in the field of landowner. A 14 years old son of the landowner saw her cutting sag. He gradually went there and started beating her with a thin stick. He tore her sari, took sag and sickle and broke her basket. In this abusive manner she was sent he house back.

Stealing Cocks, Eggs, Goat, etc.

Dalits are oppressed by the evil act of stealing cock, hen, goat etc. Stealing is such an evil act by which a person oppresses other person indirectly. Dalits rear hen, cock, goats, ducks, etc. Other Hindu castes do not like to do this profession, but they consume chicks, eggs, goat etc. They approached to buy cock, egg, goat, duck from the Dalit. But sometimes a Dalit does not want to sell a cock or hen or goat at reduced price. He wants to sell them on high price. This behaviour of a Dalit irritate the landowners who still think that they are the bread providers of the Dalits. In this situation, they want to harass a Dalit by evil act of stealing goat, chicks, hen, cock etc.

D.R. (65) of a village in Bahadurpur block of Darbhanga district informed that his family has been subjected to misery by the evil act of stealing cocks and goats. In his village, there lived Koeri landowners. They were big landowners and nowadays, many of them are in jobs. On festive and ceremonial occasion, the service holders and their relative reach in the village. They like to enjoy by eating non-vegetarian food. Once a Koeri service holder working in police came in his house for a goat. He wanted to buy, goat and cow. But D.R. did not want to sell because his son had gone in the house of relative. He asked to tell in yes or no tomorrow. Tomorrow the police had to join his duty. So he came back without goat. This was taken bad by the police and his brothers. Dalits generally go to sleep at early night. The police and his brothers went in Dalit Tola silently. They opened the Tati of a house and brought goat at his house. The goat was killed and its flesh was eaten, legs and skin of the goat were thrown outside the house of D.R. In the morning, D.R. did not see his goat. He asked the children of the house. All came out of house and saw legs and skin of the goat. After some days, they came to know that it was the work of police and his brother.

Stealing Cattle

Dalits are also oppressed by the evil act of stealing cow, calf, buffalo etc. To oppress Dalit there came thief and steal their cattle at night. They do not appear to oppress Dalits face to face. But they harass them in such a manner in which there is lack of evidence. One can just guess, but cannot say with certainty.

J.D. (53) of a village in Bahadurpur block of Darbhanga district informed that his cow worth Rs. 5000 was stolen by the Gundas belonging to landowners of the village. One day, young Gundas were uprooting the green gram from his field which he had cultivated as sharecropper. It was around 8 p.m. J.D. went to see his field of gram crops. He saw four-five young person stealing the crop. He shouted loudly and persons from this Tola ran to help him. The thieves were able to escape but they had to leave the gram crops in the field. He brought the gram crops before the landowner in whose land he had done sharecropping. He gave half crop to landowner and brought half share in his house. It was the field of a widow landowner who had only daughters. The aim of the Gundas was to oppress the widow as well as J.D.

After sometimes, the Gundas made plan to steal the cow of J.D. which was worth Rs. 5000, He had taken cow from the widow landowner on half share. the cow gave a calf and within 15 days she began to give 5 kg. milk per day. He took permission from the cow-owner to sell. It became a news in the village that J.D. had a cow to sell. Buyers began to come to purchase the cow. But J.D. was not ready to sell not less than Rs. 5000. Now the calf also became able to walk with cow. Gundas thought that it was now fit time to steal the cow. One dark night, they came with Lathi, Bhala and Gun. They cut the lock of the room in which cow was kept at night. They took the calf and cow out. In the morning, J.D. saw that his cow was not in the room. He also saw the lock cut by the thieves. He went in the house of the owner and informed her about the theft of the cow. Neither the owner nor J.D. made case in absence of any clear cut evidence.

M.M. (42) of a village in Darbhanga urban block of Darbhanga district informed about a similar case of theft of buffalo. He had taken a calf to be taken out at the time of selling. Gradually she turned in a full grown buffalo and gave a calf. Now M.M. approached to the owner to know his desire, whether he was interested in keeping the buffalo or he wanted to sell. The owner had two buffalos already, therefore, he asked to sell the buffalo. One day, a Yadava paikar (one who does the business of selling and buying the cattle) came to buy the buffalo. He purchased buffaloes in the villages and brought them in the Khatal of town to sell. He came twice-thrice time to buy, but he was not giving proper price. The owner had instructed him not to sell buffalo less than Rs. 8000. This value was decided by the owner. In his visits, he became aware of the place where buffalo was kept at night. He also saw the ways by which the buffalo could be stolen. He met a famous animal thief and made plan to steal the buffalo as early as possible. One dark night four-five persons came and took the buffalo out of house by opening another gate from back side.

Stealing Grains, Box, Ornaments form the House

Dalit are also oppressed by the evil act of stealing box, ornaments, grains, utensils etc from the house.

R.R. (25) of a village in Bahadurpur block of Darbhanga district informed that he was oppressed by the evil act of stealing his all belongings from the house. The neighbour of R.R. was a Kahar. There was a young girl in his house. The girl became the centre of attraction for the Gundas of the village. Gundas used to come and make round around the house of the Kahar. As the house of R.R. was situated just by the side of Kahar, he did not take the visit of Gundas in the Tola good. He informed the male members of Kahar family and also the Toladwellers about the visit of Gundas of the village. In this way, to some extent he attempted to organise the Toladwellers against the evil intension of the Gunda elements. Anyway, Gundas became aware of this fact. They though out a plan to teach R.R. a lesson so that he might not dare to come in their way in near future. One day. R.R. went to market with his wife. His 15 years old daughter and 10 years old son were at house. The couple could not return. The Gundas took advantage of this situation. Around mid night, they came in the Tola with arms and managed to enter in the house of R.R. They closed the door in which children were sleeping and easily took out all boxes, grains, utensils from the other rooms of the village. R.R. was put in such a situation that he had no utensil and grain in the house to cook. He had no clothes and money to buy anything. He became quite helpless. He had to take loan from the landowners of the village to run the family.

B.R. (29) of a village in Darbhanga urban block of Darbhanga district informed about a similar tragedy which took place in his house nearby 3 years ago. He had taken courage to appear as witness against a Yadava criminal. This was not taken good by the Yadavas of the villages. At caste level, they took decision not to provide work to B.R. and to harass him in various ways. The young Gunda Yadavas took decision to steal all belonging of the B.R., one dark night they approached with arms in the house of B.R., the mouths of all family members were closed with cloth. Their hands and feet were tied. They were laid on the ground. The criminals took boxes, clothes, ornaments, cash, grains, utensils etc. In the morning neighbours came and set them free. They had nothing to eat and cook. He wanted to file a case in Thana but his wife and children did not allow him to do so.

Stealing Bundle of Crops

In order to oppress Dalits, the bundles of harvested crops either from the field or from the thrashing field are stolen.

E.R. (26) of a village in Bahadurpur block of Darbhanga district informed that bundles of harvested paddy crops were stolen from his field. He owned one bigha of land. The quality of land was very good. It was situated just on the bank of a government pond. He used to take good harvest from the field. But this was a matter of jealousy for the other landowners who belonged to Kurami caste. The neighbouring Kurami landowners were ready to pay E.R. two bighas of land slightly away from the village, but E.R. was not ready to exchange. Now the landowners thought to vex and oppress him in different ways. His oxen were not allowed to enter in the field of other landowner at the time of more time. Neighbouring landowners did not cooperate him. But due to location and quality of land, he was able to get good harvest. One year he harvested the paddy crops. After a week, he made bundles but could not carry the bundles at thrashing field. Silently, the other landowners made plan to steal all bundles from the field. E.R. was not aware of this fact. He did not go to watch the bundles at night. This was also good for the thieves. At night, they gradually stole all bundles and put them in their respective fields. In the morning, when E.R. went to carry the bundles, he did not see bundles in the field. He began to weep sitting in the field. All villagers reached to show sympathy to him but he was made poor by the thieves.

G.C. (28) of a village in Darbhanga urban block of Darbhanga district informed that the bundles of harvested gram crops were stolen from his thrashing field by the Gundas of the village. He had caught a Paithan boy doing illegal sex relation with a Dalit girl. He took courage to beat the boy with shoe. The parents beat the girl, too. The boy made up his mind to put G.C. in trouble. G.C. owned 10 Katha of land. The plot was suitable for gram crop. He used to sow Grams each year in this field. He had harvested the crops and put bundles in front of his house. The thrashing field was situated in the back side of his house. Other Tola dwellers also had their Khalihan there. Now he was planning to thrash them. There were 24 bundles of Gram crops. In the same night, the Paithan boys came and stole all bundles and put them in their houses. In the courtyard of house, they took out grain by beating with stick. In the morning, he did not find his bundles. He understood what had happened. His wife and children began to weep, but in vain.

Setting the Thrashing Field on Fire

This is also a criminal act by which Dalits are oppressed and terrified.

D.D. (48) of a village in Bahadurpur block of Darbhanga district informed that his thrashing field containing 51 bundles of paddy was set on fire by the Gundas of the village who belonged to a powerful caste. One day a boy of Gareri Caste was going to see his Khesari field. A Dalit girl was cutting grass on the boundary of her own field. The boy saw the girl and made up his mind to rape her. He gradually went on the boundary of that field. He wanted to have funny talk with her. But the girl remained silent. It was going to be evening and she was waiting for the arrival of his parents who had gone to perform work in another village. The boy wanted to take advantage of this situation. He caught the hands of the girl and made her to lay on the ground. The girl resisted and cried for the help. D.D. was coming with his buffalo. He heard the cry and went to help her

He gave a good beating to the Gareri boy. The head of the boy was also injured. The boy decide to take revenge on D.D. He saw his bundles in the thrashing field. He took fire in a small earthen pot and placed in the middle of the bundles. The fire gradually broke out and all bundles were burnt to ashes.

L.R. (39) of a village in Darbhanga urban block of Darbhanga district also disclosed a similar fact. He informed that his thrashing field was set-on fire by a one-eyed barber. The barber was stealing potato in the field of a Koeri landowner. L.R. was coming from the market. He saw a man digging potato in the darkness of night. He gradually went there and caught him. L.R. gave him a good beating. He was brought in the village before the landowner. He received beating again. A fine of Rs. 300 was placed over him. He had to pay the fine in a month. This time was given on the request of the father of the accused. The barber thought to take revenge from L.D. because it was he who had made him thief in the eye of the villagers. L.D. had 125 bundles of paddy crops in the thrashing field to thrash. He was busy in sowing wheat, so he could not do thrashing soon. One dark night the barber reached the thrashing field. He had fire in an earthen pot. He placed the pot with fire in the middle of the bundle of the crops. Gradually the fire break out and all paddy bundles were burnt to ashes.

Setting the House on Fire

In order to vex and oppress Dalits, their houses are also set on fire.

L.R. (26) of a village in Bahadurpur block of Darbhanga district informed that his house was set on fire by a Malaha criminal because he had not mortgaged his land in the hand of Malaha. L.R. owned ½ bigha of land. It was very good land for cultivation. To meet expenditure on the treatment of his son, L.R. was badly in need of money. He moved door to door of landowners, but no one was ready to provide him huge loan. He approached to Gareri for loan. He had sold his sheep so, he gave Rs. 1000 as loan at 36 per cent per annum rate of interest. He again took a loan of Rs. 500 at the same rate of interest. After one year, the loan and interest went above Rs. 2000. So, he decided to mortgage his land in the hand of Gareri. A Mallah of the village heard about it. He also approached to Dalit to take the land in mortgage. The Dalit L.R. did not agree. He mortgaged his land in the hand of Gareri at Rs. 3000. The Mallah took it bad. He made up his mind to take revenge by setting his house on fire. One dark night, he approached near his house. He had fire with him in an earthen pot. He placed fire under the tiles and went away. After some time, fire broke in his house. L.D could manage to come out of house with wife and children. But his entire things inside the house were burnt to ashes. Chicks, Goats and a Calf were also burnt alive. Grains and utensils were also burnt to ashes.

T.R. (28) of a village in Darbhanga Urban Block of Darbhanga district informed that his house was set on fire by a powerful criminal of a powerful caste in the village. He had taken courage to ask the name of a person who was carrying a woman of the village forcibly. The woman was crying for help. She was a Dalit woman of the same village. He came in village and asked them to follow the criminal. By that time woman was released and the criminal had run away. The woman disclosed the name of criminal. Hearing the name of Mallah criminal, nobody wanted to follow him. The criminal heard that L.D. of Dalit Tola had taken lead to catch him. He thought in his mind to punish T.R. One night the went in Dalit Tola with fire in a pot. He placed the fire below the tiles on the roof. After some time, the fire broke out. The villagers ran to put out the fire but in vain. Three neighbouring houses were also burnt. Human lives were saved. But there was a big damage of animal life and property.

Nowadays organised crimes are being committed against the Dalits in which their house are set on fire in broad day light with armed persons. Although such phenomena were reported from Central Bihar districts, but no such case was reported in Darbhanga district.

Committing Dacoity

Dalits are subjected to atrocity by committing dacoity. In dacoity, clothes, cash, ornaments etc. are looted at gun point. On resistance, murder is also done.

U.D. (41) of a village in Bahadurpur block of Darbhanga district informed that he was oppressed by committing dacoity. It was summer season. His kiths and kins were assembled to take part in the marriage ceremony of his son. 25 female relatives and 30 male relatives were present on this occasion. All had come with clothes, cash and ornaments. The boxes of relative were kept at a separate room. There was no space to sleep in his house due to crowd of relatives. A day before the departure of Barat, a grand party was organised for kiths and kins. The party was held at night. Liquors were also consumed. There was a joyous environment. After party all went to sleep. It was dark half of the month. At around mid-night nearly 20 persons with arms came and broke the door forcibly. They asked the females of the house to surrender their ornaments, cash, boxes clothes etc. The male members were sleeping outside. Some criminals surrounded them and did not allow to shout and move. The female members were also threatened not to shout. They gradually took out all belongings of the house. Some young girls were also subjected to rape. The dacoits stayed in the house for an hour and looted property of the house and chastity of the women. The ornaments and dresses of bride and grooms were also looted. L.D. had refused to play musical instruments on the occasion of Chhathi ceremony in the house of powerful landowner. That was the main cause behind committing dacoity in his house.

M.M. (41) of a village in Darbhanga urban block of Darbhanga district also disclosed the similar fact related to a dacoity committed in his house. He had sold two buffaloes worth Rs. 12000. The villagers came to know about this fact. It was a village dominated by Yadavas and Rs. 12000 in the house of M.M., they made a plan to commit dacoity in the same night. At mid night 20 people with pistol and guns went to Dalit Tola and surrounded it. Some entered forcibly in the house of M.M. They put M.M. and his wife under custody and asked whereabout of money. When he refused to say, he was beaten badly. His wife and girl were taken away. They were subjected to rape. Anyhow, dacoits were able to know the place from his wife where money was kept. They took money and boxes and went away in the night. They took out materials from the boxes and throw them at a distance in the fields.

Rape of Dalit Women

The most sorrowful aspect of atrocity is rape on Dalit women. As they are poor, so they easily become victim. Men take advantage of their such pathetic situation. They become victim of rape by landowners, local criminals, Khatal owners, brick kiln owner, contractor, police, service holders, officials etc. Their situation is such that no one believes upon them about rape. Everybody says that for money they would have surrendered their body for rape. If the rape is disclosed, they are beaten by their own men. In this situation, they even do not like to disclose their rape.

Rape by Landowner and their Men

Landowner and Dalit women as labourers remain very close to each other. Dalit women have to visit the fields of landowners not only to work, but to cut grasses, to collect fallen grains, to collect cowdung, to bring soil for own use, to graze cattle, to cut sag, to collect fruits and dry leaves from their trees. Not only this they have to defecate in the field of landowners. On many occasions, they go for these works, where they become victim of rape by the landowner.

S. Devi (25) of a village in Bahạdurpur district became victim of rape for cutting sag in the field of a landowner. She was returning alone from the work. She thought to cut sag in the field of a landowner. She started cutting sag quickly. Suddenly the young son of landowner came and attacked her. She was compelled to surrender her body before the young boy. The young boy left her after making his mouth black.

L. Devi (20) of the same village was subjected to rape when she was collecting dry leaves in the garden of a landowner for fuel. She entered the garden of a landowner and began to collect dry leaves. Suddenly a young man of the village entered the garden. It was mid-day and there was no one nearby the garden. Seeing no one nearby, the man attacked the women who struggled hard to save her, but in vain. Her chastity was lost. She had gone to collect fuel and came back losing her chastity.

T. Devi (30) of a village in Darbhanga urban block of Darbhanga district was subjected to rape by the Barahil of a landowner. She had gone to cut grasses in the field of Arahar. The Barahil of the landowner came there. Seeing woman cutting grass amidst the field of Arahar, the Barahil attached her. She was compelled to surrender herself. In this way, she lost her chastity for a thing like grass.

B. Kumari (15) of a village in same block was subjected to rape by the son of a landowner in whose house her mother was a Gobar Kadane or Dai. Once her mother had fallen ill. She asked her daughter to go to clean the shed of her owner. She used to go to clean the Goshala. One day, the owner was not at house. He had gone somewhere. A 18 years old boy of the owner entered in the shed, while B.K. was cleaning cow dung. He started helping her by lifting the basket containing dung on her head. She quickly finished the task. She washed her hands and came back to put broom and basket inside the shed. The boy was waiting for her return. As soon as she turned to go out of house, the boy closed the door and caught hold of her hands. She was compelled to surrender herself before the boy. The boy satisfied his hunger of sex and then allowed her to go out. She went home and disclosed the fact to her mother. Her mother did not send her on work next day. When she became cured, she came to work and told the matter to the owner. The owner abused the boy before her.

Rape by Criminals

In villages, there are some Gundas and Criminals who oppress the villagers by their evil act of Gunda, theft, dacoity, etc. Dalit women becomes victim of rape of these Gundas.

M. Devi (40) of a village in Bahadurpur block of Darbhanga district informed that her 18 years old daughter was subjected to rape by a young Gunda of the village. He was a famous dacoit of the area. People were terrified by his act. One day her daughter went to ease in a neighbouring field. It was around 8 to 9 p.m. As her mother was ill, so she did not ask to accompany her. After easing, she was about to come back. Just then a man closed her mouth with hand and took her on his shoulder. The man brought her in a neighbouring sugarcane field. He compelled her to surrender her body for his sexual satisfaction. The girl recognised his face and she became silent like a dead. She neither cried nor shouted. When the men got satisfied fully, he allowed the girl to go home. The girl came and told to her mother. Hearing the name of the dacoit, her mother started scolding her as to why she had gone alone. But no member of the family could dare to ask from the criminal.

R.R. Devi (48) of a village in the same block informed about the rape of her Putoh (Son's wife) by a Gunda of the village who was also involved in murder of a powerful man of the area. Her daughter-in-law had gone to clean clothes on the bank of the pond of the village. Unfortunately, she was alone at that time. The Gunda saw a women washing clothes alone on the bank of the pond. He gradually reached there. She saw her for sometime. Then attacked her. He took her on his lap and brought in a neighbouring bushes of tree. He compelled the women to surrender. The woman had to surrender herself to satisfy the hunger of his sex. She came back home and told about the misery. Hearing the name of the murderer, the members of the village remained silent. They advised her not to go anywhere alone.

Rape by Khatal Owner

L.R. Devi (26) of a village in Bahadurpur block of Darbhanga district was subjected to rape by the Khatal owner in whose Khatal she worked as a Dai. One day, there were no other members in the Khatal. The owner himself was there. The owner asked the Dai to clean the shed and to provide water and fodder to the cow. He also made promise to pay some cash for this work. She performed all work. Then she demanded some extra cash. The owner asked him to come in the room. When she entered inside the room, the owner closed the door and looted her charity. Then he started giving a note of Rs. 100. But she started abusing her. She left work in his Khatal for ever.

Rape by a Brick-kiln Owner

S. Devi (20) of a village in Bahadurpur block of Darbhanga district had gone to perform work in brick-kiln of an owner. She had gone along with her husband. She was young and gay. The owner of brick-kiln got attracted towards her beauty. He started making funny talk with her. He was ready to provide advance cash any time. One day, her husband had gone to a local market. Some labourers of brick-kiln had also gone there. S.D. went to wash her clothes in a neighbouring bank of river. She had gone there alone. The owner of the brick-kiln also went there. He started showing as if he had come for bath. He entered the water. He pulled S.D. also in the water. Her chastity was looted in water by the owner of the brick-kiln. She did not disclose this fact to anybody but she asked other woman to remain away from the owner.

Rape by a Truck Driver

L. Devi (25) of a village in Darbhanga urban block had gone to work as Reja in a brick-kiln. She used to load and unload the truck. The driver of the truck got attracted towards the gay face. He began to wait for chance to rape her. One morning he had gone to ease in neighbouring river. He saw L.D. there who had also come for easing and bathing. The driver thought this was the best time. He went to her and started making jokes. In funny talk, he caught her in his hand brought amidst bushes. Here, she was compelled forcibly to surrender herself looting her chastity, the driver went away. She did not disclosed any one about this misery but in talk she used to abuse the driver. She used to curse him.

Rape by a Contractor

D. Devi (29) of a village in Bahadurpur block of Darbhanga district was subjected to rape by a local contractor who had taken contract for constructing school in the village. B. Devi used to work as Reja at the time of construction of school. She worked for two months. But her payment was not made. She requested the contractor again and again. The building of school was constructed. The contractor stated giving payment to labourers. B. Devi was absent on that day. The contractor made haltage in the school. Cock was cooked shared with liquor. Around 9 p.m. B. Devi came to receive the payment. The contractor asked her to come inside the room. He made payment and put her thumb impression on paper. When she turned to go out of room, the contractor pulled her on his bed. He closed the door and compelled her forcibly to surrender her body. She had to surrender herself for receiving payment.

Rape by VLW

M. Devi (26) informed that she was subjected to rape by VLW who resided at the house of a Yadava landowner. The VLW had asked her to fill up a form for a sewing machine under TRYSEM scheme. One day VLW asked her to come in the evening to receive form. He was going to block to bring the form. He resided in a separate room quite away from other villages. It was about to sunset. M. Devi saw VLW returning. After some time she approached to VLW for the form. VLW was inside the room. He asked her to come inside the room. He gave a form and took her signature on a register. He began to tell her as to how she would fill up the form. By this time, darkness spread in his lantern was lighting. Suddenly VLW woke up from the bed and closed the door. He pulled M. Devi on his bed. She was compelled forcibly to surrender her body for sexual gratification of VLW. Seeing such behaviour of VLW, she lost all her hopes of getting sewing machine. Thereafter, she never met the VLW.

Rape by Police

Dalit women also become victim of rape by the police.

B. Devi (29) of a village in Bahadurpur block of Darbhanga district had become victim of rape by the police. She had gone to file a case against the rape by a powerfui person of the village. She became victim of rape by a young Kurami, when she had gone to collect cow dung quite early in the morning. She decided to file a case. She did not know much about the complication related to rape case. She went to Thana. The Thanedar asked her to stay for a night only then to register her case. She stayed in the Thana. At night, she become victim of rape by the police. The police compelled her to surrender her body for sexual gratification of police men. After rape, they told her that now her case was referred for medical verification. The medical report verified the fact of rape. The people reached with her next day in the village. The culprit could not appear before the police. His family members gave Rs. 500 to police as Salami. The police also took Rs. 500 more to finalise the case.

GANG RAPE

Dalit women become victim of gang rape by the criminals, Gundas and police.

M. Devi (40) of a village in Bahadurpur block of Darbhanga district informed that his 20 years old daughter-in-law was subjected to gang rape by the Gundas of the village. It was summer season. M. Devi and her husband had gone to harvest wheat crops in the field of a landowner. They had left the house around 2 a.m. They had asked the daughter-in-law to bring food and water for them. She got up when there was darkness. She went to ease in a neighbouring sugarcane field. Four-five Gundas of the village were also easing there. She did not see them but they saw her. One of Gundas got up and hold her mouth with one hand. From other hand he caught her both hands. She was brought in the middle of the sugar cane field. They closed her mouth with a napkin. Her hands were tied. In this physical condition, she was raped one by one by all five Gundas. When all Gundas satisfied this hunger of sex, they released the women who gradually returned home loosing her chastity. The Gundas had threatened her to kill her husbands on disclosing the rape. But she told this misery to her mother-in-law. Her mother-in-law asked her to remain silent because they had neither property nor power.

Dalit Women as Kept

Some Dalit women had to lead a life of kept of powerful man of the village like Mukhia, Sarpanch, Biggest Landowner, Biggest Criminals etc. The woman concerned first becomes victim of rape. The incidence of frequent rape by the same person compels her to become kept. When she accepts to become kept, she has costly dresses to wear and ornaments to decorate her body. She is known as the wife of his husband, but at the same time she is called as the kept of the man concerned.

G. Devi (36) of a village in Bahadurpur block of Darbhanga district was leading a life of kept of Mukhia of the village who belonged to Yadava caste. She was wife of the Kamia. She was gay and beautiful. Mukhia used to go to supervise transplanting and other agricultural works. He saw the wife of Kamia. He was attracted towards her beauty. He wanted to have her any way. One evening all Kamias were making bundles of paddy crops to carry to the thrashing field. G. Devi was also there with her husband. All Kamia and Kamin began to carry bundles but G. Devi began to cut grasses for her cow. The thrashing field was situated at a distance. When all Kamia and Kamins went away Mukhia and G. Devi were left alone. Mukhia took advantages of this loneliness. He compelled G. Devi to surrender herself for his sexual satisfaction. As there was no one to help her, she had to surrender herself. Thereafter, Mukhia began to wait for her with cash in pocket. When she became victim of rape three-four times, she decided to take money. Gradually, Mukhia started using her as kept. When her husband knew it, he beat her mercilessly. But when she did not change her character, he left her to do what she liked. She took one bigha of cultivable land from Mukhia. He had given cash to her on many occasions and he still gives her grain and money. Dresses and ornaments are also bought for her by the Mukhia. Now she is popularly known as Mukheine. She does not irritate to hear this name for herself.

U. Devi (28) of a village in same block was leading a life of kept of Sarpanch of the Panchayat. The Sarpanch has given her 2 bighas of land to cultivate, a plot of land to construct house, cash to make house pucca. She lives with her husband.

M. Devi (30) was leading the life of kept of a famous hero of the village who belonged to Koeri caste. He vies money time to time and stays with her like her husband. When he comes, the real husband is not allowed to enter inside the house.

PART III

CONCLUSION

The present study is exploratory and descriptive in nature. It aims at highlighting the pattern of status, exploitation and atrocity on Dalits in the state of Bihar of our country.

Description of sample villages, exploration of present day status of Dalits, explanation of social areas of exploitation, delineation of economic areas of exploitation, study of religious areas of exploitation, presentation of political area of exploitation, examination of exploitation of Dalit by Dalit and analysis of atrocity on Dalits were the main objectives behind the study.

From the point of view of method, two districts situated in two ecological regions of Bihar were chosen on the basis of concentration of Dalit population. These were Gaya district in South Bihar and Darbhanga district in North Bihar. From each district two blocks were selected purposively keeping population of Dalit in mind. From each block 20 villages were taken randomly and from each village 10 Dalit households were chosen for detail study. Thus, the present study covers methodologically 2 district 4 blocks, 80 villages and 800 households.

Study of sample villages reveals that Dalits have been integral part of our social and economic structure since time immemorial. They have been major labour force and are still playing significant role in our social system. They are tied to our social structure through Jajmani System.

Analysis of data on present day social status of Dalit indicates that our secular and democratic Constitution has played significant role in enhancing the social status of Dalits. It has attacked the evil practice of untouchability. Now Dalits sit with other castes on public place. They travel with other castes in bus and train. They visit the hotels with other castes. Some Dalits have opened tea stall where all castes visit. In hotels, water and food by a Dalit is accepted by all. But in villages, the tradition-bound families belonging to other Hindu caste, still do not accept water and cooked food of Dalit family. Some other Hindu castes have started accepting food and water of Dalits. Some Dalits also maintain relationship with high caste and backward caste Hindus through invitation. This appears true in both ecological setting of the State of Bihar.

Description of present day educational status highlights that nowadays Dalit children study in schools with the children of forward and backward caste Hindus. Some Dalits have been appointed as school teachers. The children of forward and backward caste Hindus go to read from these Dalit teachers. Some Dalits have attained high educational status and they are servicing on high posts in government's jobs. They are educating their children in English medium private schools. It is beyond doubt that in both regions the Dalits have become aware of the benefits of modern education, but the phenomena of non-enrollment, non-attendance and dropouts can be seen among the poorest Dalit families who are still struggling hard for bread. Their poverty compels them to use the children as means of income.

Explanation of present day economic status of Dalits in both regions of Bihar indicates that now Dalits are free to choose occupation of their own choice. They are not under the clutches of landowner. Parcha of homestead land have been given to them. Gairmanjarua land have been distributed. Profession like vegetable selling, Feriwala, Thelawala, Tamtamwala, Rickshawala, and Coolie are common among them. Service holder Dalits have purchased land. They are now good farmers. Some Dalits do share-cropping on the land of other castes. Now they enjoy credit facilities from institutional banks. Thus, their economic condition is much better now than before independence of India.

The present day religious status of Dalits reveals that Dalits have been integral part of our religion. They participate in village level religious festivals and ceremonies. They visit freely to village temples and sacred ponds or wells. Prasad of Dalit families is accepted by all. Brahman priests also visit their houses to conduct worship. They also perform Yagya and Akhanda and invite other castes to participate. The present day political status of Dalits in both regions highlights that political status of Dalits have definitely gone up. Now they are Mukhia, Sarpanch, MLA, MP, Minister etc. They are Choukidar, Police Officials, Thanedar, B.D.O. etc. Thus, they participate in political and administrative system. In village level and inter-village level decisions, the Dalits of villages also take active part.

Undoubtedly the status of Dalits after independence have changed due to secularisation and democratisation of our Constitution, but it is also true that exploitation and oppression of Dalits in both regions of

Bihar is still going on. A thorough investigation of the problem reveals that the phenomena of exploitation, oppression and atrocity on Dalit have social, economic, religious and political dimension. The study indicates that it is not only forward castes, who have been often high lighted as the exploiter and oppressor, but nowadays backward castes are more involved in the exploitation and oppression of Dalits than the upper castes.

Analysis of data on social areas of Dalits exploitation reveals that in both iconological regions of Bihar three sections of Dalit population are worst victim of exploitation. These are children, women and aged. The children are kept engaged in household works instead of sending them to school. But the most painful aspect is selling the labour of children by the poor Dalit family. The owners, hotel owners, Garage owners, brick-kiln owners, truck or bus owners, service holders etc. utilize the service of Dalit children for selfish purposes.

Like Dalit children, Dalit women are also subject to exploitation. Like children, the exploitation of women begins in the family. Dalit women have to struggle hard to maintain their families. They not only perform work in the house, but they have to earn wages as well to supplement the income of the family. In some cases, only women have to run the family and their drunkard husbands do not perform any work. The agencies involved in purchasing the labour of Dalit women at cheap rate are landowner, Khatal owners, brick-kiln owners, truck owners, contractors, service holders, etc.

In our culture, there is a concept that old is gold. This is also true for the Dalit. But due to utter poverty, the poor Dalit families exploit the services of aged persons not only for household work but compel them to sell their labour at cheap rate in the hand of agencies like landowner, Khatal owner, hotel owner, truck owner, brick kiln owner, mill owner, contractor, service holders, etc.

The study on economic are a of Dalit exploitation reveals that poor Dalits are still not in a position to sell their labour at market value. Due to indebtedness, they are compelled to accept the terms and conditions related to bonded labour or attached labour. As bonded labour or attached labour, the bargaining capacity of a labourer is nil. Such Dalit labourers have to work on wages decided by the owner. They do not get wages prescribed by Minimum Wages Act. Child labour, women labour and aged labour are exploited on cheap rate of wages. They received less wages from the landowner, Khatal owner, hotel owner, brick kiln owner, truck owner, contractor, service holders etc. These facts are existing in both regions of

Bihar.

Analysis of religious area of Dalits exploitation presents the fact that Dalits are exploited in the name of religion and religious festival. For religious work like construction temple, preparing Yagyashala, constructing hut for the Sadhus, erecting Pandal and stage of festival occasion etc., services of Dalits are utilized. They are forced to pay subscription, to perform Shramadan and perform work at cheap wages. In the name of religion and religious work, they are not allowed to sell their labour at market value. Such phenomena were present both in North and South Bihar.

Exploration of facts on political area of Dalit exploitation reveals that in both parts of Bihar Dalits are subjected to exploitation by political and administrative authorities. Thus, they become victim of exploitation by Choukidar, Dafadar, Police, Thanedar, Lawyer, Mukhia, Sarpanch, Gram Sewak, Karamchari, Block Officials, Bank Officials etc. They also become victim of exploitation by traditional caste Panchayat and village Panchayat. Leader, MLA, MP, etc. also do not lag behind in Dalits exploitation of various kind.

Examination of the problem of Dalit atrocity in both regions highlights that Dalits have been poor since centuries. They were under the clutches of Zamindars, Jagirdars, etc. But after independence they are not under the bondage of any kind. That is why the behaviour of Dalits borne after independence is quite different than their old generations. Now they do not offer pranam to forward or backward castes. They hesitate in calling a person as Malik or Babu. They do not hesitate on sitting with forward or backward. Now they deny a landowner to perform work without wage. Present education and economic policies have become a painful development for landowners who enjoyed the labour of Dalit at cheap rate. In reactions to these developments Dalits are subject to atrocities of various kind. Dalits children and women are abused and beaten when they go to collect, cow dung, leaves, fruits, grasses, sags, wood etc. from the fields of landowners. By these behaviours, landowners try to show that Dalits cannot exist without their support. In worst situations the landowners do not allow Dalits to ease in their fields. But Dalits are being united to fight against such atrocities. Their organised reactions are helping them in leading respectful life.

Nowadays, the government is taking serious action against the persons involved in atrocity on Dalits. For this purpose Dalits Thanas have also been established. But the attitudes of these Thanas is not so helpful as was expected. These Thanas exploit and oppress both the Dalits as well as the persons involved in atrocity. To get rid of Thanas, the powerful persons have adopted indirect method of atrocity. They commit such evil acts are theft, dacoity, setting fire in field, thrashing field, houses etc. By these evil acts, Dalits oppressed and put to hardship. It is not that Dalits are not free to file case but in want of definite proof they do not want to visit Thana and fall in the trap of police.

The most heinous form of atrocity is rape of women. Dalit women are subject to rape by landowner, Khatal owner, Hotel Owner, Local authorities, Officials, Service holders, Businessmen, Contractors, Criminals etc. Women are not only women, but they are mother, sister and daughter, too. One can imaging well what will happen to a person if his mother, sister and daughter, is given the similar treatment as is given to Dalit women. Such persons who exploit them are fully responsible for this crime but Dalit Society is also not exception in this regard. When the news of rape spread, Dalits start beating the women or girl because they consider the all fault of a woman or girl. Everybody abuses such women. Therefore, woman generally do not like to disclose the incidence of rape among the members of society. Sometimes, situation compels them to sell their sex with the rapists. Some time, women go to sell their labour but have a sell their sex.

The phenomenon of gang rape on Dalit woman also comes in existence in both regions of the Bihar State. Dalit women are subject to gang rape by local Gundas, Criminals, and other powerful persons who have no regard for the chastity of other and who are not afraid of punishment as well.

Besides, rape, and arson, Dalits are subject to atrocity by murder and group murder. The phenomena of murder and group murder was not reported in North Bihar, but in South Bihar, it was common. In order to fight against the atrocity, Dalits have formed aggressive organisations. Some aggressive organisations like Naxalitis, CPI (ML), MCC etc. have come up. To counter the aggressive behaviour of Dalit organisation of sena, some senas of local castes have also emerged. These senas are involved in arson and murder. Thus these senas are in action either offensive or defensive but is constant vigil and tension like that of war.

One of the sorrowful plight of Dalit exploitation nowaday is exploitation of Dalit by Dalit. Fifty years of independence of our country has created a gap among Dalits. Now some Dalits are in prosperity, some are educated, some are service holders, some are landowners, and some are rich. They do not have sympathy for their poor, uneducated, brethren. As a result the exploitation of Dalit by Dalit has also come into existence in both geographical regions of Bihar.

In conclusion, it can be highlighted that the Dalits of today is not the Dalits of past. Now Dalits are free to lead a respectful life. They are free to educate, to make journey to sit with anyone at public place, to eat with anyone in public hotel, to contest election and to select occupation of their own choice. These developments have definitely brought changes in the status of Dalits. But all Dalits have not been brought to the same level. Undoubtedly some Dalits have become rich, landowner, service holder, factory owner, contractor, business men, trader etc., but still there are many Dalits who are leading a life of poorest of the poor. For them independence does not hold any meaning. They are born in loan, grown up in loan and die in loan. Their children do not attend school rather sell their labour for nominal wages. Their women sell labour at reduced rate and are forced to sell their sex. There aged are also forced to sell labour at cheap rate. To make their survival, they have to perform work under exploitative and oppressive conditions.

The rich and major Dalits do not have sympathy for the minor and poor Dalits. They exploit minor and poor Dalits in the same way as other castes of the villages. The rich Dalits try to utilize the labour of poor Dalits at a cheap rate. They are also involved in atrocity on poor Dalits. The phenomenon of rape of Dalits women by Dalits men have also come into existence.

It is not that only Dalits are subject to exploitation. Even the rich and powerful persons also become victims of exploitation. Exploitation is a world-wide phenomenon.

The study highlights the exploitation of Dalits by Dalit. It is beyond doubt that during fifty years of our independence, a class of Dalits has come into existence. The Dalits belonging to this class are well to do. They own land, do Bataidari or Manidari. Some family member of their family are well placed in government job. They are educated and engaged in modern means of livelihood. Thus, definitely is much better position than other Dalits. Due to emergence of this class in Dalit, the exploitation of Dalit by Dalit has come in to existence. The dominant Dalit community like the Chamar, the Dusadh, the Bhuiya, and the Pasi exploit the minor Dalit castes like the Dhobi the Mehtar, and the Nat. The numerical strength of the Dhobi, the Mehtar, and the Nat is very less in comparison to the Chamar, the Dusadh, the Pasi and the Bhuiya. Naturally, they belong to dominant Dalit community. The minor Dalit communities have very little of no say in the decision of the major Dalit community.

The exploitation of the poor Dalit by the rich Dalit indicates that like the other landowner, the Dalit landowners also utilize the services of Dalit labour at very cheap wages.

In exploitation of the labour, they take side of the other landowner. Like other landowners, they do not like to implement the minimum wages. The Dalit landowners like the other landowners do not want to work manually. They have labour to cultivate land. They also have servant and maid servant to perform household works. They have established diary farm and utilize the services of Dalit children or women in diary farm. They utilize the children of other Dalit as servant but send their children in school and college.

The Dalits serving in town areas bring the children of their poor relative or other poor family to utilize their services as household servant. These children have to work from dawn to late night. On run away, they do not get any payment but are blamed as thieves. What to say about payment of the salary, they are served food left after eating in plate by the family members. They are abused and frequently beaten up. Under such exploitative and oppressive situation, they have to work for the Dalit masters. As they are away from their parents they do not dare to escape also.

The study on atrocity on Dalits reveals that Dalits are subject to atrocities by other Hindus and Muslims. Sometimes, they are subject to atrocities by their own brethren, who are also Dalits. For minor mistakes the children of Dalits are beaten mercilessly. For do not obeying, a young Dalit is torture physically, sometimes, the hands and feet of Dalits are broken. Sometimes, they are attacked with lethal weapons. Sometimes, they are murdered. On some occasion, the cattle of Dalits are taken way, their land and house are seized and auctioned. The bundles of wheat, paddy, etc. are looted or burnt to ashes. Their houses are set on fire or demolished. The thrashing ground is burnt to ashes. On various occasions, the dacoity is done in their houses to loot ornaments, money and clothes. Their goats and cocks are consumed forcefully. When they demand any price they are abused. In this way they are subjected to wicked, oppressive and cruel behaviour.

Nowadays, Dalits have united themselves under the banner of some activist organisation. Some of these organisations have political affiliation as well. Virtually these organisation work as Dalit sena under such organisation. Dalits are agitating to get minimum wages and proper share in agriculture. They are also agitating against their exploitation and oppression. The Dalit senas have also taken up violent means to lead prestigious life in the society. They have taken revenge by killing selected status holding personalities of the rural areas. In order to counter such revengeful attitude of Dalit sena, other Hindu castes have also formed their senas. These senas have also taken up violent means to suppress the Dalit activities. These sena rape Dalit women in gang and kill them. Sometimes, the entire Dalit Tola is set on fire and sometimes atrocity results to group killing in which even infant and children are also subject to brutal murder.

Although the atrocity of Dalit is a general phenomenon, but atrocity on Dalit women in particular is more common. Dalit women have to go out of house to work. They have to remain in close contact with the men of means for whom they work. They do not have their own land to graze cattle, to cut grass and even to defecate. For these activities and for work, they have to go in the field of other. Seeing a Dalit women in lonely places, the men of means attempt to rape them. After rape, they try to please them by providing money, paddy, wheat, rice, ornaments, clothes etc. When Dalit women are attracted towards these things, they become object to rape frequently. They do not want to disclose such fact, because they are also beaten by their husbands or other family members. The men of means take advantages of such position. They know well that they would do nothing after the incidence of rape. This encourages the rapists to rape another Dalit women or the same women repeatedly. In majority of cases, the rape leads to keeping kept of the same Dalit women. Such Dalit women have to lead a life of kept in presence of their husbands and other family members. In the beginning it is not taken well by their husbands, but gradually they do not pay any attention towards such illegal sex relations of their wives with the men of means.

It is not that only the landowners are involved in rape and illegal sex relations with Dalits women, but sometimes Choukidar, Mukhia, Sarpanch, Gram Sewak, School Teacher, Bank Officials, Police etc. are also involved in the rape of the Dalits women. Sometimes, the Dalit women herself open chance for their rape. Through the medium of rape they want to have permanent illegal sex relation with men of means. Their main motive remains to wear costly dress and ornaments and eat good food without performing manual labour. In some Dalit families, even the head of the house holds compel a girl or newly wedded daughter-in-law to bring the men of means under their trap of sex so that she will be able to get good food to eat and good dress to wear without doing manual labour in the field. Thus, in some cases, the family head compels the Dalit women to become victim of sex atrocity.

In violent atrocity, the Dalits are killed in group, their houses are demolished, or set on fire. In fire their grains, ornaments, utensils or even goats, cocks, calves etc. are burnt. Thus, they are subject to loss of live and property.

Dalit Tomorrow

From the study some conclusions about the Dalit tomorrow can be drawn, which are as follows :

1. The Dalits will be conscious towards their social prestige. As a result the social status of Dalit will definitely go up. They will not go to share feast in the house of other Hindus without invitation.
2. The Dalit will become conscious towards their voting right as a result they will play significant role in the politics.
3. The organisations of Dalits will certainly help them in obtaining minimum wages and to agitate against their exploitation and oppression.
4. Within Dalit itself two groups will definitely come into existence (i) Poor Dalit and (ii) Rich Dalit.
5. The rich Dalit will try to exploit and oppress the poor Dalit in the same way as the other men of means.
6. In exploitation of the poor Dalit, the rich Dalit will take side of the other rich person of any community.
7. The exploitation of the poor Dalit will continue in some way or the other, the significant feature will be the exploitation of Dalit by the Dalit.
8. The organised activities will lead to organised atrocity on Dalit.
9. The sex atrocity on Dalit women will continue in some way or other due to their non-violent behaviour and submissive temperament, till they do not defend this strongly.
10. The Dalits serving of different responsible posts will maintain social relation with the other castes serving in the same institution

and residing in the same locality.

11. Untouchability will gradually end. The social relation with Dalit will not improve suddenly.
12. Well to do Dalit will prefer intercaste marriages.
13. There will be no religious or ritual performance by a Dalit for the upper caste.
14. The Dalit may manage their sacred performance themselves.
15. The economic development and political power at the hands of Dalit may help their quick absorption to the main stream of Hinduism.

Thus from the perusal of the data and analysis through various chapters the facts related to atrocities highlight the anger expressed by the rich and powerful persons against the changed behaviour of Dalits. With the acts of atrocity, they want to suppress the changed and aggressive behaviour of poor Dalits. Emergence of violent senas on the part of Dalits as well as other castes reveal clearly that the exploitation and atrocity on Dalits can not be controlled by violent behaviours. Attempts should be made to bring positive change in the behaviour of Dalits as well other castes. Through constructive measures violence and atrocity can be removed.

The incidence of rape indicates low status of Dalit women. Status of Dalit women even in their own society is not high. From very beginning they are made submissive. Premarital relation is not taken seriously but extra marital relation is subject to serve punishment. The incidence of rape generally takes place in lonely place both at Gaya and Darbhanga.

In order to check the incidence of rape, the women will have to come forward. They will have to attack by sickle or other weapons on the rapists. Such steps by Dalit women to accept money after rape as compensation to forget the incidence should be stopped. They should not accept such money. Otherwise, it will lead to further rape. Sometimes, the compensation received provides the ground to lead a life of kept.

Efforts should be made to bring a change in attitude of rich and powerful men that Dalit women are also like women of other castes. They have also right to lead a respectful life. They come to sell their labour not to sell their sex.

Last but not the least, it is truth of our social system that Dalits were the integral part of our society, they are today also integral part of society and they will be our integral part even tomorrow. As all parts of our body are valuable, so all parts of our society are also equally valuable. As we have regards and respects for the person of upper castes are also we should have for the Dalits too. This will bring peace and prosperity in our society and will help in solving the problem of atrocity and exploitation of Dalit of Bihar for ever.

BIBLIOGRAPHY

BOOKS

Ambedkar, B.R. (1945) : Annihilation of Caste. Bombay : Bharat Bhushan.

Ambedkar, B.R. (1945) : What Congress and Gandhi have done to the Untouchables. Bombay : Thacker and Co.

Benjamin, J. (1989) : Scheduled Castes in Indian Politics, ESS-ESS, Publication, New Delhi.

Beteille, Andre (1969) : Caste Old and New. Delhi : Asian Publishing House.

Beteille, Andre (1969) : Caste, Class and Power. Bombay : Oxford University Press.

Burman, B.K. Roy (ed) (1970) : Social Mobility Movement Among Scheduled Castes and Tribes of India, New Delhi : Registrar General of India, Ministry of Home Affairs.

Desai, I.P. and etc. (1985) : Caste, Caste-conflict and Reservation. Delhi : Ajanta Book International.

Gurye, G.S. (1961) : Caste, Class and Occupation. Bombay : Popular Book Depot.

Jha, Hetukar (1991) : Social Structure of Indian Villages. Patna University.

James Manor (1993) : Power, Poverty and Poison. University of Sussex.

Jha, Shashishekar (1972) : Political Elite in Bihar. Bombay : Vora and Co. Publication.

Khan, Mumtaz Ali (1980) : Scheduled Castes and their status in India. New Delhi, Uppal Pub. House.

Malhotra Bros (ed) (1994) : Prevention of Atrocity Act., 1989.

Panikar, K.K. (1993) : Caste and Democracy, London : Leonard and Vingina.

Sachidananda (1974) : "Research on Scheduled Caste : with Special reference to change" in a Survey of Research in Sociology and Social Anthropology, pp. 276-310. Edited by M.N. Srinivas et. al., Bombay : Popular Prakashan.

Sachidananda (1976) : The Harijan Elite. Haryana : Thomson Press.

S.C. Dubey (1990) : Indian Society. N.B.T., New Delhi.

Shyam, Lal (1981) : The Bhangi. Popular Books, Delhi.

Vidyarthi, L.P. and Mishra, N. (1979) : Harijan Today. Classical, Publications, New Delhi.

Wiser, W.H. (1958) : The Hindu Jajmani System, Lucknow Publishing House, Lucknow.

PAPERS

Haldar, A.K. (1976) : "Scheduled Castes of Bihar, their distribution and relative concentration", *Journal of Social Research* 19(1) : 74-84.

Jha, Hetukar (1977) : "Lower – Caste Peasants and Upper Caste Zamindars in Bihar (1921-25) : An analysis of Sanskritization and Contradiction between the two group", *Indian Economic and Social History Review* 14(4) : 549-59.

Kurren, C.T. (1982) : "Economic Condition of Scheduled Castes", Yojana 26 (19) : 13-17.

Mishra, N. (1978) : "Studies on the Scheduled Castes in Bihar", *Journal of Social Research* 21(2) : 47-70.

Pathy, Jaganath (1982) : "Politics of Reservation in India : Caste Study of Political Agitation in Bihar and Gujrat", *Philosophy and Social Action* 8(2).

Roy, Ramashray (1967) : "Bihar Power Patterns", *Seminar* 95 (July).

Sachidananda (1967) : "Caste and Conflict in Bihar Village", *Eastern Anthropologist* 20(2) : 143-50.

Sachidananda (1974) : "Emergent of Scheduled Castes Elite in Bihar", Religion and Society 21(3) : 55-61.

Index

S

T